THE ENLIGHTENMENT PAST

Over the last 200 years the theories and ideals of the Enlightenment have come to be viewed as the foundation of modern Western political and intellectual culture. Particularly in France they have played a fundamental role in the development of national identity. In a series of richly contextualized readings Daniel Brewer examines the cultural construction of the Enlightenment in France from the eighteenth century to the present day. He examines a range of important Enlightenment texts, explores the ways in which they defined their modernizing project, and analyzes the cultural and political uses to which they have been put by scholars, writers and intellectuals. This book presents a significant advance in the field of Enlightenment studies, in an important and timely reassessment of the heritage and continued relevance of Enlightenment ideals.

DANIEL BREWER is Professor of French Studies at the University of Minnesota. He is the author of *The Discourse of Enlightenment in Eighteenth-Century France: Diderot and the Art of Philosophizing* (Cambridge, 1993; paperback edition, 2007).

THE ENLIGHTENMENT PAST

Reconstructing eighteenth-century French thought

DANIEL BREWER

CAMBRIDGE UNIVERSITY PRESS

CAMBRIDGE UNIVERSITY PRESS
Cambridge, New York, Melbourne, Madrid, Cape Town, Singapore, São Paulo, Delhi

Cambridge University Press
The Edinburgh Building, Cambridge CB2 8RU, UK

Published in the United States of America by Cambridge University Press, New York

www.cambridge.org
Information on this title: www.cambridge.org/9780521879446

© Daniel Brewer 2008

This publication is in copyright. Subject to statutory exception
and to the provisions of relevant collective licensing agreements,
no reproduction of any part may take place without
the written permission of Cambridge University Press.

First published 2008

Printed in the United Kingdom at the University Press, Cambridge

A catalogue record for this publication is available from the British Library

ISBN 978-0-521-87944-6 hardback

Cambridge University Press has no responsibility for the persistence or
accuracy of URLs for external or third-party internet websites referred to
in this publication, and does not guarantee that any content on such
websites is, or will remain, accurate or appropriate.

```
B1925.E5 B74 2008
0134111162720
Brewer, Daniel.

The Enlightenment past :
 reconstructing
       2008.
                                           2008 10 10
```

Contents

List of illustrations		*page* vi
Acknowledgments		vii
1	Producing Enlightenment history	1
2	The event of Enlightenment: beginnings	24
3	The subject of Enlightenment: constructing philosophers, writing intellectuals	49
4	Designing the past: thinking history through Montesquieu	75
5	Literature and the making of revolutionary history	97
6	Inventing a literary past	122
7	Commemorating Enlightenment: bringing out the dead, belatedly	148
8	The Voltaire effect	162
9	Reading among the ruins	179
10	Epilogue	199
Notes		206
Bibliography of works cited		232
Index		248

Illustrations

9.1 Holland House Library after September 1940 air raid in London (1940). Photo credit: National Monuments Record. 180
9.2 Désert de Retz, Study 37 (France 1993). Photo credit: Michael Kenna. 185
9.3 Hubert Robert, *Imaginary View of the Ruins of the Grand Gallery of the Louvre Palace* (1796). The Louvre. Photo credit: Erich Lessing / Art Resource, NY. 190
9.4 Hubert Robert, *Project for the Disposition of the Grand Gallery of the Louvre* (1796). The Louvre. Photo credit: Scala / Art Resource, NY. 193

Acknowledgments

To write is to begin repaying unrepayable debts, of which I've incurred many in the course of completing this book.

I'm grateful for the critical spirit and intellectual generosity of many friends and colleagues, not all of whom, through my unintentional omission, will figure here. My thanks go to my colleagues and students at the University of Minnesota, and especially the faithful of the Theorizing Early Modern Studies (TEMS) lab – both faculty and graduate students – including Juliette Cherbuliez, J.B. Shank, and Michael Gaudio, as well as Michael Hancher, Steven Ostrow, Bruno Chaouat, and Michal Kobialka. I'm grateful to colleagues elsewhere for those sometimes brief moments (but more valuable than they know) when they've lent me a kind ear (and sometimes a skeptical eyebrow), including Bernadette Fort, Caroline Weber, Geoffrey Turnovsky, Marie-Hélène Huet, Julie Hayes, David Porter, Downing Thomas, Keith Baker, Dena Goodman, Karlis Racevskis, Lesley Walker, Ross Chambers, Marshall Brown, Lynn Hunt, Pierre Saint-Amand, Dror Wahrman, Srinivas Aravamudan, and Andrew Curran.

My thanks go to all those whose professional sociability enabled me to test ideas for this book, hopefully to refine the good ones and discard the rest. I'm pleased to express my gratitude to Patrick Coleman, David Carrithers, Peter Reill at the UCLA Center for 17th and 18th Century Studies, David Brewer, Dorinda Donato, Dianah Jackson, Karlis Racevskis, Diane Fourny, John Bender, and Robert Morrissey.

I've been intrigued to imagine how several national traditions might enter into dialogue and debate in this project, and so the chance to discuss the crossroads of literary and cultural history with farther-flung colleagues has been invaluable. For many such opportunities, my thanks go to Luc Fraisse, Anthony Strugnell, Frédéric Ogée, Peter Wagner, Robert Mankin, David Denby, Georges Benrekassa, Ansgar Nünning, Herbert Grabes, Jean Marie Goulemot, François Hartog, Henry Rousso,

Stéphane Van Damme, Georges Didi-Huberman, Antoine Lilti, Nicholas Cronk, Jonathan Mallinson, and Julia Douthwaite.

Material support for this project came in the form of a University of Minnesota McKnight Art and Humanities Summer Fellowship and a National Endowment for the Humanities Summer Fellowship, which I'm pleased to acknowledge. At Cambridge University Press, my deep gratitude goes to Linda Bree, for her confidence and her steadfast support throughout this project, to Maartje Scheltens and Jodie Barnes for their invaluable help all throughout the production process. I'm pleased to express my thanks to Jan Williams for her skillful preparation of the index, and to Jo Bramwell for her keen copy-editor's eye. I'm indebted to two readers for their thoughtful engagement with my project. Finally, words do not express or begin to repay what I owe to Mária Brewer in this labor and in many others.

Versions of some of the material in this book have appeared earlier. My thanks to the journal editors of *Modern Language Quarterly* and *SVEC* (*Studies on Voltaire and the Eighteenth Century*), and to the volume editors of *Montesquieu and the Spirit of Modernity*, *The Cambridge Companion to Voltaire*, and *Ruins in the Eighteenth Century* (Landau-Paris Symposium on the Eighteenth Century) for permission to reprint.

CHAPTER I

Producing Enlightenment history

How do we seize the foreign past?
Julian Barnes, *Flaubert's Parrot*

To articulate the past historically does not mean to recognize it "the way it really was" (Ranke). It means to seize hold of a memory as it flashes up at a moment of danger.
Walter Benjamin, *Illuminations*

We want historians to confirm our belief that the present rests upon profound intentions and immutable necessities. But the true historical sense confirms our existence among countless lost events, without a landmark or a point of reference.
Michel Foucault, "Nietzsche, Genealogy, History"

The Enlightenment has long been hailed as the foundation of modern Western political and intellectual culture. The beginnings of this historical moment, the "age of reason" of late seventeenth- and eighteenth-century Europe, are commonly located in the attempts to place knowledge on new foundations and in so doing to reground existence and action. The term 'Enlightenment' thus signifies a particular set of ideas, values, and cultural practices that grew out of an existing intellectual and socio-political order, often enough by resisting it, and that gradually gained power and prominence during the eighteenth century. Over the following two centuries these ideas, values, and practices would come to define fundamental aspects of contemporary political and social life in a liberal, democratic society, on the level of both individual and collective existence. More precisely, the term Enlightenment would designate the following tenets: the autonomy of fundamentally rational individuals, the progressive function of the state to which individuals give up their freedom in return for increased collective well-being, the essential rationality of a natural order made accessible through scientific knowledge and its technological applications designed to better material existence, and the potentially just nature of collective social relations. The desire to regulate human affairs based on these values constitutes the so-called Enlightenment project, a program aimed at reforming individual behavior and social practices.

Reformist, progressivist, and emancipatory, the Enlightenment project is fundamentally future-oriented, even to the point of being impossibly utopian, a constantly and constitutively unrealizable goal. The emergence of this project thus sets in place a changed relation between past, present, and future, instituting what François Hartog calls a new "régime d'historicité," a specific way of writing history but also of structuring historical knowledge and phrasing historicity, the historical nature of things and being.[1] No longer is the present to be understood and lived in terms of the past, whose repetition the present makes manifest. Instead, the present is to be grasped as becoming what it no longer will be. Viewed from the perspective of a future anterior, poised between irremediable loss and ultimate accomplishment, the present of the Enlightenment project is experienced increasingly in terms of what it will have been.

Michel Foucault has claimed that we must try to think of ourselves as "beings who are historically determined, to a certain extent, by the Enlightenment."[2] My aim in *The Enlightenment Past* is to examine the implications of Foucault's remark, teasing out the question of our historical determination by considering how the vast Enlightenment narrative has marked more than two centuries of intellectual thought and cultural practice. In a sense, that narrative is well known. Thanks to numerous anthologies and case studies of Enlightenment writers, as well as synthetic histories and critical interpretations of the period seen through the lens of social, cultural, and intellectual movements, the story of the Enlightenment sketched out above has become a familiar one in the cultural imaginary. It is a story often told telegraphically, as a kind of *aide-mémoire*, a way of remembering our contentedness with civilization, or perhaps forgetting our discontent. Less well understood is why the Enlightenment narrative has become so familiar. What conditions link us to the Enlightenment past? Are we bound by that historical determination, and what would it mean to be free from it, in historical, epistemological, or ontological terms? Foucault's comment underscores the urgency of reflecting not on the Enlightenment past per se, as an autonomous object or event, but rather on a present and the mode of its relation to that past. What Foucault calls for is a form of critical thought defined and constituted by its linkage to the Enlightenment past.

Reflection on the Enlightenment past inevitably must involve critical self-reflection, which can productively be located discursively, in narrative and in the stories a culture tells (of) itself. Consequently, it is pressing to ask not what the Enlightenment was, but rather how we tell its story – assuming these two issues can be separated, which is far from certain. Situating the Enlightenment past in relation to such stories may mean that we must accept that past as a constructed, imaginary object. Yet the question of the Enlightenment remains nonetheless historical in nature. Moreover, raising the question of what the Enlightenment was must also involve investigating the discursive operations and cultural practices whereby certain images of the Enlightenment were – and continue to be – constituted, circulated, contested or rejected. If the Enlightenment is of cultural value in the present moment (and my contention is that it is), then we must investigate how such value comes to be attached to the Enlightenment. We must reflect on how we come to know and valorize these constructed images, for it is in this coming to invested knowledge that we link the Enlightenment to our present moment. The aim of this book is to provide a space for such reflection by proposing a critical genealogy of the Enlightenment.

From the moment it was first posed, the question of the Enlightenment involved epistemological innovation, the project of devising new knowledge. Such writers as Montesquieu, Voltaire, Diderot, Rousseau, d'Alembert, and Condillac rejected traditional, canonical, and doctrinaire ways of knowing, proposing instead radically new ways of structuring knowledge. Their aim, moreover, was to create alternative ways of relating that new knowledge to their own times. In *L'Esprit des lois*, for instance, Montesquieu views the sociopolitical order of past cultures as essentially rational and thus comprehensible in human terms, an argument on which he bases his claim that the sociopolitical order of eighteenth-century France can be restructured in a more just fashion. Continuing the work of critical skepticism undertaken by Pierre Bayle in his *Dictionnaire historique et critique*, Voltaire delights in revealing how successive generations wrote over the truth of their past with errors of ignorance and self-interested lies. In this negative insight into the foundations of existing historical knowledge lies the promise of an ultimately rational history. The materialist epistemology of sensationalism, promoted by Diderot, d'Alembert, and Condillac amounts to a new way of knowing through the body, a body grounded in the present moment of sensation. In the realm of art, new pictorial, theatrical, and novelistic genres amount to technical experimentations with ways to relate this sensational, sentimental knowing to the present as it is experienced by imaginary characters of fiction, as well as by their eighteenth-century spectators and readers. Diderot's art criticism displays this relationship and also theorizes it, and Rousseau explores the complexity of the present apprehended as experience, both in his epistolary novel, *La Nouvelle Héloïse*, and his lyric, autobiographical writing, including the *Rêveries d'un promeneur solitaire* and *Les Confessions*.

This view of the canonical texts of eighteenth-century writing extends a vector of the Enlightenment project itself, namely, the drive to bring about a new way of knowing (in) the present historical moment. Yet the story I wish to tell in *The Enlightenment Past* cannot extend that project uncritically, just as we cannot rely unconditionally on the narrative of Enlightenment itself. One of the aims of this book is to pry apart two distinct Enlightenment narratives, two ways of organizing time and the subject's place in it – that of certain eighteenth-century writers who came to stand for the Enlightenment, and that of their successive readers. Each of these narratives represents a specific and distinct "régime d'historicité."

To begin reflecting then on how these Enlightenment texts are read, we can note a frequent recourse to an 'advent narrative' that recounts an inaugural conceptual event marking the beginnings of modernity. This move is particularly manifest in intellectual history, in such examples as Paul Hazard's *The European Mind, 1680–1715* (1935), Ernst Cassirer's *The Philosophy of the Enlightenment* (1932), and Peter Gay's *The Enlightenment: An Interpretation* (1966–69). In different ways each of these classic works was shaped by, and helped shape, the national-intellectual traditions in which they were produced and into which they have been imported. Despite these local, contextual differences, each of these three works illustrates how an image of the Enlightenment stands for an emergent modernity. Defining this modernity schematically via the proper name, these works construct the following portraits: Descartes, the first modern philosopher of rationalism; Voltaire, the first modern historiographer; Rousseau, the first analyst of modern contractual identity in its psychological, social, and political dimension; Diderot, the first modern art critic (or novelist or materialist philosopher); d'Alembert, the first modern historian of science.

Increasingly, the inaugural narrative that situates the beginnings of modernity in the idea of Enlightenment seems to possess less power to persuade. Is the Enlightenment regime of historicity over, no longer our own? Perhaps not, but certainly what compels our attention is not the narrative of intellectual origins but rather the social and institutional origin of narratives. At present, research focuses more frequently on revealing the contextual location of the idea, its place within a cultural network of texts, social relations, and interests. Symptomatic of this paradigm shift, in the United States at least, is the fact that intellectual history no longer enjoys the disciplinary status it once possessed. Considering such varied indices as academic hiring patterns, debates within scholarly publications, library cataloguing, and scholarly press publicity nomenclature, we see that it is not in intellectual history but in social and cultural history that the most appealing research agendas seem to be located, the most compelling interdisciplinary debates are taking place, and disciplinary renewal has been most spiritedly manifest. One consequence of this paradigm shift towards the sociocultural is that different stories about the eighteenth century and its significance for the present are now being told. Different texts, contexts, and events are foregrounded in the narratives of social and cultural history, which employ other explanatory logics to account for other cultural formations and practices. Patterns of sociability, strategies of self-production and resistance, newly empowered relations to knowledge, the role played by image-making and representation in determining thought, constructions of identity (gendered, national, racial, urban, domestic, colonial ...) – the significance of these research topics lies perhaps as much in the present they imply as in the past they explain (or construct).

One story these narratives do not tell, however, is that of a heroic, emancipatory, and ultimately modernizing Enlightenment such as it was told by earlier generations of intellectual historians. For some, these new narratives are the discouraging sign that research agendas have gotten highjacked by political ones, with scholarship having been pressed into service to promote ideological ends. For others, scholarship never enjoyed such protection from the political and such innoculation from the ideological. In this light the heroic story that once was told of an emancipatory Enlightenment that marks liberal thought is just as much a product of its times, from Kant to the 1960s, as any other less enchanted story about the Enlightenment, past or present. But in one case or the other, the Enlightenment now looms up from the other side of a paradigm shift. How should we grasp what we see? Is the Enlightenment to be understood from the perspective of intellectual history, cultural history, or perhaps in terms of a mode of historical thinking and analysis that cannot be reduced to such disciplinary labeling? A guiding thread of *The Enlightenment Past* is that, as historical object, the Enlightenment cannot be taken as a given, for reasons that are both historical and epistemological. One way to frame the issue of historical knowledge posed by the Enlightenment is by considering what has been called the 'crisis' of French historiography in the last half of the twentieth century.

The specter haunting the French historian is that of an instrumentalized history, based on the notion of the French nation-state and pressed into service in schools and universities to forge a patriotic and nationalist French imaginary. Easily caricatured, this was the history-writing illustrated by Ernest Lavisse, author of a primary-school history book, '*le petit Lavisse*', and a twenty-seven-volume *Histoire de France* (begun in 1892), followed by a nine-volume *Histoire de France contemporaine* (1921–2). Lavisse's texts had a massive influence in the production of Third Republic French national identity.[3] That history of France begins to break up in 1929 with the appearance of the journal founded by Marc Bloch and Lucien Febvre, *Annales d'histoire économique et politique*.[4] Responding to the trauma of the First World War, the *Annales* suggested the bankruptcy of history-writing that focused on the wars of the nation-state. Rejecting the ideology that undergirded nineteenth-century positivism, the *annalistes* shifted emphasis from the political to the economic, as well as from a Gallo-centric view to a more Eurocentric one. Their work also questioned the notion of organic evolution and teleological progress that had buttressed earlier national histories.

"Nous vivons l'éclatement de l'histoire," wrote Pierre Nora in 1971 in his description of the new series he would edit with the publisher Gallimard entitled "La Bibliothèque des histoires." What Nora's series signaled was the breakup and disappearance of History in favor of the story/history of numerous objects – regions, classes, outlooks, times, things ... Rejecting overarching syntheses in favor of the exploration of objects in their multiplicity, historians gave up on universal and universalizing history. Instead, it was sensed that 'new history' was being done in France in the 1970s. The notion takes form in the title Jacques Le Goff gave to the collection of essays he edited in 1978, *La Nouvelle histoire*. The disciplinary renewal that this 'new history' represented was based above all on the methodological model of *mentalité*. From Lucien Lévy-Bruhl's *La Mentalité primitive* (1922) and Marc Bloch's *La Société féodale* (1939) to its wholesale incorporation in the 1960s, the concept of *mentalité* was used to uncover the 'unthought' of thought, "the internalized conditionings that cause a group or a society to share, without the need to make them explicit, a system of representations and a system of values."[5] Aiming via the notion of *mentalité* to uncover structures that were impersonal and unconscious, psychological rather than intellectual, collective rather than individual, the 'new history' of the 1970s renewed history, but it did so at a price. As Roger Chartier argues, the 'new history' placed a serious limit on understanding the past by radically separating the ideas of the past that constitute a *mentalité* from those of the present that make up historical interpretation. Furthermore, this separation implies that ideas have an intrinsic signification, existing independently of their interpretation. However, as Chartier observes, this separation is far from a given. Instead, it may well belong to the covert strategy the historian employs to legitimate his or her own relation to the past. By covering over the traces of how the past is 'consumed', the individual historian can make it seem as if the concept of *mentalité*, along with other categories generated by historical analysis, were in fact universals.

The disciplinary renewal produced by the 'new history' in France resulted from the decision to work against this strategy of interpretive camouflage. One way to restore historicity to categories of thought was by locating the origin of historical understanding in the practice of making history, the various ways in which individuals and groups are discursively and disciplinarily conditioned – as well as enabled – to speak about the past, both individually and collectively. This turn to discourse grew out of the high structuralism of the 1960s, illustrated most classically in Roland Barthes's bringing narratological analysis to bear upon the historical.[6] Observing that history writing is essentially a form of narrative, Barthes argued that any historical understanding derived from that writing is narratively determined. Just as literary discourse does, the discourse of history produces its own 'effect of the real' through precise technical means, such as the pronominal absence of the "I" or the focus on 'there' and 'then' to the exclusion of any 'here' and 'now'. For that reality effect to take hold, these markers of discursive technique must be made to appear to be absent, doing their work as if they were not there. Literary scholars may have relied on Barthes's essay to indict historians for an under-theorized relation to their own craft, and historians may have rejected the insights of structuralism out of hand for being a mode of thought that is resolutely, if not imperiously and terroristically, antihistorical. Yet the disciplinary renewal brought about by *la nouvelle histoire* in France grows out of a probing concern with history's relation to language and the role it plays in determining historical understanding.[7]

Michel de Certeau extends Barthes's insight to argue that historical discourse is a disciplinary discourse, determined by a specific collective practice. Taking the example of intellectual history, *l'histoire des idées*, *Geistesgeschichte*, Certeau notes that its object, the idea as that which can be thought in a given time (be it the Hegelian 'spirit' or *Geist*, Weberian *Weltanschauungen*, or Kuhnian paradigms), is not so much a real, historical object as a sign of a constitutive need on the part of historiography. Intellectual history stands for the impossibility of eliminating the ideologies that inform historiography, Certeau claims.

But in awarding them the place of an object, in isolating them from socioeconomic structures, or in supposing, furthermore, that 'ideas' function in the same fashion as these structures, parallel to them and on another level, the 'history of ideas' can only find in the form of an 'unconscious' this inconsistent reality in which it dreams of discovering an *autonomous* coherence. What it manifests is in fact the unconscious of historians, or rather, that of the group to which they belong ... The search for a coherence belonging to an ideological level thus refers to the *place* of those who develop it in the twentieth century.[8]

The case of intellectual history can be taken to stand more broadly for doing history *tout court*. Following Certeau's lead, focus on the historical given is replaced by attention to the historiographical process, resulting in a changed relation to the real.

If meaning cannot be apprehended in the form of a specific knowledge that would either be drawn from the real or might be added to it, it is because every 'historical fact' results from a praxis, because it is already the sign of an act and therefore a statement of meaning. It results from procedures which have allowed a mode of comprehension to be articulated as a discourse of 'facts.'[9]

It was Michel Foucault who offered a relentlessly bracing exploration of the relation between historical understanding and historical praxis. A guiding thread in Foucault's writing is the problematic linkage between history and metaphysics, a connection that always risks coming undone. In the early essay, "Nietzsche, Genealogy, History," for example, Foucault defines traditional historical practice in terms of a suprahistorical perspective always implicit within this practice. Traditional history is

a history whose function is to compose the finally reduced diversity of time into a totality fully closed upon itself; a history that always encourages subjective recognitions and attributes a form of reconciliation to all the displacements of the past; a history whose perspective on all that preceded it implies the end of time, a completed development. The historian's history finds its support outside of time and pretends to base its judgments on an apocalyptic objectivity. This is only possible, however, because of its belief in eternal truth, the immortality of the soul, and the nature of consciousness as always identical to itself.[10]

The "support" of the historian's history, the latter's ground, is thus a metaphysical one, claims Foucault. In defense of the historical discipline, we might object that no 'practicing' historian believes anymore in total history, in the perfect recoverability of absolute origins, in an essence of things that preexists the world of contingency and change, in truths that will be made manifest in a teleological march towards history's end, in an enduring subject of history that remains always identical to itself. But do such denials serve less to defend the historian's method and craft than to imply that traditional history involves a metaphysics whose foundations are all too shaky, a metaphysics that has come ungrounded?

To embrace this metaphysical ungroundedness and nonetheless produce historical knowledge, Foucault calls for replacing traditional history with genealogical history. This brand of history refuses to assume the timeless truth or identity of things prior to their emergence, and in this refusal reveals the accidental and contingent aspect of these truths and identities. The genealogist does not recover the origin of events in the attempt to reveal an ultimate, total signification; rather, the aim is to make legible their descent, their ongoing construction or constant reconfiguration.

To follow the complex course of descent is to maintain passing events in their proper dispersion; it is to identify the accidents, the minute deviations – or conversely, the complete reversals – the errors, the false appraisals, and the faulty calculations that gave birth to those things that continue to exist and have value for us; it is to discover that truth or being does not lie at the root of what we know and what we are, but the exteriority of accidents.[11]

If the genealogist "listens to history," writes Foucault, what is heard is not "the timeless and essential secret of things." Instead the genealogist discovers "the secret that they have no essence or that their essence was fabricated in a piecemeal fashion from alien forms."[12] Can we quibble here and ask whether 'listening to history' suggests the latter's voice, and thus that the enigma of history could be resolved in the final expression of its secrets? Does the image of voice thus reground history and its capacity to speak truths? We should note, though, that Foucault does not state that history speaks; rather, he insists on what the genealogist discovers. History's voiced truths are an act of ventriloquism. However much we might wish to hear the voice of history, what is revealed in the critical and self-reflexive encounter with history is the inescapable contingency of its making.

Both Certeau and Foucault draw attention to the 'place' or practice of history, to the set of discursive, disciplinary, and institutional conditions that determine all historical knowledge. These are processes always at work in the confection of all history, the telltale signs that historical knowledge is a singular perspective that can never be made universal, total, or true. Consequently, to maintain belief in traditional history, these signs must be effaced. As Foucault notes, "historians take unusual pains to erase the elements in their work which reveal their grounding in a particular time and place, their preference in a controversy – the unavoidable obstacles of their pleasure." They hide these signs, he adds, by invoking "objectivity, accuracy of facts, and the permanence of the past."[13] Yet at particular moments, and in the texts that mark them, these telltale signs of history's place and its practice become particularly visible.

One such moment was the celebration of the 200th anniversary of the French Revolution. Spawning countless conferences, articles, and books, the bicentennial produced an extremely detailed view of the complex revolutionary period. Generating intense debate in France, and somewhat more detached commentary elsewhere, these bicentennial events highlighted the extent to which the legacy of the Revolution was still in dispute, certainly among historians but also in the larger public sphere.[14] While the French government continued the well-established republican tradition of representing a Revolution that best suited it, French historians reflected more publicly on the overtly ideological and polemical use that had been made – and was still being made – of the revolutionary past. In a disciplinary self-reflexive sense, certain historians wondered aloud whether it was possible to avoid such a politicized understanding of the revolutionary past, or whether, on the contrary, the moment had arrived to examine the role of the political in historical understanding.[15] This French 'historians' feud' concerning the fraught relation between memory and the political thus crystallized a debate under way within the discipline of history since the beginning of 'the new history'. Extending beyond the flashpoint event of the Revolution, this reflection questioned how to remember other particularly controversial events (such as the Occupation and the Vichy 'syndrome', the Algerian War or the Dreyfus affair). This reflection derived its theoretical impetus from French historians' desire to examine the role their own disciplinary practice had played – and could play – in constructing the narrative of French cultural identity, such as it was being formulated in the fraught context of postwar, postcolonial, post-national France.[16] Marked by a *devoir de mémoire*, a memorial duty and dutiful memory, historiographical practice became inescapably an obligatory act of civic and ethical engagement.

The revolutionary celebration spawned renewed interest in the Enlightenment, and the disciplinary self-reflection it occasioned generated explanatory paradigms forged to take the place of the by then moribund Marxist interpretation of the Enlightenment. Championed notably by Albert Soboul, the Enlightenment of Marxism was taken to reflect the interests of the rising bourgeois class, interests in conflict with those of an entrenched and empowered *Ancien Régime* aristocracy. It was the bourgeoisie that the Revolution brought to power, according to the Marxist narrative, and with them the values of their class.[17] The economic determinism of the Marxist interpretation would be forcefully contested by historians anxious to reground political agency. In 1978 François Furet's *Penser la Révolution française* helped set revolutionary historiography on a path toward what Furet argued would be a new political interpretation of the Revolution, but one not hopelessly entangled with a social interpretation. To do so, Furet argued, it was necessary to grasp the Revolution as thought. Keith Baker summarizes Furet's position thus:

Whatever its social conditions ... the Revolution was an essentially political phenomenon. It was political not simply because it represented a struggle for the possession of power, but because it transformed the symbolic grounding of an entire community and reconstituted the logic of social relations in the most profound sense. In short, it represented the supremely political act of redefining the public order.[18]

The position Furet represents is a theoretically important one, for by basing an understanding of the political on what he calls "the semiotic," he pointed the way toward a fresh understanding of the symbolic work of cultural practices, newly conceived in their political dimension. As far as the Enlightenment is concerned, Furet's work shifted the question from what the Enlightenment was to that of how it would be represented, the ways successive generations 'constructed' it as part of a larger effort to bring the Revolution to a close (which, for Furet, did not effectively occur until 1880, with the establishment of the Third Republic).[19] This closure was brought about as much by such representational practices as commemoration as by the triumph of disembodied political ideas and ideals.

This construction, moreover, signaled human agency at work in the political sphere and not economic determinism dictated by the inexorable march of history.[20] This focus on representational practices lying at the heart of the cultural imaginary makes it possible to rethink historical determinism, that is, to imagine other temporal logics and causal narratives than the commonsensical one according to which the past is the unquestionable cause of the future. It is in this sense that Roger Chartier has suggested we should do away with the teleological narrative according to which the Enlightenment produced the Revolution. Instead, he asks, how might we imagine that the Revolution produced the Enlightenment, through the revolutionaries' creation of the tradition they needed in order to legitimate their struggle? This after-the-fact origin signified the attempt "to root the legitimacy [of the Revolution] in a corpus of texts and founding authors reconciled and united, beyond their extreme differences, by their preparation of a rupture with the old world."[21] However productive Chartier's insight might be for understanding the political culture of the revolutionary moment, we might wish to extend its range considerably. For throughout the nineteenth and twentieth centuries, the French cultural imaginary aimed precisely at producing the Enlightenment it desired. Even in the early years of the twenty-first century, at a moment when the national narrative seems to be in increasing disarray, it is not by chance that the models are being produced of a more sociable, European, cosmopolitan, and thus a potentially more 'universal' Enlightenment, one that perhaps would not be inflected by – and thus held hostage to – the national specificity of French history.[22] One of the aims of *The Enlightenment Past* is to investigate the production of these belated origins.

In France, the interpretation of the Enlightenment was always – and continues to be – mediated by another set of 'local', contemporary conditions. It is perhaps a truism to suggest that the viewpoint of the present invariably inflects any given view of the past. Through a series of fine-grained analyses of instances of that inflection, I wish to suggest that the Enlightenment can be understood, as Jean Marie Goulemot puts it, as "a series of arbitrary reconstructions possessing their own historicity." This understanding of the Enlightenment may well be one of the most unsettling and unavoidable of legacies. "Receiving the legacy of the Enlightenment thus means receiving the legacy of the imaginary scenarios that it produced or confirmed. Accepting or refusing this legacy comes to the same thing."[23] Yet I don't wish to imply that our return to an Enlightenment past is destined to remain blindly determined by the mediation of the reconstructive history. For one of the intriguing symptoms of contemporary critical reflection on what in telegraphic fashion I shall call 'the current situation' is an increasing awareness of the need to grapple with the question of phrasing the Enlightenment in order to come to terms with that situation. In 1987, for instance, Alain Finkielkraut diagnoses the 'defeat' or 'undoing' of thought (*la défaite de la pensée*) in what he sees as culturally pluralized and ethically fractured French society, and he describes that malaise in terms of a decline from humanitarian, universalizing, moralizing Enlightenment thought.[24] Some twenty years later, Régis Debray conducts his own sardonic critique of the material and moral excesses of French society through a reflection on the impossible legacy of the Enlightenment.[25] Despite their differences, the Enlightenment that Finkielkraut and Debray refer to is a constructed image, both of their own making, to be sure, but also part of a powerful and unruly collective sociocultural memory. Insofar as self-reflection is an integral part of Enlightenment thought and discourse, the contemporary construction of the Enlightenment involves self-reflection on how this memory comes to be, how it functions, and to what ends (if indeed there can be an end to memory). As David Denby suggests in an article whose title performs the kind of historical-critical work he calls for, the very juxtaposition of an 'Enlightenment crisis' with a 'modernity crisis', without assuming from the outset what causal vectors link these two entities, is the condition of possibility for a bracing revision of some familiar and entrenched assumed ideas.[26]

Across the Channel and across the Atlantic, 'local' circumstances also shaped the construction of the Enlightenment. To be precise, it was only there that "the Enlightenment" as such was constructed, as opposed to *les Lumières, Aufklärung, Voorlichting, Felvilágosodás, Prosveshchenie, Oświecenie, Upplysning*, terms whose linguistic diversity itself suggests that they are far from designating the same geo-local entity, and thus probably not the same conceptual one.[27] Moreover, the opaque strangeness of such terms, at least for an Anglophone monolingual, should effectively estrange us from any 'natural' notion we might have of just what the Enlightenment is and how it came into being. To take but one example of the need to estrange the natural, we can turn to the venerable genre of the dictionary. With its apparent neutrality and linguistic objectivity, the *Oxford English Dictionary*, second edition (1989), illustrates the conjuncture of the linguistic and the local. "Enlightenment" is defined, first, as "the action of enlightening; the state of being enlightened." All examples of the word's use in this sense are taken from English writers. The second definition is the following: "sometimes used [after Ger. *Aukflärung, Aufklärerei*] to designate the spirit and aims of the French philosophers of the eighteenth century, or of others whom it is intended to associate with them in the implied charge of shallow and pretentious intellectualism, unreasonable contempt for tradition and authority, etc." Examples here are taken from nineteenth-century English commentators of German philosophy (Hegel and Kant). Given the performative nature of dictionaries, it is difficult to exempt the *OED* entirely from the anti-Enlightenment French-bashing that the entry describes, suggesting a much broader national-intellectual discursive tradition that shapes this return to Enlightenment.[28]

Such was also the case across the Atlantic. In the United States, it was the American Revolution, and arguably the English one before it, but certainly not the French one, that provided the prism through which historiography would view the Enlightenment. Consequently, the French Enlightenment was accorded far less of a causal role in the narrative about how reform and revolution came about in the broader European and North Atlantic context, which was described in terms of local and national Enlightenments. Moreover, in viewing the French Enlightenment from the United States, observers tended to overlook the postrevolutionary debates that pitted republicans against anti-republicans, and later a communist left against a Gaullist right. At best these debates were seen as the 'internal' Gallic squabbles of French nationalism. In contrast, it was as if the vantage point of beyond the Channel were an unencumbered one, beyond ideology, and so there was no need to ask what other 'internal' issues might be inflecting the interpretation of the Enlightenment put forward by historians in the United States. Had such questioning occurred, as it is beginning to, scholars and commentators might have wondered just how well Enlightenment political philosophy translates into the Anglo-American liberal discourse, and whether something significant must necessarily get lost in translation in the passage from one epistemological and political tradition to another.

Pursuing this kind of questioning, Mark Lilla has asked whether, from the French Revolution onwards, Anglo-American political philosophy has not remained "estranged" from its continental counterpart. Singularly uninterested in seeking common terms to explain such unintelligibility, this political philosophy aims instead and more insularly at self-legitimation.[29] Following Lilla, the view of the French Enlightenment produced in the United States should be read in terms of its constitutive blind spots, such as the question of the individual's freedom in his or her relation to the state. This was a central issue for the political theorists of the French and American revolutions. It was resolved in the two cases in different theoretical and structural terms, giving rise to two different ways of viewing this relation, and not only in the immediately postrevolutionary moment but throughout the next two centuries. As an example of how the trans-Atlantic view of the Enlightenment could be understood in terms of local conditions and contextual drives, Sophia Rosenfeld has argued that the liberal historiography of the Enlightenment written in the United States following the Second World War can be read not so much as the project of recovering timeless humanitarian values of the eighteenth-century past, but rather as the attempt to establish an intellectual genealogy for specifically mid-twentieth-century liberal ideals and values.[30] Although Rosenfeld does not make the point, at issue is a postwar, Cold War, and liberal American version of the Enlightenment, determined perhaps as much by a contemporary, local context as was the French postwar Marxist interpretation of the same texts and events. Rosenfeld's recontextualizing consideration of liberal historiography's version of the Enlightenment joins a more extensive questioning of that Enlightenment, beginning with the revisionist examination of the complex relations of sociability that bound individuals to one another in the eighteenth century. This revision itself will need to be contextualized in turn, set in relation to the intellectual genealogy fashioned by eighteenth-century scholars of the 1990s, who came of intellectual age not during the wars of the mid twentieth century – the 'hot' one of the '40s, the 'cold' one of the '50s or the oppositional culture wars of the late '60s and '70s – but during a moment of disciplinary self-reflexivity and hyper-professionalization.

CONTESTING ENLIGHTENMENT

This brief sketch of Enlightenment historiography, which will be fleshed out in the following chapters, conveys the methodological claim that any history of the Enlightenment, if it is to make comprehensible the latter's historicity, must engage with local micro-genealogies of 'the Enlightenment question'. The larger theoretical point underlying this claim is that all knowledge is local and situated knowledge, whether we understand this determination in a discursive, historiographical, institutional, or cultural sense. This claim concerning the situated nature of knowledge frames the argument of *The Enlightenment Past*, whose aim is to explore how knowledge of the Enlightenment takes shape in particular contexts. Insisting on contextual, situated understandings of the Enlightenment, I proceed from the conviction that any interpretation of the Enlightenment is precisely that, beginning with the version of things the eighteenth-century philosophes themselves produced and extending to modern interpretations that continue to cast the discourse of Enlightenment in contestatory, emancipatory, heroic terms. It is true that these are the terms in which the philosophes presented themselves and their writing. At issue, though, is whether these terms can be taken over uncritically in a present-day evaluation of the Enlightenment and its significance. One sign of the scrutiny to which the discourse of Enlightenment has been subjected is renewed interest in the forms of resistance, hostility, and critique the philosophes' writing encountered. The discourse of Enlightenment may present itself as a contestatory discourse, but from the moment of its appearance it was also a contested one, constructed as much by its enemies as by its champions.[31] Fréron's epic pillorying of Voltaire in *L'Année littéraire*, Palissot's parody of the philosophes in *Les Cacouacs*, the more serious critique of the *Encyclopédie* project undertaken in the Jesuits' *Journal de Trévoux* – for long these elements of intellectual and cultural history were viewed in schematic, caricatural fashion, as instances of *l'infâme* that Voltaire so repeatedly lambasted. It was all too easy to tell Enlightenment's story by adopting the adversarial stance the philosophes themselves developed towards their critics, phrasing things in terms of the opposition between the benighted and the enlightened, the old and the new. This way of recounting the Enlightenment neatly divides things up between the winners and the losers of the eighteenth-century culture wars. As we will see, this oppositional strategy was all too easy to displace onto other latter-day political and cultural battles. But this version of things presents an essentially monolithic Enlightenment, overlooking the tensions within the discourse of Enlightenment itself. Nor does it help us understand the complicated internal dynamics of the cultural battles into which this discourse would be inscribed. Consequently, it is instructive to assess the internal conflicts of the Enlightenment by considering the critical resistance to the philosophes' story of modernity that later versions of the eighteenth century mounted. For instance, by considering the anti-Enlightenment position of the proto-literary historian, Jean-François de La Harpe, we can understand the place the Enlightenment was made to occupy in the literary historical and political narratives that told the story of a certain revolutionary modernity (as well as of the beginnings of modern literary history).

Resistance to the Enlightenment characterizes not only a few benighted anti-philosophes of the eighteenth century or some arch-conservative anti-revolutionaries. Taking interest in the larger field of cultural production, and not just that of elite intellectual culture, literary and cultural historians have brought back into view the work of the adversaries of the philosophes, as well as that of other second- and third-tier writers. The story of these writers fits less well into the narrative of a heroic, emancipatory Enlightenment, and thus these figures are explained according to other heuristic models. In particular, the model of a developing sociability of urban print culture continues to gain in interpretive authority among literary and cultural historians. This interest in thinkers and writers who resisted mainstream Enlightenment provides a way to consider this cultural production in terms other than those provided by the

Enlightenment progressivist, emancipatory narrative. As such, this interest amounts to another form of revision of the Enlightenment narrative, if not even resistance to it.

Yet scholars of the early modern period have been less quick than others to theorize the need to think through such resistance. Twentieth-century literary, feminist, and cultural critics have been far more intrepid in their assessment of the Enlightenment project. For some, the Enlightenment is not a project to be embraced but a legacy to be contested. For others, that legacy must ultimately be rejected as a form of ideology whose power to situate us as subjects should no longer enthrall. According to the prevalent indictment of the Enlightenment, which owes much to the bracing critique put forward in 1944 by Theodor Adorno and Max Horkheimer in their *Dialectic of Enlightenment*, it is ultimately yet another form of Western hegemony, cultural imperialism cloaked as a higher form of rationality, a pursuit of knowledge so total – if not totalitarian – that ethical concerns are left behind. In *Modernity and the Holocaust*, Zygmunt Bauman pursues this critique of the teleological illusion of an emancipated modernity, arguing that the evil of the Holocaust was in fact a rationality of evil.[32]

Responding to Adorno and Horkheimer's critique of Enlightenment, Jürgen Habermas worries whether one can get 'beyond' Enlightenment, or forget it, without falling into unreason. "There is no cure," Habermas writes, "for the wounds of Enlightenment other than the radicalized Enlightenment itself."[33] Finding few defenders among cultural critics today, Enlightenment has ended up, it would seem, a flawed bulwark against unreason, and apparently an outdated approach to contemporary issues such as gender, race, and ecology.[34] Posing the contemporary relation to Enlightenment in the stark terms of a binary opposition and an obligatory choosing of sides, cultural critics make it seem as if one could not be a subject of Enlightenment and a thoroughly postmodern one as well.

It is of course not new news to report that postmodernism is inhospitable to the Enlightenment project. Indeed, Enlightenment thought is a choice object against which to launch a postmodernist critique, especially insofar as the Enlightenment is perhaps the 'other' discourse that critique requires. It has been suggested that a good deal of contemporary critical thought finds a constitutive alterity in the discourse of the Enlightenment, a difference over against which it situates itself in order to delineate its specificity.[35] Like Voltaire's God, if the Enlightenment didn't exist, both as historical moment and conceptual category, would postmodernism have had to invent it, in an apparently supreme unself-aware gesture of creating its own foundational narrative? But this inevitable return of the Enlightenment as the ground for postmodern critique may signal not so much postmodernism's blind spot as something quite important concerning the constitutive limits of contemporary critical practice and historical understanding.

THE LIMITS OF ENLIGHTENMENT

In discursive terms, the postmodern moment is marked by the crisis of narratives. Calling into question master tropes, universal laws, and other foundational paradigms, the critical practice associated with a postmodern stance argues for the power of the particular, the local, and the heterogeneous to undo and resist 'grand narratives' and the truths they purport to tell. But postmodernism, in its philosophical dimension, is more than the retread of radical skepticism that its critics frequently claim it to be. It also signals a crisis involving the kind of discourse of legitimation and ethical judgment that characterizes the modern. Enlightenment is a choice example for locating this crisis. In the introduction to *The Postmodern Condition*, for instance, Jean-François Lyotard offers the Enlightenment narrative as a prime instance of a modern narrative. Modern, for Lyotard, means any way of knowing that justifies itself through reference to a metadiscourse that legitimates its status, a grand narrative that underwrites its working, the rules of its 'game'. Such narratives might include the dialectics of Spirit, the hermeneutics of meaning, the emancipation of the rational or of the working subject, or the creation of wealth. The Enlightenment narrative is modern in precisely this sense. For this narrative, which Lyotard schematizes as one "in which the hero of knowledge works toward a good ethico-political end – universal peace," is implicitly legitimated by the metanarrative of a philosophy of history.[36] Once that metanarrative is questioned, or somehow fails to win our confidence, the narrative of Enlightenment runs aground. The consensual relation between like rational minds becomes impossible. Enlightenment becomes the space, sign, or site, not of modern consensus but of postmodern dissensus, an eventuality I will return to but whose problematic dimensions can be sketched out here.

In *Why History?*, Keith Jenkins suggests that from the eighteenth century to the present, it has not been possible to bring about through the application of reason, science, and technology a higher level of social and political well-being for an increasingly freer citizen-subject. The name given to that impossibility is modernity, a failed experiment in social living when judged in the experiment's own terms. If such is the case, then perhaps these terms do not apply to the present. Extending this incommensurability to the extreme, Jenkins claims that "we must accept that we live and have always lived amidst social foundations having no legitimating ontological, epistemological, methodological or ethical grounds for beliefs and actions beyond the status of an ultimately self-referencing (rhetorical) conversation."[37] It is the recognition of this ungroundedness, he concludes, that defines postmodernity, a recognition that one may dispute but cannot escape. For no other perspective is available besides that of postmodernism, which is the perspective produced and determined by the present historical moment. There can be no argument over whether the history of the present moment will be a postmodern history, for there cannot be any other. Thus, extending Jenkins's assertion, one could argue that there can be no other understanding of the Enlightenment than one that is grounded (rhetorically) in a problematic grappling with the question of an impossible modernity.

This is not the first assessment of the relation between the Enlightenment project and modernity. Already in 1784, Immanuel Kant located the place of Enlightenment in contemporary debate, publishing a short essay in the *Berlinische Monatsschrift* entitled "An Answer to the Question: 'What is Enlightenment?'" Kant's answer to the question is well known: "Enlightenment is man's emergence from his self-incurred immaturity. Immaturity is the inability to use one's own understanding without the guidance of another."[38] Enlightenment results from the courageous decision to free oneself from existing ways of knowing and to use one's own faculties in order to know otherwise. Kant encapsulates his understanding of the Enlightenment in the motto *sapere aude*, dare to know. The phrase consolidates the thinking of an age, forming a project we continue to recognize as a fundamentally modern one. According to the familiar yet bracing perspective Kant's essay provides, Enlightenment is an emancipatory process, involving a way to realize the ideal of freedom through the use of the human faculty of reason. Enlightenment thus involves contesting established instances of authority, requiring that they submit to rational examination. This general questioning of authority does not simply lead to relativism, however, even if relativizing the truth claims made in the name of absolute principles was – and remains – one of the familiar and most effective tactics of Enlightenment critique. More important, Enlightenment also implies a new attitude towards legitimation, the way in which the truth claims of judgment can be founded. If the validity of arguments cannot be justified through an appeal to exterior authoritative instances, then judgments bear the burden of proof to support their own claims to legitimacy. Judgment itself must provide its own self-reflective evidence in order to legitimate the results of its operations. Thus the aim of Enlightenment is double. It seeks both emancipation from traditional modes of authority, and a new, self-imposed, or self-generated authority that could legitimate arguments and resolve debate and conflict.

The new authoritative instance for Kant is that of criticism. The age of Enlightenment is also the age of criticism.

Our age is, in especial degree, the age of criticism [*Kritik*], and to criticism everything must submit. Religion through its sanctity, and law-giving through its majesty, may seek to exempt themselves from it. But they then awaken just suspicion, and cannot claim the sincere respect which reason accords only to that which has been able to sustain the test of free and open examination.[39]

Kritik is the ultimate instance where judgments made in the name of reason can be adjudicated. In the *Critique of Pure Reason* Kant figures this instance as a "tribunal" that reason itself sets up, a "tribunal which will assure to reason its lawful claims, and dismiss all groundless pretensions, not by despotic decrees, but in accordance with its own eternal and unalterable laws." This image of a single tribunal suggests the ideal goal, if not the reality, of being able to adjudicate competing, heterogeneous demands and thus to provide a just resolution to conflict. But the question arises as to whether the judgment that the tribunal of reason would provide could resolve conflict without suppressing difference, heterogeneous elements that cannot be governed by a sole law or criterion. The fact that Kant wrote three *Critiques* has been taken to suggest that he did not believe in a single monolithic reason, and in fact that the three forms of reason he treats – scientific, ethical, and esthetic – do not fully coincide.

The image of the tribunal suggests that the work of reason is situated in a social context as well as in a purely logical one. The question of Enlightenment is thus not a rhetorical one, at least not in any purely formal way. The power of truth claims is imbricated within the power of institutions. As a result, resolving competing claims before the tribunal of reason amounts to a social and political ideal, as well as a philosophical one. The law of reason serves as a legitimating principle for action in the social and political sphere. It is in this sense that Enlightenment acquires a public dimension. As Kant defines it, the public use of reason is distinct from the kind of speaking or writing that is limited by institutional constraints, which for him reflects the private uses of one's reason. Taking the example of the clergyman and the teacher, these eighteenth-century public intellectuals, Kant argues that their discourse represents a private use of reason in a civil post and therefore can be restricted without hindering the progress of Enlightenment. But the public use of reason is "that use which anyone may make of it as a man of learning addressing the entire reading public."[40] The ultimate addressee of Enlightenment discourse is an ideal collectivity, which goes by various names in the eighteenth century, such as the reading public in Kant's essay, posterity, or humanity. Enlightenment discourse can also claim to represent that addressee, as when the philosophe speaks in the name of that ideal collectivity. The philosophe does so ostensibly to help realize the Enlightenment program of liberal, liberating reform for the betterment of humanity by providing in the figure of that collectivity a normative, regulative value. Indeed, it may happen that Enlightenment discourse is formulated in such a way that all the positions of the discursive triangle are occupied by one instance, as the position of addressee, referent, and speaker become collapsed. ("I speak to you, humanity, of humanity, for which I am the spokesman.") This discursive totalization is not a mere discursive arrangement, for it is designed to achieve ends that have been associated with a certain totalitarianism and terrorism.

With the question he poses, Kant designates a concept and names an event, the advent of Enlightenment. His question thus provides a way to phrase modernity, a sense of being (modern). The question of Enlightenment makes it possible for us to phrase our identity as individual agents and as members of a bonded community. Through this question, I can say 'we', phrasing a collective identity in terms of the qualities Enlightenment designates, such as rationality, freedom, morality, and humanity. Phrasing modernity means phrasing being in time, and thus the question of Enlightenment is also a historical question. Being modern involves constructing foundations, searching for legitimate principles upon which to ground judgment. Designating this search, Enlightenment implies a teleological mode of understanding as well as action. It is a project, an ideal to be realized within a history that is universal, the becoming of a collective 'we'. The question of Enlightenment is a political question as well, the cosmopolitanism of Enlightenment implying a cosmopolitics, a total program for achieving the collective identity of humanity.

Now, more than 200 years after Kant's phrasing of the question of Enlightenment, the question has become ours as well. Or rather, it remains our question, one in which we – and 'the we' – are implicated. It is a limit question, which we cannot do without but that we cannot get beyond. Although Kant's essay is entitled "Answering the Question, 'What is Enlightenment?'," the question perhaps admits of no answer. For Michel Foucault, Kant's question marks the advent of modern philosophy, the mode of philosophical thought that for more than two centuries has been trying to supply an answer to Kant. Indeed, what makes modern philosophy modern, claims Foucault, is its constant attempt to answer this question.[41] Foucault's caution is helpful here as we consider the place of Enlightenment in contemporary debate. For he urges us to confront the difficulty of thinking critically about the question of Enlightenment. Rather than answer this question yet once again, Foucault proposes that we ask another question, namely, upon what principle could we found a critical understanding of Enlightenment, from which perspective could we situate it in contemporary debate? The question is all the more acute because Enlightenment itself is founded upon critique, the process called upon to supply legitimate principles for judging competing claims. How can one formulate a critique of critique, and on what ground does one stand to consider the question of foundations? What perspective would allow us to gain a critical distance from a system whose power is based on its ability to create critical vantage points?

Foucault's cautionary note suggests the complexity of undertaking a critique of Enlightenment. For the very system that Enlightenment's critics would reject relies upon critique, which it in fact needs. Producing a critique of Enlightenment is thus one of the most enlightened of projects. Producing such a critique amounts to engaging in a process determined by precisely the very system that its critics wish to gain distance from and be freed of. The empowering move of seeking to adopt a critical stance even towards Enlightenment may well backfire, placing the critic in an inescapable double bind. For if the critic's aim is to "detect and denounce all of the cases in which the system fails to improve the process towards emancipation," then "the critic's position now presupposes that the system itself is understood by criticism as being put in charge of promoting emancipation and that critiques, whatever forms they may take, are needed by the system for improving its efficiency in the direction of emancipation."[42] The critic is subjected all the more inevitably to the system of Enlightenment.

In these past several pages – and the past several decades, if not centuries, to which they refer – it seems that the question of Enlightenment inevitably leads not to answers but to more questions. But before these questions spawn even more, let us attempt to evaluate them, albeit in an interrogative mode. Just what are the consequences of considering the question of Enlightenment in this fashion? Instead of producing agreement concerning a better understanding of Enlightenment, do these questions in fact work to undermine the latter's legacy? Do they not testify to an arrogant skepticism, or worse to a corrosive nihilism, that risks destroying the positive and valuable creations the Enlightenment has bequeathed to us? Or can these questions be seen as an attempt to invent another relation to Enlightenment, one that would not be founded on the impetus to critique. And so another question: can we imagine another relation to Enlightenment besides a critical one? Is there another way of phrasing Enlightenment, another mode or genre, besides that of critique, that makes it possible to imagine resisting Enlightenment without opposing it? To be sure, it may seem that resisting Enlightenment is logically impossible, tantamount to venturing into the illogical, the irrational, the premodern. This aim may appear to jeopardize a familiar identity, placing at stake our sense of being (modern). However, it may also be the case that the venture of resisting Enlightenment involves being postmodern (or postmodern being). In considering a number of moments, texts, and cultural practices in and through which Enlightenment is constituted, the present book aims to articulate that historical and resistant mode of thought in its relation to the Enlightenment.

CHAPTER 2

The event of Enlightenment: beginnings

Writing in 1759, Jean Le Rond d'Alembert opens his *Essai sur les éléments de philosophie* with what he calls the "tableau de l'esprit humain" at mid century. The chronology may seem arbitrary, but within three or four years the Parisian intellectual scene saw the appearance of La Mettrie's *L'Homme machine* (1747), Montesquieu's *De l'esprit des lois* (1748), the first three volumes of Buffon's *Histoire naturelle* (1749), the prospectus of the *Encyclopédie* (1750), Rousseau's *Discours sur les sciences et les arts* (1751), Voltaire's *Le Siècle de Louis XIV* and Duclos's *Considérations sur les mœurs* (1751). D'Alembert's portrait or portrayal of mind can be seen as the opening conceit of an intellectual news story, as he sets out to describe a dynamic, multifaceted epistemological event that is reconfiguring the intellectual culture in France. Thought has awoken, observes the mathematician and coeditor of the *Encyclopédie*, freeing itself from the obscurantist yoke of opinion and superstition. Especially in the area of the natural sciences, true knowledge of the world has been achieved thanks to a systematic explanation of its elements. But in all disciplines and forms of thought, notes d'Alembert, new ways of knowing are taking shape. All beliefs and ideas have been reexamined, from secular science to divine revelation, from questions of metaphysics to standards of taste, from music to morals, from scholastic theology to commerce, and from the politics of absolutism to popular rights. A new way of philosophizing marks mid-century France, one that d'Alembert does not hesitate to characterize as revolutionary, in intellectual-historical terms as well as geopolitical ones.[1]

"Our age is the age of criticism," Kant writes in 1781, "and to criticism everything must submit." For Kant, the act of criticism involved subjecting truth claims to validation in the public sphere, to the "test of free and public examination."[2] In the *Encyclopédie* article "Gens de lettres," Voltaire describes this mid-century moment not so much in terms of a Kantian opposition between public and private but rather as marked by a disciplinary shift from philology to philosophy. Yet this shift redirects the interpretation performed by "l'esprit philosophique," amounting to what Voltaire hails as a powerfully new ideological critique. Turning away from establishing ancient texts, critical activity now focuses on assessing the foundations on which beliefs and doctrines are based. In a stroke, critical activity has come to rely on robust philosophy and has destroyed all manner of "infectious" prejudices: "astrologers' predictions, magicians' divinations, all manner of spells, false wonders, false marvels, superstitious custom; it relegated to the schools a thousand childish disputes that formerly were dangerous and that have been made contemptible."[3]

What d'Alembert describes in the *Essai* resembles the process of epistemological change that Thomas Kuhn will name a paradigm shift, in which one disciplinary matrix with its values, questions, methods, criteria of validity, and socializing function cedes in explanatory force before another.[4] This awakening of reason and the ensuing revolutionary way of philosophizing mark an epistemic break, in which the structuring logic organizing the relation between words and things is thoroughly reformulated, resulting in a new discursive grid-work determining the production of knowledge.[5] Following upon this epistemological shake-up is the attempt to reorder and reassemble knowledge, yet differently configured. Devising elaborate conceptual schemes and textual mechanisms, writer-philosophers such as Condorcet in the *Esquisse d'un tableau historique des progrès de l'esprit* and the encyclopedic coeditors Diderot and d'Alembert propose various ways to link information in the name of a rationalized, totalized knowledge. These systems of ordered knowledge imply moreover a universal knowing subject, figured in d'Alembert's *Essai* via the synecdoche of "l'esprit," this mind or spirit that constitutes a subject whose existence is the condition of such epistemological networking or mapping.[6]

D'Alembert's story of enlightenment is a familiar one, reappearing in the "Discours préliminaire" to the *Encyclopédie*, which recounts the long march that mind makes in moving from darkness and barbary to light and truth. This story exemplifies the founding narrative of modern knowledge, which recounts how a universal subject attains knowledge of exterior objects as well as critical self-consciousness. The story returns in various forms in all the major texts of Enlightenment epistemology, from Descartes's *Discours de la méthode* and his *Méditations métaphysiques* to Condillac's *Essai sur l'origine des connaissances humaines*, Diderot's *Lettre sur les aveugles*, his *Lettre sur les sourds et muets* and his article "Encyclopédie," and La Mettrie's *L'Homme machine*. Philosophical inquiries into knowledge, sensation, and the faculties of human thought that produce knowledge, these texts do more, though, than illustrate classical-age epistemology. With varying degrees of explicitness and self-reflexivity, they perform a new subjectivity, constructing the Enlightenment subject, both theoretically and formally, through their experimentation with a wide range of discursive and narrative practices. This performance of subjectivity is perhaps most evident in the case of Diderot's writing, exemplified by his "art of philosophizing."[7] It also takes place in numerous other experimentations with the philosophical genre, from the performative theatricality of Descartes's *discours* to Condillac's *essai*, the textual diagramming of human knowledge in the *Encyclopédie*, and the dialogical structure of Rousseau's discourses. Constructing new forms of subjectivity becomes an almost obsessive concern with eighteenth-century writers. Not limited to the philosophical genre, this undertaking extends well beyond the bounds of philosophy proper (bounds that had not yet been established in the eighteenth century and perhaps can never be). In eighteenth-century novels and plays, especially in memoirs, the epistolary novel, and autobiography, such writers as Marivaux, Crébillon, Diderot, Graffigny, Rousseau, and Sade tell the story of constructing a subject whose quest for knowledge of self and society is guided by the inner light of feeling.[8]

In d'Alembert's *Essai*, the hero of this story of emergent modernity is *l'esprit*, and the language it speaks is that of philosophy. However familiarly modern this story has become, the version of events it provides was not universally accepted in eighteenth-century France. D'Alembert and other writers may have welcomed and even promoted this intellectual revolution, but there were members of lettered society that did not. Some were more cautious than d'Alembert in embracing change, while others saw in the questioning of faith and tradition's truths a dangerous threat to institutional authority and privilege. Although the ensuing battle between the philosophes and their critics was often intensely polemical, it was not insignificant. This discursive struggle involved nothing less than establishing the values and truths that would define the intellectual life of eighteenth-century culture, who would determine them, and what cultural prestige would flow to these members of society. The eighteenth-century continuation of the previous century's *querelle* that had pitted 'Ancients' against 'Moderns', this struggle might be called, in somewhat journalistic fashion, the culture wars of early modern France.[9] It was also a battle the philosophes would soon win. Diderot may have failed to be elected to the Académie Française because Louis XV felt the writer had too many enemies, but the *Encyclopédie* that he and d'Alembert edited received permission to be published (for reasons probably having as much to do with national pride and the economic benefits France would lose if the venture migrated to Russia as with the triumph of intellectual freedom). By 1772, when d'Alembert was named perpetual secretary of the Académie Française, the major cultural institutions had ceased to be sites of opposition to the 'new philosophy'.

If the Enlightenment has been taken as the triumph of modernity, that judgment rests on shaky ground, uncertain as we often are about the modernizing project of emancipation and domination the Enlightenment signifies. Can we aspire to Enlightenment without modernity, declining to embrace the ideology of progress, the new, reason, and total knowledge? Should we go as far as Bruno Latour does in claiming that we have never been modern, that we have never entered the modern era insofar as modernity is an arrangement connecting entities, a temporality that has nothing temporal about it?[10] One of the aims of this book is to recount the long-lasting and continuing fallout of the Enlightenment event, the struggle to assign meaning to the revolutionary moment d'Alembert heralded, to establish the cultural values that would inflect how this event was to be understood. Lasting more than two centuries, that struggle would involve writing and rewriting the history of eighteenth-century texts, authors, and culture, producing literary, political, and cultural narratives to be used in schools, universities, and the larger public sphere in the service of varying ideological agendas. We can understand the Enlightenment thus more as a palimpsest than an event, or an event that becomes such by being continually rewritten. A site of collective memory, the Enlightenment is also where a struggle to remember – and to forget – occurs, a struggle that shapes the cultural imaginary. This process is ongoing moreover, for we are still connected both historically and textually to the Enlightenment, with the nature of that connection located somewhere between unquestioning adherence and uncompromising critique. By considering our link to the Enlightenment, we can grasp how our phrasing of that intellectual and cultural bond is also a way of phrasing our contemporary moment.

The term 'culture wars' is a case in point. While it may help explain tensions in early modern French culture, the term remains anachronistic. Turning up in late twentieth-century America, not eighteenth-century France, it refers to the clash between faith and reason as modes of truth and judgment, the debate concerning the proper role of government with respect to individual freedom, the struggle for control of those institutions that determine public values, such as print and electronic media and schools. The term also signals that the bond of commonality has somehow been broken, the link that supposedly joined citizens to one another and to a shared past, and without which community is, as Jean-Luc Nancy puts it, *desœuvrée* or inoperative.[11] To refer to 'culture wars' in early modern France is thus to apply an interpretive paradigm that freights considerable critical values and judgments. Is the danger here that of committing anachronism in the practice of historical interpretation, in other words of projecting a vision of the present onto the past in order to make the past comprehensible? Philosophers of history have written much on the danger of getting lost in what David Lowenthal calls the "foreign country" of the past.[12] Such caution could be the Ariadne's thread that would save my reading of the Enlightenment past from going too far astray. But can we completely avoid projecting the present onto the past? Historical understanding always involves some kind of anachronism, insofar as any understanding of the past is the result of a project and a projection from a later present. A danger more significant than anachronism might well be the failure to elaborate a historical practice that admits that such projection must inevitably occur. Could one imagine an interpretive practice that reveals this projective historiography at work? The wager of this book is that in this projection might lie the very possibility for a renewed historical understanding that does not fall for the historicist lure of an organically developing, teleological understanding of causes and effects, be it ontological or narrative.[13]

This is why *The Enlightenment Past* opens with d'Alembert and his essay on eighteenth-century philosophy. The essay sets in place a logic, both narrative and historical, that will make comprehensible what d'Alembert perceives to be happening in mid-century France. From the outset, the Enlightenment event comes about conceptually and discursively, resulting from the workings of the interpretive genre. Moreover, the ongoing advent of enlightenment involves a palimpsestic writing over of the event that begins already in the eighteenth century and that will continue for some 250 years. Generic experiments, the founding texts of the Enlightenment involve a material practice (whether we call it that of 'text', 'discourse', or 'rhetoric') that precedes and generates any particular concept of enlightenment. This generative anteriority means that stereotypical characterizations of the Enlightenment can never be relied upon totally, as visions or versions of the event somehow derived independently of interpretation. Such freedom from interpretation is of course illusory (or a sign of bad faith). For it is impossible even to imagine answering the question of what Enlightenment is – assuming it ever can be answered – without first reading the Enlightenment text. This often-invoked need to return to the text should not be taken in positivist terms to mean simply that more paraphrase is needed. Instead, reading in a strong sense requires engaging in an ongoing grappling with the text's constitutive tensions, in the attempt to come to terms both with the text's incitement to understand and with its resistance to understanding. And so we must return to d'Alembert and his attempt to figure the event of Enlightenment.

ENLIGHTENING REVOLUTION / A REVOLUTIONARY ENLIGHTENMENT

For d'Alembert, the mid-century awakening of reason he witnesses is revolutionary. The term 'revolution' carries a good deal of semantic freight when used in the context of eighteenth-century France. Such was certainly the case following 1789, as political theorists elaborated a model of change to explain the revolutionary events and their aftermath. We should be wary of using such a model to interpret the epistemological event described in the *Essai*. That model is doubly distant from the event d'Alembert writes about: it belongs to an explicitly political discourse, not that of epistemology or philosophy, a political discourse that refers to and is grounded in the revolutionary experience of 1789 and afterwards. Nonetheless, for long, French historiography has viewed the Enlightenment through the prism of the Revolution, which is presented as having been anticipated, if not caused, by Enlightenment ideas. Eighteenth-century revolutionaries and counterrevolutionaries alike presented such a view of things, invoking patterns of influence and causality that would have a long life. Recent scholarship has put aside these explanations of the relation between Enlightenment and Revolution, thereby bringing into view other aspects of seventeenth- and eighteenth-century thought and culture.[14] The connection between Enlightenment and Revolution is a methodological knot that we will worry repeatedly. In d'Alembert's *Essai*, the larger theoretical question this text raises concerns the way to articulate the relation between epistemology and politics, knowledge and power. This was a question that had considerable importance for d'Alembert and other eighteenth-century philosophes. But to understand it we need not read backwards from the French Revolution, viewing the earlier context as if it were linked naturally to the latter one according to some anticipatory, causal logic. By abandoning revolutionary teleology, we can ask in what other sense d'Alembert might have understood this new way of thinking as revolutionary.

In the more than 1,300 articles d'Alembert wrote for the *Encyclopédie*, 72 contain the word "révolution." In almost all, the term is used in an astronomical or geometrical sense, referring to rotational motion around an axis. In a handful of others, the term is used slightly differently to describe a sudden or momentous change: the impact that Rameau produced on French music ("Musique") or the influence of Descartes on philosophy ("Cartésianisme" and "Expérimental"). (In Montesquieu's *Lettres persanes*, the ever-changing fashions of women's hairstyles are as many 'revolutions.') In the *Encyclopédie* the term has a political meaning as well, signifying the sudden overthrow of a ruler or a change of government. A brief sub-article written by de Jaucourt defines revolution in this way. However, the entry's head links the term to "Histoire moderne d'Angleterre," suggesting that its field of political reference is limited to English history and the events of 1688. Even in this explicitly political context the term retains its astronomical and geometrical meaning, referring to naturally occurring changes that are regular and repetitive.[15] This is how d'Alembert portrays the advent of the intellectual revolution he refers to in the "Discours préliminaire" of the *Encyclopédie*:

For everything displays regular revolutions, and darkness will end with a new enlightened century. We will find this bright light more striking because of the time we have spent in the shadows. They will seem like an intrinsically quite harmful anarchy, but one sometimes useful in its consequences. Let us not hope for a fearsome revolution however. Barbarism lasts for centuries, and apparently that is our element; reason and good taste are transitory.[16]

The shadows may part to reveal the light of truth, but nothing guarantees that the new age of reason and taste will endure. It too may pass, as regularly as the moon and the planets. Epistemological change may be sudden, even cataclysmic. However, the story of that change is not commonly told in the eighteenth century by means of a teleological narrative of progressive becoming. Only in the next century will this narrative mode become dominant, employed in numerous disciplines to make change comprehensible.

Diderot's *Pensées sur l'interprétation de la nature* also raises the question of how epistemological change should be understood. Referring to a great revolution in the sciences, Diderot observes that philosophy has rejected speculative metaphysics, aiming instead to place knowledge on the new foundations of experimental procedures and experience. The new knowledge thus produced results from direct contact with the material world, and not from idealized, speculative abstraction. In many ways,

Pensées sur l'interprétation de la nature amounts to an eighteenth-century reflection on a scientific revolution that did not suddenly occur in eighteenth-century France but that had begun several centuries before in Italy. That earlier event is commonly seen to result from a radically new understanding of what constituted scientific inquiry and the verification of truth claims in the absence of preestablished, authoritative, and institutionalized judgments. The new way of knowing was based on the conviction that science is an autonomous epistemological practice, separate from metaphysical philosophy and technology. According to this new epistemological practice, nature could be known, but in a limited and utilitarian way, based on an experimental method of inquiry set within well-defined parameters.[17]

Placed within this larger story of a European scientific revolution, Diderot's text appears to be yet another reflection on the becoming-modern of scientific thought. We should read this text carefully, though, especially concerning the narrative of knowledge production that it implies, lest we overlook elements of the text that do not square easily with the notion of epistemological progress suggested by the model of scientific revolution. Does scientific thought evolve in linear, progressive fashion, for example, or does it transform itself according to a process of displacements, dead ends, and retreats? At one point Diderot comments on the status of geometry in Europe, which he perceives to be an all but dead science, supplanted by ethics, *belles-lettres*, natural history, and experimental physics. In less than a century, he affirms, Europe will have only a couple of great geometers. "This science will come to a standstill where it was left by the likes of Bernouilli, Euler, Maupertuis, Clairant, Fontaine, and d'Alembert. They erected the pillars of Hercules. No one will go a step beyond." Not only does Diderot understand knowledge production in terms of disciplinary transformation; more significantly, he views epistemological change as potentially non-linear and non-progressive, shaped less by teleology than by catastrophe. Pursuing his observation concerning Europe's great geometers, Diderot compares their works' future existence to that of the Egyptian pyramids, "whose massive blocks covered with hieroglyphs awaken in us the terrifying idea of the power and resources of the people who built them."[18] Intellectual monuments to past greatness, these works contain achievements that may also be unsurpassable, if not incomprehensible, to future ages.

But it is only a nagging doubt concerning the direction of epistemological change that inflects *Pensées sur l'interprétation*, not an overarching hypothesis. The dominant epistemological narrative of epistemological change that appears throughout the encyclopedic text recounts the progressive development of ever better, ever more useful knowledge. Light will always dispel the shadows, a finality figured in the first volume's frontispiece. The goal of the encyclopedic text, as Diderot puts it in the article "Encyclopédie," was to be a capacious *tableau* of human ideas, a *mappemonde* that would chart new fields of knowledge. More than that, though, the *Encyclopédie* was designed to revolutionize thinking ("changer la façon générale de penser"). It was to bring about not just more knowledge but stronger knowledge, providing an incitement to more powerful critical thinking. But alongside this meliorative narrative of intellectual emancipation and empowerment, together with the notion of writing and reading it implies, a second narrative of change is produced in the encyclopedic text, generated by an ever-nagging doubt. At one point, Diderot likens the *Encyclopédie* not to a map of knowledge but to its storehouse, a protective structure that could preserve advancements in the arts, sciences, and trades from the ravages of a future "temps de troubles." In a literal, historical reading of such 'troubled times', Diderot's phrase refers to the civil unrest during the Fronde years of the seventeenth century. But the temporal reference here is prospective, not retrospective, which is to say that Diderot imagines the return of 'troubled times'. At the very least, nothing is said of what might prevent such disruption from occurring again. Perhaps not all revolutions are beneficial to knowledge. Or perhaps the narrative of sociopolitical or cultural change is not compatible, or commensurable, with the narrative of scientific change.

Both d'Alembert and Diderot sensed their present to be a moment of great change. But it was also one in which it had not yet been established which narrative could best recount that change and thus make it comprehensible. Should change be presented as being cyclical and repetitive, or linear, teleological, and progressive? In fields of knowledge as diverse as historiography, biology, economics, ethics, and political theory, writers in the eighteenth century attempted to answer such questions concerning the nature of change. Often enough, the way they posed such questions is now understood as premodern, formulations that could not be fully understood in the eighteenth century and that anticipate at best what would later become a modern way – our mode – of understanding change. This anticipatory logic is often invoked to read Diderot's *Le Rêve de d'Alembert*, a text that presents imaginary encounters first between Diderot and d'Alembert, then between d'Alembert (dreaming then awake), the doctor Bordeu, and the inquisitive *salonnière* Julie de l'Espinasse. The text stages the experience of the geometer d'Alembert's conscious attempt to comprehend Diderot's materialist account of life forms in terms of a static, geometry-based paradigm. Diderot thus puts to the test the process that d'Alembert established in 1743 in his *Traité de dynamique*, and that would be called d'Alembert's principle, namely, the reduction of a problem in dynamics to one in physics. This initial dialogue is followed by a second section, in which d'Alembert, while dreaming, returns to reconsider the materialist thesis. His disjointed formulations become a new text for Mlle. de l'Espinasse and Bordeu to interpret, and the dialogue between the three characters provides Diderot with a fictional means to push the materialist thesis to the limits of what it can account for. Traditionally, *Le Rêve* is read as a model of conflictual understanding in the life sciences, situated between an outmoded paradigm of biological form, which the text rejects, and a modern paradigm of biological evolution, which cannot (yet) be fully formulated.[19] Nonetheless, even though we can take *Le Rêve* to stand for a mode of thought different from what we commonly take to be 'modern', or at any rate our own, it is not certain that we grasp what is most distinctive about such a text by projecting back upon it the modernity it is said to anticipate. Uncoupling the text from that retrospective projection, we would have to take seriously the text's genre of the dream, inquiring into all other forms of the hybrid, the mixed, the monstrous, and the polyvocal in this text. In other words the notion of epistemological change found in theoretical formulations in *Le Rêve*, but also in its formal matrix and its figures, signals in a broader sense the notion of historical understanding taking shape in the period. If Diderot and d'Alembert could not determine whether to rely upon a narrative of cyclical repetition, of linear progress, or even of hybridity and an ongoing mixity to formulate change, this means at the very least that the question of representing change was still a knotty and contested issue, one not resolved (yet) by intellectual tradition, discursive consensus, or institutional fiat.

PORTRAYING CHANGE

In naming his text an *essai*, d'Alembert suggests he will treat the advent of enlightenment, "the awakening of reason" and the emergence of "true philosophy," in relatively unstructured fashion. But d'Alembert is no Montaigne, and the promise of a loosely formed set of personal reflections is short-lived. As announced in the second chapter, the work is in fact a nineteen-chapter table or tableau of current knowledge ("tableau de nos connaissances réelles"). Explicitly recalling the aim of the *Encyclopédie*, whose first volume had appeared six years earlier, d'Alembert claims that only by presenting knowledge in the form of a *tableau* can the representation of that knowledge resist the winds of time. It is tempting to read the *Essai* as yet another universalizing theory of knowledge and its production, set under the heading of "philosophy." To be sure, several examples of Enlightenment epistemology are shaped by this totalizing, theorizing impulse, such as Condillac's *Essai sur l'origine des connaissances humaines* and his *Traité des sensations*, d'Holbach's *Système de la nature* or Helvétius's *De l'esprit* and his *De l'homme*. Latter-day critical assessments of the Enlightenment are quick to stress the connection between the drive for universal knowledge and a will to mastery, played out in the entwining of knowledge and power. Horkheimer and Adorno read Sade's *Juliette* as the literary allegory of such an entwining, and Foucault's Enlightenment prepared the way for the "sciences of man" that became modes of discipline and normalization, techniques for controlling bodies and souls, as the hierarchical power modeled on kingly, monarchical sovereignty became a more networked power employed in order to govern.[20] But things are not quite so simple in the *Essai*, or perhaps not quite so complicated. Philosophy may well have undone prior ways of knowing, but it is not certain that knowledge can be put back together so easily here (or in any eighteenth-century text for that matter) in the name of universalizing epistemology. At the very least, knowledge does not attain the form of an immobilizing, immutable tableau whose truth claims and validity place it above and beyond history. What exactly is the tableau of knowledge d'Alembert presents, and what discursive power does this form of representation possess and produce?

As it was used in the eighteenth century, the term *tableau* refers most extensively to a genre of visual representation, painting, that gives pictorial form to non-pictorial objects and ideas. The term also possesses a literary meaning, as de Jaucourt notes in the *Encyclopédie* article of the same name: a *tableau* is a set-piece collection of descriptions designed to produce intense emotive effects on the part of the reader ("these are the descriptions of passions, events, and natural phenomena that an orator or poet spreads throughout his composition, where their effect is to entertain, surprise, touch, frighten or imitate, etc." (15:806). It is in this sense that the *Dictionnaire de l'Académie Française* of 1798 will define *tableau* as "the natural and lively imitation of a thing, whether in speech or writing." Although there are other more specialized uses of the term *tableau* in the eighteenth century – meaning "table" in the language of commerce, and designating a kind of public bulletin board for official decrees in the judicial context – these two, painting and literature, highlight a certain duality, if not tension, that the term contains. *Tableau* designates a form of representation that both immobilizes and renders dynamic. Objects and ideas are arrested and depicted, and at the same time this representation produces intense emotional effects on the part of the reader. This duality is at work in the theatrical tableau. Here, actors' movements are arrested and dramatic development is temporarily halted, yet the emotive response this immobilization is designed to produce is dynamic, extending over the suspended time of the tableau. More important, this shifting of emphasis from stage to house highlights the interpretive work of spectatorship, which thus becomes the individually produced narrative of the play's effect, begun in the moment of the tableau.[21]

Presenting a portrait of knowledge and extending the effects of this new way of knowing, d'Alembert's text is marked by the duality of the *tableau*. The object of knowledge is not static and orderly, for the epistemological landscape is a dynamic chiaroscuro of planes and vectors. "A new light on some objects, a new darkness on others – this was the fruit or the result of this general stirring of minds; just as the effect of the ocean's ebb and flow is to wash some objects up on the shore and to wash away others." What results is a lively and creative new way of thinking, an "enthusiasm" or "a lively fermentation ... of minds," which violently collides with whatever resists it, "like a river that broke through its dikes."[22] These metaphors of growth, movement, and transformation are not embellishments of otherwise dry academic prose, however, a brief narrative moment within the larger philosophical treatise. Providing a natural causality, this tropology of nature serves the more telling rhetorical purpose of naturalizing the story of mind the *Essai* recounts. The revolutionary event of mid century is presented as possessing its own logic and as having been shaped by a number of quite natural causes. This event thus belongs to history, which is the narrative form above all that naturalizes events and in so doing makes them knowable. In other words the reader is enjoined to understand the "awakening of reason" in a historical sense, as part of a narrative of becoming.

Insofar as geometry is the language of space, not of time, d'Alembert the geometer may not be best situated to understand how the event of reason's awakening belongs to history. Can this theoretician of space think the Enlightenment in its historical dimension, as possessing an inherent historicity? It is true that in the *Essai* and elsewhere d'Alembert locates the revolutionary event of reason's awakening within a history whose events occur according to an overarching causal logic. But that history is made up of revolutions that occur with a curious regularity at mid century. The fall of Constantinople, the Council of Trent, and the development of Cartesian philosophy – these events recall the geometrical, astronomical sense of the term 'revolution'. D'Alembert's eighteenth-century advent of reason marks a revolution that is far more a repetition of the old than an emergence of the new. The image of "the awakening of reason" seems to suggest as much. If we wish to criticize d'Alembert, it should be for nothing more than simply wishing to remain a geometer, though, someone more at home in the language of space than in that of time. But in that case, the natural images used to represent the advent of reason in the *Essai* also signal the impending breakup of one epistemological matrix and the emergence of another. The world can no longer be thought of in terms of the geometrical paradigm of knowledge, which is incompatible with other emergent paradigms, notably that of the life sciences. D'Alembert the geometer does not reflect the newest of the new knowledge, then, and he fails to recognize the incompatibility between these divergent epistemological paradigms. Nonetheless, his text plays out this tension. Proposing to provide a static tableau of knowledge produced by the new philosophical spirit, the *Essai* represents that event through its recourse to natural images that figure a dynamic process of becoming. This tropology suggests how the life sciences are encroaching upon thought in the mid eighteenth century, supplying a rhetorical matrix and semantic register for an emergent discourse that had yet to receive fully unified conceptual form.[23] By narrativizing that event, the *Essai* also points to its ultimately historical dimension. Knowledge happens, producing epistemological events that can be known in the form of an intellectual history.

What makes this kind of historical thinking possible for d'Alembert? In a word, Descartes. According to the intellectual history told in the *Essai*, what defines the present moment is its having conceived of and implemented a new method for doing philosophy ("l'invention et l'usage d'une nouvelle méthode de philosopher"). The reference to this "new method" of course possesses a Cartesian resonance, and in the "Discours préliminaire" that d'Alembert wrote for the *Encyclopédie* Descartes was praised for having thrown off "the yoke of scholasticism, opinion, and authority, in short, of prejudice and barbarism."[24] But such praise is not unmixed, for d'Alembert also admits that he must turn Descartes's own weapons against him, making use of the rigorously methodical skepticism of Cartesian philosophy to probe the weakness of somewhat fanciful Cartesian science. D'Alembert reflects the philosophes' double view of Descartes – author of good philosophy but whose abstract, system-building natural science runs aground on the shoals of an increasingly experimental method.[25] Deriving a critical stance from their reading of Descartes, the philosophes aimed to free themselves from the tutelage even of the master teacher who taught them how to free themselves from the tutelage of master teachers.

But there is more. The "new philosophical method" d'Alembert hails as the hallmark of his age does away with traditional ways of linking past and present, such as dogma, superstition, or legend. In their stead it places critical reflection. The systematic doubt that Descartes used so extensively calls into question the reliability of any historical knowledge, at least the kind of knowledge gained via the historical text. For such texts can present only mediated knowledge and never direct experience. Self-learning is better than second-hand history, Descartes suggests in the *Discours de la méthode*, and in the *Règles pour la direction de l'esprit* he proposes that the historical and the philosophical are fundamentally incompatible modes. Now by 'history' what Descartes meant was primarily sacred history, the version of the past written by the church. The critique of sacred history will be pursued in increasingly polemical fashion by Locke, Bayle, and of course Voltaire. For these three, the mission of the age was to destroy error, prejudice, and partisan truths. "Pyrrhonisme" or commonsensical skepticism was a position strategically adopted to refute the claims of historical knowledge made in the name of sacred tradition and ecclesiastical institutions.[26] The power of skepticism was thus a negative one, designed to contest the truth claims of others. But what can skepticism succeed in knowing? For Voltaire, often hailed as the first modern historian, the skeptic's stance alone could never provide a foundation for knowledge. Laboring unrelentingly to overcome the corrosive skepticism of a Bayle, Voltaire's constant goal was to achieve historical knowledge. The writing of history was a way to recover the past, provided that the historical understanding thus attained could be based on a rigorous and defensible historiographical method.[27] Voltaire thus is credited with rehabilitating history, whose epistemological foundations had been shaken by Cartesian doubt.

The methodical doubt of Cartesianism dealt a powerful blow to the truth claims made in the name of ecclesiastical or royal history. Yet Cartesianism nonetheless enables an authentic historical mode of thought. This was seen early in the century by Fontenelle, who, according to Georges Canguilhem, understood that "Cartesian philosophy, in doing away with tradition, in other words the unconsidered continuity between past and present, simultaneously founded in reason the possibility of history, that is, the awareness of a sense of human becoming."[28] Cartesian philosophy makes historical understanding possible as a form of critical thought pertaining to time. When d'Alembert calls the eighteenth century "the century of philosophy," due in part to the Cartesian legacy, he can do so because philosophy has made it possible to think of the present historically, as a 'century' to be understood not as the manifestation of providence or fate, but as the result of the critical work of reason.

This opportunity for reflecting on writing history and historical understanding is not one that d'Alembert seizes in the *Essai*, though. For him, history writing remains a separate genre, an entertaining one that is especially valuable for teaching moral lessons to children. It is also a useful genre for philosophes to master, and its lessons are profitable for rulers to know.[29] But the majority of d'Alembert's comments on history are generic in nature. He notes, for instance, the merits of writing in-depth, systematic history ("l'histoire approfondie et raisonnée"), a style for which he finds Montesquieu's *L'Esprit des lois* to provide the model. He observes that the most reliable way to write history is in the form of private memoirs and letters. The kind of history-writing he favors is "l'histoire universelle et abrégée," a condensed general history that combines the colorful and entertaining description of events with interesting reflections. Ultimately, d'Alembert's rehabilitation of history writing is stylistic, not epistemological. Historiography remains essentially an art, still shaped by its own past as that artisanal and courtly craft practiced by scribes and scholars in the pay of the powerful. D'Alembert provides little reflection here on historiography as a discursive practice and as a mode of critical understanding.

But we should not write off d'Alembert too quickly for having failed to theorize historiography compellingly. Nor should his comments on style be passed over for merely perpetuating an understanding of historiography that was already becoming outmoded in the eighteenth century. More interestingly, and recalling previous comments about generic experimentation, we can read d'Alembert's text with an eye to its own style of history, the particular way of narrating events and phrasing history that it presents. Like the "Discours préliminaire" or Diderot's article "Encyclopédie," d'Alembert's *Essai sur les éléments de philosophie* is a manifesto of Enlightenment, an eighteenth-century report on the state of knowledge. But it is shaped by a historiographical impulse as well. These texts recount the advent of Enlightenment, narrating the long march of mind in its progressive development from darkness to light, from barbary to 'our century'. In d'Alembert's *Essai*, the subject of that story and of that history is mind, human intelligence, *l'esprit humain*. D'Alembert might well be called the first intellectual historian.[30]

D'Alembert is not alone in constructing this inaugural narrative of modern knowledge, the story of the struggle to establish the explanatory legitimacy of rational science and thereby to acquire a modern way of knowing. This is the same story that Voltaire recounts throughout his fiction. In numerous masterfully constructed tales, "l'esprit philosophique" assumes many characters: the initially naïve yet soon to become experienced young Candide, the two wise planetary philosophers of *Micromégas* who present an ironic view of France's claim to universal superiority, or the new-world Huron Indian of *L'Ingénu* who represents a natural philosophy superior to that of so-called civilization. In these tales, "l'esprit philosophique" confronts other vectors of subjectivity, which comprise other ways of knowing (superstition, custom, belief) that are embodied in other subjects (the ignorant, the religious, the fanatical, etc.). As Voltaire's tales also suggest, the intellectual event d'Alembert describes in the *Essai* is a highly conflictual one, involving not only a logical or conceptual kind of opposition, as suggested by the binary metaphors of darkness and light, ignorance and knowledge, unreason and reason. For the struggle here also possesses a social dimension. It is part of a larger attempt to empower those who speak in the name of science, philosophy, and reason, to claim legitimacy for those scientists, philosophers, and cultural critics who undertake to tell reason's story. This struggle also involves valorizing the social spaces within which these individuals move, lending prestige to the institutions with which they are associated, and viewing the activities taking place there and the resulting cultural products as capable of generating distinction for the subjects who move in these spaces.[31]

But it is as if d'Alembert wishes to sidestep the issue of social conflict in the *Tableau*. Far more cautious than some of his fellow philosophes, he seems to want to find a way to decouple the epistemological and philosophical revolution he describes from any consideration of the social, economic, or cultural transformations occurring at the time. Should we conclude that the story of Enlightenment told in the *Essai* is ultimately not particularly helpful for understanding this event from the perspective of social or cultural history? If there is a lesson to be drawn from d'Alembert's caution, perhaps it is to be learned by imagining that this story stands for a prototypical intellectual history, which produces an idealist, idealized version of the event of enlightenment. In its theoretical allegory, this text illustrates how intellectual history conceptualizes the event all the better to decontextualize it (or vice versa). Does this mean once again that d'Alembert steadfastly remains the geometer, someone best able to think change and process in static terms by representing them in the form of a *tableau*, a genre of presentation that freezes time and immobilizes history? But this excusing of d'Alembert for being a geometer amounts to invoking a disciplinary alibi, as if from within the limits upon thinking that disciplines impose, certain critical issues could be dispensed with. But whose alibi is at stake here – d'Alembert's or our own? For if we sidestep the question of history and avoid grappling with the foundation of historical understanding, as d'Alembert seems to do, we too repeat geometry's own inability to provide a sufficiently powerful conceptual apparatus for understanding the forces reshaping forms of knowledge in the eighteenth century, forces that are epistemological as well as sociocultural, assuming in fact that the two domains can be separated.

In his "Réflexions sur l'histoire" d'Alembert proposes that the most effective way to teach history is backwards ("à rebours"), setting out from the present in the direction of the past. *The Enlightenment Past* aims to gauge the effects of such a retrospective consideration of the Enlightenment, a working through of the Enlightenment problematic by working back to it from a series of contemporary vantage points determined over the course of some 250 years. At stake will be showing how the event of Enlightenment comes into being, acquiring discursive and institutional reality. If this process is an inevitably retrospective one, are we then free to imagine viewing the event of Enlightenment from another perspective, working back to it via another disciplinary path besides that of intellectual history, a path that d'Alembert may have blazed already?

ENLIGHTENMENT: INTELLECTUAL HISTORY OR SOCIAL HISTORY?

In "Sur la destruction des Jésuites," d'Alembert presents the mid eighteenth century as a revolutionary moment, and doubly so. Pertaining both to philosophical ideas and to realms of power ("états et empires"), revolutionary change involves intellectual and sociopolitical history. In other words the *Essai* alone and the portrait of mind it sketches out do not illustrate completely how d'Alembert grasps the event of Enlightenment. Taking up differently the question of representing the advent of Enlightenment, d'Alembert effectively rewrites the *Essai*'s version of that event, presenting it this time not as a pure intellectual historian but rather in its socially contextualized dimension. Perhaps d'Alembert should not be called an intellectual historian after all, not even a prototypical one. And more seriously, perhaps intellectual history is never purely that. In any event, d'Alembert will redraw the portrait of mind presented in the *Essai sur les éléments de philosophie*, above all in his *Essai sur la société des gens de lettres et des grands*, where Enlightenment thought is embodied in a new social type, the writer or *homme de lettres*. D'Alembert locates this figure in a social context characterized by a potentially conflictual relation between the powerful and the lettered in which the latter must rely on a system of aristocratic patronage and state support in order to survive. However, this portrait remains an ideal portrait, if not a utopian one, in which every effort is made to write out any essential, constitutive conflict between the lettered and the powerful. D'Alembert's position is ultimately one of compromise, based on the attempt to separate the epistemological, the social, and the political. For other less compromising eighteenth-century writers, such a separation is neither possible nor desirable. The following chapter examines that situation through the image of the philosophe as it is constructed in the eighteenth century, taking it to be part of a more extensive discursive strategy, a complex and multiform figure designed to articulate the linkage between knowledge, critique, and desire, modes of discourse and affect involving ideas, goods, wealth, or distinction.

It is crucial to grapple with that linkage, and for a number of reasons. First, all knowledge is situated knowledge. In other words knowledge is never simply *of* things, for knowing always already takes place within a mediating context, *in* and *through* genres of discourse, institutions, and subjects. To understand this process, knowledge must be seen as always embodied, local, and material. To be sure, forms of knowledge can be constructed and judged in such a way that their situatedness, the mediation of their context, and the desire that drives them remain camouflaged.[32] This is the approach to knowledge that d'Alembert takes. But this attempt at decontextualization can never be completely successful or permanent. Not only is all knowledge situated knowledge, but also – and this is the second aspect of epistemological linkage – each way of knowing situates other ways, which it incorporates, contests, or rejects, but which it cannot ignore. In complex ways, truth and power are always already entwined so that the truth of knowledge is located in and results from the situating, metadiscursive power possessed by a given way of knowing. Consequently, we cannot take a purely descriptive approach to epistemological questions, if only because that knowledge itself is not purely descriptive. Such an approach amounts not only to a reductive way of posing more extensive epistemological questions; more seriously, it also makes it difficult to grasp the connection between knowledge and context, those places and spaces where the enabling conditions of knowing are located and where the powerful effects of knowing are played out.

For d'Alembert, the Enlightenment is an epistemological event, the advent of the idea of reason. I have taken his portrait of mind as the starting point for this investigation of how the Enlightenment comes to be configured over the next 250 years. The choice of any beginning is strategic, and this particular inaugural moment has been selected to display the situated nature of knowledge, in other words the relation between text, context, and the production of historical knowledge. In seeking to understanding the event d'Alembert heralds, we should not sever it from other contexts, at least not if we wish to grasp how knowledge production takes place within social, political, and cultural spheres. For the new relation to knowledge that the Enlightenment represents is also historical in nature. What this means in one sense is that Enlightenment thinking is defined by a specific understanding of history and historical change. In Voltaire's "Philosophie de l'histoire" included in his *Essai sur les mœurs*, in Condorcet's *Tableau historique des progrès de l'esprit*, or in Buffon's *Histoire naturelle*, we find emblematic attempts to formulate a philosophy of history based on progressive change, teleologically driven transformations that occur in the realm of mind, society, and nature. Historians of philosophy and of ideas have provided a detailed explanation of this emergent philosophy of history, including both the idea of history as well as its practice.[33] The kind of historical relation I am interested in exploring is a different one. It involves not the enlighteners' production of historical understanding exclusively, but our own as well, generated as it is through reference to texts of the past. Numerous readers of Enlightenment texts – including philosophers, historians, cultural critics, and writers – have proposed revised interpretations of the Enlightenment. Rather than see these as randomly varied interpretations of a pre-given historical event, I propose that these interpretations may be judged by taking them to be as many ways of phrasing a relation to that event, ways of linking a past and a present. Thus they are means of producing a way of knowing that is fundamentally historical in nature because of the linkage it establishes between past and present. It is in this linkage that the Enlightenment is instituted. Once again, d'Alembert's text is helpful in understanding this historical relation. More precisely, and in a retrospective sense, the way d'Alembert's text has been recontextualized in order to provide a contemporary understanding of the Enlightenment can tell us much about the historical understanding it is still capable of producing. To illustrate this point, let me return to the *Essai* once again, this time through the lens provided by Ernst Cassirer and his *Philosophy of the Enlightenment*.

This jump forward to Cassirer and a more contemporary moment can be justified at least rhetorically by the fact that the first chapter of his compendious and highly influential analysis of the Enlightenment redraws with quotation and commentary the very portrait of mind that d'Alembert sketches out in the *Essai*. *The Philosophy of the Enlightenment* is a kind of philosophical palimpsest, inaugurating a return to the Enlightenment by writing over the portrait of mind with which d'Alembert inaugurates enlightenment. Is all intellectual history, including the kind illustrated by Cassirer, in some sense a vast palimpsest, one textual overlay upon another? Is the historical relation of ideas situated precisely in this intertextual act? If so, we would be perpetually at one remove from the historical event and its texts, always obliged to defer to texts in order to represent events. Thus, our understanding of these events would always be deferred, not enabled, by the mediating obstacle of the text. At the same time, though, we can rely on that textual mediation in order to think through and represent our own situation and our linkage to texts and events. As a discipline, intellectual history has been soundly criticized for neglecting to deal with the material determination of ideas, that is, with the stuff of which social, cultural, and economic history is made. But one response to this critique is to demonstrate how intellectual history can in fact account for this constitutive mediation, by examining how the text of intellectual history itself, given its production in particular rhetorical, disciplinary, institutional, and cultural contexts, mediates any ultimate understanding of events. What might this attention to mediation reveal in the case of *The Philosophy of the Enlightenment*?

For Cassirer, the Enlightenment is "a part and a special phase of that whole intellectual development through which modern philosophic thought gained its characteristic self-confidence and self-consciousness." It is the moment when that spirit "achieves clarity and depth in its understanding of its own nature and destiny, and of its own fundamental character and mission."[34] Dena Goodman has argued that this unfolding of spirit takes place in an ideal, conceptual sphere, in the "rationalist and idealist intellectual context that began with the Greeks and continued through the French Enlightenment to Kant, Hegel and Cassirer himself."[35] By linking the Enlightenment to that tradition, Cassirer sought to unify and rehabilitate Enlightenment philosophy as a unified concept whose place in the history of Western thought was legitimately defensible and strategically necessary. Do the reasons for such a defense of Western thought seem less compelling today, when that thought is accused of promoting Eurocentric interests and an ideology of domination? Or is that defense more necessary than ever? If it seems less necessary to rehabilitate Enlightenment, it may be that we are too distant not from the "rationalist and idealist intellectual context" Goodman refers to, which stretches from Greek antiquity to Cassirer himself, but rather from the German intellectual climate of the 1930s in which Cassirer wrote. That climate was heavily influenced by the discipline of history, and particularly by the historicist argument that all reality was fundamentally historical in nature and should be understood in terms of continual becoming. For Cassirer, given its methodology and the kind of knowledge it produced, the discipline of history – or at least turn-of-the-century German historiography – provided an inadequate means for telling the story of the history of philosophy. Nor could that story be told by philosophy, at least not that philosophy marked out by Hegel. From a Hegelian perspective, philosophy provides the philosophical version of the historical process of becoming. Thus, in the grand story of the becoming of Spirit told in Hegel's *Phenomenology*, the Enlightenment is presented simply as a philosophical-historical way-station, characterized by reflective thought which can only observe the world and not act upon it.[36] The story Cassirer the neo-Kantian wishes to tell about the Enlightenment is a different one. His aim is to reveal the "unity of [the Enlightenment's] conceptual origin" over and beyond the particular and contradictory manifestations of Enlightenment thought,[37] without presenting that unity as a momentary synthesis that announces a later, nineteenth-century form of critical philosophy. To that end, Cassirer organizes the work of eighteenth-century writers according to three main categories of thought: scientific and epistemological, religious and moral, and esthetic. Each of these categories provides the order according to which Enlightenment writers will be treated in successive chapters. Cassirer's account of eighteenth-century thought will thus display a narrative structure that is modeled on the order of the topics of Kant's three *Critiques*.

It is difficult to overestimate the role that Cassirer played in shaping the intellectual historical, liberal, and neo-Kantian interpretation of the Enlightenment that began to take shape in 1932 when his work first appeared in Germany and that held sway until fairly recently. What seems to have significantly reduced the influence of Cassirer's work is the charge, made first in the United States by Peter Gay, that *The Philosophy of the Enlightenment* represents a kind of intellectual history that fails to account for "the social dimension of ideas," their "social matrix." All ideas are multifaceted overdetermined entities, existing at once in several interconnecting realms, such as the psychic, the socioeconomic, the discursive, and the political. What is required, argued Gay, is a kind of social history that can account for this complex interrelationship. Cassirer's failure to develop such a history stems from what Gay charges is his "unpolitical idealism."[38] In calling for a more capacious view of the Enlightenment that includes both its 'high' and 'low' versions, and that takes the production and consumption of books to be as crucial for understanding the social as the production of ideas, Robert Darnton will continue to invoke Cassirer as a foil for what a new social history should avoid.[39] In her study of the role played by salon culture in developing the "republic of letters" in eighteenth-century France, as well as her ongoing work on the notion of sociability, Dena Goodman has forcefully argued that social history cannot be blind to the question of gender. Consequently, she too takes Cassirer to task, this time for an interpretive strategy "derived from his belief that the Enlightenment was misguided in its assumption that sociability, not masculine reason, was the basis of ethical, political, and intellectual activity."[40]

The critique of Cassirer formulated by Gay, Darnton, and Goodman is telling. But instead of taking it to be directed at one individual thinker, we can read it more productively as performed from within the discipline of history in the attempt to reconfigure that discipline and the way it treats the question of the social mediation of intellectual production. *The Philosophy of the Enlightenment* thus stands for the kind of idealist, idealizing intellectual history for which ex-intellectual historians have taken their ex-discipline to task for not being sufficiently equipped to analyze adequately the social and cultural contexts that mediate an understanding of texts. Viewed as disciplinary self-critique, the critique of Cassirer suggests that 'old-style' intellectual history is marked by a blind spot, that it is constitutively unable to attain a perspective from which to view itself critically as discipline and account for its limits.[41] But such constitutive blind spots can also generate insights. The disciplinary blind spot of intellectual history may in fact characterize not just this one discipline but all disciplines, which by their very definition represent a set of protocols of epistemological production, determining not so much what can be said in a given field of knowledge as what cannot. In that case, though, it is not certain just what would be gained by the shift from one kind of history (ideas) to another (the social), at least not as far as our understanding of historical knowledge and the conditions of its production are concerned. Does this mean that the discipline of history remains unable to grapple effectively with the contextualizing mediations that determine its own text? This may seem like an abstract, theoretical question that arose only recently as the discipline of history went through various paradigm shifts or 'turns', first to language and then to culture. But the question also lies at the very heart of the historical enterprise, the quest for historical thought. It is the question that Cassirer, albeit in an oblique way, confronted in and through *The Philosophy of the Enlightenment*.

To read Cassirer this way, not as representing intellectual history's flight from the social but as a knowing yet subtle engagement with it, we first must ask what writing a book on eighteenth-century European thought possibly could have meant in the intellectual, social, institutional, and political context of the 1920s and 1930s in Germany. Cassirer himself performs precisely this linkage in his introduction to *The Philosophy of the Enlightenment*, explaining first why the Enlightenment should be rehabilitated from the judgment of Romanticism, and then by claiming that rehabilitation to be all the more urgent in the present context. Enlightenment philosophy, he claims, is not mere reflective thought, as Hegel argued; "it consists not only in analyzing and dissecting, but in actually bringing about that order of things which it conceived as necessary, so that by this act of fulfillment it may demonstrate its own reality and truth."[42] Enlightenment thought possesses a certain critical agency, whose recovery has become all the more urgent. Recalling Kant's motto of Enlightenment, *sapere aude*, Cassirer writes, "We must take courage and measure our powers against those of the age of the Enlightenment, and thus find a proper adjustment. The age which venerated reason and science as man's highest faculty cannot and must not be lost even for us. We must find a way not only to see that age in its own shape but to release again those original forces which brought forth and molded this shape."[43] One can only wonder to what group the pronoun "we" refers here, or what imaginary community it can be thought to create – we moderns of the twentieth century, we European intellectuals, we German Jews, I (Ernst Cassirer) who address us all ... In any event, the act of retrieving the dynamic, critical force of enlightenment thought and resituating it, reactivating it in the present moment in order to bring about change, cannot be conducted solely in historical terms. "No account of the history of philosophy can be oriented to history alone. The consideration of the philosophic past must always be accompanied by philosophical re-orientation and self-criticism."[44] It is philosophy, not history, that ultimately is called upon to bring about a renewed understanding of the present moment, a moment to which Cassirer refers allusively, perhaps cautiously, yet tellingly.[45] "More than ever before, it seems to me, the time is again ripe for applying such self-criticism to the present age, for holding up to it that bright clear mirror fashioned by the Enlightenment. Much that seems to us today the result of 'progress' will to be sure lose its luster when seen in this mirror; and much that we boast of will look strange and distorted in this perspective."[46] This twentieth-century return to a European Enlightenment marks a way to pursue that project, in the name of the core values of modern liberalism, values that in the 1930s were being ever more forcefully assailed. In a richly detailed and cogent contextualization of Cassirer's work, Johnson Wright describes the tone of *The Philosophy of the Enlightenment* as one of "lucid nostalgia ... as if [Cassirer were] encouraging European liberalism, at its darkest hour, to begin to reconstruct its identity by means of a meditation on its happy youth."[47] At the same time, as Wright also notes, Cassirer's work was read outside Germany not as an appeal to a cosmopolitan, pan-European intellectual tradition in which national particularities were transcended, but rather as yet one more Franco-Prussian encounter in which the problems explored by French analytic thought, and put to the test by English empiricism, ultimately found their synthetic solution in German philosophy. Viewed from this other, postwar, British perspective, Cassirer's Enlightenment could seem to one historian at least to be a Germanizing annexation of an apparently not so cosmopolitan Enlightenment, the latter's so-called universal values being pressed into service to promote a national specificity and intellectual superiority.[48]

If I have chosen Ernst Cassirer as a privileged example, it is not to take intellectual history to task yet again in the name of a more encompassing, somehow more accurate social or cultural history. Such terms may be helpful for classifying the configurations and transformations of disciplinary knowledge. But such classificatory clarity may be illusory, just as it is not possible simply to choose between two ways of 'doing history', between two modes of historical understanding. The case of Ernst Cassirer and *The Philosophy of the Enlightenment*, presented here schematically as a sociocultural reading of the production of intellectual history, is offered as a cautionary tale. I have made an example of Cassirer, but not to criticize him, for he illustrates all too well that choosing between ideas and their 'situation' is neither possible nor perhaps even desirable. As this staged clash of perspectives onto Cassirer's work illustrates – should he be read as an embattled German Jewish neo-Kantian liberal or as a co-opted German nationalist intellectual? – knowledge is always situated knowledge. That epistemological situatedness, the mediation of knowledge, cannot be avoided or transcended. Thus the issue becomes not that of opposing 'the intellectual' and 'the sociocultural' but of phrasing their mutually determining imbrication.

Putting this issue in more disciplinary terms, we could observe that research agendas in the more 'literary' disciplines have undergone considerable change in the past few decades, as more empirical, archival work is carried out with the aim of writing social and cultural-historical analyses of things that were previously treated by means of textual, rhetorical methodologies. At the same time, in the more 'historical' disciplines those same social and cultural historical analyses are being carried out with an increased attention to the determining role that language and other forms of symbolic action play in shaping any understanding of the subject of history. As far as the Enlightenment is concerned, a new object of study has emerged. It results neither from a 'revised' and objectively more accurate vision of the eighteenth century, nor from a theoretically more 'refined' perspective. The question becomes, then, how are we to articulate our own critical relation to that 'new' object, that eighteenth-century Enlightenment whose history we seek to write? Certainly a modern question, it was also one that the philosophes themselves asked, as they sought ways and means to phrase their relation to their own emergent modernity, a modernity that was characterized increasingly with reference to philosophy and literature, two intellectual and increasingly social-cultural practices that were conducted by a new subject, the philosophe, to whose construction I now turn.

CHAPTER 3

The subject of Enlightenment: constructing philosophers, writing intellectuals

The story of enlightenment's advent is one of the eighteenth century's most recurrent and enduring narratives. Its conditions are suggested by the connection made in the 1694 *Dictionnaire de l'Académie Française* between scientific thought and the idea of progress. Later, Bernard de Fontenelle, permanent secretary of the Académie des Sciences, provides one of the first theoretically coherent explanations of that connection, one that breaks with a cyclical or providential notion of history, assumes the possibility of ever-increasing human knowledge, and valorizes philosophical thinking as a way to bring about such a future. Condillac explains the generation of ideas from the perspective of sensationalism in his *Essai sur l'origine des connaissances humaines* (1746), a philosophical text whose narrative recounts the stages of the body's encounter with the material world, a story of progressive becoming that many an eighteenth-century novelist would try their hand at as well. Turgot, in his "Tableau philosophique des progrès successifs de l'esprit humain," shifts emphasis from scientific knowledge production to the domain of the political and the social. Reason, freedom, and communication – eighteenth-century writers were coming increasingly to imagine that these were the driving forces of a history shaped by human agency. Was such progress inevitable? For Diderot, the Enlightenment narrative of inevitable progress at times seemed irresistible; on darker days he brooded about error, loss of direction, and a return of the shadows.[1] In *Candide*, Voltaire worries about an evil encroaching upon human happiness from all sides, all the while that he spins a tale of Candide's becoming wise, if not enlightened. It is Condorcet, though, writing at the end of the century, who represents a kind of endpoint of this progressive narrative of Enlightenment. The last Enlightenment philosopher – of the eighteenth century at least – to thematize the possibility of endless progress and infinite perfection, Condorcet sets out in the *Esquisse d'un tableau historique des progrès de l'esprit humain* to show that "no limit has been determined for the perfecting of human faculties, that man's perfectibility is truly infinite, that the progress of this perfectibility, freed henceforth from any power that would stop it, has no limit but the duration of the globe on which we have been cast by nature."[2] Progress may have been infinitely perfectible for Condorcet, yet ironically his life was all too finite. He died from poison taken while under a death sentence issued by a revolutionary tribunal, ending a life and beginning an afterlife that were long taken as a bio-allegory for the confrontation between philosophy and politics, truth and force, and either the limits of Enlightenment or those of the Revolution.[3]

For readers desirous of conclusions, this either/or characterization of Condorcet will be symptomatically frustrating. What does Condorcet's story mean? My answer can only be: it depends on what story is told and to what end. While investigating the critical reception of eighteenth-century texts in the following two centuries, I became increasingly persuaded that the telling of the enlightenment story is an event in its own right. More than a second-order descriptive discourse, the enlightenment story in fact performs enlightenment, albeit in always different manners. The advent narrative of enlightenment is a narrative event that creates ways not only of viewing the world but also of acting within and upon it. This narrative thus involves the production of the enlightenment subject, by creating interrelated subject positions, intersubjective matrices determining how individuals will assign value and meaning to things, themselves, and others. It is in terms of this narrative production of subjectivity, value, and meaning that any narrative of enlightenment can and should be judged.

What then of the micro-narrative of enlightenment set forth in the opening lines of this chapter? What subject of enlightenment is displayed in this story plotted between the appearance of Fontenelle, who thrived in the institution of scientific truth, and the disappearance of Condorcet, who fell victim to the institution of political truth? It is tempting to imagine that the story of enlightenment's advent involves pure ideas, taking place in a world of mind, an ideal space of disembodied knowledge best charted with the compass of intellectual history. But many Enlightenment writers clearly saw, well before our own cultural turn, that the ideal world of disembodied knowledge was an illusion, if not a trap, and certainly a less productive way of realizing critical knowledge. One name they gave to this less powerful way of knowing was Cartesianism, which today might be called philosophical idealism. Attributing the *bon mot* to Fontenelle, d'Alembert suggests in his

Encyclopédie article "Cartésianisme" that Descartes is a thinker who should always be admired, and sometimes followed. By and large, Enlightenment writers rejected Cartesian idealism, finding it to be an inadequate or even misleading explanation of the physical world, the way human beings gain knowledge of that world, and how they interact within it. Materialism, which derived significant impetus from Locke and aimed at explaining the interaction of physical bodies, was seen as offering a more persuasive account of knowledge formation than idealist epistemology, given the latter's reliance on the notion of innate ideas and divinely produced knowledge.[4] According to the materialist hypothesis, matter was unknowable, or at least could be grasped only in its properties as they act upon the human senses and thereby produce ideas. Helvétius, Condillac, and later Destutt de Tracy would argue that sensation is not only the origin of thought, it is coextensive with thought as well.[5] In his *Réfutation d'Helvétius*, Diderot vigorously points out the difficulties inherent in this position, all the while making manifest its appeal for him. Throughout the century, the power of the materialist position – as well as the source of virulent opposition to it – resided in its founding doubt concerning the knowability of matter, an unyielding skepticism that undermined the metaphysical certitudes of Cartesian idealism and of theological dogmatism.

This rejection of philosophical idealism has no small bearing on the stories of enlightenment I wish to consider, first of all the story told by Enlightenment writers themselves, but also the critical account of that story being told here. Intellectual historians have analyzed in detail the conceptual shift from idealism to sensationalism and materialism that occurred in the eighteenth century. Often enough, that story leads to Immanuel Kant, whose notion of critical judgment proposed a resolution for many of the oppositions with which English and French thinkers were wrestling. What I wish to read in the eighteenth-century shift from idealism to materialism is a move from a more disembodied and dematerialized understanding of thought to one that always seeks to locate the latter's contextual determination. This shift carries with it the impulse to tell the story of enlightenment differently, to perform it otherwise. As a result, our own accounts of the reconfiguration of knowledge characterizing the Enlightenment must be shaped by this narrative impulse. In interpretive terms, we must be attentive to the vectors and intensities in this story that work to contextualize and historicize it, to embody its subjects and materialize the place where it is played out. It is well worth noting that this is precisely the work of literature, which makes things seem real by contextualizing, materializing, and embodying, whether it involves ideas or desires, power or drives. This is perhaps the most telling reason why the turn to the cultural must not leave literature behind, as if it were but a remnant of an outdated, elite notion of culture and not the place where some of the most powerful narratives of culture are given symbolic form – or at least once were. Enlightenment writers took varying degrees of distance from an idealism that they found unable to provide a satisfactory basis for either an ethics or a politics. This perspective was of little help as they grappled with questions involving the good use of power, an issue that returns repeatedly in the story of enlightenment and that will acquire particular urgency during the Revolution.

As we have seen, the attempt to elaborate an ethico-political perspective causes d'Alembert to redraw the portrait of mind presented in the *Essai sur les éléments de philosophie*. His *Essai sur la société des gens de lettres et des grands* effectively reconfigures the earlier subject of enlightenment epistemology. In the former text, an abstract, ideal *esprit* was set in place, figuring a subject newly empowered to speak in the name of the 'new' science from within the expanding and self-legitimating public sphere of 'modern' science. In the second *Essai*, that subject is replaced by a different one, the writer or *homme de lettres*, who is set in a context that is all but absent in the earlier *Essai*. The *homme de lettres* belongs to a socio-political context characterized by a potentially conflictual relation between the powerful and the lettered, in which the latter must rely on a system of aristocratic patronage and state support. In this essay on the social dimension of philosophical writing, it is as if d'Alembert had reached the limits of what a purely idealist history of knowledge could explain. To treat issues of ethics, politics, and subjectivity, he must change perspectives, moving from intellectual to social history.

Ultimately, d'Alembert's portrait of the *homme de lettres* remains an ideal if not utopian one, in which any essential, constitutive conflict between the lettered and the powerful will be written out. For d'Alembert, the result of intellectual activity has been to civilize French society, not pervert it as Jean-Jacques Rousseau claimed.[6] D'Alembert's writer is a sociable creature, wishing to be a productive, well-integrated member of elite society, and viewing his intellectual skills and writerly craft as the means to that end. He is far from the alienated, victimized writer that Rousseau repeatedly describes in a pathetic, neurotic, paranoid manner. Writing is an integrative act, a way to forge social bonds and produce intellectual community. Letters pacify, not antagonize or alienate, and d'Alembert views their cultivation as one of the most certain ways to eliminate unrest in a monarchy. This pacification was certainly the objective that the cultural politics of a Louis XIV were designed to realize. But a century later, in the mid 1700s, d'Alembert's claim concerning the pacificatory role of writing seems strangely out of date. For Alexis de Tocqueville, writing another century later, the development of letters during the *Ancien Régime* brought an increase in social tensions, not their lessening. The philosophes lacked the power and prestige to transform their social critique into reality, and so the critical energy their writing generated could not be productively channeled into social reform.[7] The importance of d'Alembert's vision of the eighteenth-century *homme de lettres* lies perhaps as much in its symbolic dimension as in its historical accuracy. For what d'Alembert imagines as a conflict-free relation between the lettered and the powerful defines a symbolic sphere that could be called an Enlightenment imaginary, a construct that bears closer scrutiny.

For d'Alembert, the powerful "dispense renown," the source of social prestige and cultural capital. This relation between the *homme de lettres* and *les grands* can be read through the lens of an instrumentalizing desire, for the powerful are figured here as the means by which writers can obtain the sense of self they wish for. This is why d'Alembert will encourage "le commerce des grands," for by frequenting the powerful a writer can enhance his reputation, and even create it. The *homme de lettres* is justified in seeking out this esteem, for it provides a legitimate incentive to produce even greater works. D'Alembert goes so far as to generalize the mechanism of deriving identity from this instrumentalizing desire, extending it to the powerful as well. Once wit, "le génie philosophique," has spread to all levels of society, including the highest, the *homme de lettres* will no longer need to seek out the other's esteem. Tables will be turned, and the powerful will keep company with writers instead of merely collecting their works.[8]

D'Alembert's view of eighteenth-century writers, their intellectual work, and the level of social integration it provided is one version of the phenomenon of sociability that has been extensively analyzed by cultural and literary historians.[9] Focusing on print culture, and especially on developing patterns of social exchange among the lettered elite in 'the republic of letters', these historians have shown how new institutional spaces and intellectual practices took shape – in such places as academies and salons – that offered participants a certain autonomy with respect to monarchical and aristocratic modes of being. But the valorization of sociability points not only to a transforming public sphere but also to a reworking of subjects' affective relations to one another. De Jaucourt's encyclopedia article "Sociabilité" defines the term as "benevolence towards others," valorizing this form of social relations and giving it a valence that is normative rather than merely descriptive. Sociability is a civilizing sentiment, similar to sympathy, and thus a taming affect. As such, the valorization of sociability can be seen in relation to the larger rehabilitation of the passions that takes place in eighteenth-century psychosocial theory.[10]

D'Alembert represents a reasonable voice in this process, for he urges the lettered to take the measure of their own worth instead of relying on the values of a patronizing aristocracy, a first step towards forming a sociable community of minds. D'Alembert's reflections on writing and power voice his strong desire for such an autonomous community. Given desire's protean power to rescript reality, though, d'Alembert's text may represent a republic of letters that was more imaginary than real, a symbolic community in which autonomy appears realizable through the act of well-intentioned writing. For d'Alembert, the autonomy of such a community derives from its essentially non-contestatory nature. "The trait of true philosophy," he writes, "is not to force its way past barriers, but to wait until the barriers facing it fall, or to turn aside when they remain closed."[11] Adopting a stance uncharacteristic of his fellow philosophes, d'Alembert wishes to believe that real philosophers don't rock the boat and that the best philosophy is a non-combative one. To the extent that his essay on writers and the powerful effectively rewrites his earlier essay on mind, we can conclude that d'Alembert senses that the question of knowledge cannot be treated independently of that of power; the two are conjoined in discursive formations through which power/knowledge flows and by means of which individuals are linked. For other eighteenth-century writers these twin questions were more intractable, inflecting how writers would define what was perhaps the privileged figure of the eighteenth-century *homme de lettres*, the philosophe.

CONSTRUCTING THE PHILOSOPHE

Writers, thinkers, and sometimes activists, the French philosophes are familiar cultural figures. Authors of the texts associated with Enlightenment thought, some of them were writers who, in the shift from a patronage system of cultural support to one determined increasingly by the publishing market, succeeded relatively well in living by the pen. But the term 'philosophe' also designates other members of the literate class, the numerous *gens de lettres* whom history remembers less well and who were less successful in making a name for themselves. These are the aspiring – and sometimes soon to be failed – philosophes, who may have embraced the intellectual program of enlightenment values, but who were unable to break into the cultural establishment of the *Ancien Régime*. They belong to what Robert Darnton has called "the literary underground" of the Enlightenment, populated by marginal, low-life individuals whom editorial market capitalism exploited or ignored and who lived by their pen and their wits, writing pamphlets or pornography, tutoring or spying.[12]

Not a philosopher in a contemporary, disciplinary or institutional sense, the philosophe is a distant precursor of today's public intellectual. These two are not synonymous, of course, for they designate cultural realities as different as the *Ancien Régime* and twenty-first-century republican France. Yet each marks a specific phase in a common cultural genealogy, a particular way of imagining the relation between intellectual work, cultural value, and social community. Thus we can return to the eighteenth-century philosophe, recovering that figure as a historically determined symbolic construction. Produced in the eighteenth century and not completely forgotten today in cultural memory, the figure of the philosophe provides a way to phrase the relation between past and present, as well as to analyze a certain tension involving the aims and limits that define the public intellectual. But before tracing such a connection between present and past, we should note that the figure of the philosophe, precursor of the public intellectual, has its own precursors as well. Chief among them is the figure of the writer, whose 'birth' in seventeenth-century France made possible the emergence of the philosophe in the shape this figure would take on in the following century.

If the writer was born in the seventeenth century, it was due in no small measure to the cultural policy of the absolutist state, which set institutions in place that supported the production of elite culture.[13] This support helped produce increasingly autonomous high cultural spaces. Founded in 1635 by Cardinal Richelieu, the Académie Française is but one of the numerous institutions the Crown established to promote and regulate cultural production. Until fairly recently the significance of these institutions was understood according to the official version of their own identity that these institutions provided. This interpretation of artistic production and of the cultural institutions that shaped it was deeply embedded in a nostalgic, nationalist, and conservative postrevolutionary vision of French classicism. In other words it is as much an ideological product as the oftentimes nostalgic vision that seventeenth-century classicism produced of itself.[14] This view of *le grand siècle* has been subjected to considerable critical scrutiny, leading to an understanding of seventeenth-century cultural production in its ideological dimension, that is, as a material product designed to produce social reality by giving it a particular symbolic meaning.[15] In one such view, this ideological dimension emerges once seventeenth-century artistic and literary production is viewed through a regicentric lens as promoting royal power or as resisting it.[16] At present, a less monolithic (and perhaps less Jacobin) view of early modern culture is taking shape, and with it a more nuanced (and at times contradictory) view of cultural production as 'sociability' displaces 'ideology' as the object of cultural historians' and literary scholars' analysis.

This move from the critique of ideology to the analysis of sociability brings to light a fundamental shift in early modern political and social theory. According to the theory of absolutism, the social order was composed of individuals whose aggressive self-interests had to be checked by the state in order to maintain balance and order. This view of things was increasingly questioned by social and political theorists through the notion of sociability, that is, a natural human inclination for collective harmony that did not need state intervention and that in fact the state should promote. The idea of sociability made it possible to theorize the social subject not as the pawn, victim, or resister of a coercive state power, but rather as a relatively free agent, able to contribute to civilized society and entitled to enjoy its benefits – and its profits. The emerging paradigm of sociability, which hearkened back to an Aristotelian-humanist notion of the individual as a communal being, explains the importance of other social spaces that were developing in early modern society. Official academies, for instance, not only the well-known Académie Française but also numerous provincial academies, functioned as centers of cultural activity that socialized artists and writers, offering them contacts, mutual support, and social recognition. Because these state-sponsored academies provided privileges to their members, they risked becoming gerontocratic institutions that maintained the mediocrity of the status quo and blocked the social integration and distinction of younger artists and writers. But as one set of social spaces failed to provide such opportunities, others were created that did. A counter-force to officially sanctioned spaces developed, notably in salons, which also functioned to socialize artists and writers. Salons were places where literary issues were discussed, but also where a discourse of cultural politics was developed that provided salon-goers with a mode of strategic resistance, albeit limited, to the hegemony of court culture.[17] Constituting a network of sociability, academic and salon culture helped bring about the emergence of the writer, who was relieved, although not entirely freed, from the constraints of aristocratic patronage, yet newly subjected to the pressure of state patronage.

Language bears the traces of cultural change, and the three major dictionaries of the period, produced by the Académie Française in 1694, Antoine Furetière in 1690, and Pierre Richelet in 1680, all illustrate this socio-semantic shift. No longer the scribe of the powerful, the seventeenth-century writer is an '*écrivain*', a term that comes to designate the creator of works possessing an esthetic element. '*Ecrivain*' first becomes synonymous with '*auteur*', then in successive dictionary editions refers more to an activity to which greater and greater prestige or cultural capital is attached. A further consequence of the reconfiguration of the cultural field taking place during the seventeenth century is the development of new reading publics, whose members' sensibility the writers of fiction increasingly believe they are able to shape. Occurring during the great flourishing of court culture during the reign of Louis XIV, the event to which these end-of-century dictionaries bear witness is the production of 'literature'.

The early modern emergence of literature belongs to a larger socio-esthetic process that Pierre Bourdieu has called the development of the intellectual field. For Bourdieu, culture is a structured system of relations comparable to the forces of a magnetic field, where the power and authority of individual elements or agents are determined by their dynamic relation to other components of the field. Bourdieu's field theory aims to account for culture both structurally and temporally, for he argues that the elements of culture must be understood in an ultimately historical dimension. In the case of the intellectual field, this means considering it as resulting from a historical process defined by increasing differentiation and autonomy. The development of seventeenth-century court culture is thus one moment in the gradual organization of cultural life into an intellectual field that takes place during the Middle Ages and Renaissance, as creators of high culture free themselves both economically and socially from court and church. The intellectual field continues to develop well beyond the *Ancien Régime*, through the intensive expansion of such institutions as the school and university systems of postrevolutionary republican France, and the publishing and communications industry of more recent times.[18]

If examining cultural production runs the risk of conflating description and analysis, we do well to recall that Bourdieu assumes that the workings of the cultural field are not obvious from within the field itself. Intellectual operations may be governed by the unspoken enabling conditions of the cultural field, yet this silence is not that of what is simply unsaid. The critique of ideology insistently reveals that it is as if there were something about the cultural field that resisted analysis and understanding, a kind of cultural unconscious that could not be formulated in terms of individuals' awareness but that nonetheless receives material form in the cultural practice of symbolic production. An inevitable tension exists between what the text of culture 'says' and what remains unsaid in it. Paraphrase can never succeed in exhausting the work of the text, nor can it provide critical understanding of that work, given that paraphrase can hardly do more than simply pursue and perpetuate the ideological work that texts perform. If I raise these theoretical concerns, it is to highlight the kind of critical self-awareness required before setting out to interpret any text on early modern sociability, including those containing the figure of the philosophe.

There are numerous textual entry points for such an analysis, from prose fiction to letters, memoirs, and reception speeches at the Académie Française. The most influential of these texts is likely the *Encyclopédie* article "Philosophe." Attributed to César Chesneau Dumarsais, who contributed several articles on grammar for the *Encyclopédie*, this article is an abridged version of a short treatise that appeared in 1743. From the moment of its publication this text circulated widely, and it was to be found, says Voltaire, "among the papers of every inquisitive person."[19] The article overlaps with several others in the *Encyclopédie*, such as the unsigned article "Lettres," "Gens de lettres" written by Voltaire, "Philosophique" written by de Jaucourt, and Diderot's article "Eclectisme." The intriguingly self-reflexive encyclopedia article also belongs to a larger encyclopedic ensemble constituted by countless articles' reference to "philosophe," "philosophie," and "philosophique," a network itself linked to other articles referring to such concepts as "lettres," "littérature," and "gens de lettres." It is now possible to constitute these semantic networks rapidly and exhaustively, thanks to a searchable electronic text version of the 1751 edition of the *Encyclopédie*, made accessible via the Project for American and French Research on the Treasury of the French Language. The ARTFL database also contains most major eighteenth-century texts in searchable form, and thus these semantic networks can be linked to far broader ones. How these texts should be read once they have been identified is of course another matter, just as it always has been.[20] The article "Philosophe" is important, from a literary historical perspective, because of its place in the clandestine literature of the period.

It was highly instrumental in consolidating a semantic, intellectual, and sociological shift in the meaning of what it meant to be a writer in France.[21] Less and less was the kind of writing designated by the term 'philosophy' represented as marginal with respect to the social order, whether this marginality was viewed as harmless or as subversive. Instead, philosophy was increasingly portrayed as serving an essentially critical role within society.

This shift can be seen by comparing earlier representations of the figure of the philosophe, such as the entry "philosophe" in the *Dictionnaire de l'Académie Française*. In the 1694, 1718, and even 1740 editions, the *Dictionnaire* defined the philosophe first in relation to logical inquiry, second in terms of a mode of behavior characterized by a secluded and modest life, and third as incarnating a potentially disruptive way of thinking. The third definition reads as follows: "[philosophe] is also used in an absolute sense sometimes to refer to an individual who, through freethinking (*libertinage d'esprit*), places himself above the ordinary duties and obligations of civic and Christian life. He is someone who refuses nothing, who knows no restraints, and who leads the life of a philosophe." Linked to a critical libertinage tradition, the philosophe incarnates here a potential threat to good manners and religion. We should be wary of relying too heavily on the institutionally sanctioned dictionary of the Académie, for it does not entirely parallel a more positive view of the philosophe presented in Furetière's 1690 dictionary, as well as in the Jesuits' 1721 *Dictionnaire de Trévoux*. In the article "Patrie" (national homeland), Furetière notes that "a philosophe is always in his homeland." The Trévoux dictionary reaffirmed the cosmopolitan nature of the philosophe, calling him "a citizen of the world" and "a person who is nowhere a foreigner." Yet in 1762, that cosmopolitanism was passably threatening, at least in the dictionary of the Académie, where a cosmopolitan is defined as "someone who doesn't adopt a homeland (*patrie*) [and ...] is not a good citizen."

Dumarsais's text of 1743 is marked by these debates concerning the proper place of the thinker-writer in society, debates that Dumarsais attempts to settle by suggesting that the philosophe of the Académie's *Dictionnaire* is a philosophe in name only, that is, an outmoded figure that the article will dismiss from its opening lines. "Nothing is easier to acquire today than the name of philosophe; an obscure and secluded life, the trappings of wisdom along with some readings, these are enough for this name to be given to persons who pride themselves in the name they do not merit."[22] The strategy employed here is one of which the encyclopedists frequently avail themselves, that of affirming the relation between name and thing as a matter of convention. Socially determined and not fixed by nature, this relation is arbitrary and thus is subject to revision. Nothing is easier to acquire than the *name* of philosopher – the proper manner and some well-placed references will suffice. But this means that the conventional definition of philosophe can be rewritten according to other, more 'useful' criteria – useful knowledge being highly valorized by the encyclopedists and often referring to values critical of the status quo. The article "Philosophe" rewrites prior definitions in just this fashion, rejecting the image of the philosophe as a simple libertine, whether deist or atheist, who had "the force to get rid of religious prejudice." The philosophe fashioned here is not the scapegoat of the Académie's *Dictionnaire*, but rather a more 'modern', enlightened subject.

Two traits characterize this subject: a particular type of philosophical inquiry and a certain social behavior. As for the first of these traits, the philosophe is presented as embodying an "esprit philosophique," possessing "a mind marked by observation and wise judgment that traces everything back to its true principles." The philosophe rejects "meditation" as a source of knowledge, seeking a truth grounded on empirical observation and not on pure speculation. Exemplifying the move away from Cartesian idealism, Dumarsais's text embraces the sensationalist credo that all knowledge comes from the senses. The philosophe acquires a newly empowered self-sufficiency, moreover, for he quite literally embodies knowing. Thought itself is a kind of sense here, and thus in his search for first causes the philosophe needs go no farther than the very body. The phantasmatic image offered here as illustration of this epistemology is the clock that winds itself. No mention is made of any clockmaker, however, a silence that skirts the issues of divine existence or intervention. Other writers pursue the materialist thesis in greater detail. In *L'Homme machine*, for instance, La Mettrie proposes a mechanistic explanation of the somatic causality of thought, and Diderot explores the limit case of this way of knowing through the epistemological setup of *Le Rêve de d'Alembert*, a text that stages the fictive dream of epistemological embodiment, standing for a way of knowing through the body.

As Louis Althusser notes, words are instruments of knowledge in scientific discourse, but in social, political, and ideological terms they are not tools but weapons, explosives, tranquilizers or poisons. Words can be "the site of an ambiguity: the stake is a decisive but undecided battle."[23] The article "Philosophe" belongs to such an intellectual, social, and ideological struggle, mounting a minor skirmish in the culture wars of eighteenth-century France, but an engagement nonetheless. Affirming new 'true' principles, the article aims to found them rhetorically by contesting and displacing others. Quite expectedly, the rationalism affirmed here is radical and intransigent, designed to unseat not only speculative metaphysics and idealism, but also religion. "Reason is to the philosophe what grace is to the Christian ... Grace determines the Christian to act by free will; reason determines the philosophe, without eliminating the taste for free will." Religion too is replaced by a new sociability, an attitude towards others that constitutes a second aspect of the image of the philosophe the article develops. "The philosophe is eager for all that goes by the name of honor and probity: that is his sole religion. Polite society is the sole divinity, so to speak, that he recognizes on earth; he showers praise upon it, he honors it through his probity, a precise attention to his duties, and a sincere desire not to be a useless or cumbersome member of society."[24] Even in rejecting the wisdom of tradition, the philosophe's intellectual pursuits do not preclude his being an essentially social creature.

Here lies an important difference between the mid-eighteenth-century image of the philosophe and that of a half-century earlier. The philosophe of earlier generations was characterized by retreat, a willed withdrawal from social pressures and obligation in favor of a simpler, more honest life of philosophical reflection. This notion of speculative retreat is a commonplace in the philosophical tradition. What does it signify, however, when read in relation to the social and cultural context in which it is activated? In the highly integrated Parisian court culture of Louis XIV, the concept of retreat was a complicated one.[25] For court nobility, it meant a kind of exile, tantamount to the loss of wealth, privileges, and power. Choosing retreat was unthinkable for aristocrats who derived their sense of identity from their place within court culture. For other groups, however, whose members imagined ways of constructing social identity removed from court culture if not entirely independent of it, the notion of retreat was more appealing. As a freely chosen state, retreat was not necessarily exile, and thus it could signify a degree of autonomy. One of the best-known novels of the seventeenth century, Lafayette's *La Princesse de Clèves*, ends with a scene of retreat, as the novel's heroine leaves Paris to spend the remaining few years of her life in seclusion. Generations of the novel's readers have grappled with the meaning of this final act. Is it a tragic and fatal ending, which befalls a heroine no longer able to resolve competing exigencies of love and duty? For long it seemed that this must have been how seventeenth-century readers viewed the Princess's situation, as they interpreted the novel through the same lens as the one used to view the classical tragedies of Corneille and Racine, where the logic of the tragic genre meted out a similar mortal fate. In these plays the tragic hero is a victim whose individual death affirms the survival of a collective order, be it moral, social, or political. Recently, however, the retreat of Lafayette's Princess has been seen as a form of affirmative resistance, an act whereby the heroine removes herself from the competing demands of husband and lover, as well as from a social order that defines her place in terms of such demands.

Yet the Princess's act remains a 'literary' retreat. In actual social practice, retreat took place in a limited number of instances, the most notable of which are perhaps the literary salons established by such women as Madame de Scudéry. Retreat also occurred in such religious institutions as Port-Royal (even if convents functioned more often as spaces of imprisoning exile for girls and women). In terms of its symbolic function, however, the image of retreat may not have reflected reality but it produced effects that were real nonetheless, serving to affirm and perform the idea of withdrawal, to maintain it as an act that could be realized, if only in an imaginary, symbolic way. It would have been all the more important to make such withdrawal appear possible, given the regulative pressures of a courtly society.[26]

By the eighteenth century, the need for this symbolic escape valve was less pressing. Accordingly, the imaginary spaces of exteriority constructed in literature and other forms of educated writing were configured differently and served other purposes. The established genre of utopian literature will continue, intersecting with a flourishing new genre of travel literature. In both cases, however, the symbolic exteriority provided by the fictional, narrative elaboration of 'exotic' other spaces tends to affirm the cultural order instead of offering a retreat or escape from it. From Jean de Léry's *Histoire d'un voyage faict en la Terre de Brésil* (1578) to Louis-Antoine de Bougainville's account of his travels in *Voyage autour du monde* (1771), the grand travel narratives of the 'age of discovery' describe a distant space that all too often turns out to provide a discursive screen onto which authors and readers alike can project familiar interpretive structures and values. These screen travelogues allow readers to believe in the encounter with a real other, or another reality, all the while providing the comforting affirmation of the timeless naturalness of the knowledge that readers believe they already possess. No exile, and nothing new under the sun, indeed.

To produce critical knowledge that is not merely a replay of the already known, travel writing had to aim at establishing a vantage point beyond or outside the familiar cultural frame, which it then could estrange and make unfamiliar. Montesquieu's *Lettres persanes* tells the story of two Persian travelers in Paris, providing readers with a view of French culture seen through other eyes (and the Other's eye) and offering a paradigmatic illustration of how a text produces this critical knowledge. The drive to produce such knowledge also shapes the figure of the philosophe. Here the voluntary withdrawal of the previous century is rewritten as a speculative, intellectual exteriority, a critical perspective from which the philosophe can evaluate arbitrary and dogmatic norms. The judgments the philosophe produces from such a position are designed to contribute to intellectual and social change. Viewing themselves as agents and instruments of that change, eighteenth-century philosophe-writers claim to be necessary and valuable members of the social order. Yet they argue with equal conviction that they wish to remain free from what they see as its contingent and arbitrary determinations, expressing a tension between freedom and restraint that is one of the defining dialectics of eighteenth-century liberal thinking.

In psychological terms, this dialectic plays itself out in the countless, almost obsessively repetitive gestures of self-representation performed by eighteenth-century philosophes. Jean Marie Goulemot sees in these acts the beginnings of the modern notion of writer and writing. "To base the truth of one's words on one's unfortunate vocation, one's marginality, ego or the sternness of one's life – that represents the archeology of a contemporary discourse on writing ... What constitutes today's image of the writer as a rebel, oppositional by nature, a marginal character out of obligation and through writing, goes far back in time."[27] Goulemot's modern writer may be the last vestige of a persistent romanticism rather than the precursor of a more skeptical, less nostalgic postmodernism. Nevertheless, Jean-Jacques Rousseau is without doubt the most modern of eighteenth-century writers in Goulemot's terms, for the truth he makes public in the *Confessions*, the *Rêveries d'un promeneur solitaire*, and other intimate writing is a personal, private one that is always out of place. The truth Rousseau's text recounts is that of an alienated individual, an 'ex-centric' subject that cannot find a place in the hyper-civilized world of Parisian salons, a perverse world whose inhabitants take pleasure in falseness, perversity, and the suffering of others. Rousseau's text affirms that the truth of the alienated writer's experience extends beyond the singular case of Rousseau himself. The experience of reading he calls out for is designed to found a new social order characterized by sympathy, moral justice, and affective integration. This new order is the realization of a kind of general particularity, which can be theorized in literary terms through Rousseau's autobiographical writing and in political terms through his notion of the general will.

The case of Rousseau illustrates only one aspect of the changing socioeconomic conditions of literary activity in *Ancien Régime* France. The sphere of educated writing, *les lettres*, was reshaped as the writer's dependence on an aristocratic patronage system weakened. That system was being replaced by a market economy in which publishers' sales figures, not the will of the aristocratic wealthy, determined who would write, what would be written, and what would be published. Authors came to see themselves as producing works to which it was possible to have rights, works possessing economic value.[28] Nevertheless, the publishing industry does not yet constitute the sole source of support for the eighteenth-century writer, and so the work of writers and of writing cannot be fully explained by the mechanism of market economy capitalism. The economic sphere of the book trade intersected with another economic sphere, that of the state and its extensive system of privileges. Writers may have amassed social capital from being admitted to the salon world, but they acquired real wealth from membership in the numerous academies and other institutions of elite culture. Two different literary worlds took shape after mid century: the 'high' Enlightenment where writers formed a part of the social and cultural elite, moving easily between salons and academies, and what Robert Darnton has called the literary underground, composed of still aspiring – or already failed – philosophes, writers, and critics. These are the "demi-littérateurs" and "écrivailleurs" that Louis-Sébastien Mercier describes in *Tableau de Paris*, and the "canaille" whom Voltaire castigates unsparingly. Was the literary world as dichotomous as Darnton's binary metaphors of 'high' and 'low' suggest? Instead of reflecting a real division between two distinct social spheres, these metaphors more likely translate the desire on the part of certain writers to project a prestige hierarchy in which they could improve their perceived status by contemptuously dismissing other writers as being beneath them. In any event, sizeable numbers of mid-level writers populated Paris – journalists, editors, translators, and compilers – and although their work did not produce the values of the Enlightenment, it certainly contributed to propagating them.[29]

These entwined issues of philosophical reflection, social integration, and economic benefit traverse the article "Philosophe." The philosophe may establish a critical remove from traditional thinking, but in this text he is not some marginalized rebel who proclaims the purifying value of alienation. Such solitude is unthinkable here, tantamount to a kind of monstrosity. "Man is not a monster who must live only beneath the sea and in the depths of the forest." Invoking the idea of an intrinsic, essential sociability, the text affirms the philosophe's place in the social order. "Our philosophe doesn't find himself in exile in this world; he doesn't believe he is enemy territory."[30] It is only natural that the philosophe would be sociable in this world, if there can be no hope of gain or punishment in any future one. The religious paradigm is replaced by the social paradigm, just as it was by the sensationalist paradigm earlier in the text.

Sociability does not remain an abstract principle and universal value for long, though, for it will be linked to a system of exchange, interest, and benefits. This linkage is suggested by the following lapidary definition of the philosophe's social character: "he is a gentleman (*un honnête homme*) who wishes to please and to make himself useful."[31] The term *honnête homme* designates a complex cultural formation in *Ancien Régime* France. For seventeenth-century moralists, *honnêteté* refers to a moral character that individuals may claim to possess regardless of birth or social station. But moral values and social station are seldom so easily separated. *Honnêteté* is not a classless ideal, even if it is a key concept in an esthetic and moral discourse that seemed to transcend social class. For besides the term's use, its effect depended upon its rhetorical and ideological function within a changing social order. As court absolutism grew more powerful, the traditional nobility found it harder to assert aristocratic will, as it was made to feel increasingly dependent upon the state. It is against this backdrop of power relations that the discourse of *honnêteté* must be set, for the standards of good taste, decorum, and esthetic judgment that characterized the *honnête homme* were an essential part of a strategy allowing the nobility to articulate a new and 'civilized' identity in its relation to the state. In Méré, Saint-Evremond, or La Rochefoucauld, for instance, the discourse of taste affirms the supremacy of the monarchical-nobiliary order, making the noble subject of *honnêteté* appear as the natural social subject and subordinating others who do not share these values. For the *robins* or the newly ennobled members of the administrative order, as well as for members of the wealthy bourgeoisie who aspired to nobility, the discourse of *honnêteté* provided an important way to define identity. By subscribing to its values, the *robin* and the bourgeois could establish a common connection with traditional nobility, even if that meant denigrating the values and practices that characterized non-noble groups. The discourse of *honnêteté* marking the last half of the seventeenth century was complex and ideologically charged. It was, as

Michael Moriarty puts it, "the site of a class's renegotiation of its position, a renegotiation that took account of new recruitment to this class and a new relationship of this class to other social groups."[32]

By 1743 when "Le Philosophe" was published, the previous century's renegotiation of social position and cultural capital through the discourse of *honnêteté* was essentially a *fait accompli*. Consequently, reference to the figure of the *honnête homme* does introduce particular moral values into the discussion of what constitutes a philosophe, recalling a discursive strategy for forming an emergent social figure. Yet the values and interests that dovetail here in the construction of the philosophe are located far more explicitly in an eighteenth-century economic sphere than was the *honnête homme* of the seventeenth century. Defined as wanting to please and be useful, the philosophe's usefulness is inseparable from a certain self-interest, which is phrased in terms of pleasure and economic advantage. "[Our philosophe] wants to enjoy (*jouir*), as a thrifty wise man would (*en sage économe*), the wealth that nature offers him; he wants to take pleasure together with others, and to do so, one must be pleasing. Thus, he seeks to be found agreeable by those with whom he lives by chance or by choice, and in so doing he finds what is agreeable to him."[33] The philosophe's wisdom allows him to derive pleasure from the wealth that nature provides for him, from goods that come naturally into his possession. Seeking to combine *sagesse, économie*, and *jouissance* ("jouir en sage économe"), the philosophe works to set up an arrangement where in giving others pleasure he finds what suits him, what is appropriate, what he desires.

The philosophe's pleasure and happiness are subjected to demanding calculation. "The true philosophe knows nothing of the torments of ambition, but he does want to have life's pleasant commodities. Besides what is exactly necessary, he requires the decent superfluity (*un honnête superflu*) required for a decent man (*un honnête homme*) and which alone makes for happiness."[34] Do these "pleasant commodities" and the "decent superfluity" that constitute the philosophe's happiness refer to the creature comforts of a developing consumer society, praised by Voltaire in *Le Mondain*?[35] Or do these terms betray a thrifty wisdom on the part of this "sage économe," who is always alert to the benefits to be derived from each word and act, according to an economic calculus that legitimates excess (the "honnête superflu") without expressing at whose particular expense this excess is derived? Phrased more broadly, at issue in reading "Le Philosophe" is whether it is sufficient to borrow the Enlightenment writer's own terms to describe the writer's situation. The justification for such a borrowing rests on the assumption that the writer's terms reproduce faithfully the image that writers produced of themselves. But the price to be paid for that assumed interpretive fidelity is a failure to understand critically the desires and tensions determining the creation of such an image. We must seek ways to resist the lure of that tantalizing image, refusing paraphrase, however faithful to its object it seems to be, and aiming to realize a resistant reading strategy that resituates the concepts and values conveyed by the image of the philosophe.

First, a theoretical framing question: how we can understand "Le Philosophe" in a historical sense? Should it be read as providing an unmediated reflection of social reality, its materiality disappearing in the face of the raw givenness and ultimate comprehensibility of the real? Or does this text represent that reality by giving it discursive form, providing through a complex discursive mechanism the symbolic resolution of tensions not resolved in reality? The commentary of Herbert Dieckmann, one of the first modern interpreters of "Le Philosophe," illustrates the former, more mimetic understanding. For Dieckmann, "Le Philosophe" both belongs to and reflects a historical moment of transition, in which the seventeenth-century notion of aristocratic civility was losing its intellectual force and its regulative function. The *honnête homme* of the court was becoming the urban, cosmopolitan philosophe. As Dieckmann puts it, "the philosopher freed himself from the standards of polite society; he felt no longer bound to its code, but to the *bien public* and the *genre humain*; from an observer of the 'bienséances' and the 'délicatesses sensibles' he became a guide and leader of humanity; it was to the larger world that he was going to devote his thought and actions."[36] It is true that in the eighteenth century a weakening occurs in the power of court culture to shape significant intellectual or esthetic works. But we should be more cautious than Dieckmann in linking that historical context to a reading of its texts. Dieckmann's commentary collapses the distinction between actual writers (the philosophes, both real and would-be) and the image of this social type that writers imagined and constructed. That image performed a strategic symbolic function, and in collapsing the distinction between historical context and its representation, the interpretive perspective that Dieckmann has been pressed into service to illustrate, we risk continuing unknowingly the rhetorical, performative, and ideological work that the image of the philosophe originally was designed to do.

In presenting the philosophe as someone able to free himself from society's constraints and become a world citizen, as if at will and through the stroke of the pen, this perspective reactivates the gesture of numerous eighteenth-century writers who represented themselves as free from the determining contingency of history. Diderot may worry about state censorship of the *Encyclopédie*, for instance, but he claims to be free to write for the ideal and imaginary public of posterity. Rousseau rejects his real readership, which in his obsessional view acquires the dimensions of a horde of hostile persecutors. He desires to transcend this hostility – real and imagined – by receiving a compassionate, sympathetic response from imagined readers. This scenario is played out in a scene of self-representation in the *Confessions* in which Rousseau imagines the moment following his earthly death when he appears before God, finally freed from a personal history marked by persecution and misunderstanding. Book in hand, in other words bearing the private self-image he has fashioned to replace the contingent public image against which he struggled throughout his life, Rousseau imagines he will finally succeed in freeing himself from history by hearing divine words of personal redemption. Set in the preface of the *Confessions*, this scenario presides over the autobiographical text, presenting a privileged scene of divine reading that serves as a prompt for the reading Rousseau wishes to elicit from his own real and earthly readers. Similarly, other philosophes, believing in their ability to free themselves from historical contingency, will dialogue with earthly rulers – Diderot and Catherine of Russia, Voltaire and Frederick of Prussia. Materializing an alliance of knowledge and power, philosophy and politics, these dialogues represent a utopian moment of enlightenment. Do these writers believe in the possibility of realizing such a utopian scenario? Or do they adopt the position of believing in the alliance between philosophy and politics as part of their writerly persona? Whatever the case, history would prove this utopian moment to be short-lived.

Utopia, this *u-topos* or non-place, is a space that exists nowhere. Eighteenth-century thinkers experiment repeatedly with ways to realize the utopian impulse of Enlightenment thought. Philosophical prose offers one such means, as in Dom Deschamps's numerous works, Morelly's *Code de la nature* or Kant's *Project for Universal Peace* written at the century's mid-revolutionary end. Fictional or literary prose provides other ways to realize the Enlightenment's utopian impulse through the presentation of imaginary places whose inhabitants have realized a seemingly more perfect social order. One such technique involves inserting micro-utopias into larger narratives, as in the depiction of happy virtue in the Troglodyte letters of Montesquieu's *Lettres persanes*, the rational, deist state of Eldorado in Voltaire's *Candide*, idyllic Clarens in Rousseau's *La Nouvelle Héloïse* or the island of Tamoé in Sade's *Alice et Valcour*. Alternatively, the utopian impulse may invest the entire text. In Diderot's *Supplément au voyage de Bougainville*, the apparently harmonious marriage of desire and natural law is staged through the fiction of Tahitian society. Graffigny's *Lettres d'une Péruvienne* reveals the impossibility of an exotic, primitive utopia, for which is substituted the affective, feminine, and social ideal of the heroine's own space. Mercier's *L'An 2440* depicts an idyllic Paris situated in an elsewhere of the future.

In all these texts, a position of spatial exteriority is created (Tahiti, Peru, Switzerland, the New World) to figure a seemingly unassimilable difference, whether it is phrased in terms of race, culture, or gender. That difference is then invested with a certain critical function in order to unsettle the reader's belief in the natural givenness and legitimacy of existing codes and norms. As Enlightenment writers experiment with the critical potential of utopian writing, the reality of the outside space they create to do so becomes increasingly rhetorical. Diderot's *Supplément au voyage de Bougainville* does not claim to represent any real Tahiti, or at least not the way the eyewitness account of Bougainville does. Instead the text supplements and supplants that account, exposing a utopian conceit that was never really very well hidden in the first place. Rather than refer to a space existing somehow 'outside' the social-cultural order, the utopian text carves out an 'ex-centric' space within that order. It is a space of difference within culture itself, which remains determined by the cultural order. Because of that inevitable determination, it is an imaginary space whose symbolic exteriority runs the risk of affirming the cultural order, reasserting a version of ideology in the very act of attempting to contest it and pry it free for critical examination.

The utopian impulse of Enlightenment thinking also shapes how eighteenth-century writers understood the image of the philosophe. Roland Barthes has analyzed this situation in an essay on Voltaire, whom he calls "the last of the happy writers." Voltaire's happiness or good fortune resulted from personal genius, to be sure. But that good fortune also stemmed from the historical situation in which genius could display itself. That situation, for Barthes, is characterized above all by the transformation of class relations. Bourgeois writers enjoy ever greater fame, wealth, and freedom, or at least they believe they will. Their interests seem increasingly to correspond to those of society at large. Such a state is a paradise soon to be lost, Barthes observes, for history soon catches up with writers, as it does with all who imagine themselves beyond it. The Voltaire that Barthes describes resembles eighteenth-century writers in general, as Jean-Paul

Sartre had characterized them a few decades earlier in *Qu'est-ce que la littérature?*[37] Sartre views these writers as imagining they occupied a social sphere outside the determinations of elite court culture. Representatives of an ever more empowered bourgeois order, they believed themselves free to create and to critique. What makes this situation perfectly utopian, argues Sartre, is that writers did not experience this freedom as alienation. It was later, in the nineteenth century, that the critical impulse of literature estranged the writer from bourgeois society as well as from the historical conditions that had brought it about. Eighteenth-century writers could realize the critical impulse of writing without risking such alienation. The critique they engaged in comprised values and ideals that could be claimed to have universal application, pertaining to 'man' or 'humanity'. Yet the context from which these values and ideals were derived was not some abstract universality, but rather the very concrete, material context of the writer's particular situation. In this sense the philosophe is 'ex-centric', a subject embodying difference within the social order, yet determined ultimately by that order. Given this paradoxical utopian situation, what kind of critical practice was available to the Enlightenment writer who adopted the persona of philosophe? Was that writer destined to reassert the ideological order in the very act of contesting it?

For Louis Althusser, Enlightenment thought is based on precisely this contradiction insofar as the Enlightenment discourse of universality amounts to a discursive strategy of veiled self-interest. "When during the eighteenth century," writes Althusser, "the 'rising class', the bourgeoisie, developed a humanist ideology of equality, freedom and reason, it gave its own demands the form of universality, since it hoped thereby to enroll at its side, by their education to this end, the very men it would liberate only for their exploitation." The relation between this class and its own ideology was not "an external and lucid relation of pure utility and cunning," Althusser notes, for the bourgeois subject lives out in the ideology of freedom "the relation between it and its conditions of existence: that is, its real relation (the law of a liberal capitalist economy) but invested in an imaginary relation (all men are free, including the free laborers)."[38] Following on from Althusser's argument, one could ask to what extent "Le Philosophe" too involves a real relation – intellectual work – but one set in an imaginary relation – the writer free to become through his writing a citizen of the world, a condition presented as available to all enlightened subjects. Read thus, "Le Philosophe" deploys a strategy designed to provide a symbolic resolution to particular social contradictions. This image of the philosophe papers over the kind of contradictions Althusser describes. Skirting crucial issues, the text rechannels tensions in order to stabilize and neutralize them in the utopian, universalist ideal of freedom and unfettered social intercourse. But the image of the philosophe is an essentially unstable one, and during the century the contradictory aspects of this figure become increasingly difficult to contain. Pointing out the ideological work that the article "Philosophe" performs suggests one way to begin uncovering this figure's instability, by re-situating a universalizing discourse within the particular conditions of its elaboration, thereby revealing the situation of particular individuals behind the contours of universal subjectivity.

Other eighteenth-century writers are much more wary than the author of "Le Philosophe" when it comes to accepting the ideology of critique and social integration that the image of the philosophe conveys. Diderot's *Le Neveu de Rameau*, for instance, returns to this privileged Enlightenment image in order to play out the series of tensions and conflicts that define this historical moment. In this dialogue the character Moi represents the well-intentioned philosophe in search of truth and wisdom. He describes himself as a disinterested observer of Parisian life, habitually lost in reflection on the subject of politics, love, taste, or philosophy. He claims to rise above the desires, interests, and perversity that define the society he observes, however, and he praises art, literature, and philosophy for their moralizing, civilizing power to improve society. Throughout the dialogue Moi's self-descriptions recall the traditional attributes of the philosophe. Even Lui refers to him as "Monsieur le philosophe." The epithet conveys no respect on Lui's part for Moi, however, but rather a corrosive irony, which turns the intellectual quality of philosophe into a merely social category. For Lui, the philosophe scarcely differs from the denizens of the Bertin house where Lui leads his parasitical life, inextricably bound up in the perverse self-interest that defines the "social." As Lui sees it, no one speaks the language of goodness and truth except hypocritically. Everyone is busy posturing, and all acts are ultimately self-interested ones, especially those of the philosophe who is perhaps the most deluded member of society of all. Lui relentlessly undercuts Moi's position as uninvolved observer by exposing its fundamental paradox: Moi believes himself to be free from self-interest, but he can do so only through his exceptionally interested relation to another such as Lui. Lui calls Moi to account with the suggestion that his philosophizing may be no more than a "position," a hypocritical stance adopted out of self-interest.

The unity of the figure of the philosophe in *Le Neveu* is undermined ultimately by the fact that this figure is double, represented not only by

Moi but by Lui as well. In the text's opening lines, Moi describes Lui as an original character: "he shakes things up, he agitates; he occasions praise or blame; he brings out truth; he makes known decent people and unmasks the rascals. That's when the man of good sense listens and sorts out the world around him."[39] As Moi soon discovers, though, each of them has his own relation to truth, and the values of one will never be in accord with those of the other. Moi may think he enjoys a superior intellectual position, a better way to "sort out the world around him," to interpret reality. But his encounter with Lui reveals that his world is more complicated, more intractable, more "mêlé" than he thought. No common basis for judgment exists that can put an end to the dialogue, debate, and *différend* between Moi and Lui.

As is inevitably the case in Diderot's writing, apparent unity is destabilized in *Le Neveu* and the image of the philosophe is rent in two. In this split, any number of oppositions – between the universal and the particular, the general good and individual self-interest, the useful philosophe and the deceptive social parasite, art and philosophy – are forcefully played out in all their problematic consequences. One of these consequences involves posterity, the *philosophe*'s successors, those who may have 'the last laugh' the Nephew refers to in the closing lines of the text ("rira bien qui rira le dernier"). Diderot's open-ended dialogue reminds us that the question regarding the image of the philosophe is not, and cannot be, limited to the eighteenth century, for the cultural field of the Enlightenment is one to which we too are linked, however uneasily, sometimes, we occupy this field and despite all too justifiable misgivings towards both its utopianism and its power configurations. The image of the philosophe must be read as prefiguring, however remotely, another figure in and through which another modern moment is represented once again, through another symbolic construction or *image tutélaire*, the figure of the intellectual. How might we imagine a linkage between these two moments?

THE LAST INTELLECTUALS?

In the eighteenth century

a world is born that will later become that of the intellectuals, in which a new kind of philosophe is recognized as possessing a universal competency and an unlimited right to intervene in civic affairs. The writer wishes to be judge and guide, the only one able to inscribe the real world completely in words and on the page, a privilege that the *Encyclopédie* illustrates most fully.[40]

The subject of Enlightenment

That utopian world of proto-intellectuals seems distant at present, all the more so if, following Jean-François Lyotard, we take the term 'intellectual' to designate not a person to be described in professional, institutional, or sociological terms, but rather a specific type of discourse.

> Intellectuals are ... minds that, occupying the place of man, humanity, the nation, the people, the proletariat, creation or any kind of similar entity, that is, identifying with a subject endowed with a universal value, analyze from this point of view a situation or a condition, and prescribe what must be done in order for a subject to realize itself, or at least in order for its realization to progress.[41]

Intellectual discourse is based on the assumption that its particular subject can identify (or be identified) with a universal subject.

Thus the intellectual is completely distinct from information-managers of what Lyotard calls the new techno-sciences of language whose responsibilities are designed to realize maximum efficiency (by maximizing profit), not to question the limits and conditions of those responsibilities. The intellectual is also distinct from the writer, artist, and philosopher, whose responsibility involves testing the limits of his/her domain, questioning the accepted criteria of judgment in writing, painting, or thought. What has made the intellectual's situation critical, argues Lyotard, is that since the mid twentieth century there has been no way to think universality, to justify claims made in the name of a universal subject.[42] 'Enlightenment' is the term Lyotard uses to designate universalizing thinking, a mode of thought that has become outmoded not because it is obsolete and must somehow be modernized, but because it has fallen into disuse, its laws now in abeyance. With the decline of enlightenment thought comes the inability to mount a defense of ethical values derived from it and that would be based upon the notion of what Lyotard calls a universal victim-subject. Some of the most powerful writing of the eighteenth-century Enlightenment defends the rights of such victims – Voltaire's tireless campaign against religious fanaticism (particularly in the Calas and Sirven affairs), Diderot's portrayal of convent life in *La Religieuse*, and his more general defense of individual freedoms, always subject to infringement by the imposition of collective ethical norms.

If the discourse – and defense – of universal human rights is the most enduring legacy of the Enlightenment, it is also the most fragile. The demise of the intellectual is a sign of precisely that fragility. From Zola to Sartre, the intellectual was the person who spoke out to defend the cause of someone who had suffered an injustice. Can such speaking out still be justified? Lyotard maintains that this intervention is necessary because of "an ethical and civic responsibility." Yet he cautions against extending beyond the limits of local and defensive interventions the point of view that would justify them, that is, the position of spokesperson for universal humanity. Such a move towards universality, he claims, can ultimately be deceptive; "it can lead thought astray, as it misled Sartre." For Lyotard, the intellectual lives on, but with what seems to be little more than a kind of negative freedom to act in the postmodern condition. With the idea of universality seemingly in ruins, perhaps thinking is newly unfettered from its tantalizing universalist obsessions. But what ethical and political actions are to be performed, and what discourse can legitimate or defend them? It is in terms of these questions that the debate over the legacy and aftermath of Enlightenment must be couched.

As for the philosophe in the *Encyclopédie*, this image may have become too outmoded, too untimely, to be of much use in figuring a subject whose call we hear and wish to heed today. Perhaps the image of the intellectual has even been eclipsed. Champion of ethical modernity in the time of the Dreyfus affair, the intellectual appears more frequently now as a shady figure with an imperfect past, a figure all too often displaced by others who aspire to the role of intellectual, but who can present only a simulated image or simulacrum of that figure.[43] The role of the intellectual may once have been to mediate between injustice and ethics; the sole mediation left to perform today seems to be determined solely by the media. Zola's "j'accuse" has been drowned out by CNN announcers' "Here's the news." If we wish for authentic intellectuals, perhaps finally all we can do is gauge our distance from their images, reactivating them without nostalgia for what may have been lost, and without satisfaction over an identity regained and affirmed, acknowledging instead quite simply these images' incommensurability with our present. For in that recognition of incommensurability lies historical understanding, allowing us to resist Enlightenment without rejecting it, to put it to use once again, but hopefully without delusion.

CHAPTER 4

Designing the past: thinking history through Montesquieu

In a 1776 letter, Denis Diderot digresses for a moment to recall the funeral of Charles-Louis Secondat de Montesquieu, which had occurred some twenty-one years earlier. Ever the sensitive one, Diderot notes how deeply moved he was by this event commemorating the influential political theorist. Why might this have been the case? What meaning might Montesquieu's death have held for the writer of forty-two who had barely begun the *Encyclopédie* project and had not yet written his major works? When Montesquieu died in 1755, the work of the Bordeaux *parlementaire*, which included *Considérations sur les causes de la grandeur des Romains et de leur decadence* (1734) and *L'Esprit des lois* (1748), had already contributed significantly to reshape thinking in France concerning the need to limit the power of the monarchy. For Montesquieu, if power remained unchecked it would tend towards ever greater and more corrupt despotism. This despotism is thematized as oriental in Montesquieu's political theoretical texts, as well as in his epistolary novel, *Lettres persanes*, no less a work of political theory for being an epistolary novel.[1] This so-called oriental despotism is best read not as a literal, empirical description of Persian culture, but as a metaphor for the dangerous power Montesquieu believed was operating much closer to home, in the political order of monarchical absolutism. This despotic Orient results from a displacement, the transposing of a real fear onto an imaginary one. Thus, projecting an imaginary and phantasmatically pure power offers a symbolic counterweight to the experience of 'French' monarchical power. If the cautionary fiction of 'Oriental' despotism provided a symbolic solution to the problem of absolutist power, Montesquieu proposed a political solution as well, in the role he believed the nobility could play in limiting such despotic ascendancy. Moderation was the primary principle of the aristocracy, this class that Montesquieu defined by its renunciation of personal ambition in the name of service to the public good. Because of its ability to bring about the balancing of competing interests, the nobility could effectively moderate the monarchical will to power. Montesquieu saw in his own class, the administrative nobility or *noblesse de robe*, a way to theorize the possibility of a counterweight to absolutist power, as well as to imagine a political ethics or civics that would promote a more tempered, moderate regime.

Diderot assesses Montesquieu's stature in similar terms in his 1766 letter, referring to him as the "tutor of kings and ... the declared enemy of tyrants." Yet his digression serves another purpose, providing Diderot a way to stage his own experience of Montesquieu's death. He notes with some pride, for instance, that in the procession following Montesquieu's coffin he alone represented the cohort of philosophes.[2] What meaning might his presence have had at this event, and for whom? A remark Jean-Jacques Rousseau makes in a letter suggests one answer. Rousseau notes acidly, "I was in the country when [Montesquieu] died, and I learned that of all the men of letters that Paris teems with, only Diderot accompanied his funeral procession. Fortunately, he made the others' absence the least noticeable."[3] Rousseau is less concerned with assessing the significance of Montesquieu and his work than with taking a jab at Diderot, this Montesquieu funeral groupie. With all the heavy irony of a gossip columnist, Rousseau points out the event's theatricality, which confirms yet once again the play of appearances and hypocrisy that for him constitute elite Parisian lettered society. Given the rift between Diderot and Rousseau, the latter's snide remark can be expected. Yet it also alerts us to the rhetoric of self-fashioning in Diderot's relation to a culturally iconic Montesquieu, a rhetoric that Rousseau of all individuals would understand.

This self-fashioning takes place by projecting an affective relation to the absent figure of Montesquieu, a process that occurs emblematically in another more extensive digressive remark, this time in the *Encyclopédie* article "Eclectisme." Once again Diderot writes an imaginary return to Montesquieu's funeral, a few days after the event this time, and not two decades later.

I wrote these reflections on February 11, 1755, upon returning from the funeral of one of our greatest men, desolate over the loss of this man suffered by the nation and letters, and deeply indignant over the persecution he had undergone. The veneration in which I held his memory engraved on his tombstone these words, which I had intended earlier to use as an inscription on *L'Esprit des lois: alto quoesivit coelo lucem, ingemuitque repertâ.* May posterity hear these words and learn from them that, alarmed by the whisperings of the enemies he feared, and sensitive to frequent insults, which he would doubtless have scorned had they not seemed to him to bear the mark of authority, the loss of this innately sensitive man was the sad reward for the honor he won for France and for the important service he had just performed for the universe!

The Montesquieu depicted here wrote selflessly for the betterment of humanity, yet was persecuted by the injurious enemies of reason. He ultimately finds the vindication he merits, however, in the veneration of future generations, in whose name Diderot implicitly speaks. This is the dialectic of posterity, in which Diderot fervently believes, moreover, despite the numerous times the dialogic writer would put this argument to the test.[4] This highly stylized eulogistic aside in the *Encyclopédie* article recalls the numerous eulogies, for Montesquieu and others, delivered during the eighteenth century in reception speeches given at the Académie Française and elsewhere. These set pieces of praise marked not the passing of kings and nobility, as did the eloquent funeral orations delivered by Bossuet in the previous century, but the enduring work of "great men" who labored for their fellows and their country. These eulogies constituted a kind of "paper Pantheon" that anticipated the one founded in stone in 1791 during the Revolution.[5] In similar fashion, Diderot puts the past to work in his remarks concerning Montesquieu. More than simply offering praise for a great man departed, Diderot's comments enfold Montesquieu in the party of embattled Enlightenment philosophes struggling against the opposition of the ignorant and the powerful. By praising Montesquieu, Diderot plays out a transposed version of the drama of critique and resistance that he experienced as editor of the *Encyclopédie* during skirmishes with court and church in the early 1750s. Praising Montesquieu becomes for Diderot an occasion for self-depiction and self-justification. Montesquieu's death provides the pretext for sketching out the image of the writer-intellectual, to argue for the legitimacy of that figure's social and ethical role, and to point to the positive changes the philosophe would help bring about.

The praise of Montesquieu that Diderot interjects in the article on "eclectic philosophy" illustrates a more general rhetorical strategy the philosophes used increasingly from mid century onwards, as they attempted to intervene critically in various debates, as well as to garner social distinction and the cultural capital that flowed from it. Philosophical writing is characterized as playing not an entertaining role, or even a merely instructive one. Instead it is attributed a critical, potentially transgressive power that drives its presentation of new knowledge and useful truths. Despite the hostility it encounters, the writing of the philosophe-intellectual is defended in the name of a national interest and collective utility that transcend the sectarian. It is posterity, moreover, that will best assess the true worth of the philosophe. Through this discursive appeal to posterity's judgment and the ultimate exoneration of the philosophe, the eighteenth-century writer can imagine, if not an escape from the constraints of a hostile present, then at least a deferral of that contingency.[6] Through this leap into an imaginary future, the writer rescripts the present and redesigns the desired subject located there.

Containing a reflection on writing, Diderot's eulogistic aside concerning Montesquieu also presents a scene of reading, in which the writer returns to his own encyclopedic article written two decades earlier. This speculative moment is one privileged example of how the encyclopedic subject is marked out and filled in, through a process that is the hallmark of the discursive workings of ideology. One of the few cases in the *Encyclopédie* where this subject is designated by the first person and receives affective substance and texture ("desolate," "indignant"), the passage belongs to an array of instances in the encyclopedic text where new subject positions are staked out and new power relations are configured in ways that will define the modernity of the Enlightenment project. Montesquieu functions as a kind of tutelary image here, a phantasmatic self-projection on Diderot's part, but one that provides a model for shaping the more general image of the public intellectual that begins to emerge around the mid eighteenth century. This self-projection and rescripting of the present may well be one of the constitutive features of the historical-critical project of Enlightenment.

Like most scenes of reading, this one can be read as a critical allegory. The tale it recounts is that of a modern return to an absent yet remembered textual past, a return that takes place symbolically, through writing, and which scripts a new collective subjectivity and the values that define it. Witnessed in this scene of reading is what I would call the use value of Montesquieu within a larger strategy of self-construction. This manner of putting the past to strategic use characterizes not only Diderot's writing but also that of countless other readers of Montesquieu, both past and present. It is by examining this linkage between past and present that we can win critical insight into historical thought. In the case of Montesquieu, considering his use value provides a way not only to read Montesquieu historically, but also to think history through Montesquieu, so to speak, in order to grasp the stakes involved in designing the past.

In Diderot's reading of Montesquieu, this use value involves an intertextual relation between Montesquieu and his readers, which can be explained with the interpretive paradigms of influence and reception. It could be argued, however, that these paradigms are insufficient for understanding the historical nature of interpretation, the latter's very historicity, and thus that the resulting account of reading (Montesquieu) cannot be historical in any critical sense. These are complex questions, to be teased out here in successive chapters. But already I want to argue that reading (whether Montesquieu, the texts of the eighteenth century or reading *tout court*) cannot be simply a hermeneutic act, or not in any simple sense, insofar as it is an inescapably historical act. This claim could be based on the commonsense observation that all readings of texts occur in particular historical contexts; these contexts in turn may be described in relation to an individual and his or her conceptual field, or in relation to broader, collective groupings. But to contextualize reading in a strong sense, to grasp what it means for a text to be determined by its context, we must do more than juxtapose text and context fortuitously (or even heuristically). Once we consider how the relation between these two might involve more than chance, and how in fact this relation also results from interpretive agency on our own part, we open reflection to the question of what it is that determines interpretation historically, as well as how this determination can be thought of as historical. The critical issue appearing throughout this book involves elaborating a reading strategy that reveals how reference to texts of the past can be understood as the nexus for grasping a present context in its historical dimension. To what use are texts of the past put? How can the past be grasped as/in texts? These are the essential and foundational questions that must be grappled with before anything resembling a literary or a cultural history can be written. By engaging with the question of determining the criteria with which to judge the uses to which texts of the past may be put, a truly bracing cultural history can be written.

 The encyclopedists faced these questions, at least those contributors for whom the project called into question 'old' knowledge by producing 'new', more useful knowledge. This process is seen throughout the *Encyclopédie*, including in the use made of Montesquieu. In addition to Diderot's article "Eclectisme," some 78 other articles refer to Montesquieu by name, and 66 refer directly to *L'Esprit des lois*, making a total of 131 articles. The most extensive reference is found in an extended entry opening the fifth volume, which appeared in 1755. The entry contains eulogy, biography, and a critical commentary of the major works. But besides the article's content, what most likely captures our interest today is its rhetorical, narrative, and ultimately ideological dimension. Besides providing biographical information, the article defends Montesquieu from his critics, countering the hostile reception *L'Esprit des lois* received upon its publication in 1748 from those who attacked its author for supposedly irreligious sentiments. As part of the article's defense mechanism, a particular narrative strategy is employed, namely, telling the story of Montesquieu's becoming an "homme de lettres," "philosophe," and ultimately, in an even more praiseworthy mode, "benefactor of humanity" and "legislator of nations."[7] Through this story, the article historicizes Montesquieu, giving him over to history. In the process it hypostatizes certain values (such as duty to nation and spirit of citizenship), transforming them into universals, just as the individual Charles de Secondat is presented not as a Frenchman from Bordeaux but as "a man of all countries and of all nations." Indeed, one of the article's ideological functions lies in the way it performs this transformation by stripping values of their particularity and presenting them as universals, outside and beyond a history of contexts and particularities. The name 'Montesquieu' thus comes to stand for a universal subject finally freed from the present moment.

Yet this is a present that can be thought only in relation to a past, which can be represented but not fully recovered. The Montesquieu article performs a commemorative monumentalization, resulting in a kind of encyclopedic synecdoche. Conveying the praise of a 'great man', the article also presents a figure who stands for the work the article announces the *Encyclopédie* itself should perform in order to become a monumental depository for patriotic feelings. The *Encyclopédie* too should be a kind of textual "benefactor of humanity." If we can read the figure of Montesquieu as a form of encyclopedic self-reflection, what might this tell us, however schematically, about the entwined historical projects of the *Encyclopédie* and the Enlightenment? Paradoxically, in this epitaph-like article that apparently gives Montesquieu over to a universalizing history, what we find is an uncanny oblation or neutralization of history. The enlightened, liberal critique Montesquieu is presented as representing here is removed from history and written in stone, so to speak, in the form of a program, an agenda, a project with global aspirations. The article writes Montesquieu into a universal history of Enlightenment, revealed as the liberal political policy, and the liberating social policy, that is to be formulated "for all countries and for all nations." Ultimately, this brief article dramatizes the temptation to which Enlightenment eulogy succumbs, prefiguring the haunting temptation of universality and totality that marks if not the end of the Enlightenment project then certainly a divisive tension within it.[8]

Rather than Montesquieu's 'reception' by the encyclopedists, we might think instead of a kind of grafting process at work in the encyclopedic text whereby the figure of Montesquieu is attached to the Enlightenment narrative. This body of texts from the past designated by the proper name is strategically incorporated into a present text to produce new and so-called modern knowledge. This is the intertextual operation in general. But Montesquieu's grafting onto the encyclopedic text must be analyzed in its specificity. The encyclopedists' use of Montesquieu to represent themselves in history affords us insight into the use that can be made of the past. That insight must be recontextualized in turn and brought to bear upon future appropriations of the past, including our own, so as not to becloud that insight, making it unavailable for grasping our own historical work. This is a potentially paradoxical moment in the attempt to think history through Montesquieu. For precisely when we believe we have reached an understanding of history through Montesquieu, we may in fact participate in an imaginary, ideological oblation of history, a rechanneling of historical thinking that neutralizes its more problematic and self-reflexive aspects. Putting this claim interrogatively, what purpose does it serve to analyze the use made of Montesquieu during the mid eighteenth century if that analysis does not also open up onto the question of the use to which Montesquieu might strategically be put today?

The task of thinking history through Montesquieu has always been an urgent one. Throughout the past two centuries in France and beyond, Montesquieu has played, and continues to play, a crucial role in the constitution and regeneration of liberal thought. Reference to Montesquieu's discussion of such fundamental issues as justice, freedom, tolerance, rights, and natural law has been a central and essential part of numerous critical debates in intellectual and political history, as liberal thought repeatedly transforms itself in the face of various sociopolitical pressures, ideological conflicts, and institutional exigencies. In this sense the *Encyclopédie* represents an inaugural moment in a longer trajectory of liberal political thought and its attempts to formulate its own discursive and political self-empowerment. The place accorded Montesquieu in the *Encyclopédie* is a privileged one, which is all the more interesting given the cautious response to the publication of *L'Esprit des lois* on the part of such philosophes as Helvétius, d'Holbach, Voltaire, and Condillac. For them it was no simple affair to integrate the author of *L'Esprit des lois* into the Enlightenment program of reason, reform, and progress. Finally, the figure of Montesquieu in the *Encyclopédie* signals but one of many subsequent receptions, succeeded by that performed by enlighteners such as

Condillac, social theorists such as Rousseau, physiocrats such as Destutt de Tracy, revolutionaries and liberal postrevolutionaries such as Constant, social theorists of the Third Republic such as Durkheim, and, closer to the present, Louis Althusser, Tzvetan Todorov, and Julia Kristeva.[9] If one can still speak of an author's fortune, that of Montesquieu in the nineteenth and twentieth centuries results from his texts' being pressed into service as strategic reference points in the reconfiguration of liberal thought.

Montesquieu provides a perspective onto the liberal political tradition that flows from the eighteenth-century Enlightenment, yet his relation to that tradition is complex, insofar as he can be taken to prefigure it, illustrate it, and mark its limits. His writing also affords us the occasion to question our own relation to that tradition, a relation potentially fraught with at least as much complexity. For while the idea of Enlightenment remains a foundational one, providing an indispensable way to produce self-knowledge and critical thought, that idea itself has been subjected to intense critique. We confront the legacy of an Enlightenment perhaps always already "in eclipse," to borrow an image from Max Horkheimer.[10] To assess that legacy, can we imagine that somehow Diderot sensed the complexity of the relation to the Enlightenment in the case of Montesquieu, just as Diderot plays out that complexity later in his own writing? In any event, in the article "Eclectisme" the placement of Montesquieu introduces a certain tension within the history of philosophy that Diderot recounts, a tension that the name 'Montesquieu' will come to signify.

The article contains a rather standard history of philosophy, drawn directly from Johann Jakob Brucker's *Historia critica philosophiae* (1742–4). Eclectic philosophy is presented as one school of philosophy, one stage in the history of philosophical thought that extends from the pre-Socratics to eighteenth-century rationalism. But Diderot is less interested in rehearsing a canonical history of philosophy than in suggesting somewhat obliquely an innovative way of doing philosophy, a productive mode of conducting intellectual inquiry. Embodied in the figure of the eclectic, this mode of inquiry resembles not a thinker or school of thought from antiquity but rather the kind of critical reader the encyclopedists sought to shape and encourage. Eclecticism thus becomes a very contemporary way of engaging in critical thought and doing philosophy, and one that is quite Diderotian, moreover.[11] It is here, in an entirely eclectic manner, that the proper name 'Montesquieu' is inserted. We might imagine that for Diderot that name does not stand for the glorious culmination of a reason brought to bear upon questions relating to jurisprudence and political theory, nor that it signifies some blinding unfolding that goes by the name 'Enlightenment'. Rather, in this brief moment of digression, when Diderot turns aside for a moment from Brucker's ready-made history of philosophy and yields to the pleasure of thinking eclectically, he uses 'Montesquieu' to formulate a contemporary relation to that history. Through this proper name, he inserts a link to that history, a kind of encyclopedic *renvoi* or cross-reference. Commemorating Montesquieu also allows Diderot to stage his own relation to that history. For a brief moment he delays writing a funerary inscription addressed to posterity that would consign Montesquieu to a universal history. In that moment of digressive delay he addresses the question of his absence, staging his own sense of loss, presenting in all its dramatic particularity the feeling that the event of this passing produced in him.

Diderot's staged relation to Montesquieu stands for his refusal to take over uncritically the powerful story of the unfolding of Enlightenment universal reason, as well as his desire to stage his own particular relation to such a story. Through this example, which I read as a critical allegory, we can formulate the central question of how a resolutely historical relation can be established to Montesquieu and to the texts this proper name stands for. The operative assumption here is that it is crucial to understand our relation to texts in this historical fashion. For in this manner we can articulate not so much what the historical past might have been, but rather what constitutes the essentially historical determination of our reading practices, the historicity of our interpretive relation to texts. The objective, as Georges Benrekassa suggests, is to undertake analyses that reveal the conditions on which we are still related to Montesquieu's thought.[12] These analyses cannot amount to a reception history. The notion of reception, a scarcely evolved version of influence, ultimately remains unhelpful for thinking what constitutes the historicity of the interpretive act itself, especially if by historicity we understand the manner in which one is exposed to the event, the way one is subject (or subjected) to it. As this chapter's somewhat tortured title suggests, "thinking history through Montesquieu" involves determining how we continue to be related to Montesquieu's text, subject to it in a way that allows us to reflect (upon) what constitutes the subject of history.

Such reflection is not unavoidable, and there exist ways of reading Montesquieu that elide the issue of our relation to him and his texts. Such readings fail to consider either the historical nature of his writing or the historical nature of the paradigms and premises employed to read it. For example, as Jean Ehrard has observed, it is crucial to determine whether

Montesquieu is being read onto one side of the revolutionary break or onto the other, or indeed in terms of that break at all.[13] Are we involved in discovering something anticipatory, perhaps familiar, just as de Tocqueville's *Ancien Régime* announced the postrevolutionary state, or is there in Montesquieu's writing something that remains resolutely prerevolutionary, ante-Hegelian even, as Benrekassa calls it, an unassimilably other way of formulating the question of history and a relation to it? Such decisions are crucial, for they determine the significance that Montesquieu's writing will acquire for establishing essentially historical thought.

HISTORY – PROVIDENTIAL, BELLICOSE, OR RATIONAL?

Montesquieu is the first to undertake to think history in his texts, a project to be considered in its own terms before we read these texts through the lens of other historical-narrative perspectives. His first step is to take a critical distance from specific historical perspectives available to him. Already in the *Considérations sur les causes de la grandeur des romains* he moves beneath the surface of past happenings such as they might be presented in chronicles. He wishes instead to unearth what brought these happenings about, to reveal an underlying causality that determined what happened. In the *Considérations* he writes, "Fortune is not what rules the world: we can ask the Romans, who knew continued prosperity when they ruled one way, and uninterrupted upsets when they acted in another. There are general causes, either moral or physical, that are at work in each monarchy and that cause it to rise up, support it or bring it down; all events (*tous les hasards*) are subject to these causes."[14] Chance does not govern the world, but rather a structured set of causes. Events are ultimately intelligible, and by seeking ways to formulate the causality of the past can the historical event as such be understood.

For historical thought in the Renaissance and early Enlightenment, the case of Rome provided the primary if not unique model for political and ethical reflection. For Montesquieu as well, Roman greatness will hold paradigmatic importance. In pursuing his reflection on historical causality, he later turns from the specific historical case of Rome to consider, in *L'Esprit des lois*, what determines historical events in general, in whatever local context they occur. But in both texts the event is comprehensible above all. *L'Esprit des lois* opens with a litotes that recalls the earlier claim in the *Considérations* that it is not fortune but an intelligible structure or logic that governs the world. In conceiving of this project,

Montesquieu assumed that "amidst the infinite diversity of laws and mores, [men] were not led by their fancies alone."[15] In the Roman nation and all others treated in *L'Esprit des lois*, historical causality is located in a fully self-explanatory secular realm. This shift from sacred explanatory paradigms to secular ones is a familiar move in Enlightenment writing. But we should guard against assimilating Montesquieu too quickly into a so-called Enlightenment tradition based on a required set of foundational precursor texts. Although the *Considérations* mark a shift from sacred to secular causality, they do not belong entirely to an enlightenment philosophy of history. Montesquieu may believe it possible to grasp the ultimate *raison d'être* of history's movement, yet the *Considérations* are guided by no overarching desire to persuade of the triumph of universal reason, such as one finds in Condillac or Condorcet, for instance.[16]

To explain the events of Roman history in secular terms, Montesquieu must take clear issue with the theological-political notion of providential history, such as it is formulated in Bossuet's *Discours sur l'histoire universelle* (1681) and *Politique tirée de l'Ecriture Sainte* (1709). Bossuet's vision of universal history had the advantage of bringing order to things, but it was less than divine. For the order of Bossuet's sacred history was that of a providential eschatology, with its apocalyptic ultimate end, an order that was a screen or alibi for secular history. The theological end of history justified political ends in Bossuet's sacred history, as altar and throne merge in the solution to contemporary French social issues that absolutist monarchy claimed to provide. Refusing Grotius's notion of an originary sociability that joined individuals, Bossuet saw the beginnings of the social order in a divisive sinfulness. Corrupt by nature, individuals could not succeed in forming a social order based on freedom. Instead only force could establish and maintain that order. It is probably an exaggeration to label Bossuet a simple apologist for absolutism, for he carefully distinguished between absolute power and arbitrary power. Yet his insistence on this distinction can also be viewed as his attempt to legitimate absolutism, to cover over the arbitrary, in other words motivated, nature of power as figured in his political theory. In this gesture he seeks to naturalize power absolutely, and in a manner repeated endlessly in the texts, images, and spectacular events of the absolutist court of Louis XIV.[17] Given this interplay between historical theory and political practice, we can imagine that the distance Montesquieu takes from Bossuet signifies far more than his opting for one philosophy of history over another. Thinking history for Montesquieu cannot be divorced from reflection on the historical context in which such thought is located. His insight regarding Bossuet is to have understood precisely the extent to which history in the bishop's providential history, both as theory and as practice, remains imbricated ideologically and inextricably in political practice, as well as in the social order and the court culture that practice promoted. Above and beyond any particular history theory or narrative that we might derive from Montesquieu's writing, be it that of nations, economic systems, or values, it is crucial to stress how these writings are shaped by the desire to formulate a discourse on history that is not blind to the place of the political within such a discourse.

This desire helps explain Montesquieu's comments on Thomas Hobbes as well. For just as this Bordeaux *parlementaire* with a Huguenot past refuses the apologetic religious history of the Jesuit bishop of Meaux, he staunchly rejects the bellicose history that flows from the vision of a fearful and aggressive human nature that Hobbes presents in the *Leviathan* (1651). For Hobbes, or at least the Hobbes we can read through Montesquieu, individuals possess an innate desire for domination. Their will to power and to mastery is originary, preexisting the social order that emerges as a bulwark against an otherwise potentially merciless war of absolute destruction. Success in preventing such violence depends upon creating a sovereign, in and through whom is constituted the commonwealth, "that great Leviathan." By entering into a contract or covenant one with another, individuals reduce the set of collective wills to one sovereign will, to whom all are subjected and subjugated. In Hobbes's theory, then, the figure of the sovereign stands for that displacement of will, its ongoing alienation. Montesquieu was not alone among eighteenth-century readers in taking issue with Hobbes's view of society, happiness, laws, and nature.[18] For Montesquieu, certain natural principles preexist the positive laws that were designed to establish them. But he is less interested in examining any pre-social order, arguing instead for the logical priority of natural principles over positive laws. "In [the state of nature], each feels himself inferior; he scarcely feels himself an equal. Such men would not seek to attack one another, and peace would be the first natural law." "The idea of empire and domination is so complex and depends on so many other ideas," he adds, "that it would not be the one they first have."[19] The universal desire for domination that Hobbes imagines is quite simply unreasonable, concludes Montesquieu, and war and its bellicose history represent a departure from reason. But why is such a view of power unreasonable? Where is reason located in Montesquieu's view of things?

For Montesquieu, history is rational, a conviction that should be understood less in teleological terms than in epistemological ones. To speak of the rationality of history does not mean for him that all social structures and their development in time are determined by a particular finality, but rather that their order is intelligible. Belief in this intelligibility presides over *L'Esprit des lois*, the opening line of whose first book concisely defines laws as "the necessary relations deriving from the nature of things."[20] The keystone of Montesquieu's thought, this formulation presents laws not as orders, comparable to divine laws, but as a set of complex interrelations. Like the "constant rules" of the physical universe, these laws are not statutes and decrees but explanatory concepts, structuring principles containing the condition of possibility for understanding the mechanism of social order. Another name for the law governing this mechanism is human reason. "Law in general is human reason insofar as it governs all the peoples of the earth; and the political and civil laws of each nation should be only the particular cases to which human reason is applied."[21] Montesquieu's conviction of the rationality of history has led some interpreters to conclude that he justifies certain abuses, a seemingly logical conclusion given the claim in the preface to *L'Esprit des lois* that "each nation will find here the reasons for its maxims." Yet history's rationality means its explicability for Montesquieu, and not the legitimacy or desirability of all events flowing from a society's laws. This intrinsic comprehensibility does not function as the acceptance of the status quo; instead it is the condition without which meliorative political intervention cannot be imagined.[22]

Montesquieu's rejection of Bossuet's providential history and of Hobbes's bellicose history illustrates the kind of critical questioning to which the claims to historical knowledge were increasingly subjected in the eighteenth century. This questioning was conducted in the name of a growing skepticism, a 'pyrrhonism' that marks the limits, the impossibility even, of well-founded historical knowledge. If we wish to keep that critical questioning at bay, safely contained within the eighteenth century, then we should refuse to see a commonality or resonance between it and contemporary philosophy's ongoing and critical questioning of the foundations of knowledge, writing that examination off as postmodern 'nihilism' or 'antifoundationalism'. Yet a good deal of contemporary philosophical work returns to such early modern philosophical writers as Descartes, Pascal, and Leibniz to recover their way of grappling with the question of founding knowledge. Rather than an inflationary postmodernism, these returns retrieve a question that stands for the ongoing attempt to found a modern approach to knowledge.

As historical texts are subjected to such skeptical scrutiny, the facts of history reemerge for the eighteenth-century historian in all their facticity, as *faits*. These disjointed, heterogeneous bundles of deeds were given to the historian's gaze with no essential linkage connecting them and making them comprehensible. As Voltaire observed in his *Remarques pour servir de supplément à l'Essai sur les mœurs*, this work appeared to some as no more than "a chaotic mix of events, factions, revolutions, and crimes." But this observation does not mean that human history, from Charlemagne to the rebirth of letters and the arts, was chaotic because men and women are irrational creatures. Rather, "this means in a more fundamental way that historian history itself, devoid by definition of philosophical reason, is condemned to the chaos of counting."[23] This chaos of the enumerable is the disorder that Montesquieu attempts to avoid. He seeks to remedy the lack of understanding that otherwise results not just from a plethora of information, too much to know, but more seriously from a fetishizing of factuality designed to dispel doubt concerning the objective reality of the factual.

To exorcize the specter of skepticism, Montesquieu adopts a viewpoint from which the various physical and moral causes determining human action, as well as their interrelation, appear susceptible to being explained rationally. Laws are explanatory concepts and regulatory principles, and thus they instantiate rationality. The category of law provides the base upon which Montesquieu rests his explanation of the nature of government, the structure of republican, monarchical, and despotic rule. This same category also guides his analysis of each system's particular principle, its *ressort* or distinctive governing mechanism. In the republic, for instance, virtue is what determines legal process, political structures, and above all the actions of individual citizens. In the monarchy, the principle of honor provides just as strong an impetus; it can inspire the noblest of actions and, when joined to law, can realize the goals of government as effectively as virtue. As for the despotic system, fear is not only the consequence of this type of rule but its necessary condition, if the despotic state is to maintain itself.

The category of law also enables Montesquieu to explain historical change, understood as structural changes viewed in their diachronic dimension. Change occurs when decisions are taken or actions performed that do not respect the principle of a particular government. In a democracy, for instance, equality is the principle that defines such a system. Yet that principle is corrupted when the equality people desire is extreme, as when individuals wish to be the equals of those selected to govern them. "So the people, finding intolerable even the power they entrust to the others, want to do everything themselves: to deliberate for the senate, to execute for the magistrates, and to cast aside all the judges." As a consequence, the chief *ressort* of the democratic republic is weakened and disappears: "there will no longer be mores or love of order, and finally, there will no longer be virtue."[24] Similarly, monarchy becomes corrupted when the power that nobility derives from honor is made arbitrary, which occurs once nobility is made hereditary. Increasing the number of noble families in this way may make the monarchy less violent, but it will become less virtuous as well. Moreover, "as there will be little virtue there, one will fall into a spirit of nonchalance, laziness, and abandon, which will make a state with neither force nor spring."[25] As for despotism, its order is absolute: "no tempering, modification, accommodation, terms, alternatives, negotiations, remonstrances, nothing as good or better can be proposed. Man is a creature that obeys a creature that wants."[26] Yet even in the despotic state, the latter's "inner vice" causes it to perish: "the principle of despotic government is endlessly corrupted because it is corrupt by its nature."[27] Whereas other forms of government perish by chance, so to speak, the despotic state endures by chance, since specific circumstances resulting from climate, religion, geography, or natural character prevent its further degeneration and eventual overthrow by revolution.

L'Esprit des lois represents the most thoroughgoing attempt in eighteenth-century France to offer a rational explanation of political structures and the processes of transformation to which they are subject. Indeed, an essential inclination to change seems to be the fate of all such structures, which Montesquieu describes as inherently unstable and inevitably subject to the vicissitudes of time. A letter from the *Lettres persanes* offers a striking image of this dynamic yet non-linear view of historical change. As Rica, a Persian visitor to Paris, enters a library he hears from his interlocutor, a wise "dervish," the following description of French history: "Here are the historians of France, where royal power is at first to be seen in the process of formation; dying twice, being reborn twice more; later, going into decline for several centuries, but gradually recovering its strength, making gains on every side and reaching the peak of its development; like rivers which on their way diminish in size or disappear underground, then emerge again and, swollen by the rivers which flow into them, sweep away rapidly everything which lies in their path."[28] This image of history as a constantly flowing, unstoppable, and undirected river flowing its natural course may have been a dying metaphor already in 1721. This view of historical change also comes to us doubly filtered by the fictional, discursive structure of the epistolary novel, for it is not

Montesquieu who speaks, but the Persian visitor to Paris who writes to his compatriot.

This interpretive caution notwithstanding, other examples in the novel illustrate the principles Montesquieu presents as presiding over social change. In the celebrated story of the Troglodytes, for instance, this fictive people's political history is made legible as moral history. The Persian traveler Usbek writes, "with truths of a certain kind, it is not enough to make them appear convincing: one must also make them felt. Of such kind are moral truths."[29] If the Troglodyte episode has more of an effect on Usbek's correspondent than would "subtle philosophy," it is once again because moral principles are presented as the *ressort* or explanatory mechanism of political structure and historical change. What this episode in the *Lettres persanes* makes legible is that an unregulated society is incessantly riven by conflicting interests. By definition unstable, social structures cannot prevail against a process of transformation in which the state may attain a momentary utopian ideal – the flowering of republican virtue that follows violent injustices – yet tends inevitably towards a moral inertia in which public laws come to replace private ethics. It is significant that this final outcome in the allegorical tale is described as the moment when the Troglodytes decide to select a king in order to guarantee their social harmony, a monarchical unification of individuals that the letter presents in dark tones, won at the cost of freedom and spontaneous virtue.

What we read in the Troglodyte episode, as well as throughout Montesquieu's writing, is that a given political order is always located on the brink, on the verge of change. Such change results most often from the principles of government having been perverted. "Once the principles of the government are corrupted, the best laws become bad and turn against the state." The contrary is of course also imaginable, namely, that when principles are healthy, bad laws will have the effect of good ones. But this is because "the force of the principle pulls everything along."[30] Examples of such causality are numerous in *L'Esprit des lois*, and what they massively demonstrate is how fragile the principles of governments are, and how easily corrupted. It is as if any change in the sociopolitical order is likely, in some sense, to be for the worse.

It is true that Montesquieu imagines the possibility of two kinds of change, at least in a limited, constitutional way. In a discussion of the relation between laws, political freedom, and the constitution, he writes: "A state can change in two ways: either because its constitution is corrected or because it is corrupted. If the state has preserved its principles and its constitution changes, the latter corrects itself; if the state has lost its principles when its constitution starts to change, the constitution is corrupted."[31] Examples of the corruption of government's principles abound in *L'Esprit des lois* and need not be multiplied here. Of more interest is Montesquieu's reference to the possibility of positive change ("[the constitution] corrects itself"). But we should guard against interpreting this action, together with the change of a state it describes, in too optimistic a fashion, as heralding a meliorative transformation towards enlightened government. For the phrase lends itself to two readings. It suggests that a constitution may be corrected (*se corriger*) in a jurisprudential sense, made better and thus more apt to promote happiness and prevent injustice. But it also means that a constitution may correct itself (*se corriger*) in a mechanistic way, as adjustments are made that do no more than simply reestablish a balance of forces.[32] This second reading is entirely consistent, moreover, with Montesquieu's more mechanistic understanding of social order.

Montesquieu's discussion of revolution provides an especially pertinent example of the conceptual framework within which he formulates historical change. Now, as has been noted, the sole example of a single, founding revolution is to be found in Roman history, treated only in the *Considérations*.[33] But there are other kinds of revolutions as well. In a complex reflection on the nature of the revolution that could occur in a democracy, Montesquieu writes:

> If there has been some revolution and one has given the state a new form, it could scarcely have been done without infinite pain and work, and rarely with idleness and corrupt mores. The very ones who made the revolution wanted it to be savored, and they could scarcely have succeeded in this without good laws. Therefore, the old institutions are usually correctives [*des corrections*], and the new ones, abuses. In a government that lasts a long time, one descends to ills by imperceptible degrees, and one climbs back to the good only with an effort.

Older institutions in this case are better ones. The people who shaped them possess a simple and austere morality, in which resides the wisdom of their laws and manners. Thus Montesquieu can conclude, "recalling men to the old maxims usually returns them to virtue."[34] It would seem that the general conclusion to be drawn here is that if a good revolution can be imagined, it must in fact be a restorative one, bringing about a return to better days.

But such a return is exceptional at best. The common objective of all states, whether their particular objectives are expansion, war, commerce or glory, is to maintain themselves in time. The political theory that results from this view promotes stability and equilibrium by making the corrections that establish and maintain a balance of forces. History can be read in the *Considérations* as a wearing away more than as a series of transformations, which means that political history amounts to the various accounts of the struggle to withstand time.[35] Yet in a corruptible world this struggle cannot be won. Invoking a view of history devoid of providentialism and relying instead on a more organic paradigm of development, Montesquieu suggests that nothing withstands time. Particularly telling in this regard are comments about the English constitutional government, which may well represent the system that best promotes citizens' freedom. But even this government cannot endure: "Since all human things have an end, the state of which we are speaking will lose its liberty; it will perish."[36] History, writes Jean Starobinski, offers Montesquieu "no more than the chance for degeneration."[37] The name Montesquieu gives to this state of ultimate degeneration is despotism; it is there that all three forms of government meet once monarchy, as well as democratic and aristocratic republic, yield to those forces that unbalance them and undo their natural principles. If this is Montesquieu's view, though, did he see things clearly? Is this view of things a misapprehension of history? This is the conclusion we might draw from Henry Vyverberg's suggestion that "if this view of the dynamic individuality of civilizations restrained Montesquieu from seeing the main historical course in terms of a unitary and purposeful evolution, it encouraged a view of constant world movement and flux."[38] For Vyverberg, Montesquieu remains on this side of an Enlightenment understanding of history as linear progress, embracing a more somber, pessimistic view of societies' development. All civilizations, those entities Montesquieu calls "nations," follow a pattern of development particular to each one. Each is an individual entity existing in a specific space and time, each possessing its own particularities and its own finality.

This sense of the particular and even the fragmentary is suggested by Montesquieu's style, the formal, discursive manner in which he formulates historical understanding. For the great eighteenth-century theorists (and writers) of history, historical truth was best sought by recasting the manner in which it was presented. The eighteenth-century reform of historiography thus entailed an esthetic reform as well, for in moving from annals to history, the great Enlightenment historians stressed the fundamentally narrative determination of historical understanding. Representing history meant narrating events, as narrative became a means to make things 'rational'. The development of historical narration corresponds to the advent of perspectival representation in painting, each being a newly fashioned yet conventional way of presenting truth. By offering events in narrative fashion, the eighteenth-century historian sets up the reader as ironic spectator of the historical scene. The reader is invited to judge freely the truth of the events, to draw some meaning from their presentation. The eighteenth-century historian resembles the novelist of the same period, for in the texts of both it is more the persona of the narrator that unifies and organizes, not the narration itself. In the case of Montesquieu's writing, the reader enjoys a similar freedom to interpret the version of events presented. But at the same time Montesquieu's writing resists a unifying, overarching understanding of history that presides in advance over the representation of events. The presentation of history in Montesquieu's writing is fragmentary, by which I mean not that it is incomplete but rather that it resists narrative development into a whole. The same kind of critical resistance is to be found in the texts of writers with whom Montesquieu has a curious esthetic affinity, namely, in Montaigne's *essais* and Pascal's *pensées*, a resonance that is not merely formal but intellectual and critical as well, at least concerning the question of history.

Determining Montesquieu's place in Enlightenment historical theory thus is not a simple matter. But trying to situate him among shadowy pessimists or sunny optimists only complicates the issue, which involves history itself. As Jean Starobinski has argued, Montesquieu understands history to be driven by a perpetual force; thus history is the expression of something that is not historical. Like a map, it unfolds, spreads out, and becomes more comprehensible over time. Yet also like a map, it does not change because it cannot, unless and until it is reconceptualized in terms of progress, according to a theory (or a philosophy) of becoming that we have come to recognize as modern. Starobinski goes on to argue that this view of history itself needs to be situated historically, as belonging to a moment between what he calls the age of theology and the age of historicism. It is a view no longer governed by the imperative to achieve one's salvation and not yet shaped by the powerful need to make one's history. Manifestly, this historical moment is no longer our own, and what Starobinski calls the age of historicism is doubtless past. In more Foucaldian terms, we belong to another epistemic formation. One of the most difficult historical enterprises involves thinking the structure of knowledge that is no longer of our age, knowledge that is obsolete, historically alien, a *savoir mort*. Our contemporary way of knowing history may provide a ready means for ascribing a place and significance to Montesquieu in an evolutionary development of political thought. But must we not confront the possibility that this contemporary, seemingly enlightened notion of history contains its own blind spots, and thus that it also obscures an understanding of the historicity of Montesquieu's thought, blurring what is historically the most particular to it?[39] In other words terms such as 'conservative', 'aristocratic', 'baroque', or 'pessimist' may well designate what must be rethought if we are to formulate Montesquieu's currentness or *actualité*, both in his own time and in ours. To undertake that rethinking, we will ultimately have to give up reading Montesquieu uniquely as a theorist, and especially as a theorist of history. For this rethinking will aim to grasp the relation between historical discourse and political discourse, above all as they are realized in the practice of writing.

To think history through Montesquieu we must return to his critique of absolutist monarchy, which is located at the center of his thought. Montesquieu brought despotism home to France, presenting it not as an exclusively exotic and so-called oriental form of government, but rather as a fatal tendency inherent in monarchy as well.[40] "Political liberty is found only in moderate governments. But it is not always in moderate states. It is present only when power is not absurd, but it has eternally been observed that any man who has power is led to abuse it; he continues until he finds limits. Who would think it! Even virtue has need of limits."[41] To understand the historicity of Montesquieu's writing, we should move beyond describing the historical context in which it was produced, examining instead how that writing reflects upon its particular mode of being subjected to events. Thus the historicity of Montesquieu's writing must be phrased in terms of the specter of monstrous abuse, instability, and misery that he names absolutism, a form of power that could not be avoided, but only checked and limited. "So that one cannot abuse power, power must check power by the arrangement of things."[42] In political theoretical terms, this call for a limitation of powers is met in the constitutional system of government, with its system of checks and balances that moderate otherwise potentially absolute power. But this passage also contains a more general reflection on power, and not that of an exclusively political, jurisprudential nature. Montesquieu's writing contributes to the broad attempt in early modern Europe to reconceptualize the direct, univocal, and potentially disastrously violent exercise of power, and to formulate power instead in a more balanced, delegated, and ultimately mediated and thus moderate fashion. Power comes to be imagined as being lodged not so much in decrees that express sovereign will, but in morals and manners, institutions and laws, that together form a vast series of *ressorts*, a network of counterbalancing forces that if properly attended to will preserve harmony and equilibrium.

This network is what Montesquieu calls "l'esprit général" of a nation. Several things govern individuals' behavior and existence, thus constituting this general spirit. Among them Montesquieu includes climate, religion, laws, political maxims, the examples of times past, customs, and manners. In a more contemporary idiom, what Montesquieu describes here might be called national culture. This determination is not absolute determinism, though. This network of forces does not offer constraints to freedom, but rather the field upon which freedom is deployed. "Liberty is the right to do everything the laws permit."[43] It is for this reason that "l'esprit général" of a nation must not be changed: "The legislator is to follow the spirit of the nation when doing so is not contrary to the principles of the government, for we do nothing better than what we do freely and by following our natural genius."[44]

Julia Kristeva has taken up this concept of "l'esprit général" as a way to maintain the idea of nation as a bulwark against the social atomization and fragmentation brought about by nationalisms, regionalisms, and religious conflicts. For her, Montesquieu's "esprit général" figures that totality into which particularities can be inserted and have their place, yet without being censored, repressed, or denied in the name of some totalizing imperative. Through the concept of "l'esprit général" Kristeva imagines the possibility of a nation based upon the integration of its citizens yet without this process implying their absorption, a nation based on the recognition of otherness in all others, including ourselves.[45] But the critical issue of nation and nationalism is only one of the contemporary problematics into which Montesquieu's writing can be injected, in order to reflect upon our own subjection to the event. Another is the law of gender, consideration of which has sparked numerous vibrant rereadings of the *Lettres persanes*.

Through this critical injection of Montesquieu into the contemporary, history can be thought through his writing. As Jean Ehrard succinctly puts it, paradoxically Montesquieu is "anachronistic yet always present-day,"[46] for in fashioning a response to monarchical absolutism, a state of political affairs belonging now to a perfectly bygone time, he articulates a technique of power designed to exorcize specters that are all too much of our own time. The relatively limited plays of power imagined during the reign of Louis XIV are followed by what Georges Benrekassa calls "other terrifying scenarios," other totalizing projects that will not fail to deploy themselves in the years following the advent of Enlightenment. Montesquieu contributes to our historical understanding of those projects, and the risk that dwells within them, "the risk of alteration or alienation that a love affair with the universal is always about to impose."[47]

CHAPTER 5

Literature and the making of revolutionary history

On July 28, 1794, Maximilien-François Robespierre, president of the National Convention and member of the much-feared Committee of Public Safety, was executed. Robespierre's fall, followed by the purging of the powerful Jacobin clubs, promised the end of the Great Terror, which had claimed tens of thousands of lives throughout France (1,300 in the preceding month alone). Certainly the worst was over after the events of 9 Thermidor, as the day was known according to the new revolutionary calendar. The National Convention reasserted its authority, prisons were emptied, and more freedom was experienced under the Directory, although more corruption as well. But Thermidor did not put an end to terror, for it marked the passage from the Great Terror to the White Terror, with anti-Jacobin reprisals taking place throughout France.

The events following Thermidor were shaped by the haunting question of how to move on from terror.[1] Originally conceived as redemptive and purifying violence, the Terror had quickly become excessive and perverse, a self-justifying ritual that had to be brought to an end. Yet the Terror had been conducted in the name of the revolutionary state, the political instance that claimed ultimate authority to protect rights and property. To repudiate the Terror wholesale thus meant questioning those very principles of the Revolution in whose name the Terror had taken place. Indeed, for the Revolution to have lasting meaning, those principles had to be reaffirmed all the more forcefully. Yet how to move on from Terror? The sole way around the impasse was to ascribe to Thermidor a double and seemingly contradictory significance. It had to signal both a break in revolutionary history and the guarantee that the Revolution would continue. Thermidor had to represent the renewal and regeneration of an originally purifying, founding event. Otherwise, the perception that the Revolution had gone hopelessly adrift would play into the hands of the counterrevolutionaries. The challenge faced by post-Thermidoran authorities was to dismantle the Terror without resorting to a terroristic anti-Jacobinism. The problem was all the more acute because the way to eradicate terrorism most efficiently involved maintaining the revolutionary purity that the Jacobins had put in place and refined during the Terror itself. Thermidor is thus an especially illustrative example of the problematic relation between the Revolution and the political institutions of the *Ancien Régime* that the revolutionaries sought to reform or replace. The Revolution was supposed to mark a complete break with all that had gone before, signaled by the new revolutionary calendar that began with Year I. At the same time, however, revolutionary discourse could not bypass the powerful discourses of the past. They continued to have an effective existence, if only as counter-discourses against which the new revolutionary discourse set itself in antagonistic fashion, either to repudiate and reject them or to reshape and reintegrate them in a new idiom.

One of the challenges facing historians is to avoid replaying the very contradictions that define their object of investigation, as they constantly risk acting out these tensions instead of working through them to achieve historical knowledge. Thermidor and the French Revolution in general pose this same challenge, crystallized in the question of whether the violence of the Jacobin Terror was necessary or contingent. Could the Revolution, as event but also as a political concept, be contained? Did it necessarily have to spill over into Jacobinism in the eighteenth century, socialism in the nineteenth, and communism in the twentieth? Historians of the Revolution kept this question at bay by viewing the Revolution as comprising two political tendencies (one more liberal, the other more radical), which they saw in chronological terms as the Revolution's two phases (the second, more violent, phase of Jacobinism being either the perversion of a more liberal first phase, or else its radicalization, depending on the overall view of the Revolution being promoted). Ultimately, though, both interpretations of the Revolution repeat the essential debates of the revolutionaries themselves, playing out the Revolution once again, this time on the stage of historiography. Here, though, the work of history seems unable to free itself from a script written long before and which it can only write over (and over) in an obsessively palimpsestic gesture – unless of course the work of history is located precisely in this constant unwriting and rewriting.

In light of the question of interpretation's relation to the past, the event of Thermidor takes on broader, if not emblematic, significance. "It is as if the event that remained fixed in history as 9 Thermidor could offer at the time no clear meaning for its own episodes, which chaotically succeeded one another, or for the actors participating in them. It was as if the event was only seeking its political meaning."[2] Extending Bronisław Baczko's remark, we can view Thermidor not just as one particular event in history but as exemplifying the historical event itself. Possessing in the moment of its occurrence no meaning beyond the call to constitute its meaning, the event has no essential, original signification to be uncovered. Instead, it is 'in search of its meaning'. If Thermidor designates putting an end to revolutionary terror, this moving on from Terror does not mean rejecting the left-wing Jacobin interpretation of the Revolution. This interpretation is the one refused by the Thermidoran intellectuals, who sought to separate the Republic from the Terror by upholding 1789 as the moment of a founding freedom, perverted by the Jacobin Terror, which itself was ended following Thermidor by the power of law. In a slightly different sense, the question of the Terror can be said to involve a political hermeneutics rather than a political pragmatics. To determine the meaning of the Terror, the interpretive principles must be established on which the Revolution's meaning can be phrased, and so moving on from Terror also means attempting to put an end to the interpretive problem of interpreting the Revolution, if the end of the hermeneutic process is indeed possible.

Whether or not we accord this paradigmatic significance to Thermidor, the question remains as to how it or any event acquires meaning. The way this process is understood to occur stems from the theoretical model adopted (or tacitly at work) in investigating the event. In the model presented here for understanding the historical event to which Thermidor has led, I wish to stress the determinant role played by narrative, discursive, and symbolic practices in general with regard to historical understanding. At times appearing to stem from the event and thus to translate or represent it, such practices also seem to constitute the event as an object of understanding, to construct its meaning after the fact, however plural and contested that meaning may be. The theoretical issue involved here is not new, for some twenty-five years ago Roland Barthes pointed to the constructedness of history by stressing the role that narrative plays in determining historical understanding. Taking up the relation between the historical text and the real, Barthes argued that "the 'fact' can only exist linguistically ... yet we behave as if it were a simple reproduction of something on another plane of existence altogether, some extra-structural 'reality'."[3] Historical discourse aims for an unreachable referent 'outside' itself. As Barthes succinctly put it, historical discourse does not follow the real; it only signifies it.

This reference to Barthes's often-cited text illustrates the so-called 'linguistic turn', especially as it bears on history, historiography, and historical understanding.[4] The positions in this critical debate have been well established for some time, and in at least its more polemical version the debate is probably over. The sign of a specific moment of disciplinary change, the debate more interestingly can be taken to designate a constitutive tension within the practice of history itself. In this connection, I will make only three observations. First, the argument for (or against) what I am calling the symbolic determination of historical understanding – through language, discourse or representation – should itself be understood as contextually determined. Any model of historical analysis is part of a discourse that belongs to a social, institutional, historical context. Not only is it reductive to think of rejecting the 'linguistic model' to analyze history in favor of other models, it is also unhistorical to do so. In itself the turn to language and to methods of analysis supposedly borrowed from literary scholars is neither good nor bad, for any such turn can be judged only "in terms of arguments for, or assumptions about, history's critical function in society at large."[5] Second, if language and symbolic practices more generally not only mediate but largely constitute our understanding of culture, then by analyzing them we can gain a critical understanding of culture writ large. This is the goal of the fairly recently emerged interdisciplinary field of cultural studies, for instance, whose object is the contextualized mediation between events and signification, between acts, their understanding, and their effects. Third, what became reified via scare quotes as the 'linguistic turn' should ultimately be viewed not as stemming from something outside and different from history (literary theory, say) but as belonging to the historical discipline's own internal transformation. Like the disciplinary debates involving literary studies in the 1960s, current disciplinary debates regarding history concern the precise constitution of historical research: its methods, objects, and purposes. What rules pertain to the form in which historical argument may be phrased? On what common basis, if one exists, can differing historical arguments be judged?

Methodological and theoretical debates such as these have perennially marked the historical discipline. They are constitutive of that discipline, not tangential to it. For if the objectivity to which the contemporary study of history aspires derives from an essentially narrative art, the historian sharing at least some techniques with the novelist, then this objectivity must constantly be won anew. For the historian to deliver on the promise to speak with the authority of historical reality, this discourse must prevail over other versions of the events in question. By definition, then, historical discourse is an agonistic discourse, engaged in contesting, refuting, or even denying the discourse of another. Paul Ricœur's statement that the historian always writes in a "situation involving dispute and trial" is pertinent here, but on the condition that we understand Ricœur to refer not to a psychological situation but to a discursive, institutional, and disciplinary one.[6] Conflict is not just one theme among many that the historian may choose to treat; it is intrinsic to historical discourse itself, marking the institutions in which historical discourse is produced and circulates. In discursive terms, this means that no narrative can ever establish one particular view or version of things; no historical narrative can situate all other narratives without in turn being situated by them. One can, however, seek to gauge the conflictual, agonistic relations into which historical discourse enters, in specific contexts and situations. While this evaluation provides no sure guarantee of objectivity, it does highlight the need to consider critically the essentially political nature of historical discourse.[7] To think critically about the fundamentally political nature of historical discourse, we must analyze it not only in its formal, narrative dimension but also in terms of its rhetorical, argumentational, agonistic force as it is deployed in specific social, institutional contexts.

Despite the theoretical nature of the preceding remarks, we have moved not so very far from the initial question, 'How do we move on from Terror?' Political historians might answer that question by considering the policies that the post-Thermidorans elaborated, the institutions they created, and the programs they put in place. My objective is different, for I wish to argue that only by reflecting on what constitutes an event in its historical dimension, by considering how it is situated within history through the mechanisms of historical understanding, can we hope to 'move on' from events in order to participate critically and knowingly in the process whereby they acquire meaning.

CONSTRUCTING THE REVOLUTION

Reflecting on events in France in 1790 from across the English Channel, Edmund Burke was struck by the revolutionaries' seemingly total rejection of the past, a break at complete odds with the British notion of revolution as restoration. Burke's own more British experience of historical time may have caused him to misapprehend that this rejection marked the attempt to reconceptualize the relation between present and past, to theorize in other terms the role of the past in determining historical understanding. What Burke did not see in his *Reflections on the Revolution in France*, and only partly because this new relation to the past took clearest shape only a few years later during the Jacobin ascendancy, was that the Revolution did not at all break with the past. Instead it created the past it needed in order to define the revolutionary moment as a break with prior ideas, institutions, and leaders. That past was the newly created *Ancien Régime*, an 'old' order whose invention signaled that the 'new', revolutionary order existed, if only in contradistinction and opposition to what had come before. The Revolution acquired its identity in relation to a past in whose future the Revolution had culminated, for the break with a political monarchy marked the continuation of the work of enlightenment, the culminating event of a *siècle éclairé*.

The revolutionary reconfiguration of historical time occurred in debates concerning such topics as sovereignty, law, and political representation. It also took place in particular cultural contexts and through specific material practices, involving the production, distribution, circulation, and competing reception of texts, pamphlets, images, civic festivals, coins, maps, calendars, and clothing.[8] A new notion of historical determination was played out in these practices, in and through which took shape the revolutionary identity of an emergent political and cultural subject. Later we will consider how the Third Republic of nineteenth-century France would define the republican subject through carefully staged commemorations of an imagined eighteenth century. But from the Revolution onwards, that construction of political-cultural identity had always already begun.

A striking example of this identity construction, and one with a haunting afterlife, is the double 'pantheonization' of Voltaire and Rousseau during the Revolution. Both writers having died in 1778, their remains were transferred to the Eglise Sainte-Geneviève in 1791, when the Constituent Assembly transformed the church into a secular site honoring the "illustrious men" of the nation. Jacques Soufflot's architectural monument was the culmination of a broader cultural practice in the eighteenth century involving the cult of civic heroes rather than royal ones, figures celebrated in the countless published *éloges* and reception speeches given at academies that produce an eighteenth-century "paper Pantheon."[9] In a city where previously no public statues but those of the king could be erected, the designation of a site honoring writer-philosophes – and especially the

Literature and the making of revolutionary history 103

desacralized church named after the patron saint of Paris – suggests the extent to which the power of the pen, or at least that of publicity, had succeeded in challenging the power of the crown.

Voltaire and Rousseau were at once the most influential thinkers of the eighteenth century and the two writers of the period who were most intensely involved in constructing and managing their public image. Thus there is no small irony that in honoring these two men, the revolutionaries take over their image to make them into the precursors of the Revolution. In the elaborate theatrical-political events marking the pantheonization of Voltaire and Rousseau, including speeches and the circulation of images, both figures incarnate the 'enlightened century', the 'century of philosophy and of reason' that had produced the Revolution. The commemorative recognition of Voltaire and Rousseau contributes to bringing that century into symbolic and historical existence as the precursor of the revolutionary event that marked an end to both prejudice and tyranny. The Marquis de Pastoret had first proposed carving on the pediment of the Panthéon the phrase *Aux grands hommes, la patrie reconnaissante* (To great men, a grateful country), an inscription that would not occur until 1837. Yet already during the Revolution, the nation constructs itself by calling out to the imaginary spectator-reader-citizen, expressing its grateful recognition of civic heroes and marking the fundamental unity and historical necessity of the national present. Through a strategic and instrumentalizing use of the philosophes' very bodies, the revolutionaries bring Voltaire and Rousseau together in a display of national unity, a unification that suggests the possibility of reconciling the Voltairean critique of injustice with the Rousseauean notion of the sovereignty of popular will. "The Revolution projected onto the Enlightenment the shadow of its rifts and conflicts," writes Bronisław Baczko, implying that the imaginary past the Revolution fashioned could not outlive the revolutionary present that created it.[10] However much the revolutionaries based their political-cultural work on their desire to produce a new citizen, a new and regenerated nation, the unified civic identity that the pantheonization of Voltaire and Rousseau was designed to create would not endure. Or rather, as we shall see in later chapters, that subject could live on in the nineteenth century only in phantasmatic fashion, through a vampiristic identification with the dead, be it in the Romantic historiography of a Jules Michelet or the popular commemorative practices of the Third Republic.

The pantheonization of Voltaire and Rousseau represents but a moment in the revolutionary scenario, but one whose significance is emblematic. It reveals the intense work the revolutionaries performed to re-theorize the political. In their efforts to reconceptualize such notions as the political subject, law, legitimacy, and sovereignty, the revolutionaries' work can be understood in terms of political theory. But the revolutionaries were intensely engaged not so much in rewriting history or producing an alternative and contestatory historical narrative, however radical its program might have been, as in re-theorizing the very conditions of possibility for historical understanding. This theoretical work performed by the revolutionary 'new historians' remains under-read, however, so long as we fail to reflect on the interpretive assumptions it brings into play. Conversely, by engaging with the self-reflexive questioning concerning what Michel de Certeau calls "the historiographical operation,"[11] we can understand better the value, strength, and productivity of competing historical narratives.

French revolutionary history provides fertile ground for questioning the theoretical premises of historiography. Keith Baker, for instance, has drawn attention to how the Marxist explanation of the Revolution as 'advent' served to obscure its nature of 'event'.[12] But the Marxist advent narrative is just one version of the classical teleological narrative that Michel Foucault has insistently critiqued for its reliance on the structuring notions of totality, continuity, and causality. As Roger Chartier notes, such a narrative succumbs to "the chimera of origins," and in so doing

it burdens itself, perhaps unconsciously, with several presuppositions: that every historical moment is a homogeneous totality endowed with an ideal and unique meaning present in each of the realities that make up and express that whole; that historical becoming is organized as an ineluctable continuity; that events are linked together, one engendering another in an uninterrupted flow of change that enables us to decide that one is the 'cause,' another the 'effect'.[13]

Although teleological narratives possess considerable explanatory power, the understanding they provide comes at a cost. The story of causes and effects makes seamlessly evolutionary what might otherwise be perceived in terms of breaks and divergences; more generally, the narrative of becoming might well be the result of a historiographical projection onto an imaginary past. As François Furet observes, "the postulate that 'what actually happened' did so of necessity is a classical retrospective illusion of historical consciousness, which sees the past as a field of possibilities within which 'what actually happened' appears *ex post facto* as the only future for that past."[14]

It was Michel Foucault who demonstrated the critical possibilities of a genealogical mode of analysis that rejects teleological master narratives.[15] Adopting a genealogical narrative does not mean that the category of origin needs to be dismissed, though; the story of origins can be told, but otherwise, rewritten to reveal how origins are produced after the fact. This belated production of the past may be the work of ideology, shaped by interests and institutions. But refusing to accept this historiographical belatedness, and thereby refusing to work through it, means overlooking and indeed denying the investment of the present in a constructed past. In the case of the French Revolution, as Chartier suggestively observes, the crucial question is not whether the Enlightenment produced the Revolution, and if so how, but rather whether the Revolution invented the Enlightenment. Did such a belated invention occur "by attempting to root [the Revolution's] legitimacy in a corpus of texts and founding authors reconciled and united, beyond their extreme differences by their preparation of a rupture with the old world?"[16] Chartier's hypothesis is consonant with my own, namely, that the Enlightenment has already always been produced after the fact, in the attempt to prepare and legitimize modernity's break with the past. The past is constructed through the historical operation, that is, a discursive, disciplinary, and institutional practice that generates historical knowledge. In other words the past cannot be known without reflection upon the practices in and through which it becomes a knowable object. In a sense, the past is not past, at least until it is read as such. But the historical operation is not exclusively an epistemological operation, involving knowledge alone. It possesses an ontological dimension as well, involving the subject of history and self-construction, a dimension that can be explored through the revolutionary reading of Rousseau.

STAGING THE VIRTUOUS CITIZEN: ROBESPIERRE READS JEAN-JACQUES

In 1790, a bust of Rousseau was placed in the hall of the National Assembly, along with a copy of the *Contrat social*. Eager to create a past whose legacy the Revolution would embody, the revolutionaries found inspiration for the new constitution in Rousseau's political theory. In a speech to the Assembly, Pierre-Louis Ginguené asked:

With what sovereignty were you invested in order to regenerate a great empire, to give it a free constitution? With the inalienable and imprescriptible sovereignty of the people. On what base did you found this constitution, which will become the model for all human constitutions? On the quality of rights. Well, Messieurs, Rousseau was the first, under the very eyes of despotism, to establish systematically the equality of rights among men and the sovereignty of the people.[17]

Throughout the nineteenth century, historians will see Rousseau as prophet and guide for the Revolution, stressing the impact his ideas had on revolutionary theory and practice concerning natural man, popular sovereignty and voting rights, natural law, and the ideal of equality. This understanding of Rousseau's influence was complicated by Daniel Mornet, who, in attempting to provide methodological rigor to the then fledgling discipline of literary history, asked the simple question of who was reading what texts at a given historical moment.[18] Mornet rejected the hypothesis of Rousseau's political influence for the simple empirical reason that the political texts – including the *Contrat social* (1762), the *Discours sur l'inégalité*, and the *Encyclopédie* article "Economie politique" – were not widely known before 1789. Consequently, argued Mornet, the source of Rousseau's influence upon the Revolution could be located only in the texts that were widely read at the time, such as the eighteenth-century bestseller *La Nouvelle Héloïse* (1761), or the moral works, such as *Emile* (1762). Knowing that a book existed in a given library or circulated in the public sphere doesn't guarantee that it was read, however, and even knowing that a book was read provides no way of knowing how it was read and what it meant to a specific readership. Book historians can provide a good deal of empirical knowledge, which is but the beginning of understanding the role that writing and reading play in a particular cultural context, understanding that can be reached only by investigating the reading process itself – in other words, ultimately, by reading.

Significant parallels can be drawn between Rousseau's moral works and revolutionary discourse. *Julie, ou la nouvelle Héloïse*, for instance, presents the experience of two lovers, Julie d'Etanges and Saint-Preux. Through the exchange of letters between them, the story is told of intense, transgressive desire that is rechanneled and sublimated. Saint-Preux comes to know Julie as a lover only to lose her, first when she marries and finally when she dies, drowning in the attempt to save her child. This personal loss is recuperated symbolically, however, as Saint-Preux realizes that he can continue to love Julie, but only by affirming the ethical values of the domestic order – fidelity and maternity above all – that make her no longer attainable as a lover. This sublimation is repeated in the novel's closure, but collectively. In the final pages Julie is transformed through death into an object of desire whose very absence symbolically unites into a community the group of all those who had loved her, including Saint-Preux, her husband Wolmar, and her friend Claire, to say nothing of the novel's readers.

La Nouvelle Héloïse dramatizes moral regeneration and renewal on an individual level, presenting it as the basis for a renewed social bond.

Other works by Rousseau also articulate this process. The village festival, described in the *Lettre à d'Alembert*, is a civic spectacle in which nothing in particular is represented on any designated stage. But the spectacle's function is to unite all participants in a common spectacular experience. The civic spectacle is the antithesis of the theater of hyper-civilized Paris, which for Rousseau stands for the experience of modern alienation: "people think they come together in the theater, and it is there that they are isolated" (*on croit s'assembler au spectacle, mais c'est là où l'on s'aliène*).[19] The theatrical, 'civilized' gaze for Rousseau leads the self astray in false and phantasmatic objects of inauthentic, narcissistic desire. In opposition to this model, Rousseau imagines a village festival in which participants see themselves in and through the gaze of the other. The village spectacle thus provides a visual model of selfhood that corresponds structurally to the political model of the social contract, in which individual rights are alienated, given over to others, in order for each to be guaranteed self-identity within the larger social whole.

The most significant parallel to be drawn between Rousseau's works and revolutionary discourse is not thematic in nature, despite the unmistakably Rousseauean resonance of the revolutionaries' "republic of virtue."[20] Rather, what Rousseau describes and enacts throughout his writing is an experience of self-production, whether that of Saint-Preux writing of Julie, the participants in a village festival, the contractual self, or Rousseau 'himself', the autobiographical self of *Les Confessions* or the lyric self of the *Rêveries d'un promeneur solitaire*. The self the Rousseauean text also solicits is the reading self, the addressee who is interpellated and enjoined to experience an integrative, self-performative act of virtue. The epistolary novel highlights this reading experience in a highly self-reflective way, and displaying how characters read it provides an allegory of the reading experience. The fictional community of the novel's final pages figures symbolically the imaginary community of the virtuous that the reader is called to construct and enact, phantasmatically, through the reading experience.[21] James Swenson has argued that the relation between Rousseau's thought and the Revolution should be assessed in theoretical terms rather than ideological ones, adding that Rousseau's thought "is operative by the understanding of the dynamics and aporias of democratic politics that it makes available, and not merely by the 'influence' its themes, even its rhetoric and tonality, had on individual revolutionaries."[22] Or as Bernard Manin puts it, "Rousseau's works give actors a way to name and conceptualize the new reality into which history plunges them, to find their place in this reality, and to give meaning to their actions."[23]

The historical self-fashioning that takes place through the activity of reading Rousseau occurs in an early text by Maximilien Robespierre, "To the Memory of Jean-Jacques Rousseau" (*Dédicace aux mânes de Jean-Jacques Rousseau*).[24] Writing in April 1789, the soon to be revolutionary leader presents Rousseau as a paternal figure of mythic proportions, a precursor of the Revolution characterized above all by an absolute dedication to the cult of truth and inflexible virtue. For Robespierre, Rousseau stands apart from all other philosophes of the century, that 'sect' of the *hommes de lettres* that included a few respectable men but many "ambitious charlatans." Introducing a view of the philosophes that Tocqueville will later take up, Robespierre describes the essentially compromised if not hypocritical position of these writers who railed against despotism but were happy to receive court stipends, and who criticized the court but were the favorites of courtesans. "They were proud of their writings and servile as they awaited an audience," he writes.[25] Rousseau stands alone among these writers, singled out by Robespierre for the purity of his virtue, his unwavering hatred of vice, and his uncompromising disgust at the sophistry of his fellow philosophes.

What is remarkable in the cult of Rousseau to which Robespierre gives voice is the notion of 'the life'. Rousseau not only wrote about purity but lived it, his own life incarnating the virtues that his writing valorized. What is left unsaid in this cult is that Rousseau's 'life' is a life staged and written, a product of narrative, the exemplary result of an 'enlivening' reading that brings Rousseau to life. Rousseau himself already reflected upon the process whereby the experience of narrative turns the account of living into a life, both in the preface to the *Confessions* and in "Rousseau juge de Jean-Jacques." Here, Robespierre's cult and cultivation of Rousseau not only bring the philosophe back to life as an object of faithful veneration; Robespierre appropriates the absent other as a mirror or screen upon which to project the image of self the revolutionary seeks to fashion. "Oh, divine Rousseau," he writes, "you taught me to know myself ... I wish to follow your venerated path ... Happy will I be if, in the dangerous course that an unprecedented revolution now lays out before us, I remain constantly faithful to the inspirations that I have drawn from your writings!" National regeneration was an obsessive concern for the revolutionaries who had done away with the old order in France. For Robespierre, Rousseau offers the model of such self-generation, as the analogical shifter "like" (*comme*) in the following remark indicates:

The awareness of having wanted the best for one's fellows is the recompense of a virtuous man; then comes the gratitude (*reconnaissance*) of the people who surround his memory with the honors denied him by his contemporaries. Like you, I wish to acquire this fortune by dint of living a hard-working life, even by meeting a premature demise.[26]

Robespierre's reference to self-sacrifice, "a premature demise," should be read in a strong sense, as reflecting not only the laborious generosity of the committed revolutionary, but also as the rewriting of the 'real' person through the symbolic production of the virtuous self. Such a self was crucial, moreover, to realizing the objectives of the Revolution, as Robespierre and the Jacobins understood them.

In his speech of February 5, 1794, "On the Principles of Political Morality that Must Guide the Convention," Robespierre seeks to justify in moral terms the politics of the Terror. The latter, he claims, "is none other than prompt, severe, and unbending justice. Thus it is the emanation of virtue." As the performative realization of virtue, Terror can brook no opposition. Terror involves "submission to the law as the expression of the general will extended to its ultimate consequences."[27] The only condition limiting Terror is the virtue of those who are its executive agents. Consequently, even though general will cannot be represented, as Rousseau claimed, the virtue of the Terror's agents must be, just as the immorality of the Jacobins' opponents has to be constantly demonstrated. Rousseau provides a privileged model for writing and for reading that production of the virtuous subject, and in his praise of Rousseau, Robespierre reveals himself to be a canny reader, well on the way in 1790 to making use of general will, incorporated in the symbolic, phantasmatic virtuous self, as a force with which to realize the goals of the Revolution.

Roederer recounts that in 1800, when Napoleon visited Ermenonville and the room Rousseau occupied there, he exclaimed, "Your fellow Rousseau was crazy. He's the one who got us to where we are now."[28] We could define in political terms what Napoleon might have meant by the term 'Rousseau's "madness"'. It is tempting to imagine that Napoleon understood all too well that to bring the revolutionary events to an end, a certain 'mad' logic of terrorism had to be contained. Perhaps it was Robespierre, then, who had to be contained, not the Robespierre who had been dead for six years by the time Napoleon visited Ermenonville, but the Robespierre produced through the experience of reading Rousseau, the self brought to life through an experience of the texts of the past. In any event, prior to 1800 other less 'imperial' attempts will be made to move beyond (the) Terror, including the lectures and writing of Jean-François La Harpe. One of the first to write literary history in France in the modern sense of the term, La Harpe provides an important look into the political culture of revolutionary France, especially as it involves the construction of the idea of literature, philosophy, and history.

STAGING THE VIRTUOUS CITIZEN AGAIN: LA HARPE READS THE EIGHTEENTH CENTURY

Between 1786 and 1791, Jean-François La Harpe gave twice-weekly lectures on literature at the newly founded academy in Paris known as the Lycée. Designed for a clientele with an interest in intellectual fashions as much as in erudition, the Lycée soon became a successful and profitable enterprise. Classes in science were offered, but those on literature drew the largest crowds. The Lycée's success was shared by other institutions founded and supported by the urban bourgeoisie to promote the transmission of knowledge.[29] The popularity of La Harpe's lectures reflects this group's thirst for learning and its members' eagerness to participate in discussions regarding literature. These lectures also afforded the opportunity to acquire social distinction. La Harpe tirelessly invoked the classical principle of unchanging good taste as the criterion for esthetic judgment, a principle that suggested a universality safe from the vicissitudes of the historical. "Beauty is the same in all times because nature and reason are unchanging," he writes.[30] But for all his slightly worn classicism, La Harpe could not ignore the obvious. Political events soon produced repercussions both within the Lycée and in La Harpe's discourse, reconfiguring the terms whereby literature, taste, and esthetic judgment would be discussed. By 1789 he had begun to describe his lectures as those of a "citizen writer," adopting a political stance that blended commitment, necessity, and opportunism. In the early days of the Revolution, La Harpe's income and social status rose appreciably; yet following the fall of the monarchy, he and the Lycée came to know harder times. Associated through many of its founders with the *Ancien Régime*, the Lycée was carefully watched by the government. Granting the academy's request for 10,000 *livres* in 1792, Jean-Marie Roland, minister of the interior, made it clear that the authorities were not pleased with the institution's record. Teachers soon realized how much it behooved them to display a more appropriately republican spirit.

Elected to the Académie Française in 1776, when the Revolution began La Harpe had already succeeded in positioning himself as one of the prominent and powerful intellectual heirs to the Enlightenment. Not surprisingly, this "disciple of Voltaire," as one study presents him, initially favored the social and political reforms proposed in the early days of the Revolution.³¹ He too, though, fell victim to the Terror. He was arrested in March 1794 on the orders of the Committee of Public Safety, despite his participation in the Lycée's public ceremony of purging itself of antirepublican sentiment. Four months later, immediately following Robespierre's fall, La Harpe was released and hailed as one of the heroes of Thermidor. Recommended to head the Bibliothèque Nationale, he chose instead to return to teaching at the Lycée. Rather than supervise the preservation of books, he wished to direct the writing of literature, as well as its righting. He converted to Catholicism and soon became a vitriolic enemy of the reformist, philosophe movement. La Harpe's anti-Jacobin attacks on Robespierre and the Terror were standard fare for the time, but his critique of the Revolution was so impassioned and comprehensive that he was soon identified with the political and subversive right. In October 1795, La Harpe went into hiding, having been implicated by the Convention in royalist plots to overthrow the government. A year later he returned triumphantly to the Lycée, where he held forth as spokesman for the Catholic royalist revival. During this time he worked on his four-volume *Lycée, ou Cours de littérature ancienne et moderne*, which appeared in 1799.

The first work in France to provide a detailed overview of literature from a historical perspective, the *Lycée* soon became the standard reference book on literature. Its authority lasted through the Consulate and the Empire, and some eighteen complete editions appeared between 1815 and 1830. Even a century after its appearance, the admittedly conservative literary historian Ferdinand Brunetière claimed that La Harpe deserved a wider readership.³² But before placing La Harpe in any larger historical narrative, whether that of literary criticism or of the Revolution, we should consider how he himself links his text to such a narrative. For the *Lycée* marks La Harpe's own attempt to "sortir de la Terreur," to enter into a new phase of a post-Robespierre revolution by both political and discursive means. At first glance, La Harpe seems to belong to the conservative Catholic reaction, a literary version of political theorists such as *abbé* Augustin Barruel or Joseph de Maistre.³³ Unlike other counterrevolutionary writers like Jacques Mallet du Pan, who embraced the rationalist philosophy of the philosophes and even the initial revolutionary reforms, yet rejected the Revolution once it seemed to career toward anarchy, these three writers lash out at the philosophes as perverse conspirators and wrong-headed thinkers responsible for the social and moral corruption of the *Ancien Régime*. All three invoke providential intervention to explain the advent of the Revolution, brought on to punish France for its corruption. Barruel and de Maistre are more thorough political thinkers than La Harpe, however, for their critique of the Jacobin Revolution leads them to grapple with the founding of legitimate authority. Barruel argues for maintaining a monarchy of unlimited authority and de Maistre for establishing a new form, a theocracy, to supplant all European governments. But La Harpe is not a political theorist, and the interest of his writings does not stem from his strictly political pronouncements. Nor does it lie in his views on esthetic doctrine, literary taste, or individual authors. What is of interest in the *Lycée* is how it reveals the politicized discursive practice of literary history. Barthes has argued that the teaching of literature is essentially tautological in that literature *is* what is taught as literature.[34] La Harpe's *Lycée* merits an attentive return because of its role in constituting and institutionalizing 'literature' as a pedagogical, a historical, and a political object.

In the preface to the fourth volume, La Harpe seems to claim just the opposite. "This work went through difficult times: it was composed in part during the revolution, whose different periods naturally can be made out in it, but they don't influence the work's general spirit which is, and had to be, the same throughout in a book that by its nature is to be for all times and nations."[35] Allowing that the *Lycée*'s composition may be marked by the historical context in which it was produced, La Harpe maintains that his objective has been to transcend the historically particular and thus attain universality and thereby truth. In this sense he proves himself to be not only Voltaire's former protégé but also the philosophe's spiritual heir. Invoking the universal criterion of good taste, he adopts Voltaire's approach to esthetic judgment which appealed to personal, individual intuition as well as to universal, anonymous reason. Yet La Harpe argues more rigidly for the need to respect rules and preordained models, hardening many of Voltaire's esthetic positions by eliminating the well-drawn nuance that so often tempered them. The notion of genius, for instance, allowed Voltaire to valorize individual artistic creativity, albeit regulated and circumscribed. In La Harpe, on the other hand, blind faith in good taste as exemplified by the canonized classics leaves little room for the possibility of artistic experimentation or esthetic change.

Good taste is the linchpin of La Harpe's conservative, rule-based esthetics. But does it transcend historical particularity or instead actually signal it, although in displaced, masked fashion? In La Harpe's writing (as elsewhere), the notion of good taste provides an oblique yet effective way to assert class identity and promote social self-recognition. Thus the

Lycée's appeal can be traced to the identity and distinction it afforded affluent members of the *Ancien Régime* through the discourse of literary history and the esthetic judgments it shaped. Consider the following passage, in which La Harpe refers both to his lectures and to the institution of the Lycée:

> Here will appear the immortal authors whom time has preserved, no longer as the heavy trappings of scholastic pedantry presented them ... but rather with fitting greatness and the simple majesty of their genius ... To you, their dishonored glory will turn for refuge, and surrounded by your praise their monuments, threatened with disfigurement, will remain intact ... My feeble voice will not be alone in singing their praise; your admiration will bring out their beauties. I believe I will have achieved my most desired goal if my thoughts seem to you to be none other than your own memories.[36]

An instance of pedagogical salesmanship, the passage sets up a mirror to lure its readers. Inverting by sleight of hand the positions of "I" and "you," speech and memory, present and past, La Harpe's discourse derives its power from its ability to hail individuals and thereby allow them to occupy and fill out a subject position that that discourse configures. The discourse of literary history in La Harpe thus operates like ideology as Louis Althusser analyzes it.[37] The identity fashioned by ideological discourse may be perlocutionary, but it exerts a powerful pull nonetheless. For the claim made here to speak to all times and all nations refers obliquely to a particular discursive and historical context. In this way La Harpe's claim for universality is linked to his own attempt to make one set of contextually bound values prevail over others.

Despite La Harpe's wish to transcend social strife in the name of universal esthetic judgment, conflict traverses the *Lycée*. The supposed natural principles on which such judgment would be based cannot be guaranteed, and the cause, quite expectedly, is the Revolution. Thus the fourth volume of the *Lycée*, devoted to eighteenth-century literature, contains a brief appendix titled "L'Esprit de la Révolution." Another, less universal spirit is at work here, and it is located squarely in the same historical context in which La Harpe situates himself and his work. Written in 1793, at the height of the "revolutionary lunacy," this scathing indictment of the group of "Robespierre's bandits" anticipates the anti-Jacobin discourse that became common currency following Thermidor. Significantly, La Harpe locates the essence and cause of the Revolution in language, for the complete title of the appendix is "The Spirit of the Revolution, or Historical Commentary on Revolutionary Language." The title of La Harpe's several-hundred-page defense of the Catholic Church, its doctrines, and its institutions, *Fanaticism in Revolutionary Language*, also links revolution and language. But "The Spirit of the Revolution" is designed to show how language had become an instrument of the Revolution, for what La Harpe wishes to counter above all is the politicization of language resulting in the production of revolutionary discourse. Lynn Hunt describes this phenomenon thus:

> Revolutionary language did not simply reflect the realities of revolutionary changes and conflicts, but rather was itself transformed into an instrument of political and social change. In this sense, political language was not merely an expression of an ideological position that was determined by underlying social or political interests. The language itself helped shape the perception of interests and hence the development of ideologies. In other words, revolutionary political discourse was rhetorical; it was a means of persuasion, a way of reconstituting the social and political world.[38]

The mark of political discourse is an intensification of the rhetorical nature of language: established truths are revealed as mere claims to the truth, and certain claims prevail over others, acquiring the power to pass for truth and to constitute "the social and political world."

La Harpe also fears that the Revolution works not only through language but on language, transforming it to its core. Madness invades language to the point of making speech incomprehensible and critical thinking impossible. Reflecting on the type of book needed in revolutionary France, he writes:

> The book that should be written today seems to be one whose title would be "Destroying Mistaken Ideas" (*Des préjugés à détruire*). This book doubtless must be written, but it can't be published until it can be understood. And how could it be understood today? These mistaken ideas of late are like a sickness at its paroxysm: these are not errors but fits of rage, madness, and fury. Quite the moment to set about reasoning! Moreover, to speak to one another, mutual understanding must be possible. A common language is needed. As I have said already, all the basic words of language have been overturned, and the natural meaning of all primary ideas has been distorted. We have a brand new dictionary in which *virtue* means *crime*, and *crime* means *virtue*. We have a brand new logic that boils down to this kind of reasoning: two plus two is four, so three plus two makes six, and whoever questions this is a rascal who deserves to be put to death.[39]

Not only has the Revolution factionalized thinking, the meaning of words has become so altered and perverted that language has lost its intrinsic rationality. There no longer exists a single shared language, the meaning of whose terms remains above question because it is determined by the authority of law or by that of convention and consensus.

La Harpe is not alone among his contemporaries in remarking upon the relation between language and historical change. Georges Cabanis, in presenting to the Council of Five Hundred the new edition of the *Dictionnaire de l'Académie*, dryly observes that "the change from monarchy to republic caused language itself to undergo an interesting revolution."[40] Elsewhere, language is more than a mirror to those who find in it the means to effect change, especially in the political arena. *Abbé* Grégoire claims that because of the Revolution language must change, and if it doesn't it must be 'revolutionized', along with those who speak it.[41] In response to those who would control language in order to control people, J. S. Mercier imagines an absolute linguistic individualism: "I make up my language, and too bad for those who don't make up their own. French is my servant ... because I don't receive orders, thank God, I give them." Throughout the seventeenth and eighteenth centuries, a courtly standard of usage had prevailed; in the absence of that standard the Revolution may well have led to a linguistic democracy that Mercier suggests is indistinguishable from a continual jousting for power in and through language, which he views essentially in terms of its legislative instrumentality: "Legislative authority will rest with those who can get their neologisms adopted," he writes.[42] Linguistic change is the outcome of a fierce struggle over which version of reality would prevail.

These political observations regarding the relation between the revolutionary event and language can be phrased in a more properly linguistic idiom as well. For at least a half-century, grammarians and philosophers had sought to account for how the classical age's linguistic and epistemological paradigms were destabilized by a temporalized, historicized understanding of language.[43] La Harpe's bitter complaint about the revolutionary transformation of language echoes the eighteenth-century discussion of linguistic flux and whether it was intrinsic to language, and thus inevitable, or instead could be regulated if not arrested. The grammarian-philosophers could always hold, however precariously, to the Cartesian notion of "primitive ideas" to counter linguistic flux, certain essential ideas whose meaning was so elemental that it could not change. But for La Harpe no such intrinsic rationality exists in language. Power, not reason, dictates the meaning of words; rhetoric, not rationality, determines how they will be understood. Power has come to reside in words themselves, bestowing on them a dynamic performativity through which nothing less than revolutions occurs. For La Harpe, the kind of book that can and must be written will show how language's loss of intrinsic rationality led to the unique event of the Revolution: "I want to reveal how things were done, principally through the power of words, and that things were absolutely unprecedented because for the first time words were absolutely devoid of reason."[44] The revolutionary event has destabilized language just as it has destabilized politics, and thus to write literary history, at least that of the eighteenth century, La Harpe must reveal the problematic yet determinant relation between language and power.

The conjunction of language and power during the French Revolution was played out endlessly. It is not enough, though, simply to thematize it, as the writers of the time do so well themselves, and so tirelessly. How did words acquire such power as to be held responsible for the Revolution itself? What is it in language that provides history's motive force, thereby holding the promise of making the workings of history comprehensible? More succinctly, how might the relation between language and historical understanding be phrased? Such questions suggest that reflection on the workings of history cannot be severed from reflection on the workings of language, at least not without risking an event-bound positivism for which truth is located in the historical object itself rather than in a discursive relation to it.

François Furet grounds historical understanding of the French Revolution in an analysis of the language whereby the Revolution is represented, that is, in the symbolic practices in which it took place. Significantly, Furet justifies this emphasis on language not in formalistically theoretical terms but in historical ones. Following the collapse of royal authority in 1787, he argues, French society came increasingly to be characterized not by class struggle or political jousting for authority but by competition to fix the public meanings of a language that no one person and no one group could determine. Once freed from state control, French society could affirm and reconstitute itself only by overthrowing symbolically and repeatedly the state that no longer existed. As a result, the revolutionary struggle played itself out in "a world where representations of power governed all actions, and where a network of signs (*le circuit sémiotique*) completely dominated political life."[45] For Furet, the Revolution was a "semio-political event, that is ... a revolution in, of, and by the signs of power."[46] Power was not transferred from one locus of sovereignty to another, for instance from king to people or to the bourgeoisie. Instead, as Claude Lefort observes, it migrated

from the fixed, determinant but occult place it occupied under the monarchy to a place which is essentially unstable and indeterminate, whose existence is indicated only by the incessant work of its enunciation; it becomes detached from the body of the king ... and moves into the impalpable, universal and essentially public elements of speech. This fundamental change marks the birth of ideology."[47]

For Furet, during the Revolution the natural (or at least conventional) forms of political symbolization were suspended and radically new ones had to be invented. This politicized semiosis (or semiotic politics) thus distinguished the Revolution from both monarchical and republican political culture. But does Furet's characterization of the Revolution define it in terms of what was specific to it, or does he seek to contain it as a specific kind of political event, essentially discontinuous from all other political events? Lynn Hunt has suggested that Furet's argument that the "semiotic circuit" of the Terror came to an end with Thermidor does not explain why the revolution in and of language during the Terror gave way in 1794 to the revolution of interests, with the linguistic somehow shifting to the social. How, Hunt asks, does a network of signs end? How, and at what cost, can one extricate oneself from the semiotic relation of power and language? Perhaps there is no way out, in which case, and following Claude Lefort's argument, the Revolution would mark the advent of the ideological, defined in terms of the way power is expressed in contemporary political culture. Thus we return to our initial question, "Comment sortir de la Terreur?," which it seems cannot be dissociated from language. The question is also La Harpe's, and we should take him seriously when he suggests that the Revolution was driven by "the power of words."

In the section devoted to "eighteenth-century philosophy" and first presented at the Lycée in 1797, La Harpe diagnoses how this event came about. The eighteenth century may have been the century of philosophy, but it was also "the most disastrous age of degradation," marked by "the most shameful abuse of wit and reasoning in all genres." Posterity will take the name "philosophical century" as a "ridiculous nickname, a kind of counter-truth."[48] In his vitriolic treatment of eighteenth-century philosophy, La Harpe adopts well-established patterns of thought, rehearsing already familiar criticisms of philosophes launched earlier in the century.[49] He rejects all forms of atheism, materialism, and even skepticism wherever he finds them. Thus, although "healthy metaphysics" appears in France only with Condillac's works, his sensationalism is still too materialistic. Instead of situating the origin of ideas in the body, La Harpe attributes it to the mysterious union of body and soul, "one of the Creator's secrets." Other positions adopted are equally familiar. The *Encyclopédie* is a "rallying of conspirators," an "arsenal of unreligion." D'Alembert's "sublime philosophy" quickly degenerates into *"sans-culottisme."* Not surprisingly, Rousseau's critique of private property, and the Jacobins' application of it, render him "the most subtle of sophists, the most eloquent of rhetoricians, and the must impudent of cynics." Although La Harpe criticizes the sect of economists made up of Quesnay, Turgot, and du Pont de Nemours, he saves his harshest words for the false philosophers Voltaire, Rousseau, and especially Diderot. It is they who made the Revolution by trampling underfoot all religious, moral, and civic laws.

The political nature of La Harpe's literary history should not obscure the crucial issue here. It is true that his political critique of what we now recognize as mainstream Enlightenment thinking echoes the polemics directed against the philosophes by the Jesuits around mid century, against the Jacobins after 1793, and eventually against the revolutionaries in general. But the *Lycée* should not be written off as proto-literary history reflecting the philosophical stance of the religious and/or political right in postrevolutionary France. La Harpe's critical object is not so much a given philosophical position, even one that might have brought about the Revolution, as the philosophical act itself, or what he perceives as the newly politicized act of judging the truth value of statements. La Harpe does not react to the philosophes so obsessively solely because of their materialism or atheism, for he seeks to counter a destabilization of critical judgment in the philosophes' writing. In contesting reigning paradigms, the *doxa* inherited by eighteenth-century thought, the philosophes engaged in a spirited competition to determine the interpretation of things. Their work foregrounded the necessarily contestatory nature of critical thinking, with the result that any absolute ground for thought, even that of thought itself, was unsettled. In response, La Harpe seeks to right philosophy by wresting it from those he calls the sophists. He argues fervently for preserving "philosophy such as it must be, the noble contemplation of the Creator's work and all that he himself allowed us to appreciate there," and for rejecting "would-be philosophy, whose sole vain motive is to overturn established truths [and which] is strictly limited to seeking out the study of falsehoods."[50] This division leads to a literary history of the eighteenth century that sorts out the good philosophers and the impostors: on the good side appear Fontenelle, Montesquieu, Buffon, d'Alembert, and Condillac; on the bad, the *Encyclopédie*, Helvétius, Diderot, and Rousseau.

La Harpe's attempt to reground philosophy repeats a gesture as ancient as philosophy itself and that constitutes it as such. Philosophy maintains its identity by designating a threatening other, whose danger can be contained only through vigilant denunciation. This threat is embodied by the sophist, who is able to lead listeners to take false appearances for truths through a skillful yet perverse mastery of language. The greatest threat, though, is that sophistry is but a figure already produced from within the monological discourse of philosophy to counter its own determination by language. This figure is the other lodged within philosophy but not contained there. The truth that philosophy seeks to uncover and refer to is no more certain or stable than the language in which such reference takes place, as language is traversed by the affects of its speakers and subject to the most egregious plays of power. This is the threat that La Harpe constantly alludes to yet never can name, the 'unsaid' of his own discourse, always displaced onto other figures.

Not unexpectedly, the Revolution provides a prime example of this displacement. Just as reference to the philosophe-sophists is a shorthand figure for the destabilization of the ground of judgment and what might be called the rhetoricization of thought, reference to the Revolution illustrates how the *Lycée* attempts to reground judgment absolutely. For La Harpe, the Revolution is a terrifying event that must be made to mean. To produce that meaning, he introduces divine causality in the form of providential history. "The revolution is a singular event, from which no conclusion can be drawn because nothing like it can happen twice." The Revolution is a "miracle of divine justice, without which it would scandalize human reason; history will explain it only through the character of one man, a character so uncommon that history has yet to find it in any other person, especially not in a king. Consequently, this character itself is another kind of miracle that enters into the plan of Providence, the only plan that is clear and consistent."[51] To figure how the Revolution comes to mean – as an element in providential history – La Harpe must extricate himself from an absolutely rhetorical situation by salvaging the event from interpretation and according it intrinsic meaning. Whether he succeeds or not depends, of course, on whether there exist terms such as "Providence" whose meaning is not subject to dispute; in other words, on whether one can ever extricate oneself from the rhetorical situation.

But there is more. La Harpe's solution to the problem of the terrorism of language, the network of signs, by embracing providential causality is neither his most characteristic response nor his most interesting one. La Harpe cannot extricate himself from the rhetorical situation, but perhaps because he does not wish to. Through the *Lycée* La Harpe desires to restore to eloquence its ancient role as the instrument of the orator, whose role it should be to guide the populace and restore order.[52] La Harpe imagines assuming this role himself, as the literary critic who rises up as arbiter of taste and morality. He cannot help affirming the unavoidable and even desirable moment of the rhetorical situation, when conflicting interpretations occur but no predetermined resolution is available because no absolute ground for judgment exists. From within the rhetorical situation, by virtue of what La Harpe calls eloquence and through what might be called the deployment of discursive power, he will seek to reground esthetic and moral judgment. The *Lycée* marks both the culmination and the (dead) end of the belletristic tradition that developed in French court society and classicism, and the halting beginnings of a postrevolutionary discourse on literature that ascribed to classicism an instrumental role in the shaping of moral judgment.

La Harpe seeks to re-contain the Revolution and its effects, above all by reconstituting the language that it perverted. Ending the Terror, then, means giving back to words their authentic meaning. Can that meaning depend on rhetoric, though, on the orator's eloquence and the persuasive 'power of words'? This is precisely the question that La Harpe tries to avoid as he seeks to put the Revolution behind him by writing its history. But in an irony that jeopardizes his entire project, he cannot write history in such a fashion because he can never put an end to the rhetorical moment. For in a sense, this return to rhetoric also returns La Harpe to pre-Thermidoran Jacobinism, a discourse whose powerfully rhetorical effect is to form the political and civic subject.[53] Far from dismissing the *Lycée* for its bombast and right-wing polemics, we can reread it for the instructive lesson it provides in the politics of literary history (and the literarity of political history). The notion of literature La Harpe presents derives from his attempt to regenerate a language taken over and perverted by the Revolution. What he desperately desires is to exorcise the political from literature, but the depoliticization of literature is more rhetorical than real, more desired than possible. To preserve literature from the intrusion of the political, La Harpe scapegoats philosophy, and in terms that compromise his own enterprise. In the end, paradoxically, he invokes a depoliticized literature in a thoroughly politicized manner, wresting 'good' philosophy from sophistry in the most eloquently sophisticated way. La Harpe's analysis of the Revolution brings him far closer to the eighteenth-century writers whom he so virulently criticizes than he would admit, given that he invents a phantasmatic history of ideas in which ideas actually have real force. The *Lycée* inaugurates a literary history that will repeatedly replay the drama it wishes to end and be through with. La Harpe terrorizes letters, displacing and perpetuating the Terror he himself so narrowly escaped, which is to say that terrorism is not of the left or of the right. As one of the first master teachers in imperial and republican France, La Harpe helps found a pedagogical and ideological discourse designed to suppress, re-contain or rechannel terrifying events that go by many names, not the least significant being "philosophy" and "the eighteenth century."

We have come quite some distance since first asking Baczko's question, 'how to move on from (the) Terror?' Signifying a local and strategic problem confronting the post-Jacobin authorities, the question also involves the relation between events and our historical understanding of them. In this larger sense, as La Harpe's text shows, it is perhaps not possible to 'move beyond' the event in an absolute sense. In experiencing the politicization of language during the Revolution, La Harpe recognizes that the meaning attributed to events is traceable only to symbolic operations. Unwilling to embrace the logical implications for literature, La Harpe at the same time senses the power of literary discourse, as well as of discourse on literature, to shape anew the meanings of events. Much later in the history of literary history, as it comes to be institutionalized in postrevolutionary France, language will come to be seen as a means of understanding one's relation to events and not as an obstacle to that understanding. La Harpe represents the beginnings of that understanding, vexed and contradictory though they may be.

CHAPTER 6

Inventing a literary past

In the story of the French Revolution its participants produced, the event was so powerful that it could wipe away the past, eradicating the signs and cultural practices representing a former order. In the revolutionary calendar, for instance, September 22, 1792, became Year I of the Revolution. Time was reset to produce a 'revolutionized' history. Subjected to the temporal disjunction that this new calendar produced, individuals underwent a new temporal and collective beginning, the political subject's 'regeneration' as citizen. The revolutionary calendar is but one example of the extensive revolutionary reworking of the cultural practices of everyday life, involving a reconfiguration not only of time, but of space and language as well.[1] The destructive power of the Revolution stemmed in a sense from a willed amnesia, as words and images of the past were repressed in order ultimately to forget them. At the same time a new present was being forged through the production of intensely symbolic forms and practices that were to be experienced as if they had taken the place of the real that had been eradicated or at least made to seem forgotten. The new present of the revolutionary event was marked by a potentially irremediable ungroundedness. As we saw, for La Harpe this loss of foundations will be recounted through the experience of literature, for it is in writing literary history that he describes being 'terrorized' by the eighteenth-century past, by which he means a politicized, instrumentalized, and ultimately critically ungrounding use of language. Yet the writing of literary history offers La Harpe a way to rework this ungrounded experience, to get beyond the Terror via an experience of a historicized literature. The example of La Harpe suggests that the beginning of modern political culture in France occurs paradoxically in the experience of the loss of foundations, in coming to grips with the absence of an anterior moment that can no longer – if it ever could – supply meaning to the present moment. This beginning is also marked by the attempt to forge political and cultural practices that would reground experience by negotiating a sense of self and collective relations in the absence of pre-given foundations.

The beginning of modern political culture in France occurs in the clash between two political paradigms and two symbolic systems (and folklores) for figuring political cultural identity – one revolutionary, the other counterrevolutionary. The clash between these two systems will be played out throughout the nineteenth century, in fierce and drawn-out fashion. Arguably, the Revolution that pitted these two paradigms against each other does not end until the electoral victory of republicans over monarchists in 1876–7. Only then was a republican regime established that could maintain civic equality and political liberty, by guaranteeing the rights affirmed by the revolutionary principles of 1789.[2] The Parlement returns to Paris in 1879 from Versailles, where it had taken refuge in 1871 during the tumultuous early days of the Commune, and it passes a number of measures symbolically marking the Republic's certainty in itself: the Marseillaise becomes the national anthem, July 14 is adopted as the annual national festival, and amnesty is granted to the *communards*, effectively integrating them – or at least those who survived the bloody insurrection and subsequent execution or deportation – into the republican collectivity. The triumphant story of republicanism, finally established in late nineteenth-century France as political concept and practice, invokes powerful Enlightenment principles, such as the power of reason, the rule of progress, and the development of political institutions designed to promote modernization, understood as the technocratic administration of people and things. Insofar as the principles of French republicanism are proclaimed to have a universal extension that transcends the national, then historians, social scientists, and politicians can rightly take the Republic for no less than "the conquest of the modern world by the Enlightenment [which] signified the end of the exceptionalism of individual nations ... the triumph of the public sphere and democratic consensus, and the end of politics – even of belligerent confrontations between nations."[3]

Is French republicanism in fact the long-awaited culmination of Enlightenment principles, or is the Enlightenment what the republican historical narrative presents as the intellectual and social antecedent that republicanism requires in order to lay claim to political legitimacy? "The French are probably the all-around champions of the politics of memory," writes François Furet, underscoring the retrospective manner in which French cultural identity is produced.[4] If republicanism remembers the Enlightenment, it does so in the politically retrospective way Furet suggests, reconstructing the past in order to imagine the France of the future. More specifically, the canonized version of French history produced by the republican imaginary tells the story of a strong and at times violent French state that was invented as a means to unify a fragile internal situation marked by political contradictions and cultural differences. This account of how the modern French state developed has the added advantage not only of describing the republican state in the late nineteenth century, but also of relying on the same logic to explain the formation of the monarchical and imperial state (under Louis XIV in the seventeenth century and Napoleon I and III in the nineteenth).

One of the objectives of nineteenth-century republicanism was to win the culture wars of memory. Numerous practices were created to recall a past swept away by the Revolution as well as by nineteenth-century modernization. One of these practices was the development of historiography. In the works of the great Romantic historians, including Thierry, Guizot, Quinet, and especially Michelet, history-writing takes shape as an evolutionary narrative, reclaiming the past in order to recount the becoming of the nation and of the French people. The historical narrative's institutional home is the school and the university, sites where the academic discipline of history establishes a relation to the past as national history, and where history as cultural memory practice is played out. Nineteenth-century republican historiography presented the nation as the guarantor of cultural unity, grounding this unity in the national-historical narrative. As Hayden White remarks, the power of narrative form lies in the way form relates events to one another to make it appear that moral meaning is naturally attached to them. Thanks to the working of narrative form, not only do events appear to be significant; it also seems good that they occurred as they did. This narrative interconnection of events, in other words plot, provides what Christopher Prendergast calls an alibi, "which saves us from having to live the contingency and randomness of the world."[5] The plot of nineteenth-century historiography provided the alibi of a nationalized past, a national narrative of the modern French nation, in which the past was not so much recovered as constructed. The past as such is irrecoverable and thus unknowable.[6] Yet its effects "remain relentlessly present":

Unknowable the past may be, but the discourse on the past possesses a truth value in so far as it acts as a principle of legitimation, sanctioning political power, justifying social hierarchies, determining rights and responsibilities. The past, retrospectively, reconstructed as history, functions as a source of authority, overtly in the shape of jurisprudence and covertly in the form of the ways of feeling, the attitudes of mind, the norms of behavior which are transmitted to future generations and are internalized by them through the process of socialization.[7]

The generation of historians of 1820 faced their "relentlessly present" situation head-on, seeking to reestablish continuity in the aftermath of the break in national destiny that the Revolution had produced. No longer would the immediate past be experienced negatively as irremediable loss, phrased in terms of an impossible to bear nostalgia for a shattered unity. The national-historical narrative that took shape at this time was designed to recover and legitimate that experience of loss and, in the name of a communal becoming, to incorporate it into the cultural imaginary, thereby transcending its negativity. That, at least, was the historiographical wager.

The epistemological-narrative problem the Romantic historians faced was not unique. For centuries the 'history of France' has been a canonical genre used by countless writers and historians and supported by various forms of governments, whether monarchical, imperial or republican. If Heinrich Heine could liken France to "this persevering Penelope who each day makes and unmakes her web,"[8] it was because for centuries the 'history of France' had been a palimpsest. Its function was to "to ensure the continuity of national existence over the longest stretch of time possible and in an almost biological mode; to establish a community of destinies; to prove the exemplary nature of French destiny."[9] As a discipline, history may have been born of the "noble dream" of objectivity,[10] yet it possesses such an identity-forming function. The opening text of the *Revue historique* in 1876 recommends future contributors to "avoid contemporary debates, to deal with the subject treated with the methodological rigor and impartiality required by objective research, and not to seek arguments for or against only tangentially involved doctrines."[11] Seen in this light, Romantic historiography had to be rejected as being historical literature at worst and political history at best, that is, as proposing a political solution to problems of historical knowledge. Yet even positivist history cannot escape being implicated in the production of French national identity. Any historical discourse can be used politically, as a foundational narrative, a legitimation narrative, an apologetic narrative or even as a 'silent narrative' that removes voice from certain actors and events. Positivist history is but another strand in the web of Heine's French Penelope, whose historical narrative, especially in its academic, scholastic version, has provided French culture with a set of authorized ways of imagining, representing, and phrasing historical identity.

History writing plays a powerful role in creating the nation as an "imagined community." Benedict Anderson's well-used term calls attention to the fact that a national sense of common belonging and shared experience may indeed be intensely felt, yet all the while stem from a reality that is imaginary, sign- and image-based, and representational.[12] Imagined communities have a historical dimension, produced by what Eric Hobsbawm refers to as the "invention of tradition."[13] This cultural identity formation can be seen in the emergence of French national citizenship and the attempt to 'regenerate' a new political subject symbolically in the revolutionary festivals,[14] as well as in a variety of cultural memory sites throughout the nineteenth century. The workings of this cultural identity formation have been closely studied in recent times, so much so that one might wonder to what extent such studies are symptomatic of the condition they seek to analyze. It is time to weigh the consequences of this critical insight into the invented, imaginary nature of national identity. For if national identity is constructed and not given, the result of cultural contingency rather than historical necessity, then that identity must be seen as arbitrary and thus susceptible to being contested by alternative constructions. In the case of French historians, this logic forces them to face a particularly critical situation.

French historians represent a group of academic professionals to whom has been confided in a quasi-official way the responsibility of maintaining collective memory and national self-awareness. It is the historian who contributes to setting the standards for preserving historical literacy, understood as a set of performance standards (what needs to be known). But historical literacy also involves the way a society regulates its relation to its past as a social practice. We could refer to a kind of 'historian function' to suggest that 'the historian', like Michel Foucault's 'author', is less an autonomous individual than a discursive-cultural construct designed to produce a specific set of regulative effects. (A visual example of the construction of 'the historian' is the decision on the part of the Presses Universitaires de France to market history titles in their "Premier Cycle" series with full-color covers showing well-dressed and serious-looking authors. Even before opening the book, the reader can be comforted to see that French history is being well looked after.) But just when French historians are given the responsibility of maintaining collective memory and national self-awareness, national history as such seems to be losing its legitimacy. It has become far more difficult to tell *the* national story, if that story is not in fact in total and postmodern disarray. Raising a question that would have been incomprehensible in the nineteenth century, Marcel Detienne has asked, "How does one denationalize national histories?"[15]

One answer to Detienne's question lies in examining the practices whereby histories become nationalized in the first place. By revealing the constructedness of the national, a critical genealogy of national thought can be produced that could also help lay the conceptual foundations for thinking post-nationally. Such a genealogy would have to grapple with the national narrative's complex relation to a present situation. The production of a collective national identity in France is the backstory of this chapter and the next, which aim to examine some of the versions of eighteenth-century Enlightenment that will be presented in the nineteenth century. Of particular importance here is the instrumental role that literature will play in the emerging genre of literary history, itself an important element of French national history. Not only an object of consumption and circulation, literature in postrevolutionary France will become an object of study, an esthetic object, and one that the critic-teacher incorporates into a social and socializing practice. By considering how literature is established as an object of instruction, we can see how the eighteenth century will be institutionalized, in other words selectively remembered and at once strategically forgotten, as it is pressed into service in a civic, political, and ideological sense, in the construction of modern France.

The following pages read this process through two influential figures, Abel-François Villemain and Charles-Augustin Sainte-Beuve. At issue are not these individuals' literary preferences and critical idiosyncrasies. Despite the differences between Villemain and Sainte-Beuve, their writing shows how the newly historicized object of 'literature' is constructed in postrevolutionary France and why the historicizing discourse of the critic is the most productive means of apprehending that object. The writing of these two critics also highlights the institutional location of critical discourse (in the public sphere of the university or the newspaper). Finally, through these figures we will see that understanding the esthetic value and the cultural function of literature is mediated by the subject of critical discourse on literature (the academic critic and his student-listeners, or the journalist critic and reader-consumers of literature).

From 1816 to 1829, the literary critic and university professor Abel-François Villemain delivered a series of lectures at the Sorbonne devoted to the literature of the eighteenth century. Along with Victor Cousin and François Guizot, Villemain was one of the few university professors of the time who achieved considerable celebrity and influence beyond the university. Upwards of 1,000 persons attended his lectures, following which heated debate and criticism would occasionally appear in the press, most notably concerning the rehabilitation of Rousseau. Villemain wrote and revised his *Cours de littérature française* from 1816 to 1838, a particularly tumultuous period in French political history, a context in relation to which the *Cours* must be read. The period saw a relatively liberal constitutional monarchy (1814–20) give way to the government of the *ultras* (1820–7), which was marked by an intense conservative reaction (especially following the assassination of the duc de Berry in 1820 and the death of Louis XVIII in 1824). Villemain is removed from his teaching post between 1820 and 1822, and Cousin's and Guizot's courses are suspended during the conservative *ultra* reaction. Villemain's teaching, writing, and the institutional frame in which they are located raise the question of the relation between the academic-pedagogical discourse of the literary critic and political discourse, the latter involving the process of authorization, legitimation, and socialization that produces the truth value of historical discourse. In Villemain's case these two discourses are far from distinct, a problem highlighted by Villemain's place within the French university.

Founded in 1806 as the *Université impériale*, the university in its Napoleonic form was shaped by the Emperor's desire to achieve national unification. To that end the *corps enseignant* was established, instructors charged with providing French youth with a clear view of their civic and national identity. Writing in 1805 Napoleon noted:

Of all the political questions, the latter [the creation of the University] is possibly the most important. There can be no fixed political state if there does not exist a teaching body with fixed principles. So long as people are not taught as children whether they must be republicans or monarchists, Catholics or non-believers, etc., the state will not constitute a nation. It will rest on an uncertain and imprecise foundation, and it will constantly be subjected to disorder and change.[16]

Part of the "fixed principles" Napoleon required of imperial teachers was a clear sense of the limits to be placed on Enlightenment ideals. Intellectuals formed in the previous century could not be allowed to constitute a body in opposition to the state. With the *Université impériale*, Napoleon succeeded in imposing state control over educational policy by creating administrative structures that would continue throughout the nineteenth century. But a lasting monopoly over education could not be wrested from the church. Following Napoleon's downfall, the university was intellectually isolated, administratively weak, and politically suspect, viewed by conservative factions as having supported the 'usurper'. The conservative *ultra* government set about to undo what was perceived as the centralizing state secularism of the Napoleonic university. Denis-Luc Frayssinous, a titular bishop, member of the Académie Française, and

Inventing a literary past

charismatic author of *Les Vrais Principes de l'Eglise gallicane* (1817) and *Défense du christianisme* (1825), was named Minister of Ecclesiastical Affairs and Public Instruction in 1824. Under Frayssinous and the *ultra* government, the university pursued its task of indoctrinating youth, yet in accordance with other views. A bill passed in 1821 observes prescriptively that professors "are responsible not only for the instruction of letters and the sciences; they take advantage of every opportunity to teach their students what is owed to God, their parents, the king, and their country."[17] Unreliable instructors were removed, and it is estimated that between 1820 and 1830 one-tenth of all Parisian instructors either were suspended, lost their appointment, or were forced to retire for political or religious reasons.[18] One of the battlegrounds in the struggle for young minds was the teaching of philosophy, a situation that made the curricular role attributed to the eighteenth century, the age of the materialist and atheist philosophes, all the more ideologically determined. Before being replaced in 1830, the *ultra* administration made great strides in gaining curricular control of the discipline, placing priests in three-quarters of the philosophy positions in the *collèges royaux* and the *grands collèges communaux*.

It is against this political backdrop fraught with ideological tension that Abel-François Villemain was named Minister of Public Instruction in 1830 under the new government. He served in this position once again in 1841, taking over from his university colleagues François Guizot, who was named to the post in 1832, and Victor Cousin, who held it briefly in 1840. Representing the disciplines of literature, history, and philosophy, these three individuals stand for the complicated way in which the academic institution of the university, the emerging disciplines of the humanities, and the political institution of the state mesh in early nineteenth-century French culture. In the case of Villemain, this interconnection is legible in his four-volume history of eighteenth-century French literature, the *Tableau de la littérature du XVIIIe siècle*, in which the literary history of the eighteenth century and the political reality of the early nineteenth collide. The *Tableau* brings together the teaching of literature and the practice of politics, and in a way that Villemain both desires yet cannot completely master.

Villemain's *Tableau* is not unique in its genre. In 1804 the French language and literature section of the Institut de France had organized a competition on the topic of the eighteenth-century "tableau littéraire de la France."[19] In the immediate post-Revolution period, once the eighteenth century began to be seen as such, that is, as belonging to the past, considerable energy was expended in determining its meaning as a way to (re)construct the present. This effort takes place publicly and officially in the Institute's *tableau* competition. Representing a past that was both literary and national, interweaving esthetic values and ideological ones, the competition belongs to a process extending well into the nineteenth century (and beyond). Late nineteenth-century French literary histories such as those of Ferdinand Brunetière or Gustave Lanson have their proto-historical beginnings in the works of Jean-François de La Harpe, Jean Marie Napoléon Désiré Nisard, Jules-Gabriel Janin, Abel-François Villemain, and Charles-Augustin Sainte-Beuve.[20] In each, the narrative of literary history resembles that of history in that it aims to produce an imaginary unity out of the experience of contingency and fragmentation by making the past meaningful. Rejecting rhetorical criticism or the study of 'pure' form, as well as biographical criticism that is limited to the sole 'life' a work reflects, literary history historicizes the production and consumption of texts, transforming them into literature. Texts' meaning and significance are presented as historically determined and informed by developmental change. That change, which can be grasped in and through literary form, is represented as the unfolding of some suprapersonal idea or entity.[21]

If these are the recognized characteristics of the literary historical genre today, they were not at the time of the 1804 competition. Without a generic matrix, producing a literary *tableau* of the previous century was a daunting task, as one of the candidates, Eusèbe Salverte, notes:

The eighteenth century! What a mix of memories this word awakens! ... What passions still more varied! ... People least familiar with literature begin to consider this topic only by introducing opinions determined in advance. Partiality isn't limited to historical periods or to literary genres; it affects the personal aspect of authors as much as their works, showing us in these works only cherished masters or heinous adversaries.[22]

One example of reading eighteenth-century texts through the lens of "opinions determined in advance" is the submission of Prosper de Barante, a liberal protestant closely linked to Anne-Louis Germaine de Staël and Benjamin Constant. For Barante, one of the errors of the *Ancien Régime* was that these writers were prevented from exercising any positive and meaningful social role, which forced them into an aggressively critical and anti-religious position. Philosophical excess led to Jacobinism, but it was *Ancien Régime* governmental politics that had contributed to that excess. Barante saw letters as but one symptom of society's general illness and dissolution. Distancing himself from a materialist eighteenth century,

Barante strives to reestablish the connection between literature and the social context that had been broken in the last century. As his literary history indicates, political concerns infuse the discussion of literature during the Empire and Restoration as much as esthetic ones. Unsurprisingly, the joint winners of the competition, Victorin Fabre and Antoine Jay, were the authors of the most traditional and least profound of the literary histories submitted.

Villemain was well aware that the business of literary criticism was an inescapably political one. In a preface to the *Tableau* written in 1840, he signals the political use to which the eighteenth century had been put by the most consummate of politicians, Napoleon. Under the Emperor, he remarks, the only public exercise of thought was "the debate over the literary superiority of the seventeenth century or the eighteenth, over good taste or bad. That was how the ruler had influenced the thinking of people under his authority."[23] In a sense, Napoleon's cultural politics simply continue those put in place and refined by the French monarchy during the *Ancien Régime*. Whereas Louis XIV had created the bedazzling impression of the state, Napoleon transformed the mirage of a state into that of the French nation. To do so, a certain unruly subject had to be brought to order, namely, literature: "a literature whose speculative boldness had transformed the social world had to be regularized, surveyed, crowned with awards if necessary, but made submissive."[24] Villemain does not raise the issue of whether one way to obtain such submission was by creating a docile teaching body, which was clearly how Napoleon viewed things. More evident for Villemain is that literary criticism, because of its repression during the Napoleonic reign, becomes a thoroughly political and politicized discourse. "The contradictory debate concerning the literature of the eighteenth century had been one of the last arenas left half-open by the hand that had closed all the others ... and since no opportunity for politics was left elsewhere, a good deal of politics took place in literary criticism."[25] This situation was not to change with the fall of Napoleon, however, and writing in 1840 Villemain still remarks on the politicization of the eighteenth century. "The well-known names of the eighteenth century, either exalted or belittled deliberately, became instruments of political group warfare."[26]

For Villemain, the politicization of literature can be traced to the eighteenth century, a period characterized in somewhat overblown terms as "this great period of literary activity and social transformation, which begins with bold books and ends with the renewal of the world."[27] In the course of the century, literature moves outside itself, so to speak, coming to play an increasingly significant role in the social sphere and instrumentalized as a way to bring about reform or to cause the revolution. "Letters themselves had become the universal instrument of revolution … they merged with politics; they literally took on the same language as politics instead of receiving their inspiration from it."[28] There emerges during the Revolution "a literature that became entirely political, and whose last act brought political oratory into being."[29] The revolutionary period, as Villemain's terminology suggests, is a transgressive one, when apparently unrelated genres and discourses – those of letters and of politics – intersect and recombine. A hybrid genre emerges, "political oratory," whose place is the *tribune*, the podium, that space between literature and politics in which the two are linked.

For a critic like La Harpe, who had written his own history of eighteenth-century literature in the shadow of the anti-Jacobin, post-Thermidor reaction some thirty years earlier, this politicization of literature is nothing less than the latter's perversion, brought about when philosophy infects esthetics. Villemain will repeat, albeit in less vitriolic and less hysterical terms, La Harpe's critique of materialist, sensualist, atheist writers, that sect of perverse sophists whose incendiary writings alone La Harpe held responsible for the French Revolution. For Villemain, however, the politicization that literature undergoes in the eighteenth century and that reaches its high point during the Revolution is not necessarily an undesirable thing. Writing in the 1820s and 1830s, Villemain imagines the empowerment of literature as a forceful, effective agent of social change rather than the latter's reflection or, worse, merely a play of esthetic form to be appreciated. Villemain imagines a version of literature in which author, critic, and professor all play important roles. The *Tableau* contains a perspective onto the eighteenth century that offers a way to restore, recontain, and rechannel something of a dangerous yet fascinating force that postrevolutionary readers found there. Villemain's position is by no means a commonplace one in the early nineteenth century. Standard practice in the imperial university was instead to praise the *grand goût* of the *grand siècle*, seeing only the former's pale afterlife in the century following that of Louis XIV, and by no means the beginnings of a socially and historically determined reformist discourse.

This is precisely the process that Villemain locates in eighteenth-century literature. Or rather, through reference to the previous century he can begin to tell the story of such reform. "In terms of moral chronology, the eighteenth century began on the day of the first protest, initially timid and discreet, against the monarchical splendor of Louis XIV, the religious domination of Bossuet, and the classical authority of antiquity; these three naturally quite dissimilar things came together and were integrated into the spirit of the eighteenth century."[30] To mark the shift from one century to another, Villemain invokes the notion of "moral chronology." Literary and social history is readable as *moral* history, as the story of protest against power (but also, as we shall see, the power of protest).[31] This is the story Villemain wishes to tell, at least, for it would allow him to lead the eighteenth century to its apparent culmination in the French Revolution and then move fairly quickly and confidently beyond it. For curiously enough, Villemain's eighteenth century extends into the nineteenth, and his last lessons are devoted to discussion of the protestant liberal de Staël and the reactionary theocrat Joseph de Maistre. In fact, Villemain's "moral chronology" has no end. In his closing lesson he writes, "I have brought the eighteenth century to the moment when it becomes everything we understand and everything we see before us, the moment when it is in you and becomes one with a new age that you are beginning. I shall stop at the moment when I find myself here before you."[32] The present interlocutionary relation is highlighted not only for rhetorical and pedagogical impact. The effect Villemain wishes to realize is to extend the past into the present, to establish a continuity in the name of a "moral chronology," a history in which he too would have his place. It is that place that the *Tableau* works to define and to construct. With this finality in mind we can consider the larger contours of the eighteenth century that the *Tableau* presents.

In schematic terms, Villemain's eighteenth century comprises four great writers: Montesquieu, who understands the notion of modern, non-courtly freedom far better than even Voltaire, and whose *L'Esprit des lois* is "the eighteenth-century book that has the most ideas and ... the most ideas that belong to the future";[33] Buffon, whose natural history advances scientific discovery without giving in overtly to the excesses of materialist metaphysics; Voltaire, whose life and intellectual evolution are presented as emblematic of the century itself; and Rousseau, the most problematic figure for Villemain and whose rehabilitation in his courses during the 1820s and 1830s is innovative and indeed fairly remarkable. Over against this implicit pantheon are other writers whom Villemain wishes to delineate, circumscribe, and exclude from consideration by accusing them of a kind of thinking that goes by many names: epicureanism, philosophy, skepticism, materialism, and the catchall term of doctrines. Clearly the anti-Jacobinism of a La Harpe persists in Villemain's views on the pernicious nature of atheist materialism. Yet his criticism of eighteenth-century skepticism stems from his own cautious relations with conservative clergy in the 1820s, who were attempting to retake the university following the fall of Napoleon and to weed out the unreligious among its professors. Villemain found himself caught between the atheist materialism of the eighteenth century and the religious right-wing censorship of the early nineteenth.

Villemain's treatment of Diderot reveals the tensions traversing both the *Tableau* and ideological discourse of the 1820s. The Diderot presented here is essentially a contradictory figure: "a mind that is vast but inconsistent, by his nature in scarce agreement with his own opinions, enthusiastic and skeptical, a good fellow who sometimes expresses outrageous wishes, able to be virtuous and to destroy all morality. An entire school can be summed up in Diderot."[34] Diderot is a "mixture of the sophist and the philosopher, the orator and the scholar: he corrupts morality with an outpouring of emotion and good-heartedness, and he corrupts good taste with an eloquence sometimes filled with vigor and simplicity."[35] To gauge Villemain's strategy here – whether he was aware of it or not is of lesser importance – we must put aside received ideas of a 'modern' Diderot. This 'modern' image has been in the making for some 150 years, a process whose beginnings are visible in Villemain's portrayal of Diderot. Villemain forges a rift in this dual figure, circumscribing by means of negative terms such as 'doctrine' and 'school' a perverse materialist philosophy in order all the better to contain it, distancing it from that other figure found in Diderot, the critic. Thus one 'Diderot' reflects the transformation of dogmatic, intolerant skepticism into full-blown materialism. "His doctrine soon became not only a negation but a faith: after unobtrusive doubts, shrewd insinuations, partial attacks, mocking remarks that held at least a few great principles in respect, there followed the serious and systematic destruction of every religious and moral belief."[36] Yet another 'Diderot' all but prefigures the contemporary Romantic critic with whom Villemain almost seems to identify. "As a critic, Diderot possesses something of the freedom of the German school, along with a few of its affectations. What he wants and admires is naturalness, spontaneity, and simplicity – a person, in a word, and not an author." "Diderot is an excellent critic, even though he often lacks the correct exactitude. But he feels what he judges, and he analyzes passionately. His imagination takes on the hues of that of another; he adopts the language and the accent of what he wants to praise."[37] Villemain's conciliatory yet contradictory compromise papers over the problematic reception and refraction of eighteenth-century materialism, a history in which Diderot plays a telltale role. Ultimately, Villemain's denial of conflict figured by the proper name 'Diderot' invites his nineteenth-century listeners to perpetuate similar denials, including the excision of what is called 'philosophy' from the critical enterprise in the name of democratic free speech.

During the 1820s Villemain opposed the church's attempt to limit public debate and critical investigation. In the next decade, he became Minister of Education in the liberal government. From the position of critical outsider, he passed to that of more conciliatory, compromising insider for whom power could no longer be criticized for being oppressive, at least not in good faith. Viewed through this contextual lens, Villemain's initial return to the eighteenth century in his *Tableau* signals his attempt to keep alive a certain liberal, reformist tradition, insofar as his literary history of the eighteenth century recounts the story of literature's empowerment through its acquisition of critical force. But Villemain's literary history founders in a compromising denial: the force of literature is ultimately reduced to a question of eloquence. No effective means is provided for judging the effects of literature in that eloquence represents a utopian notion of language, neutralized and emptied of value, a formal performance that provides no possibility for grounding moral judgment. Does this compromising denial of moral judgment that literary criticism performs by invoking the criterion of eloquence in the nineteenth century reappear in the twentieth, when literary criticism becomes enthralled with form and develops sophisticated formalisms to prop up that denial? Already among Villemain's contemporaries, Charles Baudelaire best reveals the stakes involved in valorizing literary eloquence.

Baudelaire can hardly be accused of impartiality towards Villemain, who held the position of *secrétaire perpétuel* to the French Academy, whose doors remained closed to Baudelaire. But more than just bitterness, spite, and revenge motivated Baudelaire in his unpublished essay entitled "The Spirit and Style of M. Villemain," written after 1862. "I aspire to pain," the essay begins, "I tried to read Villemain."[38] Baudelaire has no end of disparaging remarks concerning both Villemain's *Cours* ("banal compendium worthy of a rhetoric professor") and Villemain the man ("Villemain is obscure, why? Because he doesn't think"). More telling than these acerbic *ad hominem* attacks is the obsessive criticism that focuses on the social determination of Villemain's language: "the style of a civil servant, the formulaic style of a prefect, the amphigory of a mayor, the fulsomeness of an innkeeper." Elsewhere Baudelaire refers to Villemain's "mind of an employee and a bureaucrat" and his "morals of a servant." Even in his disparaging description of Villemain's teaching – "the servile professor courts the insipid youth of the Latin Quarter" – it is the social role played by Villemain that Baudelaire highlights. "Villemain's sentences," he writes, are "like those of all the prattlers who don't think (or those prattlers who are interested in hiding their thoughts – laywers, stockmarket traders, businessmen, society people." What Baudelaire's evaluation of Villemain's literary history underscores is that esthetic judgments are never neutral insofar as they are socially and affectively determined. In his own esthetic writing, Baudelaire openly embraces this determination, finding it to be the hallmark of a certain modernity. In Villemain's case, Baudelaire keenly senses something in this teaching of literary history that, for being denied, is spoken without being said, a 'political unconscious' that plays itself out in an intensely invested relation established with the symbolic construction that is "the eighteenth century." What Baudelaire locates in Villemain's view of literature is a pedagogical and ideological imperative that colors much nineteenth-century criticism, a notion of literature tellingly visible in the countless manuals, anthologies, and literary histories produced during the Second Empire and the Third Republic. Designed to reform a shattered and contested cultural memory, to generate a new republican *habitus*, these texts were devised to produce civic students, civil servants, and new imperial and later republican citizens, united by shared moral and national values.[39] Thus, rather than view the *Tableau* as reflecting ideology, we should take it as ideology as/at work, producing through the institutionalization of literature "the liberal imaginary."[40]

Schools and the university in France were cultural sites where this identity would be forged in the nineteenth century. This process occurred all the more efficiently following the Jules Ferry reforms in the 1880s that made primary education free, secular, and obligatory. But another equally important site where national literary culture was being formed was the press, and it was Charles-Auguste Sainte-Beuve who contributed the most to shaping that culture. Although he taught briefly at the Collège de France and the Ecole normale, Sainte-Beuve's writing is journalistic criticism. It first appears in 1824, when at the age of twenty he published an essay in the Parisian liberal daily *Le Globe*, in which later essays also appeared. In 1828 Sainte-Beuve tried his hand at the *tableau* genre with his *Tableau historique et critique de la poésie française et du théâtre français au XVIe siècle*, in which he promoted a certain Romantic critical agenda through his literary history of the Renaissance. At his death in 1869,

Sainte-Beuve was the acclaimed master of the literary portrait, the term he used to describe the roughly 150 essays published between 1827 and 1849 in *Le Globe, La Revue de Paris,* and *La Revue des Deux Mondes.* From 1849 to 1869 he continued this genre in *Le Constitutionnel* and *Le Moniteur,* the official government organ of the Second Empire after 1868, writing weekly Monday essays entitled *Causeries du lundi.* These 'Monday chats' eventually numbered some 600, on almost 400 separate topics.

Yet Sainte-Beuve was hardly the most productive journalist-critic of the time. Jules Janin, the self-styled 'prince' of literary critics, authored some 2,240 articles that appeared weekly between 1830 and 1874 in the *Journal des débats.*[41] Numbers alone do not tell the story of the role played by journalist literary criticism in nineteenth-century France. The crucial issue involves the ways that the notions of writer-critic, literature, and history were being woven together in the cultural imaginary taking shape in – and shaping – post-revolutionary, bourgeois, and republican France. Sainte-Beuve's writing is particularly valuable in helping us trace that interweave. But how should we approach this somewhat antiquated journalistic criticism? Should it be read in light of what literary history would become? Retrospection runs the constant risk of establishing false causalities, reading into the past not what was but what is wanted. In Sainte-Beuve's case, this retrospective desire to find the beginnings of modern criticism would give us a backlit reading of the critic that rejects him for being unmodern or forgets him for being premodern. Marcel Proust will denounce Sainte-Beuve for precisely this reason in his *Contre Sainte-Beuve,* writing 'against' Sainte-Beuve for espousing an unmodern notion of literature, a literature that has not yet won a formal, esthetic freedom from all that imprisons it, including author, context, and history. Proust and the notion of esthetic modernism he advocates, continued perhaps in the idea of literarity promoted a half-century later by structuralism, may have made Sainte-Beuve all but unreadable. But instead of continuing to write 'against' Sainte-Beuve, or to write him off, we can return to his journalistic criticism, reading it not as a pre-literary moment but rather as one in which literature is engaged in order to think through the complexity of the present, an engagement in which the eighteenth century would be invoked strategically.

At the heart of Sainte-Beuve's critical practice lies the assumption that the literary work cannot stand on its own. Incomplete at best, potentially deceptive, the literary work must be read in relation to the set of factors that influenced its author and led to its production. Sainte-Beuve is far removed from the Romantic notion of literature, and art in general, as the product of the poet-seer of genius. Much more mundane factors shape literature, such as "blood, relations, family, race, land, and climate."[42] Sainte-Beuve's insistence on extra-literary, 'extrinsic' factors is not the biographical and historical determinism of late nineteenth-century academic literary criticism that developed from the reductively mechanical 'race, milieu, and moment' approach that Taine laid out in the introduction to his *Histoire de la littérature anglaise* (1863–4). Rather, Sainte-Beuve aims to humanize and socialize literature by relating it to its author, set within a certain social and historical context. In contextualizing literature, though, Sainte-Beuve's literary criticism only appears to historicize it, for ultimately the historical is reduced to a matter of style. Beuvian criticism is driven by the impetus to create a stylized literary portrait of the author, but one that evacuates the historical and behind which the critic ultimately disappears.

> Criticism for me is a metamorphosis: I attempt to disappear in the character I am reproducing. I become familiar with him, even through his style; I borrow and take on his diction: sentimental and delightfully nebulous with Mme. de Krüdner, slightly abstract and taut with M. Vinet, clear and fluent in an eighteenth-century fashion with Mme de Charrière. That's my aim: to observe my subject's manners this way.[43]

Elsewhere he characterizes his method of portraiture thus: "to penetrate my author, settle in there, produce him in all his various aspects; make him live, move, and speak as he must have done, following him towards a private, inner space and in his daily habits."[44]

When viewed from a more 'modern' literary theoretical perspective that separates writer from text, and lived history from esthetic form, Sainte-Beuve's biographical method appears to be prehistorical impressionism at best. But from his own perspective, the biographical method affords the critic an essential freedom.

> The critic must be partial to no one and belong to no coterie. He embraces people but for a moment, and he passes among various groups without ever becoming bound to them. He moves resolutely from one camp to another, and the justice he rendered on one side never causes him to refuse to render it on the other.[45]

The freedom Sainte-Beuve attempts to win through the biographical literary portrait is from rule-bound esthetic theory. Represented by La Harpe, Népomucène Lemercier, and Désiré Nisard, this normative, authoritarian approach to taste and esthetic judgment could only seem moribund and suffocating in the heady days of Romanticism. Criticism for Sainte-Beuve involves not so much respecting rules as crossing borders.

"The critic is never home, he moves, he travels; he adopts the tone and the air of various milieus; he is the constant guest."[46] Likening criticism to travel, Sainte-Beuve defines the critic in terms of a curiosity and openness that free him from the constraints of the familiar.

But can such freedom be won in writing, through an act of style? Is Sainte-Beuve free to travel, never to be confined *chez lui*, imprisoned in his own space and his own context? Or is the literary portrait an alibi concept, elaborated in order to deny context and repress the historical by invoking a timeless formalism and a phenomenological essentialism of esthetic freedom? Ultimately, these questions must be historicized in turn. Why, for instance, was it precisely in 1850 that Sainte-Beuve claimed that the critic must be impartial and belong to no camp? At the risk of chronological shorthand, the issue here is '48. Marking the social tumult of the Second Republic (1848–52), when the forces of socialism and democracy led to the overthrow of the constitutional monarchy of Louis-Philippe in February 1848, the date refers by anticipation to the authoritarian solution to civil disorder, Louis-Napoléon's *coup d'état* in 1851 and the Second Empire that succeeded it a year later. To consider how Sainte-Beuve grapples with 1848, in other words how he phrases the relation between the literary and the political, we can turn to the image he constructs of eighteenth-century writing, focusing specifically on how he links the eighteenth century to the nineteenth, the not too distant past of the *Ancien Régime* to what for him was an all too disquieting present.

Sainte-Beuve's role in determining which writers would signify the French literary tradition, and indeed literature itself in republican France, is massive.[47] The Beuvian Pantheon comprises Rousseau, Chateaubriand, Pascal, Voltaire, Molière, Bossuet, Montesquieu, Montaigne, La Bruyère, La Fontaine, La Rochefoucauld, and Chénier. Moralists are privileged over writers of other genres, and the seventeenth century over the eighteenth. Personal taste doubtless played a role in these critical choices. But beneath the hierarchical cataloguing of literature we can read a larger process involving the symbolic construction of the past, a cultural memory work that may possess a subjective and personal dimension, but that also reflects manifestly political and ideological vectors of a collective nature. Sainte-Beuve's criticism relates past and present in a way that is based on specific values of the true and the good. His criticism has a canon-producing imperative, moreover, and part of his legacy is to have helped shape what would be taught as 'good literature' in Third Republic France. His writing is also canon-producing in the sense that it generates laws of esthetic judgment, principles on which to assess what good literature is, how it should be used, and what effects its frequenting should produce. One of Sainte-Beuve's primary canonical laws of literature is that the political must be rejected – or repressed – whenever it threatens the established order. This prescriptive approach leads to the question of whether the rejection or repression of the political is part and parcel of the kind of memory work in which Sainte-Beuve wishes to involve literature. Does he herald a literature that can free itself from the political, just as the critic wishes to? Or does he wish all the more to free literature from the political precisely because he senses the increasingly inevitable imbrication of the two?

To tease out this set of questions, we can consider what Sainte-Beuve means when he refers to the eighteenth century. Two very different things, it would seem, as suggested in the following passage, taken from the article "Marie Antoinette" of July 14, 1851:

> When one thinks that a century called enlightened, and that had the most refined form of civilization, leads to public acts of such barbarism, one begins to doubt human nature and to fear the ferocious animal, as brutish as it is animalistic in fact, that this nature contains within it and that wants nothing more than to emerge.[48]

From the so-called Enlightenment, the height of refined civilization, emerges the Revolution in all its ferocious monstrosity. Decades of anti-Jacobin rhetoric had already rendered such phrases mere clichés by the 1850s. In locating the cause of the Revolution in fanatical passions that took over philosophy, Sainte-Beuve rehearses a worn explanation for that monstrous revolution. In his *causerie* on Rivarol he writes:

> The great new passion that produced the national fever and the delirium that gripped France was philosophical passion, philosophical fanaticism. Up until then it was thought that the word *fanaticism* applied only to religious ideas and beliefs. But the late eighteenth century was destined to show that the word applied no less to philosophy than to religion, and something monstrous was the result.[49]

The eighteenth century alone is not at stake in Sainte-Beuve's critical narrative, however. In the tumultuous political climate of nineteenth-century France, aftershocks of the Revolution continued to be felt, and no reference to any aspect of the eighteenth century remained neutral. Names were cover words for political perspectives, the encoded expression of polemical positions. The discourse on literature became a politicized discourse, as authors and texts were classified and reclassified according to the contours of an emerging and dynamic political field. Literature itself became the site of an identificatory practice, as texts were pressed into service to designate subjects and groups in nineteenth-century society, whether they were named romantic, socialist, revolutionary, republican or bourgeois. Reading literature became part of the same identificatory practice, implicated in the cultural construction of historically specific subjectivity.

In linguistic terms, the third-person narrative of history produces the impression that events relate themselves, as if on their own. Yet no historical narrative can sever itself from its narrative determination. Consequently, the historical narrative must be read not only in relation to its object, the historical referent, but also in relation to its narrative determination, which it cannot totally escape. For no history (or story) of the past can prevent itself – or be preserved – from being situated in the present, in the moment of its narrative actualization. We should not fail to notice – nor is it easy to do so – how Sainte-Beuve's vision of the eighteenth century is projected through the prism of a present moment, a present that will take on the dimensions of an obsession and will go by the name of 1848. Referring at one point to the bloody riots of early 1848, Sainte-Beuve writes of "the accident of February, that immense catastrophe we are all a part of and of which we are the survivors."[50] Just as Jean-Louis Géricault's painting, *The Raft of the Medusa*, gripped the cultural imagination in the 1820s by presenting an image of shipwrecked sailors that allegorized a shipwrecked society, so too Sainte-Beuve invokes the image of shipwreck to explain his own relation to the events of 1848. Like most other writers of his generation in France, he is gripped by the sense of living an aftermath, writing in the wake of events. Consequently, he believes he must "promote the work of civilization" (*faire œuvre de civilisation*) by protecting an imperiled civilization, and especially by safeguarding *l'esprit français*. "What is important is preventing *l'esprit français* from going astray and becoming perverted."[51] These are times when dispersion and confusion have reached their limit, when democratic, socialist leveling has undone all hierarchies, and when what is being written is, as Sainte-Beuve terms it referring to Balzac, "industrial literature." In such times, what is called for is "la bonne politique," the right policy as well as a political solution, in order to direct public opinion:

The right policy is to work one way or another to contain the growing coarseness, the immense coarseness that at a distance resembles a rising tide, to set up against it whatever dikes have not been destroyed, and to lend a hand, in short, to everything that used to be called taste, politeness, culture, civilization.[52]

What role can literary criticism play in stemming this tide of cultural perversion?

Sainte-Beuve's own esthetic policy regarding the eighteenth century is shaped by his view of the present social and political conjuncture. This policy involves a double strategy of repudiation and rehabilitation. On the one hand he will reject certain writers and works he finds manifestly philosophical, in other words excessively and threateningly political. The *Causeries* thus contribute to the afterlife of the virulent anti-Jacobin discourse witnessed following Thermidor and the fall of Robespierre in 1793, a discourse illustrated in its most vitriolically literary historical version in La Harpe. Yet there is more in the *Causeries* than this somewhat reactionary stance. For on the other hand, and more interestingly, Sainte-Beuve attempts to forge esthetic as well as social categories to justify his rejection of the philosophical and political nature of certain eighteenth-century writers. The language of the eighteenth century had not yet become thoroughly politicized, he claims, for it served above all as the medium of a refined sociability. It is this sociable dimension of language that Sainte-Beuve seeks to rescue in order to found a new literary-cultural imaginary.

If a number of things were already ruined by the late seventeenth century and throughout the eighteenth, at least language remained intact, and prose in particular was excellent when Voltaire and those around him were speaking and writing. So I would like to put us, and myself first of all, back on the regimen of clear, precise, and fluid language. In dealing with the witty men and women from a century ago, I would like us to begin to speak the way they spoke then, with lightness, politeness if possible, and without too much bombast.[53]

In a comment that does not refer simply to eighteenth-century diction, Sainte-Beuve establishes a distinction that will remain throughout the *Causeries*, namely, between fanatical, impassioned politics, which receives its impetus from philosophy, and a mode of sociability based on polished, precise, and restrained conversation, the *causerie de salon*. Hippolyte Taine would portray the aristocracy of the *Ancien Régime* as 'salon people', removed from any meaningful role in society by an overly centralized political system and whose true social function consisted in inviting each other and being invited.[54] Yet Sainte-Beuve valorizes the salon in the above passage, for it is that space where the sociability of the previous age flourished. Sociable speech is perhaps the most valuable legacy of the *Ancien Régime*, especially given the threatening incivility Sainte-Beuve senses all about and that is signified for him by the political events of 1848.

Political action versus sociable speech – these are the terms of the opposition Sainte-Beuve wishes to establish, as if language, and above all literary language, could be safeguarded, even severed, from the political in order to be returned to a mythical, pre-revolutionary purity of pure sociability. From our contemporary vantage point, Sainte-Beuve may seem hopelessly embroiled in an under-theorized view of literature, if not a pre-theoretical one, that marks a retreat from the encroachment of the political. His return to the literary sociability of prerevolutionary times thus would parallel the escapist consolation that poet-painters took in images of the eighteenth century, with its graceful and elegant beauty, as depicted in the rococo paintings of Jean-Antoine Watteau, François Boucher, Jean Honoré Fragonard, and Nicolas Lancret.[55] This other, sociable eighteenth century appealed to the nostalgic longings of all those who sought refuge from life in a bourgeois capitalist society whose *mot d'ordre*, expressed by François Guizot, minister in the government of Louis-Philippe until 1848, was "Get rich, through work and through thrift." An escapist predilection for the eighteenth century also marks Arsène Houssaye's *Le Dix-Huitième siècle* (1843) and his *Galerie des portraits du XVIIIe siècle* (1848), as well as Edmond and Jules de Goncourt's *Portraits intimes du XVIIIe siècle* (1857), *La Femme au XVIIIe siècle* (1862), and *L'Art du XVIIIe siècle* (1859–75). But is this mid-nineteenth-century image of the eighteenth century merely an alibi for intellectual and esthetic isolation?

It is tempting to read in Sainte-Beuve's call for a return to the literary sociability of prerevolutionary times not so much the denial of the political (and consequently not its failed repression) but rather a way of resisting it. In this sense Sainte-Beuve illustrates what Richard Terdiman has called the "symbolic resistance" of nineteenth-century writer-theorists, who devised literary and theoretical strategies for responding to the political with equally powerful forms of counter-discourse.[56] These strategies define a tension between the esthetic and the political that is constitutive of literature in its modernity.[57] Furthermore, Sainte-Beuve's promotion of salon sociability helps us understand the recent interest in sociability in contemporary eighteenth-century studies. Sociability has become a tantalizing lens for investigating several critical issues, from the appearance of the intellectual in early modern European culture, to gender politics, the development of citizens, political moderation, and the emergence of the modern writer.[58] In each case, the greater the critical investment in the notion of sociability, the less it appears to be an unmotivated research topic defined by its place in an objective past. Instead, sociability is constructed precisely as a way to return to the eighteenth century in order to reflect obliquely yet significantly upon various forms of contemporary engagements with the political. The disciplinary, institutional, and national determinations of these engagements are not negligible. The figures of sociable intellectuals – writers and philosophes – that contemporary European scholarship portrays, for instance, are far more devoted to contributing to the collective social order than their US counterparts, who are more contestatory and more deeply engaged in the politics of identity.

Sketching out one dimension of this argument with an admittedly broad brush, one could argue that very contemporary realities on each side of the Atlantic determine the production of two markedly different sets of images of the eighteenth century. French scholarship, at least in its most institutionally valorized instances, is engaged in investigating an eighteenth century in ways that serve the larger purpose of theorizing social integration and non-conflictual intersubjective relations. This theoretical work, and the conceptual paradigms it produces, should allow a generation of scholars and students to imagine the sociable past intensely sought for by a contemporary Europe whose social fabric at present is being severely stretched. As the literary and cultural history of sociability is written, the past that the present needs comes into view. Europe is being built one palimpsest at a time. The image of the eighteenth century currently being produced in the US is far less accommodating. Instead of an integrative sociability, what is valorized is an autonomous individualism that allows for the challenging of commonly accepted ways of knowing in the name of ideological critique, a positive and powerful understanding of things, but one that may also produce isolation and marginalization.

As should be clear, I want to suggest that no construction of the eighteenth century is neutral, for all are shaped by constitutive investments in recovering that past through a process of introjection into the present where the figure of the past takes on historical meaning. Herein lies my interest in Sainte-Beuve's desire to enter into "commerce with the previous century's witty men and women," as he creates an imaginary form of literary intercourse with the past that provides him with the longed-for illusion of social integrity and integration. His portrayals of Rousseau and Diderot offer particularly telling examples of the stakes in this involvement with and investment in the eighteenth-century past.

Representing Jean-Jacques Rousseau in 1849 was a particularly thorny matter. The revolutionaries had praised him for the model of republican citizenship he both formulated and illustrated, yet beneath the concerted attacks of anti-Jacobinism, the Catholic revival, and royalist restoration the fortunes of Rousseau did not fare well.[59] The simplest approach for the critic or literary historian was to discount the author of the *Contrat social* as a leading instigator of the Revolution. Sainte-Beuve was well aware of the difficulty before him. "The present moment is not particularly favorable for Rousseau, who is charged with being the author and the instigator of many of the ills from which we are suffering."[60] His strategy will be to identify a more tractable image of the philosophe. Lumping together Diderot and Rousseau, he writes:

Diderot and Rousseau, these inconsistent powers, contained great and beautiful forms of inspiration; they opened up magnificent insights onto the soul and nature around us. But they also took pleasure in unleashing the shadows. They're a disordered sort, and their company is unhealthy. Reason becomes inflated and the heart disturbed; they provide no healing solution.[61]

Wary of the shadowy disorder Rousseau is accused of having unleashed, Sainte-Beuve sets out to rehabilitate him by proposing a way out of the political reading. Directing attention to Rousseau the writer and not the political theorist, and invoking the imaginary construct of a non-political language, Sainte-Beuve aims to preserve the esthetic from the political. Clearly these two categories cannot remain unproblematically distinct for long, and certainly not in the case of Rousseau.[62] But Sainte-Beuve proceeds as if unaware of such issues, laboring valiantly to enclose the esthetic with a kind of protective *cordon sanitaire*. Consequently, the Rousseau of the *Causeries* is the author of the *Confessions* and not the *Contrat social*, *Emile* or any other political text. Sainte-Beuve's Rousseau is Rousseau the writer, "the writer who [wrought the greatest transformation since Pascal upon] the pure, delicate, and unemphatic language, marked by fluidity and ease, that the late seventeenth century handed over in part to the eighteenth."[63] Rousseau is "the best prepared writer to express with fresh vigor and an energetic logic the churning mix of ideas that sought to emerge."[64] Possessing an "unpolished accent" and "an earthy coarseness," Rousseau nevertheless regenerated the French language and made it into the instrument for expressing humanity's true feelings. But if such is the case, and if Rousseau's most lasting work of civilizing morality is to be found in his lyric writings, why read the *Contrat social*, *Emile*, or "Discours sur l'inégalité"? Why indeed? might respond Sainte-Beuve, who separates the thinker from the writer in a move that evacuates the political from literature as well as from the kind of literary history Sainte-Beuve proposed be written following the resurgence of the political in 1848.

An equally difficult case is that of Diderot. But which Diderot? The publishing history of his works alone reveals the author's ongoing and essentially belated construction during the nineteenth century. Explaining what texts were read but not how they were read, these material factors do not tell the whole story. In Sainte-Beuve's case, reading (Diderot) is an allegorical, self-identicatory process. The Diderot that Sainte-Beuve treats is not the philosopher, novelist, playwright or polemicist, but rather the salonnier, the art critic of the *Salons*. To be sure, Diderot may have been an atheist and a materialist, but this is a matter Sainte-Beuve finds too delicate and thorny to take up. What attracts his gaze instead is the image of the critic, an image in which Sainte-Beuve sees himself mirrored: "if the *Encyclopédie* was the principal social work of Diderot in his time and moment, his principal accomplishment for us today is that he was the creator of emotive, zealous, and eloquent criticism."[65] One always receives the imaginary forebears one desires, at least once is revealed the work of desire in writing the text of the past. The eighteenth century Sainte-Beuve sees before him in Diderot's texts, and those of innumerable other writers, is one that is both dangerous and attractive.

We have other, more familiar images of these writers today. Does this mean that we are finally able to read Diderot, Rousseau, and other eighteenth-century writers as belonging to an Enlightenment past that no longer haunts our present and that we can safely remember? Or is remembering, because of the uncanny connections it makes, ever a totally safe enterprise? Does remembering the Enlightenment not open up the space of an unsettling questioning? We certainly do not read Diderot as he was read during the nineteenth century. He is no longer viewed through the prism of the Revolution and its avatars, appropriated or reviled by one camp or the other, used as the ideological screen upon which politically motivated power struggles between monarchists, Jacobins, clerics, and republicans are played out. As literary scholars and cultural historians, we can take no small amount of solace in this change of perspective that modern literary history affords, and with it a supposed exteriority from the ideological.

Yet a gnawing doubt must haunt this belief in the emancipation from the ideological. Can we be so certain we have freed ourselves entirely from identificatory readings in general, such as they are found even in the more equitable and less caricatural nineteenth-century readings of Sainte-Beuve, Nodier, or Michelet, readers who succeed in finding themselves in the past they conjure up? To put this question in its most pointed form, does not historical understanding consist of projecting a present onto a past, a project that occurs in the very act that introjects the past into the present and thereby makes both past and present knowable through their relation? This is the constitutive tension of history itself, the discipline whose practice materializes in one and the same act the way a society is joined with its past, all the while striving to separate itself from that past.[66] If we are to evaluate this complex and conflictual relation to the eighteenth century, it can be by situating it in the larger context of emergent social discourses in the subsequent present of the nineteenth century, the present constructed by literary history in such sites as the university, the school textbook, and the newspaper. These are discursive sites, yet they are memory sites as well, where discursive mechanisms producing a complicated and at times contested cultural memory are at work. Analyzing the workings of these mechanisms is one way to begin the longer, indeed interminable process of analyzing the practices and pressures, the drives and power plays, that shape our own present construction of the eighteenth-century past.

CHAPTER 7

Commemorating Enlightenment: bringing out the dead, belatedly

One of a society's most telling traits is the complex and fascinated relation it entertains with death. That relation can be understood in psychocultural terms, as defining what French historiography would call the underlying *mentalité* of a period, a collective psychic structuring principle.[1] In nineteenth-century France, the relation to death is intensely cultivated, producing a cult of death that cuts across social classes and geographic regions. One factor among many that shape this cult is a political culture marked by what Avner Ben-Amos calls a "necromantic" tradition of French republicanism. Beginning with the French Revolution and the ritualistic killing of the king, marked by an inflationary spiral of death during the Terror, the republican tradition entertains "an infatuation with and a feeling of close intimacy with death."[2] That intimacy will be voiced repeatedly throughout the nineteenth century, as the inaugural story of violent beginnings is told and retold in histories, novels, plays, and memoirs. It will also be staged in the numerous state funerals and other commemorative exercises organized during the Second Empire and Third Republic. Whether these commemorative events served to integrate some groups within the national union or to exclude others, they remembered the dead in order to forge living memory and thereby promote a shared civic identity. Tradition was being invented in these events that brought the dead out, but symbolically, theatrically, performatively, in order to create a past that could engender a future in which a disruptive relation to the dead could be contained.

This cultural-historical perspective recalls Sigmund Freud's view that a ritualistic killing of the father lies at the center of the totemistic rituals of early societies, followed by an attempt on the part of murderous sons to atone for this disruptive violence. Freud takes this paternal postmortem moment, which Juliet MacCannell has called "the regime of the brother," as emblematic of how collective order is instituted.[3] Through attempts at commemorative atonement that take the form of religion and law, community is produced, a communal relation between subjects founded on a symbolic relation to a dead father who, as Freud notes, "[becomes] stronger than the living one had been."[4] An absent dead father occupies a central structuring position in the practices and discourses that order society and generate the social bond.

For Michel de Certeau, one such practice is historiography, a way of writing (about) the dead. In the historiographic operation, death is that absent other, that other absence, an ultimate alterity that can be given only in representation and through stand-ins. Absolute negativity, death marks the fact that "something has been lost that will not return." Viewed in its relation to that loss, "historiography is a contemporary form of mourning. Its writing is based on an absence and produces nothing but simulacra, however scientific they may be. It offers representation in the place of bereavement."[5] It is in representation, through fundamentally mournful symbolic work, that knowledge of the past is produced, knowledge that constitutes 'fraternal' subjects bound to one another in the present. French historiography of the nineteenth century is shaped by the need to find ways to perform this mournful symbolic work, to move beyond the fear and denial of melancholia to the expression of sublated mourning. What of the Enlightenment in this process?

The wager of this chapter and the next is that the 'influence' or the 'reception' of the Enlightenment in nineteenth-century France cannot be understood solely in intellectual-historical terms, reduced to the story of how one set of ideas wins out over others. The intellectual-historical narrative of an increasingly rational and progressive social, political, and ethical order, despite all the good sense it makes, may well be one of the mournful simulacra to which de Certeau refers. Perhaps the narrative of progress is nothing so much as a highly abstract way to rejoin the absent past and redeem it through the affirmation of our modernity. If so, we will need not to deny this work of mourning but rather to engage in it explicitly, in order to see how the Enlightenment past attains representation and acquires a symbolic place in the historical, national, cultural narrative of France. Through a fine-grained analysis of the working of the cultural imaginary, this chapter and the next propose ways of thinking through an engagement with the Enlightenment past, first by tracing Diderot's belatedness in nineteenth-century France, and second by analyzing 'the Voltaire effect'. The ultimate question resulting from these analyses concerns what a contemporary (and explicitly critical) relation to that past might be at present.

"Do you think, my friend, that posterity will like me?"
                    Diderot writing to Falconet, December 4, 1765

On July 30, 1884, on a square in Paris off Saint-Germain-des-Prés, a ceremony was held to honor the memory of Denis Diderot.[6] Present at this centennial celebration of the philosophe's death were leaders of the Société positiviste (who had organized the two-day event), members of the *Conseil municipal*, senators and deputies (including Georges Clemenceau), representatives of Masonic lodges, and students from the *Ecole technique Diderot*. The festivities had begun two days earlier with a grand event at the Trocadéro attended by some 3,000 persons. The purpose of the smaller outdoor gathering of July 30 was to unveil a statue of Diderot, sculpted by Jean Gautherin and still visible in the same location in Paris today. The selection of the boulevard Saint-Germain site seems rather unmotivated. Other sites were symbolically stronger. Earlier in the century Sainte-Beuve had suggested that a statue to honor Diderot the critic-artist, author of the *Salons*, be placed in front of the Ecole des Beaux-Arts. Others had proposed that the editor of the *Encyclopédie*, this precursor of 'industrialism', should be 'statufied' across from the Conservatoire des Arts et Métiers. The Société positiviste finally opted for the Saint-Germain-des-Prés location, which at least had in its favor its proximity to the former rue Taranne, where Diderot had lived. No site in the urban landscape is completely unmotivated, though, utterly devoid of symbolic meaning. So it might be noted that Gautherin's statue was erected a stone's throw away from the place de l'Odéon, site of another statue commemorating the revolutionary Danton, with whom Diderot, somewhat phantasmatically and obsessionally, had been associated earlier in the century.[7]

The commemorative event of 1884 was accompanied by numerous official speeches whose function might now seem merely decorative and ultimately ephemeral. Yet these speeches performed the essentially symbolic work of commemoration, giving meaning to the great man whose memory posterity had preserved, expressing the values according to which posterity was honoring him. These speeches thus served as a screen onto which the image of the great man was projected, a discursive Jumbotron. Represented there was not so much Diderot as his image, and not only an image of Diderot shaped by his commemorators, but that present moment itself, caught in the act of creating itself through its (re)creation of a past. We might wonder whether any commemorative act can function otherwise, as if all commemoration were inflected by a desire for self-definition and the production of identity.

The story of that desire has been told in political-historical terms. All of the numerous commemorative events held during the Third Republic's seventy-year existence can be understood according to the republican struggle for legitimacy against a monarchist and clerical right. This struggle was the prism through which the centennial celebration of the 1789 Revolution was given to be viewed, as was the double centennial celebration of Rousseau's and Voltaire's death in 1878.[8] Although Diderot's centennial too was determined by similar political objectives, its republican message was inflected by its organizers' desire to affirm the political and ideological primacy of nineteenth-century positivism. In his *Catéchisme positiviste* of 1852, Auguste Comte had already praised "the great and immortal school of Diderot," whose legacy was emancipation from both politics and religion. This freedom, claimed Comte, made it possible to imagine reorganizing society, not so much through the Revolution as through positivism and the "regeneration of the West" it would bring about.[9] Positivism represented a way to theorize the 'reconstruction' of society. The lineage of Diderot, David Hume, and Condorcet, Comte's own "essential precursor," provided the nineteenth-century positivist with an historical and intellectual narrative that served as a bridge back to an Enlightenment that could, he suggested, be erected to resist the ravages of the Revolution.

In mobilizing Diderot, the Société positiviste sought to do just that, essentially bypassing the Revolution and thus short-circuiting the endlessly repetitive debate over its causes and effects, including the nationalistic turn that debate had taken following the French defeat by Prussia in 1870. Of passing interest is the invitation the Société extended to Ludwig Büchner on the occasion of the unveiling of Diderot's statue in July 1886. Younger brother of the German playwright Georg Büchner, Ludwig Büchner was a fairly controversial champion of atheistic materialism, and publication of his *Kraft und Stoff* (*Force and Matter*) in 1855 had led to his forced resignation from the University of Tübingen. The image of Diderot that Büchner sketches is not an unfamiliar one.

> Diderot is not only one of the famous men of France, he is claimed by all the friends of unfettered scientific investigation and freethinking, whatever their language or their country. Diderot is the cosmopolitan man of science and free thought; it was for the entire world that he wrote and lived! ... Henceforth, nothing can subtract from his glory, not even the insults of the eternal enemies of all progress.[10]

In the reference to the "eternal enemies of all progress" we can hear the muffled echoes of the intense debates that had marked the 1884 centennial, along with all the other republican centennials of prior years.[11] Büchner's goal is to free Diderot from those debates, to depoliticize his image in the name of a cosmopolitanism whose objective is unfettered scientific and philosophical inquiry. Büchner's Diderot was a precursor of French positivism; more important, though, he embodied a cosmopolitan Enlightenment, which Büchner suggests can be understood only by overcoming the particularity of a constrictive nationalism. In (re)turning to this Enlightenment, the German academic attempts to preserve Diderot for the world by saving him from French history, encouraging his French listeners to transcend their national particularity (the 'glory of France') and view it instead as belonging to a properly universal intellectual history.

Büchner's Diderot hearkens back to the image of the philosopher that Diderot himself had sketched in the character of Moi in *Le Neveu de Rameau*, the selfless philosopher striving for the betterment of humanity under the banner of the Enlightenment project. The image contains nothing of the shortcomings and blind spots exposed in Moi by the text's other character, Lui, who thereby reveals the internal contradictions of Moi's ethical position. For above all, Büchner's Diderot is designed to counterbalance an image of Diderot painted and constantly retouched by Diderot's adversaries throughout the nineteenth century, an image that resembles nothing so much as Lui, Rameau's nephew seen in all his turpitude. Writing in 1763 in *Les Trois Siècles de littérature française*, for instance, *abbé* Antoine Sabatier de Castres portrays Diderot in the following terms: "inaccurate writer, unfaithful translator, brazen metaphysician, dangerous moralist, bad geometer, mediocre physicist, overly emotional philosopher, and finally a writer who authored many works even if we cannot say we have one good book from him." De Castres continues, accusing Diderot of being someone who is tempted by "intemperate ideas, [claims to] announce truth in fits of delirium, [makes] reason bellow like a rowdy, [casts forth] gigantic maxims, [combats] received feelings, [adorns himself with] pride that is more burlesque than philosophical."[12] The family resemblance between Diderot the philosopher and his character Lui is uncanny. Ironically, it is as if this dialogical text ventriloquized a response to the accusations of persons like de Castres, responding through the Nephew's response to Moi's accusations of immorality, "I believe I told you that."

De Castres could not have known Diderot's text in 1763, when *Les Trois Siècles* was written, and probably not either in 1778, when his literary history was reprinted. Thus the full impact of de Castres's disparaging portrait was felt only belatedly, once it was known that Diderot authored *Le Neveu de Rameau*. Reading Diderot is always an exercise in belatedness, however much one might wish to deny that interpretive temporality. Such was the wish of a certain Eusèbe Salverte, who spoke in praise of Diderot at the Institut de France in 1800. Seeking to free Diderot's image from the polemics of the revolution, Salverte invoked a "unanimous chorus of praise" for the philosophe. Posterity began late for Diderot, said Salverte, yet he claimed that by 1800 it had begun.[13] Numerous reception histories have amply demonstrated that Salverte's belief was wishful thinking, and that his retrospective assessment of a belated posterity would turn out to be a prognosis of an ongoing deferral.[14] For throughout the nineteenth century and into the next, posterity would continue to begin late for Diderot, both within France's borders and beyond.[15]

This belatedness may be the author's inevitable fate, due not so much to ungrateful readers and critics but rather, as Michel Foucault has argued, to the nature of authorship in general and the way it is constructed by the discipline and epistemology of literary history.[16] To be sure, material factors impinge on the belated construction of the author 'Diderot', and most notably the publishing history of his writing. That history is a particularly complicated one, and its story has been told elsewhere.[17] Certain of its elements should be recalled, however. At the time of his death in 1784, Diderot was known mainly for his association with the *Encyclopédie* and as the author of *Le Père de famille*. The existence of his earlier more philosophical writing (the *Pensées philosophiques*, *De l'interprétation de la nature*, and the letters on the blind and on deaf-mutes) was known, yet these texts' impact was eclipsed by misattributions of authorship, which associated Diderot with Morelly's *Code de la nature*, for instance, an error that endured for long. The texts that designate our 'modern' understanding of Diderot – including *Le Neveu de Rameau*, the *Supplément au voyage de Bougainville*, *Jacques le fataliste*, and the *Salons* – were not widely known during Diderot's lifetime. Editions of his texts would stretch over a century, with that of Naigeon (1798), Brière (1821), Paulin (1830), Assézat-Tourneux (1875), and finally the DPV edition begun in 1975. Individual texts also appeared throughout the nineteenth century. Publication of the *Salons*, for instance, contributed to producing a more 'esthetic', Romantic Diderot, in whom Sainte-Beuve saw the first modern critic (and his own precursor). The most celebrated example of Diderot's belated construction is certainly the publication of *Le Neveu de Rameau*, which only appeared in France after being published in Germany in a translation done by Johan Wolfgang von Goethe. Diderot became 'Diderot' not only late but after the fact, *après coup*.

If this reception history is to be understood as symbolic cultural construction, it cannot be enough simply to catalogue what texts of Diderot were available to be read, when, and by whom. Far more interpretive pressure must be brought to bear on a larger and more complex cultural field in order to understand just how these various texts could be read. One of the immediate results of raising this hermeneutic question is that it leads us to consider how the story of Diderot's belated becoming is woven into another violent and contested narrative of becoming, that involving the construction of a national, republican French identity.

Unlike Rousseau and Voltaire, Diderot hardly figures in the highly charged political debates that mark the revolutionary period of 1789–95.[18] Following Thermidor and the downfall of the Jacobins, when counter-revolutionary opposition becomes more open and extensive, Diderot's name acquires greater significance. Such figures as Antoine Rivarol and Augustin Barruel develop the explanatory notion of a revolutionary conspiracy, a plot to overthrow society concocted by the philosophes (including Diderot), the Freemasons, and other 'illuminés'. This conspiratorial logic continues throughout the Napoleonic era and into the Restoration, when proponents of a restored monarchy and a reestablished state Catholicism mount fierce opposition to what they see as a free-thinking, atheistic, and materialist Enlightenment. In Hugues-Félicité Robert de Lamennais, for instance, or in François-René de Chateaubriand's *Génie du christianisme*, eighteenth-century writers are allegorized and demonized, symbols of political and moral positions to be stoutly resisted. Partisans of Restoration institutions of order view the publication of eighteenth-century philosophes' works as a threatening political act.[19] The appearance of some of Diderot's more important works, previously either unknown or not widely circulated, does begin to modify his often virulently negative image. His materialism will continue to be problematic, the least easily assimilable element of his writing which must either be overlooked or rigorously cordoned off from the rest of his thought. Michelet and Louis Blanc see in Diderot the historical precursor of new times; Sainte-Beuve and Baudelaire praise Diderot the art critic; and Balzac and Stendhal view him as master of the short story.

During the nineteenth century, more recognizable images of Diderot begin to take shape, images that resemble more closely our present-day reception of Diderot. It would be simplistic, though, to conclude that writers and critics slowly began to get Diderot 'right' following a long series of benighted readings that had gotten him 'wrong', due to the polemical, political, and ideologically motivated use to which his texts were put. These images of Diderot, and of the eighteenth century more generally, can be assessed more productively, both intrinsically and in relation to the larger cultural context to which they belong. But it is not certain that past readings can be evaluated according to an unquestioned interpretive superiority of our modern understanding of Diderot – which one might wish to view as based on the 'scientific' nature of the finally established dependable corpus or on the putative ideological neutrality of the discipline of literary studies. Instead, we can return to those sometimes quaint, antiquated readings and the image of the eighteenth century they convey in order to see how Diderot was – and continues to be – pressed into service to bring that modernity about, or at least to represent it and make it legible.

Thus, it must be remembered that in the tumultuous political climate of nineteenth-century France, where aftershocks of the Revolution continued to be felt, no reference to any aspect of the eighteenth century could remain neutral. Particular writers implicitly signified political perspectives, and reference to their name alone was a way to encode polemical positions.[20] The discourse on literature became a politicized discourse, and the criteria used to classify authors and texts belonged not to an autonomous esthetic field (if such a thing exists) but to an emerging, dynamic political field. The experience of literature became an identificatory one, as the text was pressed into service to designate subjects and groups in nineteenth-century society, whether they were named romantic, socialist, revolutionary, republican or bourgeois. Reading literature became part of the same identificatory practice, involved in the cultural construction of historically specific subjectivity. The nineteenth-century reception history of Diderot can be seen as a long series of reductions, annexations, and mimetic interpretations – in short, as ideologically determined readings. But what exactly did it mean to 'read' literature during this period? What reading practice was involved in producing these images of Diderot? Did the reception process constitute reading as the term is understood in a more contemporary sense? More problematically, what exactly was the 'literature' that was 'read'? How are we to characterize the emergent notion of literature, considered especially in its relation to the social and to history? How might the story we are telling of Diderot's belated reception help us understand the construction of that notion of literature? These are capacious questions. To consider one set of critical issues to which they point, let me propose one select angle: the narrative of literary history and the privileged site of its deployment, the classroom.

Roland Barthes has suggested that what defines literature as such, its essential trait, is that it is taught as literature.[21] Following Barthes, and historicizing this insightful tautology, one could argue that only in the nineteenth century does literature become literature, a pedagogical object supported by an extensive textual, discursive, and institutional apparatus. One way to understand the stakes of the debate over Diderot's reception in nineteenth-century France is by examining his place in this process of literature's becoming. How does Diderot become 'Diderot', a historical figure who is transformed into a sign, one signifying element inscribed in the larger narrative of France, its literature, and their mutually affirmative connection? As we have seen, key elements of this process are located in the assessments of individual literary critics, writers, and historians. Yet we also need to return to the countless literary histories, manuals, anthologies, and *aides-mémoire* that were produced for use in the schools and the university of post-Napoleonic France. Dismissed as no more than pedagogical ephemera, these all but forgotten texts freighted powerful values and did massive cultural work in the nineteenth century. Just as the peasants of rural France were turned into Frenchmen, through a process Eugen Weber has elegantly analyzed, so too the nineteenth-century French state school was the institutional site where French children were turned into republican citizens.[22] The textual supports of that site were far from inconsequential. Through the pedagogical practice they enable, these literary histories and anthologies represented cultural memory and present values, thereby instituting the identity of the republic nation as it was constructing itself.

These histories, anthologies, and manuals performed several culturally crucial functions. They "condense the choices of a society and the image that the latter claims to produce for itself of its own past. They transmit images and stereotypes, the expressions of this society and the values it intends to safeguard and promote."[23] These scholastic texts were designed to produce a mnemonic understanding of literature as something collectively remembered rather than as a source of individual reflection. But this collective memory was won at the expense of the text itself, for the text as an object that required interpretation was ultimately made to disappear. Through their organization and treatment, these scholastic texts produced the impression of an artificial clarity, implying that interpretation needed to be a process of thinking, speaking, and writing that aimed for a monological view of things. Removed from consideration were all alternative and conflicting interpretations. These scholastic texts presented authors or works in reductive fashion, in terms of generally accepted dominant characteristics. Aimed at youth, these manuals also sought to win the confidence of parents by presenting impersonal generalities and conformist points of view. These works were careful not to separate the question of literature from that of morality, but the morality expressed by literature was one that rocked no boats, for the criterion for judging a work's literary quality was consistently presented as the manner in which the work defended the established order.[24] If, as Stuart Hall has remarked, "identities are the names we give to the different ways we are positioned by, and position ourselves in, the narratives of the past," then these histories, anthologies, and manuals offered a powerfully effective way for French educational culture to promote this identity formation.[25]

In the literary manuals produced during the July Monarchy that brought Louis-Philippe to power in 1830, Diderot was largely ignored. Indeed, as one might imagine, the entire eighteenth century was viewed far less favorably than the conservative and Christian seventeenth century,[26] which is the profile the *grand siècle* came to acquire. During the Second Empire and Third Republic, however, Diderot did receive a certain attention in the manuals, almost all of it hostile. His materialism, his atheism, his populism, and increasingly his 'Germanic' character came under relentless criticism. (It was Sainte-Beuve who first called Diderot "the most German of our brows.") Reductive and repetitive to the point of being self-parasitic, these now mostly forgotten schoolbooks from the outset were palimpsests, produced for a rapidly expanding scholastic system in need of texts to prop up the cultural values it aimed to inculcate. One hears in these literary manuals the muffled echo of earlier treatments, such as that of La Harpe, for instance, whose *Lycée, ou Cours de littérature ancienne et moderne* of 1786 contains extensive commentary on Diderot, but is designed to serve as a springboard from which to launch a devastating critique of this materialist instigator of the Revolution. La Harpe's influence will continue to be felt well into the nineteenth century in the accounts of literary historians such as Abel-François Villemain, Eugène-Nicolas Geruzez, Désiré Nisard, and Alexandre Vinet (to say nothing of later virulent critics of the Enlightenment such as Emile Faguet and Ferdinand Brunetière).[27]

This intensely hostile assessment of Diderot and the eighteenth century began to lose credence and interpretive legitimacy towards the end of the nineteenth century. A more familiar image of Diderot emerges, one resembling his present-day reading. To explain the appearance of this 'new' Diderot, one might point to the prestige of individual partisans of the philosophes such as Auguste Comte and his positivist followers (including Diderot's editors Jules Assézat and Maurice Tourneux, authors of the scholarly edition of the complete works that would last a century, and Emile Littré, known for his influential dictionary that freighted more of the Enlightenment message than might be suspected of a simple dictionary), as well as the literary historian Gustave Lanson, who quite explicitly preferred the eighteenth century over the seventeenth. For a century or so, we have been able to read Diderot as belonging to the Enlightenment, that is, as an integral part of a past moment that no longer haunts our present because that present has succeeding in accommodating the past in the narrative of modern becoming.

It is entirely plausible to tell the story of Diderot's nineteenth-century reception by invoking a political narrative of dualistic and conflictual oppositions, such as Jacobin vs. royalist, materialist vs. catholic, philosopher vs. writer, to say nothing of 'premodern' vs. 'scientific' literary history. Nevertheless, it must be noted that the justificatory logic underwriting these oppositions is a component of that explanatory narrative itself. The struggle for political power in the nineteenth century was also a narrative struggle for the authority to relate the past, both struggles involving competing versions of events and experience. In attempting to explain this conflictual situation, we must be cautious not to rely unquestioningly upon the narrative that won out, namely, the narrative of progress, liberalism, and republicanism – in short, the narrative of state history – together with the view of literature it required to support it. In taking over that narrative unquestioningly, we risk explaining Diderot's becoming 'modern' in tautological fashion, by invoking and relying unself-reflexively upon a notion of literary history that is the outcome of precisely the process we wish to understand. To explain Diderot's becoming 'modern', we must view the cultural practice that produces this becoming through lenses other than the ones that these practices themselves hold up for use. One of these lenses is that of literary history, such as it was being reconfigured by massive institutional and disciplinary transformations taking place in the French university between 1875 and 1914.

As Antoine Compagnon has shown, the most significant of these transformations is the reconfiguration of the relation between history and literature in the French university of the time.[28] The theoretical underpinnings for this disciplinary change were provided above all by Gustave Lanson, professor at the Sorbonne, director of the Ecole normale supérieure, and author of *Histoire de la littérature française* (1894). History, argued Lanson, must achieve the status of a science, possessing its own rigorous methodology and capable of providing positive, factual knowledge. For history to attain that new status, historiography no longer could be thought of as a literary genre, determined more by rhetoric than by factual truth. History must break from literature, and historians must free themselves from their own Romantic and novelistic prehistory.[29] Literature, too, must break from literature, just as history should, for the study of literature to become a true discipline, subject to the same 'scientific' and methodological imperatives as the discipline of history. This at least is the critique made of 'lansonisme' and its historicizing imperative, which Lanson's critics believe will inject an empiricism into the study of literature that cannot adequately account for the latter's esthetic dimension. For the 'new' literary historian, excessive attention to the esthetic could lead only to impressionistic criticism (which Lanson found to inflect the writings of his teacher, Ferdinand Brunetière).

This disciplinary reconfiguration of the relation between literature and history was not the result of a Parisian theory tempest in a closed, academic teapot. For it signaled an explicit rethinking of the role literature should play in the university curriculum of the Third Republic and, by extension, the function of the university in the larger, post-1870 social order. Lanson's aim was to rescue literary instruction from the insignificance to which it would be consigned so long as it presented literature as a repository of models of esthetic taste and rhetorical style. As Compagnon notes, concerning the literary teaching that Lanson rejected, "essentially directed towards rhetoric and its supreme exercise, discourse, it could produce only novelists, lawyers, journalists, and in this sense it reproduced the class of word-makers, in other words the bourgeoisie."[30] For Lanson, that way of teaching literature only reproduced the bourgeois social order, which he viewed as antidemocratic, selective, and elitist. Instead, literature should be taught in such a way as to bring about a new social order, by providing what Lanson calls "civic education" in order to produce "free citizens." By modeling the study of literature on that of history, literary study will engender a new intellectual, moral, and civic consciousness, better in tune with the imperatives of Third Republic ideals. "The historical study of literary works," writes Lanson, "... will have communicated the deep and beneficial sense of the relative, in other words the effort that is always necessary in a world that always changes."[31] What is needed in a changing world, realizes Lanson, is not just a changed curriculum, revised and brought up to date, but rather one that makes the process of change comprehensible and moreover desirable, a curriculum in short that valorizes the eighteenth century. "It is absurd to make use only of a royalist and christian literature for education to educate a democracy that does not allow a state religion," writes Lanson, adding that from the writers of the age of Louis XIV – Boileau, Racine, La Fontaine, Mme. de Sévigné – "not one iota of patriotic or social thought is to be gotten." The eighteenth century, on the other hand, has much to offer.

We recognize in this age the origins of the intellectual and social order in which we are living. We recognize the sentiments that are still today the driving forces of our actions. Voltaire, Montesquieu, Diderot, Rousseau, and Buffon are nearer to us and instruct our children to receive our legacy and to continue our efforts better than Bossuet and Racine do.[32]

Viewed through the phenomenon of 'lansonisme', what seemed initially in this chapter to be the belated construction of Diderot's image in nineteenth-century France now helps us understand republican culture's valorization of the eighteenth century at the turn of the nineteenth. Lanson's rehabilitation of the eighteenth century is thus part of a far larger process. Taken in charge by a national education system shaped by the Jules Ferry reforms, the texts of the past become the literature of the nation. French literature becomes French, the repository of narratives through and in relation to which subjects will (learn to) phrase their individual and collective identity. We can certainly understand this process in empirical, socio-institutional terms. In regard to literature itself, however, in other words the idea of literature that is produced in the late nineteenth century, this moment is one in which literature takes shape as such and becomes entwined with history, thinkable in terms of a certain historical process. In schools, disciplinary reconfigurations will present literature not as an instance of language, but as a distinct entity, as students are given to study not "elements of the French language" but "language and French literature" as an official program of study in 1882 puts it.[33] Presented in its canonical form, literature will be presented to be experienced through the lens of literary history, not only as the literature of a nation in its historical dimension but also as the 'becoming-literature' of writing, a 'pure' literature that ultimately aims to transcend the historical. Literary scholars have revealed the resulting collusion between the literary and the national, as they expose the many ways in which the literary text remains inescapably marked by its inscription in multiple geopolitical contexts. But why has that problematic relation become visible now? Denis Hollier has suggested that we no longer live in an age of literariness, in which identity, values, and thought are phrased in relation to literature. Instead, ours is the age of "postliteracy," claims Hollier, in which literature "has been mapped back onto the national, but only after the national itself has been disaffected, defamiliarized, invested with a simulacral dimension."[34] It is because we no longer believe in a literariness that could be safe from the intrusions of history that we see there the marks of nationalities.

But this turn of events was not perceived in late nineteenth-century France. Through the institutions of literary criticism, literary history, and historiography, the French cultural imaginary was the space in which the relation to the past was both acted out and worked through, in the move from an obsessive repetition of that past to its symbolic commemoration and its pedagogical institutionalization in the French university.[35] Beyond the singular version of Diderot that the nineteenth century produced, its commemorative acts in a more general sense return France to its past, resuscitating its dead, in order to design a new present. Analyzing that process is doubtless always an exercise in belatedness. Consequently, my objective in this chapter and in this book has not been to update some very complete and valuable reception studies of the Enlightenment, for they can never really be brought up to date, given that reception is an ongoing act and thus an always already belated one. The *état* of literary knowledge is never *présent*. Perhaps all one can do is take the measure of that belatedness, seeking to make explicit the historical impulse of reading by striving for ways to make explicit the linkages it performs between past and present. Besides aiming for a richer understanding of the complex cultural field upon which nineteenth-century commemorative and pedagogical acts are inscribed, we need to ask what there is to be learned of our own relation to that eighteenth-century past by considering the commemorative practice of earlier readers.

In a doubly belated way, we can return to the nineteenth-century return to the eighteenth century in order to reflect on our own relation to author, literature, history, and community. Are we (finally) the posterity that the eighteenth century deserves, the posterity Diderot so ardently desired? If so, is it because the modern institution of literature and literary history has succeeded in developing methods of textual interpretation, bolstered by pedagogical practices and research agendas, that refuse in the last instance to serve ideological ends? Or is every 'image' of the eighteenth century and its writers, every reading of these texts of the past, not mediated by the desires of its producers, shaped by forces and vectors located in the present that must be articulated as well? Finally, moving from one turn of the century to another, can the eighteenth century still serve as a way of understanding cultural change and modernization as Lanson believed it could in the French university of the early twentieth century?

CHAPTER 8

The Voltaire effect

In contemporary media-infused society, the cultural significance of writers may seem limited to glittery fame, if not mere transitory notoriety. Yet the case of Voltaire tests this skeptical view of the writer's importance in society and of literature's value more generally. In his own time, Voltaire enjoyed a literary significance that extended well beyond fame, both in France and among Europe's lettered elite. The best-known living writer in the eighteenth century, 'the patriarch of Ferney' would live on during the next two centuries, as a deeply haunting presence in France's collective cultural memory. Repeatedly, Voltaire's name was invoked in the pitched battles over the contested meaning of France's past and the direction of its future. Referred to more often than read, Voltaire acquired a cultural significance that was often decoupled from the philosophe's works themselves. The name 'Voltaire' became a token or signifier, a telegraphic way of staking claims, phrasing values, and intervening in the political arena. Voltaire's influence can certainly be understood as the legacy of engaged, liberal, reformist writing of the eighteenth century. But it must also be seen as having been generated through 'the Voltaire effect', in the auratic afterlife of a culturally iconic figure.

Whether that afterlife is in its end-stages will remain to be seen. But we do know that afterlife begins as a double life, resulting from the way a writer fashions himself or herself as an author. Michel Foucault's theoretical reflection on what constitutes an author has been especially helpful in understanding authorship as a fundamentally discursive effect, the 'author function' characterizing how certain forms of language exist, circulate, and function within a given society.[1] Foucault's idea of the discursively constructed author implies a break with other, more ontologically grounded notions of author, authorship, and authority. In other words he announces the negation or 'death' of one kind of author in order to examine, in this short essay and throughout his writing, the emergence of another relation to writing and to subjectivity, a relation that is hauntingly modern. Scholars of the early modern period have explored the question of authorship in ways that are resonant, although not always consistent, with Foucault's analysis. Their work reflects, in rough terms, two positions concerning the question of authorship and agency. On the one hand, eighteenth-century writers are seen to enjoy increasing freedom to fashion themselves as authors, independent agents who are no longer strictly bound to a courtly patronage system, and able to benefit from new laws and practices concerning literary property that let them at least aspire to increased economic and intellectual autonomy. The figure of this new author is that of the *homme de lettres*, created in the conjuncture of a modernizing literary market and political system.[2] On the other hand, that autonomy can be seen to be more illusory oftentimes than real. Robert Darnton's exploration of "the literary underground" in the late eighteenth century shows that the market did not emancipate writers but rather exploited and marginalized them, foreshadowing a notion of authorship that would be more closely experienced by the alienated, anti-bourgeois writer of the nineteenth century.[3] A more democratic political culture might have freed writers from the system of privileges that characterized the *Ancien Régime*, with its academies, salons, guilds, and pensions, but the literary market system imprisoned them all the more with another logic of authorship involving systems of production, ownership rights, value, commercial exchange, and finally identity.[4]

Both views of authorship can help us understand how such eighteenth-century writers as Rousseau, Diderot, and Beaumarchais, as well as the largely forgotten hack writers of the low Enlightenment, came to view themselves as authors, and how they struggled, some more than others, to have themselves viewed as authors and to have their works read as the creation of authors. The following pages explore that process of becoming an author in the case of Voltaire. To tell that story in all its rich complexity, though, would require at least another book. Fortunately, we have such fine-grained accounts of Voltaire, on which I shall rely. But the larger arc of the story I want to tell follows the construction of authorial identity as it moves from writer to reader, and from texts that historically become separated from their producer and, in a postmortem afterlife, acquire a larger cultural and symbolic function. The question of authorship to be examined here through the case of Voltaire, his 'effect', involves once again the cultural construction of the past as a way of scripting the authorized foundation of the present, a recovered memory that rests ultimately on a fraught dialectic of memory and oblivion.

Voltaire's fame as an author mixes literary celebrity, social critique, and political controversy. Early in his career his public skirmishes with church and government led to brief periods of imprisonment in the Bastille and exile from Paris, notably in England (1726–8). His *Lettres philosophiques* (1734) grew out of that experience, presenting an oblique yet highly critical view of France by praising England's promotion of religious tolerance, commerce, science, and personal freedom. Official response to the *Lettres philosophiques* was swift and tempestuous: the book's publisher was imprisoned and an arrest warrant was issued for its author, who prudently fled Paris for a time. (The book continued to be brought out in pirate editions, a highly successful yet risky enterprise; it soon disappeared from the market completely, yet was read throughout the century in partial, camouflaged versions.) Voltaire was allowed to return to Paris the following year, and with the protection of the powerful, including the *favorite* of Louis XV, Mme. de Pompadour, he negotiated a successful reentry into court life. His poetry earned him critical acclaim and comparison to Virgil, but perhaps not only for poetic reasons but propagandistic ones as well, given his poetry's celebration of French military exploits. But Voltaire's poetry could be sharply topical, as was the epic poem "La Henriade," which celebrated Henri IV and his efforts to end the wars of religion. Voltaire's neoclassical dramatic writing was immensely successful, with his twenty-seven tragedies and twelve comedies earning more for the Comédie Française than the plays of Corneille and Racine combined. Voltaire was also known as the author of historical works, including histories of the courts of Louis XIV and of Charles XII of Sweden. But histories were hardly the kind of writing with which a writer would achieve fame in the eighteenth century, when history-writing was considered only a step above fables commissioned by royal patrons. It was rather for his acts of social engagement that Voltaire would become especially well known – or notorious. He mounted several highly public letter-writing campaigns to obtain justice for victims of religious intolerance, such as the Calas family, and he wrote several works harshly critical of intolerance, including the *Traité sur la tolerance* (1763) and the *Dictionnaire philosophique* (1764).

In promoting the cause of reform, Voltaire was as indefatigable as he was canny. *Ecrasez l'infâme*, the phrase he began appending to his letters in the early 1760s, encapsulated the Enlightenment project of rooting out error, superstition, and intolerance by means of reasoned argument, common sense, and often a healthy dose of biting irony. Quickly becoming a battle cry, penned at the end of his letters in condensed, symbolic form as "ECRLINF," the phrase had preserved all its caustic energy when, a century or so later, Friedrich Nietzsche inserted it throughout his *Ecce homo*.

But in addition to all Voltaire did to advance reform (and to promote an image of himself in order to promote reform all the more effectively), he had the good fortune to have history on his side.[5] He represented the idealized, utopian figure of the writer-intellectual that numerous eighteenth-century writers were imagining and aiming to become, a figure described in his *Encyclopédie* article "Gens de lettres" as a more independent, freethinking, and socially useful individual, whose writing should be protected and promoted because it contributed to civilizing society. Besides Voltaire's literary and intellectual brilliance, there were material circumstances that made it possible for him to occupy that idealized position as well. His substantial wealth, amassed early on, granted him freedom from the patronage system and a certain distance from court life. He could enjoy the pleasures of civilized society without having to confront the disillusion, compromise, and alienation of materialist, bourgeois culture that the nineteenth-century writer would experience. He also embodied the engaged, sociable, and useful writer that liberal, reformist elements of French society were arguing was so necessary to France. During the reign of Louis XIV the 'great men' praised in state funeral orations, academic paintings, and official sculptures were kings and nobles. Voltaire criticized this official prestige-granting, just as he reproached Bossuet for having praised only the aristocratic great of the reign of Louis XIV and not Jean-Baptiste Colbert, the king's invaluable finance minister. During the eighteenth century, as the bourgeoisie became more central to state administration, they claimed due recognition for their services, arguing that other 'great men' should be accorded a place of honor in cultural memory for having served their nation by serving the state. "O memory! O names of the handful of men who served the state well," exclaims Voltaire in his funeral ode to the officers who died in 1741 in the War of the Austrian Succession. (It should be noted that the 'great men' of France would be joined by a woman, Marie Curie, only in 1995.)

It is one of literary history's ironies that Voltaire too would be made into an author who served the state well. During the following centuries his fame acquired a useful plasticity during the 'hot' moments of French history, these grand clashes of ideas and ideologies. But his fame was invoked during quieter moments as well, in micro-cultural practices such as the designing of school curricula and the erection of city monuments. Voltaire was overtaken by history almost as he entered it, recovered, made usable, and put to use, just as elements of the past in general are taken in hand to forge a present (or that surge up in a present trying to forget them). Voltaire remains 'a man and his works', a truly great writer who merits careful reading. But he surely also became an effect, a product of his readers (or his would-be readers). 'The Voltaire effect' resides in the relation between his texts and the cultural practices that gave meaning to them, acts such as reading, teaching, or commemoration that recover Voltaire's texts and thus establish (their) meaning in and for the present moment.

CONSTRUCTING AN AFTERLIFE

In 1778, at the age of eighty-four, Voltaire made a triumphant return to Paris from his estate in Ferney on the Swiss border. His brief stay in the capital before his death was a moment of celebration, an apotheosis that helped fix in cultural memory the image of the philosophe that would endure as synonymous with the Enlightenment. For some twenty years, the home of 'the patriarch of Ferney' was a destination point for grand tourists, and the 'visit to Voltaire' had become a literary sub-genre, exemplified by such writers as Casanova and Edward Gibbon. These visits were not without their theatrical side, and Voltaire cleverly staged his appearance before his guests to heighten the dramatic effect of the experience. (The ritual of a theatricalized visit to Ferney continues today, through to the guided tour, "Impression-Voltaire," offered by the local tourist bureau.)

Champion of tolerance, witty and acerbic polemicist, wise philosopher-hero portrayed most iconically in the marble sculpture Jean-Antoine Houdon exhibited in the Salon of 1781, Voltaire by the time of his death had become both a catalyst for liberal reform and a lightning rod for its opponents. He could play this role in no small measure because of the attention he paid to questions of authorship involving the publication and diffusion of his writings. Above all, it was the production, circulation, and reception of the Voltairean text – first poetry and theatre, then letters followed by the edited works – that produced the idea of Voltaire as a writer-author, and not just another person who wrote. His personal letters and his works were diffused throughout Europe. Written in an age known for its great letter-writers, the Voltairean correspondence remains staggering in numbers alone: some 15,300 letters still exist, from a correspondence that included over 1,500 readers. Across this vast epistolary network, Voltaire's letters were copied, circulated, and discussed, producing an identity that was known throughout Europe. The enterprise of writing resulted in creating a 'life' for Voltaire, who through his writing worked to achieve a cultural afterlife as well. He closely oversaw the production of various 'miscellanies', 'collections', and 'complete works of

M. Voltaire'. During his last years he helped prepare what would be the most complete edition of his works to date. Published across the Rhine from Strasbourg between 1783 and 1790, the posthumous Kehl edition had as its prime movers (in both an intellectual and a financial sense) Pierre de Beaumarchais and the marquis de Condorcet. The edition reached a remarkable seventy volumes in octavo format. Illustrating how material factors can contribute to an author's impact, the octavo edition acquired a far wider readership than did the larger, more 'aristocratic' quarto volumes. The edition was even more popularly affordable and easier to read and transport in the smaller duodecimo format, which ran to ninety-two volumes.

From the moment of his death, the construction of Voltaire's legacy by others began in earnest. Hostage to the process, his very remains were made into the site of legacy production, taking on a powerfully symbolic significance. Fearing he could not obtain a proper burial and would end up in a pauper's grave, Voltaire had made a partial retraction of his writings, an act the church nonetheless deemed insufficient. This intransigence gave concern to those close to Voltaire, who then arranged to transfer his remains to Ferney, resorting one last time to the well-tested strategy of flight from the capital. Voltaire's family had other plans, and his remains were buried in an abbey near Paris where Voltaire's nephew served as *abbé*. This compromise between religion and freethinking philosophy was short-lived, however, for Voltaire's remains would not remain his own. Instead, they would soon be expropriated to play a role of national significance. In 1791, the revolutionary Constituent Assembly decreed on behalf of the nation that these remains should be interred in the newly nationalized and secularized Panthéon. Built to replace the ruined church of the Abbey Ste. Geneviève, the neoclassical edifice, designed by Jacques Soufflot and named in honor of the patron saint of Paris, had been commissioned by Louis XV in 1744. The church was to rival St. Peter's in Rome, providing symbolic affirmation of France's long-standing affirmation of Gallican liberties, the principle of independence that French kings had claimed with respect to Rome. Announcing on its pediment France's gratitude to her great men, *Aux grands hommes, la patrie reconnaissante*, the building became the site where the French state has continuously performed its history by expressing the idea of a grateful nation, as well as of a national subject, produced in the gesture of national recognition. The process continues, recently in the case of the lavishly orchestrated reinterment of André Malraux's remains in the Panthéon in 1996, a celebration that was designed to affirm, even if it was not entirely successful, a connection between Gaullist politics and the cultural heritage of art and letters.[6]

Voltaire's 'pantheonization' continued the symbolic work the edifice had been called upon to perform, a work that was not without political consequences. For in claiming Voltaire as one of its own, the Revolution celebrated itself through him, aiming to legitimate itself and its policies. Voltaire might have been somewhat amused by his revolutionary apotheosis. In his *Dictionnaire philosophique* he had taken great pleasure in revealing how institutions rewrite their history as it suits them, and he had constantly exposed the unreliability of religious documents and practices designed to promote self-interested individuals. He might have understood less well the notion of revolution espoused by the revolutionaries who appropriated him, since he tended to use the term to designate a slow and extensive process of change rather than a sudden and violent disruption. This instance of a difference between Voltaire's thought and the use to which the writer was put highlights a constant feature of the Voltaire effect, the act of cultural appropriation in which Voltaire becomes a text referred to more often than read. As if to signal this transformation from writer of words to author of works, and from text to effect, on the hearse bearing Voltaire's coffin in the interment ceremony were placed several volumes of the Kehl edition, including the one containing Condorcet's *Vie de Voltaire*. The coffin itself had three inscriptions: one proclaimed his efforts in numerous *causes célèbres* to root out intolerance; the second praised him as poet, philosopher, and historian, who had prepared the way for freedom; the third celebrated his fight against atheists and fanatics, and his struggle to reclaim the rights of man against serfdom and feudalism. Thus, already in 1791 Voltaire had become a collage, the collection of *idées reçues* that Gustave Flaubert will represent ironically a half-century later in *Madame Bovary* through his savagely ironic portrayal of the anticlerical, republican character of Homais, an 'enlightened' provincial pharmacist whose so-called medical science is used to promote not the public good but his own social and economic aspirations (and with tragic results).

Voltaire's revolutionary appropriation is one of numerous attempts to tell the story of the new republic, to script a narrative of national unity that would heal deep wounds in political culture. The Republic itself, the revolutionaries claimed, would unite the men and women of France, transforming monarchical subjects into republican citizens. Although the republican calendar began with Year I, symbolically making 1792 the dawn of a new political age, the Republic's incorporation of Voltaire demonstrated how republican political culture could conjoin past and present, and thus overcome the jolting break represented by 1789. The same fate of appropriation befell Jean-Jacques Rousseau, who had died in the same year as Voltaire and whose entry into the Panthéon was decreed by the National Convention in 1794. The act brought together two figures who, in eighteenth-century prints and popular thinking, were viewed as irreconcilable enemies – Voltaire the representative of rationalism and group tolerance, and Rousseau the champion of lyric sensibility and the individual. But the reconciliation the revolutionary leaders hoped to achieve both symbolically and politically was not so easily realized. Joined symbolically in the Panthéon, the two writers continued to signal a profound and enduring tension in French political culture. The political history of nineteenth-century France, at least until the establishment of the Third Republic in 1870, when secular republicanism wins out over religious monarchism, can be written as the struggle between these two positions, a struggle that crystallized in the debate over the cause of the cataclysmic, traumatic events of the French Revolution. Was the Revolution *la faute à Voltaire ou la faute à Rousseau*? So went the ditty sung by Gavroche, street urchin and son of Paris, as he dies in a hail of bullets on the barricades in Victor Hugo's *Les Misérables* of 1862. So long as 'Voltaire' or Voltaireanism meant an intransigent anticlerical liberalism, and 'Rousseau' signified an uncompromising socializing populism, any political reconciliation between these positions was impossible. Hugo would associate them in the overarching emancipatory work of the Revolution, declaring in the oration he delivered in 1878 on the hundredth anniversary of Voltaire's death that in railing against the oppressors of the weak, the poor, and the downtrodden, Voltaire was waging "Christ's war," and doing so better than the church did. If this union beneath the revolutionary banner was rhetorically possible for Hugo, the republican synthesis was still too fragile a solution to the vexing and long-standing problem of political differences in 1878, when it was prudently decided that the centennial commemorations of the death of Voltaire and of Rousseau should be held separately.

This commemoration of the Revolution and its republican heritage would help fix a largely positive image of Voltaire in cultural memory. Yet throughout the nineteenth century, he had been a prime target for monarchists, Catholics, and conservatives. Prior to 1848, all threats to social order and the status quo were viewed with alarm by those in power, whether the power in question was that of the Napoleonic state or the Bourbon Restoration that followed Napoleon's ouster in 1814. Eighteenth-century philosophy was one such threat, for it was seen as promoting atheism, materialism, and a resurgence of the popular violence that contributed to revolutionary excesses. This nineteenth-century antiterrorist discourse had its own strategic ends. By denouncing the bloody excesses that had occurred during the reign of Robespierre and the Jacobin party, which ended with the Revolution of Thermidor in 1794, an argument could be made indirectly, yet no less effectively, for maintaining the status quo. Within this antiterrorist discourse, the names of the philosophes were interchangeable. Diderot, Rousseau, Voltaire, D'Alembert – these authors represented a philosophical 'sect' whose sole aim was to overturn established order and whose works could remain unread, covered over and silenced beneath shopworn slogans. In the highly charged atmosphere of nineteenth-century politics, no reference to the eighteenth century remained politically neutral. Politicizing the previous century was often the aim of political discourse, rather than an unfortunate outcome it sought to avoid.

But even in literary historical terms, assuming they can be kept separate from political intent, Voltaire did not fare well in the early nineteenth century. He was equated with the pleasure-seeking superficiality of the *Ancien Régime*, and his writing, like that of the eighteenth century more generally, was not considered to exemplify great literature. Held up as model instead was the literature of the seventeenth century, the *grand siècle* that was appropriately aristocratic, monarchical, and Catholic. In comparison, the writing of the eighteenth century seemed frivolous, mannered, and artificial – no more than light entertainment. In addition, Voltaire represented the century of wit, analysis, and rationalism, in other words all that the Romantics saw as being hostile to religious and poetic sentiment, stifling creativity, and preventing genius from producing great poetry. Charles-Augustin Sainte-Beuve, whose literary portraits would mark literary history for the rest of the century, was categorical: "As an artist, Voltaire excels in mockery alone, that is, in a genre that by definition is antipoetic." Gustave Flaubert put the opposition between wit and poetry genius most succinctly: "Who was wittier than Voltaire and who was less a poet?" Octave, the alienated young hero of Alfred de Musset's *Confessions d'un enfant du siècle*, expresses the period's antiphilosophical hostility to eighteenth-century rationalism. "Poisoned as a youth by all that was written in the last century, early on I nursed on the sterile milk of impiousness."[7] For Musset's 'child of the century', the sour milk of eighteenth-century atheist materialism expresses Romantic aspirations negatively, by referring to all that the previous age supposedly lacked and the legacy it had failed to provide. In literary discourse as in political discourse, Voltaire and the eighteenth century mediated a sense of present and past, signifying a dissatisfaction with the present that was experienced as a vague sense of loss. If Voltaire's writing was devalorized for being either too witty and frivolous or too rational and critical, it was so that nineteenth-century literary innovation appeared all the more striking. A cutout figure, the image of Voltaire served as floating signifier, a foil expressing nineteenth-century writers' and critics' sense of their own plight, caught in a moment they experienced as being hostile to all forms of creative genius. At times, nineteenth-century cultural imagination will attempt to recover that lost past, as do Jules and Edmond Goncourt in their resuscitation of a delicate, feminine, and pleasure-loving eighteenth-century salon culture. With the return of the aristocratic émigrés, a bygone world is invoked that existed prior to revolution and exile, a recreated world that provides an antithesis to the pale and conflict-ridden present. In clothing, hairstyles, Louis XV furniture, and pastiches of the nostalgic *fêtes galantes* paintings of Jean-Antoine Watteau and Nicolas Lancret, eighteenth-century salon culture returns as the ghost-like model of harmless esthetic production and disengaged cultural life. Yet even in this depoliticized, estheticized version of the eighteenth century, Voltaire cannot be presented in a positive light. The Catholic right cannot forgive him his anticlericalism, the populist left cannot accept his praise of luxury and commerce, the nationalists take him for a cosmopolitan, believers see him as an atheist, and materialist non-believers reject his deism. The witty deftness of Voltaire's style will receive universal praise, but only because style can be appreciated as no more than that, with no need to embrace the ideas it conveys.

THE STATE OF MEMORY

In today's scholarly view of the eighteenth century, the philosophes are seen as having had less influence on the French Revolution than earlier generations of researchers accorded them. An intellectual history of political ideas is being rewritten as a cultural history of discursive and material practices, a revision that does more than rebaptize influence as effect, for it makes it possible to examine all the more closely how and why the philosophes were read – or not – by subsequent generations. This shift of perspective has resulted in reading the philosophes' writings otherwise than through the lens of the Revolution, which for a century or more shaped interpretations of the philosophes and the prerevolutionary period in general. Besides reading the philosophes' texts more carefully, literary and cultural historians are subjecting to critical scrutiny the view of the eighteenth century that was produced by the myth-making imperative of nineteenth-century republican culture. Republicanism was successful precisely because it could overcome political fractiousness in the name of the Republic, rewriting socioeconomic particularisms through the script of national unity. Yet republicanism did not – and likely could not – expose its own need for myths. Increasingly, the question being asked in France is whether those same myths are wearing out. Can national unity still be achieved by appealing to French history as a long march to republicanism, the solution designed to overcome intense social conflict by uniting individuals as citizens in a republican society? Has republicanism become too closely associated with nationalism? Or can republicanism become something other than a myth, founded on another finality besides the unspoken rewriting of its cultural past? Such questions could not be posed during the nineteenth century, so long as the outcome of the struggle to impose republicanism was still uncertain. In the twenty-first century, they cannot be repressed at a time when the utopian and unifying legacy of republicanism in France appears to many to be in ruins.

In the nineteenth century, the political and cultural struggle to construct what would become the republican legacy took place symbolically, through the diffusion of books, in the development of educational curricula, and in forms of public commemoration. In the case of Voltaire, some 32 editions representing 1.5 million volumes were published between 1830 and 1848. Later in the century the Moland edition of the complete works appeared between 1877 and 1885, at the time of the centennial of the Revolution. A less scholarly 1,000-page edition was also prepared for the centennial celebration. The Catholic, monarchical right had always viewed this increased availability of Voltaire's text with alarm. With one-quarter of the popular centennial edition given over to texts on religion, it was decried by Mgr. Dupanloup, the firebrand anti-Voltairean bishop of Orléans, who claimed that it would empty the churches and contribute to fomenting social unrest. But Voltaire could always be read selectively and strategically, in such a way as to generate support for either progressive or conservative positions. His widespread popularization throughout the nineteenth century reflects the attempt to transform France's past into a shared cultural heritage. Schools and universities play a crucial role in making that heritage accessible to a greater number of citizens. The past becomes a national narrative, designed to bridge conflicts by inculcating moral and civic values – both religious and republican – that remain socially conservative.

A new discipline in nineteenth-century curricula, the teaching of history becomes that place where the past is conserved and where cultural memory is created and maintained, sometimes at the cost of being rewritten. Literature is pressed into service in this enterprise, as the great texts of the past are taught as examples of a national heritage. An entire apparatus of anthologies and literary histories had to be produced to teach the new national history, forms of instructional texts that mediate access to the literary text and thus make it easier to promote certain values and marginalize others. Voltaire fares far better than other eighteenth-century writers in these anthologies and literary histories, but he receives much less space than do such writers of the 'great century' as Corneille, Fénelon, and Bossuet. The publishing house Hachette begins bringing out its "Great French Writers" series in 1887, but only in 1896 does the national education ministry suggest that the term 'classic' may be used to refer to any other writers than those of the seventeenth century. After 1880, the education reforms put through by Jules Ferry contribute to secularizing education, and as a result Voltaire occupies a much more prominent place in the curriculum and state examinations. Gustave Lanson's work in the late nineteenth century assures Voltaire's entry into scholarly sanctioned research topics, an incorporation into the academy guaranteed by the 1905 law officially separating church and state. But once again, the crucial question is: which Voltaire – the writer of brilliantly crafted verse or the *engagé* polemicist? Ironically, either Voltaire could be brought into the national pantheon. Eugène Geruzez, author of several uninspired nineteenth-century literary histories, observes that in his poetry, "Voltaire ... sums up and improves upon all the qualities of French *esprit*: naturalness, clarity, witticisms, finesse, and good sense."[8] A century and a half later, a website maintained by the French Ministry of Foreign Affairs calls Voltaire "one of the great symbols of our cultural memory, along with the Louvre and the Marseillaise ... Among national writers he is probably the one who best defines French identity."[9] Memory, like the unconscious, is a *bricoleur*.

No writer was as vigorously commemorated during the nineteenth century as Voltaire. A form of cultural memory, commemoration involves forgetting as well as remembering, as the story of Voltaire's statues suggests. The Houdon and Pigalle sculptures having never received widespread public display in Paris, a campaign was launched in 1867 by the anticlerical daily *Le Siècle* to erect an open-air statue of the writer, who had been linked once again to national imperatives in 1864, when his heart had been presented to Emperor Louis-Napoléon on behalf of the nation. The Emperor had already begun this symbolic linkage in 1852, with an architectural project joining the Louvre and the Tuileries, which included Voltaire among the eighty-six statues of France's great. Later, on the rebuilt Hôtel de Ville, burned during the Commune uprising of 1871, a statue of Voltaire would be placed next to one of Molière, thereby joining two centuries that many political scripts had placed into opposition. The open-air statue of Voltaire was finally installed in 1870, a week after the Prussian army declared a state of siege on Paris. After the establishment of the Third Republic, the statue was still too strongly associated with Louis-Napoléon and the Second Empire. Removed from its public location in the Place Voltaire in a militant area of Paris, it was reinstalled in the rue Monge, a quiet academic neighborhood in the fifth *arrondissement*. Voltaire was inscribed on Parisian toponymy, remembered in the urban landscape, but in a way that amounted symbolically to a contained depoliticization and a memorializing forgetting.

But Voltaire could not be so easily dealt with a few years later. In 1878, the Third Republic was only eight years old as the eve of the first centennial of the French Revolution approached. The period was marked by fierce political and ideological battles, whose outcome involved control of the state, the role of education and of the church, and resolution of 'the social question', that is, achieving economic progress despite the condition of the working classes. The Universal Exhibition was held in the same year, which was designed to demonstrate France's revival from the Franco-Prussian wars of 1870 and the bloody civil strife of the Commune by displaying advances in the area of technology, as well as French colonial expansion.[10] Commemorations of Voltaire's death were planned in 1878 throughout the nation and indeed beyond, and staunchly anti-Voltairean events took place as well, with expiation masses and the placing of wreaths at the statue of Joan of Arc. But a century later, in 1978, bicentennial commemoration took the more restrained form of conferences organized by scholarly specialists, with special emphasis accorded to Voltaire, this time invoked as the champion of tolerance and human rights. Perhaps overshadowed by preparations for the revolutionary bicentennial celebrations planned for the next decade, commemorations of Voltaire signaled forgetting rather than memory, as if these academic events had to rescue their author from the fate of personifying witty irreverence to which much of twentieth-century literary history had consigned Voltaire.

As should be apparent, at issue in 'the Voltaire effect' is not just the fate of one writer. To make explicit the theoretical and more broadly cultural stakes involved in the story of 'the Voltaire effect', we can take up for a moment the lens offered by Pierre Nora, editor of the multi-volume *Lieux de mémoire* project. By promoting an investigation of memory sites, these material objects and real places where ritualized events occur and symbolic meanings are produced, Nora has helped focus attention on what he calls the political use of memory.[11] The French are not unique in developing practices designed to invent tradition, but they do have a particularly intense investment in the systematic construction of national and cultural memory. "The French are probably the all-around champions of the politics of memory," observes François Furet.[12] To understand the historical determination of this politics, Nora turns to Third Republic culture and its particularly intensive cultivation of memory. The Republic's leaders were certainly prone to remembering. Taking only official commemorative acts, one finds that during the Republic's seventy-year existence, eighty-two state funerals were organized, and not only for political leaders and military figures but for writers, musicians, scientists, and explorers. Explained in political terms, these events reflect the attempt on the part of government leaders to manipulate popular memory in order to bolster their own legitimacy. Yet Nora suggests that commemorative events may be considered differently, from a perspective not directly generated by this familiar political explanatory model. In these commemorative events, he observes, a particular kind of civic training takes place. Republican culture presents itself as a "permanent educational spectacle," thus reactivating the civic theatricality at work in the revolutionary *fête*. In both cases, the possibility of a new subjectivity is made manifest for participants in the ritual of commemoration. In the elaboration of these 'realms of memory', a republican, national identity is constructed through a process of display, interpellation, and appropriation. In these commemorations, the past dead and the dead past are brought out once again, yet symbolically, through language and ritualized events. The living invoke the dead in order to affirm a desired continuity between past and present, the existence of a seam joining absence and presence, thus guaranteeing the possibility of knowledge and self-understanding.

The *Lieux de mémoire* project has focused historical analysis on the numerous commemorative practices that define Third Republic culture, which in turn has helped shape research on other historical periods and national contexts. In so doing, this historical project has itself become a memory site, performing cultural memory work no less significant than that of the memory sites it analyzes. Nora's research project, together with the theoretical paradigm of the memory site, belong to the disciplinary context of French historiography, which itself is related historically to the political culture of the 1970s and 1980s in France. The *Lieux de mémoire* project performs the epistemological work of commemoration, that of a particular mode of knowing whose social dimension is collective, whose representational practice is symbolic, and whose temporality is that of belatedness. What did these commemorative acts make it possible to know in the nineteenth century, and why was the intense, obsessional need for such knowledge expressed through the theory and practice of history in France in the late twentieth century?

If much of nineteenth-century political history amounts to the acting out of the Revolution, endlessly and repeatedly, the commemorative events organized during the Third Republic can be seen as offering a potential solution to that impasse. For these events amounted to a way to work through the trauma of the Revolution. Far more than the result of a manipulative political strategy, commemorative events appeared as a way to provide closure to a traumatic history through an essentially narrative and theatrical process. These events offered to public view a symbolic form, the celebration of the great immortals, in and through which the trauma of the past could be mastered and made comprehensible. To be sure, the grand Romantic histories of earlier in the century performed a similar function.[13] Yet the commemorative events of the late nineteenth century constituted a far more immediate and far more public working through of revolutionary trauma. In short, these commemorative acts were less the reflection of a particular version of history than a kind of historical practice themselves, the outcome of which was the production of historical knowledge. Commemoration was played out as a way of knowing.

The knowledge produced in and through the memory site is always belated, constantly remade, never complete; it stands as testimony more to the present impossibility of adequate knowledge than to the fully constituted possession of the past. Phrasing the epistemological issue of memory in more affective terms, we could say that the memory site itself is also a site of trauma. Following Freud, and referring to the case of individual trauma, Cathy Caruth characterizes the traumatic event as one that the subject does not assimilate or experience fully at the time of its occurrence. That event is experienced only belatedly, in its repeated possession of the subject who initially experienced it. Traumatic possession thus amounts to an impossible history that the traumatized bear, a history they cannot entirely possess and that in its telling possessed them. The epistemological question thus becomes: how can the truth of trauma be expressed? The paradox of trauma, claims Caruth, lies in a struggle to gain access to the pain of historical experience to whose truth there is no immediate access. "Trauma ... does not simply serve as record of the past but precisely registers the force of an experience that is not yet fully owned ... The phenomenon of trauma ... both urgently demands historical awareness and yet denies our usual modes of access to it. How is it possible ... to gain access to a traumatic history?"[14]

Returning to Nora, French history, and French historiography in general, we might ask: to what extent do we find in the obsessive commemorative acts of the Third Republic the memory traces of traumatic experience? Furthermore, in what sense is the theoretical construct of the memory site a late twentieth-century attempt not only to provide historical knowledge of these events, but also to bring to a close the trauma they point to? Fervently desired as a way to put an end to violent and painful dissension, these commemorative events link past and present in an impossible-to-complete working through of history. Extending this view of trauma and its representation to the context of the Third Republic might suggest the need to revise the notion of a republican 'closure' to revolutionary trauma. Moreover, the proliferation of memory sites witnessed in the *Lieux de mémoire* project testifies to the impossibility of any such closure, both in the nineteenth-century past and at present. Numerous concepts have been invoked to put an end to the conflict and traumatic violence that characterize French history – the republic, the nation, community. Historians have been called upon for more than a century to tell the story of that closure. But if French historiography has undergone a crisis of late, perhaps it is due above all to its no longer knowing how to heal traumatic wounds, or not remembering how to. In seeking a way adequately to recognize this lack, French historiography is still engaged in working through a vexed relation to its national past, to a moment when the writing of history was an integral part of nation-building in that it was the chiasmatic institution of remembering and of amnesia. As Benedict Anderson puts it, "having to 'have already forgotten' tragedies of which one needs unceasingly to be 'reminded' turns out to be a characteristic device in the construction of national genealogies." The more chilling version of Anderson's observation is provided by Maurice Barrès in a 1899 lecture on "La Terre et les morts" sponsored by La Ligue de la Patrie française, in which he claims that to found a nation, "a cemetery and history-teaching are needed."[15] How does this dialectic of memory and forgetting, whose dimensions are disciplinarily historiographical and politically national, play itself out in the case of Voltaire?

Before Emile Zola and his 'j'accuse' launched against anti-Semitism in the nineteenth century, or Jean-Paul Sartre's unflagging social activism in the twentieth, it was Voltaire who first characterized the modern intellectual. Exasperated by Voltaire's tenacious criticism, Louis XV was supposed to have asked, "Can't that man be kept quiet?" Two centuries later, when deciding how to deal with Jean-Paul Sartre and his association with a public manifesto denouncing the French government's Algeria policy, Charles de Gaulle remarked, "Let the intellectuals do what they want ... one doesn't arrest Voltaire." The modern intellectual would consistently be defined through reference to Voltaire, be it to embrace that legacy, to resist it, or to bemoan its eclipse. Thus Paul Valéry, in a speech given at the Sorbonne in late 1944, following the liberation of Paris, praised Voltaire's combat to denounce "crimes against humanity" and his ability to remake his century "with the sole power of the pen, by *esprit* alone." Yet Valéry also asks in a more somberly historical sense whether the Voltaires of the present were destined to fail to realize their legacy in 1944, when Voltaire's name had been invoked to promote anti-Semitism and when victims of *l'infâme* numbered not a handful but in the millions. A half-century later, should we read in Voltaire's reduction to 'the Voltaire effect' the eclipse of the French intellectual? Perhaps, but in that eclipse still resides the possibility of engagement with that past. 'Voltaire' still marks the space of a problematic ethical imperative: "Can one still ask the question, 'What is tolerance?' as Voltaire did in the first sentence of his article on the subject in the *Philosophical Dictionary*? How would this article be written today? Who would write it, with and without Voltaire?"[16] Voltaire cannot be used as he was in the nineteenth century by partisans of one fundamentalism or another. Nor can we fail to remember Voltaire, any more than the past must not be ignored. We must write "with and without" Voltaire. As Jean Marie Goulemot has cautioned, commemorative memory should not erase the antagonisms that define the cultural field, producing the illusory and amnesiac image of a unified cultural past.[17] Instead critical commemoration must involve a reflection upon how Voltaire, and an irrecoverable past in general, are nonetheless introduced in and through the institutions and the discourses that shape the cultural community.

CHAPTER 9

Reading among the ruins

> The concept of progress must be grounded in the idea of catastrophe. That things are 'status quo' *is* the catastrophe. It is not an ever-present possibility but what in each case is given.
> Walter Benjamin, *The Arcades Project*

> ... our general fascination with decay and decadence...
> Georg Simmel, "Ruins"

This chapter considers the construction of the ruin in the eighteenth-century imaginary as a way to understand how writers and artists viewed their relation to past and future through their craft. I also wish to read this fascination with ruins in a conceptually allegorical manner, imagining that this fascination provides us with a way to phrase our own relation to that past via the ruin. Through this relation to the ruins of the past, we can reflect self-consciously on that phrasing as a mode of historical knowledge, perhaps the one most readily available to us today. The point of departure for this reflection will be located not in real ruins and the events that produced them, but rather in an image, and more precisely in a photograph that we immediately recognize as not belonging to the eighteenth century (Figure 9.1). What do we see here? What is there to be read?

This image presents the signs of two distinct events. One of them is the violent, perhaps cataclysmic event of the past that has reduced most of the building to the jumbled pile of rubble seen in the lower quadrant of the image's x-axis. The other event is the act of reading, seen through the three figures, their backs turned to the rubble, their gaze directed outwards from the frame and their attention focused inward, on books that remain in the tidy rows framing the image left and right. Reading here is a calm and all but immobile act, performed by individuals resigned, oblivious, or perhaps somehow resistant. Overall, the photograph has a stark and enigmatic quality, one all the more compelling because no visual markers help us explain the relation between past and present,

Figure 9.1 Holland House Library after September 1940 air raid in London (1940). Photo credit: National Monuments Record.

between catastrophic violence and eerie calm, between the framing contextuality of history and the subjective experience of the text. Do we see in these figures humanist readers located in the ruins of elite culture, or booksellers who preserve systems of exchange even amidst the rubble? This image, perhaps like all images, is not a mirror but a screen, onto which we may project what we think we see, what we wish to view. Given the inevitability of this visual desire, what sort of explanation might we provide, and what sort of story could we tell, that would link these elements of past and present?

Tracing the thematics of library and book, we might see here an allegory of reading, where the experience of the text is represented as a sublime moment, a way to register cataclysmic violence yet at the same time to transcend it. Just as the three men may have gazed upon the rubble only to have turned to the books, so too the viewer's gaze first fixes on the material signs of destruction but then is drawn to the open vault of the library's no longer present ceiling and beyond it to the open sky, in a visual trajectory that suggests both destruction and its transcendence. But is the meaning found in this image of ruins in any sense immanent to them, or is it a secondary effect, produced after the fact in a reading? Perhaps this image instead provides an allegory of temporal linkage, suggesting that nothing guarantees beforehand, *avant la lettre*, that any sense can be made of past and present prior to the past's inscription into the present, prior to the event's becoming a text. This a priori uncertainty concerning ways to link past and present is all the more pressing when the past appears as disaster, an event we cannot experience and whose time is not our own.

We can begin to gauge the effects of this photo, even if we cannot experience what it gives to be seen, by noting that it was taken by a photographer whose name remains unknown on October 23, 1940, following a September 27 air raid in London.[1] The site is the bombed-out library of Holland House, a seventeenth-century Tudor mansion, which from the mid eighteenth century until 1840 had been a social, political, and intellectual center for the Whig aristocracy. The crumbling of 'Old Europe' is signified in this site, in which are located the ruins of culture, certainly once the bombs started falling, but perhaps well before. That disaster is represented, moreover, through a relation to the broken yet somehow readable book, the object whose very legibility seems to be conditioned by the disaster it signifies.

There is much to say about this image, which in an uncanny way re-marks and retraces another image, Nicolas Poussin's second version of *Et in*

Arcadia ego (1640). The photograph depicts a more modern experience, yet perhaps for that very reason it can be used to begin teasing out here the complex issues in the eighteenth-century cultural encounter with ruins. By making visual reference to a more contemporary image and event, however, I do not mean to suggest that there exists a universal, timeless experience of ruins. It is more productive – and certainly more postmodern – to think about this image of the ruin in terms of an irresolvable diachrony, or even a polychrony, rather than a potentially universal synchrony. Aiming to examine an element of fascination in the eighteenth century's cultural imaginary, I have begun with the more contemporary image of ruin, the Holland House Library, in order to suggest that the temporal matrix in which the conceptual work of investigating the cultural imaginary of the eighteenth century will involve not a double temporality but a triple one, for we must interrogate our own gaze(s) onto the double time-frame of the eighteenth century's fascination with the figure of the ruin. It is not despite the fact that this image does not belong to the eighteenth century, but precisely for that reason, that we view it as a visual allegory for the question of reading ruins in/of the eighteenth century. Figuring a temporal threshold, designating a present moment that is not that of the eighteenth century, it reminds us of our desire to read among the ruins.

ENLIGHTENING RUINS

Ruins fascinate, and we can begin to historicize this fascination in the eighteenth century by locating it in the scientific excavations at Herculaneum and Pompeii that began around mid century. These places quickly became destination points on 'Grand Tours', inscribed into numerous travel narratives of cultural encounter and discovery.[2] It is not surprising that ruins abound in the *Encyclopédie*, where, as a cursory electronic search reveals, more than 600 instances of the term "ruines" appear.[3] These references map onto an encyclopedic grid that is geographical and historical, as well as metaphorical and philosophical. The extensive entry "Herculanum" by de Jaucourt reveals particularly clearly the encyclopedic strategy for representing the ruin. As do all encyclopedic entries, de Jaucourt's text turns Herculaneum into an object of knowledge, a richly sedimented sign located at the nexus of several ways of knowing. Geography and history make the Italian city knowable in time and space, and rhetoric gives it an intertextual dimension through reference to the description of Vesuvius's eruption in 79 CE given by Pliny the younger, as well as to other texts by Velleius Paterculus, Florus, and Columella. But the newest way of knowing the ruin is provided by archeology, which was emerging as the eighteenth-century discipline *par excellence* for managing and interpreting the past in its material manifestation, as remnant.[4] The significance of Herculaneum extends beyond the epistemological boundaries of archeology, though, for de Jaucourt's text presents the city as a model for a civilized society, that is, as an object to be understood philosophically, viewed through the lens of political philosophy. The philosophical impact of this ruined city extends into the present as well, since by presenting the ruins of Herculaneum philosophically de Jaucourt makes their significance pertinent and contemporaneous with other present-day issues. One effect of this philosophical actualization of the ruin is that de Jaucourt can bring together the question of power and knowledge, which he does in his call, addressed to the Bourbon king of Naples and Sicily, for additional funds to finance research excavations in the Italian city.

The fascination the ruins of Herculaneum exert over de Jaucourt is symptomatic of their strategic function in the century's cultural imaginary. Whether in the writings of sedentary scholars or of traveling humanists, ruins acquire immanent meaning and symbolic value. In these writings, we can read many of the familiar vectors of eighteenth-century thought: a curiosity with distant difference that is driven by the desire to loosen the constraints of inherited thought; a relativizing and universalizing historicism that naturalizes that difference and brings it home to affirm emergent forms of thought and social practice; a relentless secularizing of the transcendental concepts of religion in the name of reason, history, and culture.[5] Repeatedly, the ruin becomes a kind of cultural trope, standing (in) for something else.

A tropology of ruins is at work in the *Encyclopédie*, offering a way to figure the encylopedic text and time's mediation of knowledge. In the article "Encyclopédie," for instance, Diderot imagines a future moment when "some great revolution would have suspended the progress of science, interrupted the work of the arts, and plunged a portion of our hemisphere back into darkness."[6] On the other side of such a cataclysm, the encyclopedic text will endure, but as a monumental storehouse of past knowledge that survives intact and unruined. This, writes Diderot, will be "the most glorious moment" for the *Encyclopédie*. Like the epistemological monuments referred to in Diderot's *Pensées sur l'interprétation de la nature* or the Egyptian pyramids and Mayan temples that fascinated the philosophes, the monument testifies both to the ancients' lost wisdom and to the principle of epistemological progress. The figure of monument is one of the powerfully ordering tropes in the *Encyclopédie*. It makes the connection between present and future thinkable, projecting imagination into the future anterior as it expresses what Enlightenment will have become. In so doing, the trope of the monument shifts focus from the disorder of history to the order of discourse. The encyclopedic text gathers together the otherwise fragmented, disparate references to ruins, gives them a figural valence, and places them in a narrative of universal history. The individual ruin becomes historicized, part of a process of becoming. Ultimately, the ruin disappears in the process, not beneath the sand, though, but upon the page. The Enlightenment narrative of progress does not forget the ruin so much as subsume it, as each epoch of progress becomes the foundation upon which the next will be built, with each chapter of progress anticipating the next. Such is the case in Anne-Robert-Jacques Turgot's "Plan d'un ouvrage sur la géographie politique" and his "Plan de deux discours sur l'histoire universelle."[7] No ruins of the past remain in Turgot's text, as if the enlightened present could subsume the past entirely, integrating it absolutely and with no remainder into the seamless narrative of civilization. Paradoxically, however, the total recall of Turgot's Enlightenment narrative is also absolute oblivion. For in transforming the past into the luminous sign of a rational, progressive history, the past disappears as such, pillaged in the name of progress rather than preserved. But the past can never be preserved as past, for it can exist only in the present, in a form of presentation that must deny its existence as past but without which the past could not exist at all. This is the essential dialectic of historiographical knowledge, which is ultimately both destructive and commemorative.

IMAGINARY RUINS

As de Jaucourt's entry on Herculaneum suggests, the eighteenth-century cultural imaginary of the ruin appears at first encounter to be founded upon direct experience. Jean-Jacques Rousseau recounts in the *Confessions* the impression that viewing the Pont du Gard made upon him, and the sublime longing it instilled in him to be another person of another time.[8] Edward Gibbon's experience in Rome of "musing amidst the ruins of the Capitol" in 1764 impels him to write *The Decline and Fall of the Roman Empire*. William Gilpin finds that the ruins of Fountains Abbey fall far short of the picturesque landscape he describes in his illustrated tour books of England. The narrative of the experience of visiting Palmyra sets the stage of Constantin François de Chasseboeuf Volney's *Les Ruines* (1791), a text that will shape the entire nineteenth-century Romantic

Figure 9.2 Désert de Retz, Study 37 (France 1993). Photo credit: Michael Kenna.

meditation on ruins. But the experience Volney relates is more textual than real, which raises a problematic point concerning the temporality of the ruin, as well as the ontology to which it gives rise. Just what kind of direct, unmediated experience of the ruin occurs in the eighteenth century, if indeed such an experience can be had and subsequently related as such?

Symptomatic of the problem posed by ruins is that besides the apparently real ruins on the century's cultural landscape, we also find artificial ones. Notable examples of such constructed ruins include the folly house of the Désert de Retz (Figure 9.2), designed and constructed between 1774 and 1789 for François Racine de Monville, and the gardens of Ermenonville, where Rousseau initially was buried, which were created for the marquis de Girardin and include the artificial ruins of the Temple of Modern Philosophy.[9] A real taste for fake ruins is displayed in these gardens, whose owners received members of the aristocratic and intellectual elite. In these picturesque encounters the ruin is both commodified and reified, appearing as an object that the privileged elite can have designed and that they acquire as property in order to produce an intense experience, yet one ultimately produced on demand and thus in a sense entirely predictable. The artificial ruins of eighteenth-century gardens thus form the matrix for generating a virtual reality in which the experience of the so-called natural is in fact the sign of something intensely cultural.[10] What then is longed for in the desire for the artificial ruin?

Victor Hugo may have declared war on the demolishers of the past in his *Guerre aux démolisseurs* of 1825, but he begrudgingly recognized the esthetic lure of the ruin. "Alas, more beautiful is the debris of a beautiful palace."[11] Diderot had already gone a step farther in the *Salons*. Commenting on one of the numerous ruin paintings by Hubert Robert, he writes: "A palace must be in ruins (*il faut ruiner un palais*) to evoke any interest; how true it is that, regardless of the handling, without the ideal there can be no true beauty."[12] For Diderot, it is the ruin that fascinates, not the edifice it once was, for the ruin provides the imaginary material for judgment. The ruin may be of interest as a historical memorial that symbolizes nation and culture, as was the case with Joachim Du Bellay's Roman ruins in "Les Antiquités de Rome" (1558). But Du Bellay's collective nostalgia is not the affective mode in which Diderot casts the ruin's interest. Refusing to be drawn back to what was, Diderot anticipates what someday no longer will be.

The effect of these compositions, good or bad, is to leave you in a state of sweet melancholy. Our glance lingers over the debris of a triumphal arch, a portico, a pyramid, a temple, a palace, and we retreat into ourselves. We contemplate the ravages of time, and in our imagination we scatter the rubble of the very buildings in which we live over the ground; in that moment solitude and silence prevail around us, we are the sole survivors of an entire nation that is no more. Such is the first tenet of the poetics of ruins.[13]

The realm of the ruin is not the real, where archeology and history claim to know it, but the imaginary, where the ruin is involved in the production of poetic subjectivity. As the above passage from the *Salons* suggests, the temporal dimension of the experience of ruins is not an analeptic return to a long-gone past but a proleptic anticipation, an imaginary expansion and dispersion of the present self into an imagined future. This process of expansion and dispersion is the work of the esthetic imagination, which for Diderot functions most productively and poetically by ruining the real, so to speak, as it effaces the primary object or referent and sets a fantasy object in its stead, the material of meditative reverie. This is the understanding of the imagination that Diderot the *salonnier* will reach as his growing understanding of the esthetic experience requires that he free himself from the academic, prescriptive notion of mimesis as reduplication. If Diderot lingers over Robert's ruin paintings, which arrest him physically as he strolls through the gallery and narratively as he recounts that experience, it is because he sees in these paintings the visual analogue of the work of the imagination. Robert's ruin canvases interest Diderot not because of subject matter, but because they enact the ruining experience of painting with regard to the real. Through his meditation on Robert's images of ruins, Diderot comes to understand the undergoing of ruin as a fundamentally esthetic experience, one in which esthetic subjectivity is performed.[14]

Robert's visual technique of producing the experience of imaginary ruins has its eighteenth-century narrative counterpart. In *L'An 2440*, for instance, published in 1770, Louis-Sébastien Mercier presents a narrator who falls asleep in eighteenth-century Paris, to awake some 672 years later. Just as imaginary travel in space provides such authors as Montesquieu and Graffigny with a narrative distancing technique for presenting critical observations concerning French society, so too does this imaginary travel in time. Time wreaks change if not destruction, the narrator discovers, and nowhere more than at Versailles, which has become a collection of ruins – "debris, gaping walls, mutilated statues." Among the ruins, the narrator encounters an old man who turns out to be Louis XIV, brought back to life. The frail king, embodying the frailty of empire, observes the outcome of his glory and meditates on the vicissitudes of time. "This is all that remains of the colossus that a million hands erected with such painful effort," he remarks. "May these ruins cry out to all sovereigns that those who abuse momentary power reveal their weakness to the following generation ... Divine justice relit the flame of my days so that I would see more closely my deplorable work ... each palace that a monarch erects is the seed of a subsequent calamity."[15] Mercier's narrative produces the imaginary ruining of Versailles, which has not only an esthetic finality but a political one as well. The ruin serves here as the foil for a lyric voicing ("may these ruins cry out") in which expression is given to suffering in the name of a retributive justice. Mercier's poetic lyricism in his meditation on ruins is driven by a philosophical project. What is made legible in this imaginary space is the idea that civilization may fall into decay, and thus that even Versailles can be imagined as one day being mere rubble. This imaginary ruining of the past amounts to an act of willful violence that frees the present from the past, even at the risk of having to find ways to mourn for what once was or will have been. But this potential loss can be compensated for ultimately by the opportunity this imaginary ruining provides to construct another future.[16] If the relation between past and future is a compensatory one, involving loss and redemption, does this mean we cannot think the future without the notion of ruins? Must we engage in the workings of a destructive, ruining imaginary in order to think historically, to think things in their historicity? To consider this question, we can return to the visual imaginary of Hubert Robert.

LIVING AMONG THE RUINS

Known as the "Robert of ruins," Hubert Robert encountered the phenomenon of the ruin, as many grand tourists did, in Italy, where he spent eleven years. Deeply influenced, we are told, by the work of two eighteenth-century Italian artists, the engravings of Giovanni Battista Piranesi and the paintings of Giovanni Paolo Panini, Robert visited Naples in 1760 where he viewed the excavations at Pompeii. He and Fragonard visited Hadrian's villa in Tivoli, outside Rome, where both artists produced several red-chalk sketches of the site. While there, the two young men promptly scratched their names in the villa's plasterwork, where they were read later by another grand tourist, René de Chateaubriand.[17] An act of touristic defacement, even minor vandalism, the gesture has perhaps no more than anecdotal significance. Yet we can read it as Robert's attempt to appropriate the ruin for himself, to make it his own by inscribing the name, the sign of the self, into the ruin in its very materiality. Robert's self-affirming graffito brings the ruin into a scriptural present, yet it also embeds the self in the process of decay and destruction that the ruin signifies. This is an act Robert will repeat obsessively following his return to Paris in 1765, producing a number of immensely popular paintings of romanticized ruins. These paintings reflect Robert's keen entrepreneurial ability to cater to a rich public's taste, that is, to produce, channel, and focus spectatorial desire. Quite possibly, as Diderot suggests in the *Salons*, they also reveal the artist's attempt to keep up with his wife's taste for fine clothes. But these paintings' immense popularity cannot be accounted for unless we read them with a view to understanding their symbolic work, as figural systems in and through which viewers located themselves and saw themselves represented.

The effects of this symbolic work are strikingly visible in Robert's *Imaginary View of the Ruins of the Grand Gallery of the Louvre Palace* (Figure 9.3). If Diderot was correct in suggesting that things must be ruined to become interesting, then of all Robert's ruin paintings, this one is of particular interest. Painted in 1796, the painting depicts a key moment in the Louvre's transformation from royal collection to public museum. Signaling the emergence of a modern notion of public display and esthetic consumption, this ruin painting can be read as making visible the process of the Louvre's 'invention'.[18] Notable first of all is that the painting is structured according to a number of visual juxtapositions. The heavy linearity of vertical columns contrasts with the jagged angularity of the collapsed barrel vault. These columns and the roof frame the painting's main scene, located in the center foreground, which portrays the painting's human drama. The somber hues and cluttered disorder of this foregrounded scene contrast with the all but empty patches of light blue sky, framed by the outlines of the absent barrel vault. The painting's vanishing point is both an infinitely receding wall of the Louvre, as well as the emptiness beyond it, as if the gaze were caught in some undecidable tension between containment within the building represented here and escape from that constraint. To the undecidability of this infinite recess corresponds the double point of view the painting constructs, a gaze that is at once drawn in close to the human figures in the foreground and infinitely distant from them. The gaze both participates in the human drama and views it from a distant, transcendental position.

The structural reading of the painting sketched out above only sets the stage for analyzing the painting's effects. The most immediate effect of the *Imaginary View* is the meditation it produces on time and the human subject. Robert's painting invokes the familiar thematics of ruined monuments in a pictorially commonplace way, recalling other sketches or paintings by Piranesi and Panini, as well as Clérisseau, Challes, and Natoire. Yet the *Imaginary View* reconfigures that pictorial commonplace by setting it in another space-time. The past is not projected into the present, as is the case with representations of ruins of former times; rather, the painting projects the present into an imaginary future. In a visual gesture of defamilarization, such as is found in narrative form in Mercier's *L'An 2440*, the painting invites viewers of the eighteenth century (and of the twenty-first century for that matter) to recognize a Louvre familiar to them, and at the same time not to recognize it in some future ruined state. This tension is resolved, and the dialectic of defamiliarization is completed, once the viewer comprehends what is seen,

Figure 9.3 Hubert Robert, *Imaginary View of the Ruins of the Grand Gallery of the Louvre Palace* (1796). The Louvre. Photo credit: Erich Lessing / Art Resource, NY.

when visual image is translated into meaning and concept. But sense and concept can never fully take the place of the image, just as stating what the image means never accounts entirely for what the image does. Consequently, we must ask whether the *Imaginary View* is more than just another image of ruins that gives itself to be read according to the thematics of natural decline and decay, the vicissitudes of glory, the smallness and fragility of the human subject over against the inevitable slide towards oblivion and nothingness, represented in the emptiness of these swatches of blue. To be sure, these concepts can be pressed into service to resolve the difference between real and imaginary in this painting, and we can certainly read this painting, and indeed all Robert's other ruin paintings, in this fashion. But what is remarkable in this particular painting is how it insists self-reflexively on painting itself as a way of understanding the ruin.

Many ruin paintings foreground figures gazing upon the architectural remnants of past civilizations. This contemplation produces a number of visual contrasts – now and then, smallness and grandeur, viewing and creating, etc. In Robert's *Imaginary View*, we see a solitary artist sketching not architectural ruins but the remnants of an artwork, the Apollo Belvedere. This self-reflexive location of artworks within the artwork appears elsewhere in the painting, for, besides the Apollo, Michelangelo's "Dying Slave" can be identified on the lower right. It is as if amidst all that crumbles, art endures. Peasants and looters may squabble over the wood of the picture frames they burn for heat, suggesting what is outside the frame of the artwork – the world, the everyday, material needs, struggle and strife. But within the frame, the timeless calm of esthetic contemplation appears to reign. The self-reflexive gesture is more complicated, though, for the figure contemplating the Apollo is also an artist who produces yet another work of art, his own sketch of the Apollo. (Indeed, the figure of the artist *is* an element in an artwork and thus the Apollo's double, which is suggested by his upraised hand that repeats the statue's gesture.) We might conclude that the role of the artwork is to record the effects of decay and decline, to capture and arrest the ruinous march of time, transforming the latter's effects into a work of art. Thus the artist figure's gaze upon the Apollo, which stands for an interior meditation upon the effects of time, prefigures an imaginary spectatorial gaze directed upon Robert's *Imaginary View*, a gaze that would arrest time, estheticizing its effects within the realm of the imaginary.

Esthetic meditation upon the ruin may seek to arrest time in this fashion, but it cannot block out history, an impossibility that can also be read in

Robert's painting. The Apollo Belvedere, like Michelangelo's "Dying Slave," may be read as signifying the timelessness of art, its ability to transcend death and destruction. But the *Imaginary View* questions such transcendence by locating the Apollo within the Louvre, in a gesture that contextualizes and historicizes the esthetic experience. For the twenty-first-century viewer, the experience of viewing the Apollo takes place in the Vatican Museum in Rome. In the eighteenth century, however, the sculpture was displayed for a short time in Paris in the Musée Central des Arts (the future Louvre Museum), as part of the thousands of artworks that were confiscated during the military campaigns in the newly conquered territories, where French art specialists employed by Napoleon directed French soldiers in the selection of artworks to send back to France. In official terms, the Apollo Belvedere was ceded by Pope Pius VI to the French in early 1797. It arrived in Paris in a triumphal procession the following year and was displayed from 1800 until 1815, when it was returned to Rome following Napoleon's defeat and exile.[19] But beginning in 1796, when the *Imaginary View* was painted, it would have been difficult not to read the reference to this particular statue historically and contextually. This reference to a mythical past signals the creation of new mythologies, marking the present's appropriative, transformative power as one empire is pressed into service to represent another.

But there is more. Through this overdetermined reference to the Louvre, Robert invites a reflection on art not only as esthetic object but also in its institutional determination. Joseph M. Gandy performs a similar gesture a few years later with his 1830 watercolor, *A Bird's-Eye View of the Bank of England*, an aerial cutaway view that depicts in Piranesian-like ruins the 3-acre complex that stood as a monument to British empire. Commissioned by John Soane, architect to the Bank of England, Gandy's watercolor offers a reflection on the relation between culture and its institutions.[20] In the case of Robert's painting, the institution in question is the museum. Were we reading the *Imaginary View* alone, we might conclude that the ruined Louvre signals the inevitable transience of precisely that institution whose current function is to preserve the artwork from physical ruin, as well as to establish and maintain the artwork's value, preserving the latter from another kind of ruin. But the museum the Louvre will become is not necessarily the museum that Robert depicts it becoming. Consequently, the ruins of the *Imaginary View* must be read alongside another imaginary view, one that was displayed in 1796 as its pendant, the *Project for the Disposition of the Grand Galery of the Louvre* (Figure 9.4). This reconfiguration of the Louvre was

Figure 9.4 Hubert Robert, *Project for the Disposition of the Grand Gallery of the Louvre* (1796). The Louvre. Photo credit: Scala / Art Resource, NY.

not at the time an imaginary one. Plans to remodel the Louvre as a showcase of national and royal glory had been under way since before the Revolution. Following the downfall of Louis XVI, these plans changed somewhat, at least in what this reorganization of the space of art would mean. With the royal collection declared national property, the decision was made to 'revolutionize' existing collections (along with other newly acquired artworks seized from the church, from émigrés, and in other countries). Art would be made accessible to the people, as had been planned before the Revolution, and the practice of floor-to-ceiling display, now seen as a sign of 'feudal' disorder, aristocratic mismanagement, and irrational obscurantism, would be reorganized. In the Renaissance *Kunstkammer*, artworks were displayed according to various typologies, whether more conceptual (*natura* and *arte*) or more pragmatic (genre and size). In the emergent museum that the reorganized Louvre exemplifies, artworks would be displayed by historical provenance, in relation to their place in the objective linearity of history. In sixteenth-century Florence, the Medicis may have displayed art in the Uffizi Palace according to provenance and other categories, but in the reconfigured Louvre, presented here by Robert, we see a very modern sense of display that is underwritten by a fundamentally historical narrative.

In his reflection on museums, art, and history, Didier Maleuvre reads the historical event of the Louvre's reorganization as cultural allegory, one made especially legible when grasped in relation to Robert's two imaginary views. In the second depiction of a 'modern' Louvre, it is history and a historical understanding of art that determine the organization of the museum. Art concretizes the historical past, and "in the museum, art became a thing of the past."[21] But this relation between art and history, claims Maleuvre, is precisely what Robert shows in the *Imaginary View*. The sight of a museum in ruins does not simply suggest the past glory of a now defunct museum. Rather, and more strikingly, this sight leads us to ask whether the museum, by definition, is not already always defunct, caught inextricably in the relation to the past that it creates, destined to be that cultural institution designed to make the past visible as art. "The new museum cancels art's involvement in historical praxis but then reintroduces history into the work of art, only this time as a historiographic sediment. Art is no longer the force of history but a bearer of its representations ... art begins to represent *what is left* of history." In other words, in the museum, art comes to be visible as a ruin. "Insofar as the ruin is shaped equally by what remains and by what has been stripped away, by the presence of what still stands as well as the absence of what no longer remains, it makes the process of passing – of historicity – appear."[22] The art of the museum, this museal technique, involves making the past visible, but in a ruined state, in which it bears the marks of its passage from past to present. The past is a damaged one, but a damage that cannot be remedied and overcome, for it is a damage without which the past does not exist, except in its damaged state in the present. The historical past "does not precede its transplantation in the present: history is precisely the recognition that the past does not exist outside of the reminiscing present."[23] The figure of the ruin marks the sense on the part of modern consciousness of an acute separation and alienation from the past, yet a past that returns specter-like to haunt the present. If we can speak of the experience of modern selfhood, it is perhaps, as we shall see, in relation to this haunting historicity of the ruin.

THE STORY OF THE SUBJECT OF/IN RUINS

If one text offers a paradigmatic voicing of subjectivity in eighteenth-century culture through a reflection on ruins, it is Volney's *Les Ruines ou méditations sur les révolutions des empires*. "Hail, solitary ruins, holy tombs, silent walls! It is you I invoke, and to you I address my prayer."[24] Volney had traveled in the Levant in the 1780s, and his detailed account of the journey, *Voyage en Syrie et en Egypte* (1787), would be used by Napoleon during his Egyptian campaign. *Les Ruines* (1791), which opens with the above apostrophe, contains an experiential narrative that grounds Volney's extensive and more philosophical reflection on historical change. *Les Ruines* merits extended attention, and not least of all because soon after its appearance it became a major intertext in the Romantic, nineteenth-century narrative of cultural identity and cultural transformation. Echoes of Volney's text can be heard in Senancour, Chateaubriand, Lamartine, and Hugo. Chateaubriand, for example, brings Volney home, so to speak, domesticating the latter's reflection on defunct Levantine cultures in his account of his own travels to Bordeaux in the *Mémoires d'outre-tombe*, where he too contemplates ruins, or elsewhere, in *Le Génie du christianisme*, where Chateaubriand describes the "revolution of empire" that France has undergone on its way to becoming "this heritage of mourning, resignation, ruins, and debris."

To phrase the relation of self to past and present, Chateaubriand adopts the affective mode of nostalgia, melancholy, and mourning. However well *Les Ruines* lends itself to such an enterprise, Volney remains closer to Enlightenment thought, which the nineteenth-century Romantic writer effectively under-reads. *Les Ruines* opens with a narrator's reflection on the general condition of empires, be they located in Asia, the Levant or "on the banks of the Seine, the Thames or the Zuiderzee." The relation to the past is presented here in terms of blind fate and the incomprehensible judgments of a mysterious God. But that position turns out to be but a foil for the explanation provided by a genie that recounts to the narrator the order of history according to the laws of nature and human passions. The silent and mysterious ruins initially invoked by the narrator of *Les Ruines* become legible in Volney's text, made to yield their lessons. They come to stand for human miseries resulting from ignorance and self-interest, a human state that can be perfected by following natural laws and the principles of reason. Ultimately these ruins become the foundation upon which Volney proposes the construction of a new and enlightened social and moral order.

We should take care not to domesticate *Les Ruines* too easily by reading the text as another version of a familiar Enlightenment narrative of progress and improvement. Viewed thus, the Levant becomes yet one more utopian space invested with concepts and values whose ideological neutrality is suspect, as has shown the intense critical scrutiny to which the ideology of Western progress has been subjected. That scrutiny is driven by the following premise. The Enlightenment project amounts to the attempt to bring about through the application of reason, science, and technology a higher level of social and political well-being for an increasingly freer citizen-subject. But it seems evident that the Enlightenment project has not been fully realized and may in fact be unrealizable. Rather than designate a utopian goal or some other desired finality, the very terms of the Enlightenment project seem increasingly inapplicable to the present moment. Instead of offering a firm ground for our accomplished sense of modernity, the Enlightenment stands for an ungroundedness that defines an impossible modernity, if not a problematic postmodernity. This perspective, produced and determined by the present historical moment, is the only standpoint available to us, moreover. Thus, there can be no other understanding of the Enlightenment than one that is grounded (rhetorically) in a problematic grappling with the question of this impossible modernity. This question of how to ground the concept of Enlightenment suggests that we must reread Volney's attempt to found an enlightened order by building it through narrative upon the ruins of the past. These foundational ruins, like many others, turn out to be less stable than at first imagined.

As a travel narrative, *Les Ruines* grounds reflection on ruins upon experiential reality. The traveler, both observer and writer, transforms the experience of other space-times into a text, which recounts the alienation from the here and now while attempting to recover from the loss of the familiar by producing a traveling self that can bridge spaces and span times. In *Les Ruines*, Volney's visit to Palmyra is presented as creating a richly subjective experience, narrated after the fact, as are all travel narratives, but with a lyric intensity designed to reproduce the intensity of the original experience. But it turns out that this original experience never occurred, or more precisely that it was a textually mediated one (just as all original experiences perhaps always already are). For Volney's knowledge of the ruins of Palmyra is derived from his reading of Robert Wood's travel narrative, *The Ruins of Palmyra*, published in London in 1753 and translated into French the following year. Volney's deictic phrase, "here an opulent city once flourished," refers not to a place he saw in the Levant, but to a book he read, a textual space of encounter with the imaginary alterity of the past, a 'here' that designates the ruined foundation of subjectivity and historicity.

This discussion of actual eighteenth-century ruins, which began with de Jaucourt and the *Encyclopédie*, has led through representations of ruins, both real and imaginary, to the esthetic experience of imaginary ruins. In this experience, what is at stake is the ruinous loss of foundational grounds. What conclusion is possible to such an experience? Or can we put an end to such ruin? Instead of bringing this discussion of ruins to a close with a reading of Volney imagining Palmyra in Paris through Wood's travel narrative written in London, I shall resist the lure of closure by imagining yet another scene of reading. In this other scene, Volney is not being read directly. Rather, a reading of *Les Ruines* is overheard, or more precisely a reading of Volney's text in translation, displaced or rewritten in another idiom. It is not a real reader who overhears the story of past cultures, but a character of fiction, a phantasmatic subject. I am referring to chapter 13 of Mary Shelley's *Frankenstein*, in which the monster overhears the character Felix reading *Ruins of Empires*. As Shelley's narrator notes, it is through Volney that the monster learns both history and ethics, weaving the two together in his understanding of humanity as well as of himself. Frankenstein's monster is that monstrous place, that phantasmatic site of subjectivity, where past and present are shown to be stitched together. Never identical, never seamlessly joined, past and present can be understood less through what they are than by what joins them, a historical and ontological stitch. Just as the monster in Shelley's narrative is pieced together from lifeless body parts, with technology providing him with what can only be the simulacrum of life, so too ruined bits of empire are appropriated and apprehended esthetically, stitched together to form an experience – of culture, of the self – that can then be recounted in the form of a narrative, a work of art, an object-as-monstrance that displays the self's ruined relation to the past.

CHAPTER 10

Epilogue

"Une raison doit se laisser raisonner" (a reason must let itself be reasoned with).

Jacques Derrida, *Voyous*

In this epilogue to a book on the Enlightenment and its ongoing legacy, it is fitting to ask whether we are living in a post-Enlightenment age. Are Enlightenment ideals and values no longer viable? But how could that be the case? Have we outlived them? Or can we remember them as being anything other than outlived? And if these ideals and values are the ones on which a new critical and emancipatory humanism was once founded, who are 'we' to have outlived them? A sense of self grows from the discourses available to us to phrase that selfhood, both as it defines ourselves and our relation with others. If the discourse of Enlightenment is outmoded, in abeyance, unable to be remembered in all its legitimacy, authority, and urgency, then how otherwise are we to phrase our self and ourselves? In short, what might it mean to think of ourselves as post-Enlightenment subjects? The 'Enlightenment question' seems to have no end, an endlessness upon which a post-Enlightenment age seems called endlessly to reflect. Such reflection can be found in many a body of knowledge, not simply as one question among others, but as these disciplines' central question, marking the very possibility of knowledge at present, as well as the limits of such knowledge.

The question of Enlightenment is both an epistemological and a historical question, bringing under scrutiny the basis on which critical knowledge can be founded, as well as the foundation for historical knowledge (if these two ways of knowing are totally distinct). A remark by the historian Philippe Ariès is telling in this regard. Writing in 1978, Ariès observes that the last third of the twentieth century witnesses the end of the Enlightenment, that is, the end of the belief in the irreversibility and absolute beneficence of scientific and technical progress.[1] That end is not absolute, though, and Ariès hedges his bets, for the ending he wishes to see is not that of progress itself but of the religion of progress. The distinction is worth noting. 'Religion' here connotes an excessive, unexamined belief that binds us to progress, a link that with the end of Enlightenment comes undone. Paradoxically, however, in the very phrase that announces the end of Enlightenment through a critical and desacralizing reappraisal of the place of science and technology in contemporary society, Ariès perpetuates Enlightenment by invoking the critique of irrational beliefs, by rejecting the mystified 'religion' of progress. The figure is not as strong as Voltaire's *infâme*, to be sure, yet Ariès's comment repeats a no less Voltairean gesture. His remark invokes a different and desirable kind of progress, one that is critical and not irrational, and one that the historian's diagnosis of the modern moment seeks to preserve. Apparently it is not so easy to announce the end of Enlightenment after all, at least not in terms of the discourse of history. For such an announcement risks undermining the critical discourse in which such an announcement could be made.

French historiography is marked on the whole by the sense that something has ended. In a way that is symptomatic of the cultural memory problems I have wanted to explore in this book, 'Enlightenment' designates not so much a bygone age as a contemporary and critical moment, in this case the experience of that ending from within the discipline of history. Ariès's essay appeared in *La Nouvelle Histoire*, a collection of historians' reflections bearing on the major conceptual shifts marking the field – and the state – of history in France in the late 1970s. In a retrospective issue of the *Annales*, published at the journal's half-century mark, Jacques Revel pursues that reflection, as he wonders whether in 1979 historians had to face the fact that a "a body of knowledge has been coming apart during the last twenty years. The field of research in the social sciences is breaking up."[2] Was structuralism the culprit here, with what Revel calls its violent and sometimes terroristic anti-historicism? In "The Discourse of History" Roland Barthes had certainly contributed to the undoing of a certain historical constellation, denouncing the "historicist illusion" by which the historical narrative places the referential illusion at the heart of historiography, fusing the referent with the signifier and thus confusing language and the real. As Barthes concludes, "historical narration is dying because the sign of History is henceforth not so much the real as the intelligible."[3] But we need not demonize structuralism once again. Philosophers of history too had been worrying about history's undoing. Revel himself suggests that the 'fragmentation of history' stemmed from the advent of the end of a certain humanism. "Man, the central figure of the previous arrangement, ceases to be the founding referent, becoming instead the fleeting and dated object of a particular arrangement of the discourse of knowledge."[4] Before Barthes and Revel, though, Raymond Aron had written of the "dissolution of the object" of history. "No such thing as a historical reality exists ready made, so that science merely has to reproduce it faithfully. The historical reality, because it is human, is ambiguous and inexhaustible."[5] No longer at home in the age of science, history enters the age of interpretations. In intellectual historical terms, Aron's remark is completely in tune with his unyielding critique of the radical left in postwar France and the 'scientific' knowledge of society it claimed to offer. The science Aron holds powerless is not nineteenth-century Comtean positivism, though, but twentieth-century postwar Marxism. The latter is itself only one version of the kind of thinking Aron calls the "opium" of the intellectuals, a self-intoxicating fanaticism of the engaged left, another religion of progress that is called to the bar.[6] In weaving together here the historian's announcement of the end of Enlightenment, an event whose meaning we have not yet fully teased out, and a reflection upon the way this event can be known, I want to suggest that the disciplinary and critical self-reflection found in postwar French historiography may indeed be symptomatic of a historical crisis, but one that cannot adequately be grasped in and through the discourse of history. For the historical crisis – the crisis of history – possesses a philosophical dimension, involving both epistemology and ethics.

Explorations of that dimension typically take Theodor Adorno and Max Horkheimer's *The Dialectic of Enlightenment* as a starting point (and sometimes as an ending point). But a decade before 1944, when this indictment of reason was published, Edmund Husserl had sounded the alert over a mode of thought he argued was responsible for a European "sickness." "The European nations are sick," he announced in a lecture delivered in 1935. "Europe itself, they say, is in a critical condition." From Vienna, already displaced from a Germany gripped by spreading national socialism, Husserl echoes d'Alembert in announcing that "the consistent development of exact sciences in modern times has been a true revolution in the technical mastery of nature." He recalls the Kantian critical spirit, encapsulated in the motto *sapere aude*, in invoking "the characteristic universality of the critical standpoint, with its determination not to accept without question any pregiven opinion, any tradition, and thus to seek out, with regard to the entire universe handed down in tradition, the true in itself." But Husserl sounds a far more chilling note than his eighteenth-century philosophical predecessors when he observes that reason has become over-specialized, unilateral, and instrumentalized, resulting in a "one-sided rationality [that] can become an evil."[7] The sickness of Europe in 1935 thus cannot be isolated geographically or politically, the philosopher suggests. At stake is a sickness of reason itself.

Eighteenth-century philosophes would have been hard pressed to conceive of the kind of reason Husserl imagines in the Vienna lecture, committed as they were to a rationality that set up unreason as reason's diametrically opposed other, in order all the better to undertake to eradicate that unreason. Husserl's reason, however, is more problematic and dangerous, if not more pernicious. As Jacques Derrida observes, commenting on Husserl's lecture, it is the progress of reason itself that produces the crisis of reason, spontaneously and as if from within. This crisis is not only a splitting apart of reason, as the term's etymology in *krinein* suggests, indicating judgment, discernment, and separation; it is also, in a medical sense, the telling moment when the symptoms of a sickness become legible. "Scientific reason, in its very progress, spontaneously produces the crisis. It is reason that throws reason into crisis, in an autonomous and quasi-autoimmune fashion," writes Derrida.[8] Is such a crisis over? Can it ever be? The question is perhaps badly formulated. The issue, as Derrida phrases it, involves finding ways to think rationally reason's future, its becoming (*l'avenir de la raison* or *la raison à venir*). It is by experimenting with ways to phrase this kind of thinking, adds Derrida, that one may hope to free thought from kinds of power that are military, techno-economic, and capitalistic. Such freedom cannot be thought of as absolute or utopian, however, somehow outside and beyond the crisis of reason that Husserl diagnoses. "To be responsible, to keep within reason (*raison garder*), would be to invent maxims of transaction for deciding between two just as rational and universal but contradictory exigencies of reason as well as its enlightenment."[9] In reason, there is no *hors crise*.

How do we tell the story of that kind of Enlightenment crisis? How do we write such a history? These are questions I grappled with in emplotting this book. Following in the steps of many others, I have sought to reflect on the relation between historical understanding and narrative, both in the writers and texts analyzed in each chapter but also in the way these chapters themselves form a narrative of cultural memory of Enlightenment. From d'Alembert, Diderot, and Montesquieu presented in the opening chapters, to Husserl and Derrida discussed in this epilogue, passing through La Harpe, Villemain, Sainte-Beuve, and the nineteenth-century's construction of the eighteenth, the narrative suggested here seems chronological and linear, implying the ongoing revealing of the idea or project of Enlightenment, a story told in literary-historical or social-historical terms. Yet I have also wanted to resist this teleological narrative. Mindful of Walter Benjamin's suspicion of the kind of historicism that presents history as something that can successfully be narrated, I have offered a series of singular, perhaps fragmentary encounters with the Enlightenment question. Each chapter marks afresh that question's inevitability, as well as cultural memory's inability to get beyond that question by making it seem as if the crisis that the term 'Enlightenment' signifies could be recalled and retold once and for all, through a narrative that somehow could resolve the antagonisms and contradictions the event contains.

The Enlightenment crisis of reason, then, is bound up with a deep-seated crisis of cultural memory, a crisis that may well be one of the defining characteristics of modernity. Where do we situate the beginnings of such a crisis? Or does this historicist question of beginnings mark a retreat from the crisis, distancing the crisis by placing its beginning elsewhere, suggesting that what begins must surely end but avoiding the question of how we might ever know if we have survived the crisis, or whether instead it is ongoing and endless? But allowing for a moment the historicist question of beginnings, we could note, with Richard Terdiman, that between 1789 and 1815 the French experience a radical post-revolutionary break with familiar signs of the past, be they institutions, habits, images, or words. This was a break that memory was unable to integrate within consciousness, and thus the coherence of time and of subjectivity seemed to come undone.[10] Hallmarks of the nineteenth-century experience of modernity, this disruption of the past and the ensuing memory crisis led to repeated and diverse attempts throughout the century to institutionalize memory and thus history. The development of both the novel and historiography was designed to overcome the crisis of diachronicity by phrasing new relations to time that were at once narrative, ontological, and civic. These highly self-reflexive formal experimentations with ways of speaking about the past marked a new regime of historicity, as François Hartog terms it.

In many respects, this cultural memory crisis appears to be ongoing in France. Confronting the geopolitical reality that it no longer occupies the preeminent place it once did on the world stage, France also finds itself in a geo-migratory situation that insistently and violently has called into question the very models that used to define and constitute France as a civic entity. What kind of historical methods and models correspond to such a situation? With the idea of progress in crisis, the 'new history' embraces a presentism that immobilizes time. Events are seen in their singular occurrence, displaying heterogeneous temporalities that cannot be ordered and related according to some sense of overarching change, evolution, or becoming. For François Dosse, this new historicity, which characterizes the *Annales* school, is symptomatic of social distress and civic disarray. The *Annales* historian "becomes the specialist of an unchanging time in a fixed present, filled with fear in the face of an uncertain becoming. He is the vestal of an anguished society in search of certainty and which rushes back to the past as if it were a new religion."[11] Algeria, Vietnam, the Holocaust and its deniers, May '68, the crisis of the *banlieues* – all are signifiers of a rift in France between past and present, scars on the ideal of modernity that the rhetoric of emancipatory progress will not heal. As Jean-François Lyotard remarks, that rhetoric is far from therapeutic.

For at least two centuries modernity taught us to desire the extension of political freedoms, science, the art, and technology. It taught us to legitimate this desire because, it said, such progress would emancipate humanity from despotism, ignorance, barbarism, and poverty. The republic is the humanity of citizens. Today this progress continues, assuming the more shameful name of development. But it is now impossible to justify development by promising emancipation for humanity as a whole. This promise has not been kept. It was broken, not because it was forgotten, but because development itself makes it impossible to keep.[12]

Perhaps there can be no progress without anamnesis, without a recalling of unhealing scars, even if the more 'shameful' call of development urges us to forget them (and to become oblivious to much else). What has been lost is not some mythical past but the illusion of the future.

Memory work, together with the disciplines and discourses in which it takes place, may provide a way of responding to such a situation. That at least is the wager of a certain contemporary French commemorative historiography. For Pierre Nora, member of the Académie Française and France's national historian in all but name alone, France can no longer be thought of as a historical nation, whose past guarantees its future. Rather, it is a memorial nation. "In the past ... there was *one* national history and there were *many* particular memories. Today, there is *one* national memory, but its unity stems from a divided patrimonial demand that is constantly expanding and in search of coherence," writes Nora. By cultivating and commemorating its past, by producing that past as and in memory, France generates its identity; it generates itself as remembered and commemorated identity. "France as identity is merely preparing for the future by deciphering its memory." This intense commemorative moment, this involvement in diverse *lieux de mémoire* in which the aim is to "reassemble the shattered whole," will be a defining moment in the

French contemplation of France, believes Nora. Yet it will not be an endless moment. Another way of living together will succeed the present one, eliminating the need that has been occasioned by the current crisis to explore these *lieux de mémoire*. "The era of commemoration will be over for good. The tyranny of memory will have endured for only a moment – but it was our moment."[13]

In a book that aims at diagnosing the "contemporary disarray," Jean-Claude Guillebaud notes that in France during the last few years, commemorating has become as natural as breathing. "Literature, film, music – we take great pleasure above all in 'revival', re-editions, rediscoveries, all the while taking great precautions to manage our national heritage" in a fervent attempt to prevent all that is wrong, *le mal*, from returning.[14] Yet this "militant nostalgia," however incantatory it might be, masks the underlying danger that results from focusing attention on an imaginary past and away from the present. At what point, one must ask, does memory work shade off into an alibi, if not bad faith? As far as our venture of thinking the Enlightenment past is concerned, can we indeed consider it as a *lieu de mémoire*, a reference point for countless writers and thus a concept-place richly invested by cultural memory? But is such a modernizing revision enough? Must we not also grapple with the Enlightenment according to a temporality, a critical impulse, and indeed an ethical stance that avoids both a nostalgic and thus mystified look towards the past, as well as a utopian and illusionary projection into the future? For centuries, the Enlightenment past has been in ruins, and it cannot be reconstructed or even propped up through any kind of commemorative return. But it is in these ruins that we find the Enlightenment. Unable to perform some epic 'return' to find the Enlightenment intact, we nonetheless do find it in ruins, inescapably, along with the ideals and values they signify and which we cannot do without, especially not at present. Our turning to the Enlightenment cannot allow us to hope to put back together in any enduring way the past to which these ruins seem to belong. Yet perhaps we can return to these ruins only to think of the Enlightenment according to a future anterior, as we attempt to phrase what this event will have become – both *l'avenir des lumières* and *les lumières à venir*. We cannot remember the Enlightenment sufficiently or well enough, and our skepticism towards the universal ideals of the Enlightenment is perhaps the surest sign of our wish to consign it to oblivion. Yet we forget the Enlightenment perhaps all the better to remember it, losing the Enlightenment past in order to safeguard its future, to clear a space for phrasing yet again what it will have been.

Notes

1. PRODUCING ENLIGHTENMENT HISTORY

1 François Hartog, *Régimes d'historicité: présentisme et expérience du temps* (Paris: Seuil, 2003).
2 Michel Foucault, "What is Enlightenment?," trans. Catherine Porter. In *The Foucault Reader*, ed. Paul Rabinow (New York: Pantheon Books, 1984), p. 43.
3 Pierre Nora, "Ernest Lavisse: son rôle dans la formation du sentiment national," *Revue Historique*, 228 (1962), pp. 73–106; and "Lavisse, instituteur national: Le 'Petit Lavisse', évangile de la République," in *Les Lieux de mémoire*, ed. Pierre Nora, I, *La République* (Paris: Gallimard, 1984), pp. 247–89.
4 François Dosse's study of this breakup is suggestively entitled *L'Histoire en miettes: des "Annales" à la "nouvelle histoire"* (Paris: Editions La Découverte, 1978), translated as *New History in France: The Triumph of the "Annales,"* trans. Peter Conroy (Chicago: University of Illinois Press, 1994).
5 Roger Chartier, "Intellectual History or Sociocultural History: The French Trajectory," in *Modern European Intellectual History*, ed. Dominick LaCapra and Steven L. Kaplan (Ithaca: Cornell University Press, 1982), p. 23. See also Jacques Le Goff, "Les Mentalités: une histoire ambiguë," in *Faire de l'histoire*, ed. Jacques Le Goff and Pierre Nora, 3 vols. (Paris: Gallimard, 1974), III, pp. 76–94; Philippe Ariès, "L'Histoire des mentalités," in Jacques Le Goff *et al.*, *La Nouvelle Histoire* (Paris: Retz, 1978), pp. 402–23; and Robert Mandrou, "Mentalité," *Encyclopaedia Universalis* (Paris: Encyclopaedia universalis, 1992–5), VIII, pp. 436–8.
6 Roland Barthes, "The Discourse of History," trans. Peter Wexler. In *Structuralism: A Reader*, ed. Michael Lane (London: Jonathan Cape, 1970), pp. 145–55.
7 See Philippe Carrard, *Poetics of the New History: French Historical Discourse from Braudel to Chartier* (Baltimore: Johns Hopkins University Press, 1992). For a "present state" of the textual model's impact on intellectual history in the early 1980s, see Dominick LaCapra, *Rethinking Intellectual History: Texts, Contexts, Language* (Ithaca: Cornell University Press, 1983).
8 Michel de Certeau, "Making History," in *The Writing of History*, trans. Tom Conley (New York: Columbia University Press, 1988), pp. 28–9.
9 *Ibid.*, p. 30. See Lionel Gossman's reflection on historical knowledge, discourse, and discipline in *Between History and Literature* (Cambridge, MA: Harvard University Press, 1988).

10 Michel Foucault, "Nietzsche, Genealogy, History," in *Language, Counter-Memory, Practice*, ed. Donald F. Bouchard (Ithaca: Cornell University Press, 1977), p. 152.
11 *Ibid.*, p. 146.
12 *Ibid.*, p. 142.
13 *Ibid.*, pp. 156–8.
14 Steven Kaplan, *Farewell, Revolution: The Historians' Feud, France, 1789–1989* (Ithaca: Cornell University Press, 1995).
15 Steven Kaplan provides a synthetic overview of this moment in *Farewell, Revolution: Disputed Legacies, France 1789–1989* (Ithaca: Cornell University Press, 1995).
16 Examples of this self-reflexive historiography include Henry Rousso, *The Vichy Syndrome: History and Memory in France since 1944*, trans. Arthur Goldhammer (Cambridge, MA: Harvard University Press, 1991); and Christophe Charle, *La Naissance des "intellectuels": 1880–1900* (Paris: Minuit, 1990).
17 Albert Soboul, *The French Revolution, 1787–1799*, trans. Alan Forrest and Colin Jones (New York: Vintage, 1974). See also Soboul's "L'*Encyclopédie* et le mouvement encyclopédique," *La Pensée*, 39 (1951), pp. 41–51, reprinted in his *Textes choisis de l'Encyclopédie* (Paris: Editions Sociales, 1952).
18 Keith Michael Baker, "Enlightenment and Revolution in France: Old Problems, Renewed Approaches," *Journal of Modern History*, 53 (1981), p. 284.
19 See François Furet, *Revolutionary France, 1770–1880*, trans. Antonia Nevill (Oxford: Blackwell, 1992).
20 Furet's recurrent critique of Marxism culminates in *Le Passé d'une illusion: essai sur l'idée communiste au XXe siècle* (Paris: Robert Laffont, 1995). For a treatment of the French left's disillusionment with Marxism, see Tony Judt, *Past Imperfect: French Intellectuals, 1944–1956* (Berkeley: University of California Press, 1992).
21 Roger Chartier, *The Cultural Origins of the French Revolution*, trans. Lydia G. Cochrane (Durham, NC: Duke University Press, 1991), p. 5.
22 An interesting phenomenon in this regard is the recent *Dictionnaire européen des Lumières*, ed. Michel Delon (Paris: Presses Universitaires de France, 1997). Instead of claiming the existence of a European Enlightenment that transcends national specificity, the title of this work suggests that it is the dictionary itself that produces the Enlightenment in its cosmopolitan, European dimension. Whether this venture – that of both the dictionary and Europe – succeeds in transcending the particularities of nationalism remains to be seen.
23 Jean Marie Goulemot, *Adieu les philosophes: que reste-t-il des Lumières?* (Paris: Seuil, 2001), pp. 14, 17.
24 Alain Finkielkraut, *The Undoing of Thought*, trans. Dennis O'Keefe (London: Claridge, 1988).
25 Régis Debray, *Aveuglantes lumières: journal en clair-obscur* (Paris: Gallimard, 2006).
26 David Denby, "Crise des Lumières, crise de la modernité?," *Dix-Huitième Siècle*, 30 (1998), pp. 257–70.

27 Cf. Roy Porter and Mikulas Teich, eds., *The Enlightenment in National Context* (Cambridge: Cambridge University Press, 1981).
28 See James Schmidt, "Inventing the Enlightenment: British Hegelians, Anti-Jacobins, and the *Oxford English Dictionary*," *Journal of the History of Ideas*, 64:3 (2003), pp. 421–43. I have put aside here the question of the Anglo-American construction of the Enlightenment. For the British case, see Seamus Deane's *The French Revolution and Enlightenment in English, 1789–1832* (Cambridge, MA: Harvard University Press, 1988). *What is Enlightenment?: Eighteenth-Century Answers and Twentieth-Century Questions*, ed. James Schmidt (Berkeley: University of California Press, 1996), provides a broad overview of the German perspective on the question.
29 Mark Lilla, "The Legitimacy of the Liberal Age," in *New French Thought: Political Philosophy*, ed. Mark Lilla (Princeton: Princeton University Press, 1994), p. 34. Although such self-justification is not absent in France, this estrangement remains a perennial puzzle for French political and cultural commentators in their concern with American 'liberalism'. See Philippe Roger, *The American Enemy: A Story of French Anti-Americanism*, trans. Sharon Bowman (Chicago: University of Chicago Press, 2005).
30 Sophia Rosenfeld, "Writing the History of Censorship in the Age of Enlightenment," in *Postmodernism and the Enlightenment*, ed. Daniel Gordon (New York: Routledge, 2001), pp. 117–46.
31 Didier Masseau, *Les Ennemis des philosophes: l'antiphilosophie au temps des Lumières* (Paris: Albin Michel, 2002). See also Darrin M. McMahon, *Enemies of the Enlightenment: The French Counter-Enlightenment and the Making of Modernity* (New York: Oxford University Press, 2001).
32 Zygmunt Bauman, *Modernity and the Holocaust* (Ithaca: Cornell University Press, 1989).
33 Jürgen Habermas, *Autonomy and Solidarity: Interviews*, ed. Peter Dews (London: Verso, 1986), p. 158.
34 These are the articles of the brief against the Enlightenment that Robert Darnton rehearses in "George Washington's False Teeth," *La Recherche Dix-Huitiémiste*, ed. Michel Delon and Jochen Schlobach (Paris: Honoré Champion, 1998), pp. 149–66. See also John Gray's *Enlightenment's Wake: Politics and Culture at the Close of the Modern Age* (New York: Routledge, 1995). Gray notes that the present age is "distinguished by the collapse of the Enlightenment project on a world-historical scale" (p. 1) and proceeds to explore the possibility of an "agonistic liberalism" that could supplant a bankrupt traditional liberalism. An unrelenting indictment of Enlightenment racism is found in Louis Sala-Molins, *Dark Side of the Light: Slavery and the French Enlightenment*, trans. John Conteh-Morgan (Minneapolis: University of Minnesota Press, 2005).
35 Daniel Gordon, ed., *Postmodernism and the Enlightenment* (New York: Routledge, 2001).
36 Jean-François Lyotard, *The Postmodern Condition*, trans. Geoff Bennington and Brian Massumi (Minneapolis: University of Minnesota Press, 1984), pp. xxiii–xxiv.

37 Keith Jenkins, *Why History? Ethics and Postmodernity* (New York: Routledge, 1999), p. 4.
38 Immanuel Kant, *Kant's Political Writings*, ed. Hans Reiss (Cambridge: Cambridge University Press, 1970), p. 54.
39 Immanuel Kant, *Critique of Pure Reason*, trans. Norman Kemp Smith (New York: St. Martin's Press, 1968), p. 9 (preface to 1st edn.).
40 Foucault, "What is Enlightenment?," p. 55.
41 Michel Foucault, "Qu'est-ce que les Lumières?", *Dits et écrits* (Paris: Gallimard, 1994), IV, pp. 222–43.
42 Jean-François Lyotard, *Political Writings*, trans. Bill Readings and Kevin Paul (Minneapolis: University of Minnesota Press, 1993), pp. 113–14.

2. THE EVENT OF ENLIGHTENMENT: BEGINNINGS

1 Jean Le Rond d'Alembert, "Sur la destruction des Jésuites en France," *Œuvres complètes* (Paris: Belin, 1821), II, p. 15.
2 Immanuel Kant, *Critique of Pure Reason*, trans. Norman Kemp Smith (New York: St. Martin's Press, 1968), p. 9 (preface to 1st edn.).
3 In Denis Diderot and Jean Le Rond d'Alembert, eds., *Encyclopédie, ou dictionnaire raisonné des sciences, des arts et des métiers* (Paris: Briasson, 1751–65), VII, p. 600.
4 Thomas S. Kuhn, *The Structure of Scientific Revolutions* (Chicago: University of Chicago Press, 1962).
5 See Michel Foucault, *The Order of Things* (New York: Vintage Books, 1970), and *The Archaeology of Knowledge*, trans. A. M. Sheridan Smith (New York: Pantheon Books, 1972).
6 See David Bates, "Cartographic Aberrations: Epistemology and Order in the Encyclopedic Map," in *Using the 'Encyclopédie': Ways of Knowing, Ways of Reading*, ed. Daniel Brewer and Julie Candler Hayes, *SVEC*, 2002:05 (2002), pp. 1–20.
7 Daniel Brewer, *The Discourse of Enlightenment in Eighteenth-Century France: Diderot and the Art of Philosophizing* (New York: Cambridge University Press, 1993).
8 See Jean Marie Goulemot, "Literary Practices: Publicizing the Private," in *A History of Private Life*, III: *Passions of the Renaissance*, ed. Roger Chartier, trans. Arthur Goldhammer (Cambridge, MA: Harvard University Press, 1989), pp. 363–95. See also David Denby, *Sentimental Narrative and the Social Order in France, 1760–1820* (New York: Cambridge University Press, 1994).
9 See Joan DeJean, *Ancients Against Moderns: Culture Wars and the Making of a Fin de Siècle* (Chicago: University of Chicago Press, 1997); Marc Fumaroli, *La Querelle des Anciens et des Modernes* (Paris: Gallimard, 2000).
10 Bruno Latour, *We Have Never Been Modern*, trans. Catherine Porter (New York: Harvester Wheatsheaf, 1993). "There are no longer – there never have been – anything but elements that elude the system, objects whose date

and duration are uncertain ... We have all reached the point of mixing up times. We have all become premodern again" (p. 75).
11 Jean-Luc Nancy, *The Inoperative Community*, trans. Peter Connor et al. (Minneapolis: University of Minnesota Press, 1991).
12 David Lowenthal, *The Past is a Foreign Country* (New York: Cambridge University Press, 1985).
13 Karl Popper's *The Poverty of Historicism* (1957) mounted an influential critique of the belief in natural laws of development in human history, and in human beings' ability to discover them. See Paul Hamilton, *Historicism* (New York: Routledge, 1996).
14 In *Citizens Without Sovereignty* (Princeton: Princeton University Press, 1994) Daniel Gordon argues for precisely this uncoupling of the Enlightenment from the Revolution in order to understand a non-hierarchical eighteenth-century sociability.
15 On the changing notion of 'revolution', see Keith Baker, "Inventing the French Revolution," in *Inventing the French Revolution* (Cambridge: Cambridge University Press, 1990), pp. 203–23.
16 "Discours préliminaire," in Denis Diderot and Jean Le Rond d'Alembert, eds., *Encyclopédie, ou dictionnaire raisonné des sciences, des arts et des métiers* (Paris: Briasson, 1751–65), I, p. xxxiii.
17 For a discussion of whether the scientific revolution should be viewed as a historical fact or as a constructed concept, see *Rethinking the Scientific Revolution*, ed. Margaret J. Osler (New York: Cambridge University Press, 2000). Cf. Steven Shapin, *The Scientific Revolution* (Chicago: University of Chicago Press, 2000); and Margaret C. Jacob, *Scientific Culture and the Making of the Industrial West* (New York: Oxford University Press, 1997) and *The Cultural Meaning of the Scientific Revolution* (New York: Knopf, 1988).
18 Diderot, *Pensées sur l'interprétation de la nature*, in *Œuvres complètes* (Paris: Hermann, 1981), IX, pp. 30–1. In the article "Encyclopédie" Diderot notes, "in the sciences there is a point beyond which they are almost not allowed to go. When this point has been passed, the monuments of this progress that remain will forever astound humanity" (V, p. 637).
19 On *Le Rêve* see Jacques Roger, *The Life Sciences in Eighteenth-Century French Thought*, trans. Robert Ellrich (Stanford: Stanford University Press, 1997).
20 Foucault distinguishes between sovereignty and governmentality in "Governmentality," in *The Foucault Effect: Studies in Governmentality*, ed. Graham Burchell, Colin Gordon, and Peter Miller (Chicago: University of Chicago Press, 1991), pp. 87–104.
21 See Jay Caplan, *Framed Narratives: Diderot's Genealogy of the Beholder* (Minneapolis: University of Minnesota Press, 1985).
22 Jean Le Rond d'Alembert, *Essai sur les éléments de philosophie*, in *Œuvres complètes* (Paris: Belin, 1821), I, pp. 122–3.
23 See Roger, *The Life Sciences*; and Alexandre Koyré, *From the Closed World to the Infinite Universe* (Baltimore: Johns Hopkins University Press, 1957).

Notes to pages 36–42

24 D'Alembert, "Discours préliminaire," in *Encyclopédie*, I, p. xxvi. On d'Alembert's defense of Descartes and his critique of Cartesian "sectateurs," see Martine Groult, *D'Alembert et la mécanique de la vérité dans l'"Encyclopédie"* (Paris: Honoré Champion, 1999). For a study of how modernity is constructed through reference to Descartes, see Stéphane Van Damme, *Descartes: essai d'histoire culturelle d'une grandeur philosophique* (Paris: Presses de Sciences Po, 2002).

25 In *Entretiens sur la pluralité des mondes* Fontenelle writes, "Before Descartes, reasoning was easier; previous centuries are fortunate not to have had this man. It seems to me that he brought this new method of reasoning, much more estimable than his philosophy itself, a good portion of which is false, or highly uncertain, according to the very rules he taught us. There reigns not only in our fine works of physics and metaphysics, but in those of religion, ethics, and criticism, a heretofore unknown precision and soundness of judgment." Bernard Le Bovier de Fontenelle, *Fontenelle: Entretiens sur la pluralité des mandes*, ed. Robert Shackleton (Oxford: Clarendon Press, 1955), p. 167.

26 See the articles "Le Pyrrhonisme de l'histoire" and "Certain, certitude" in Voltaire's *Dictionnaire philosophique*. Voltaire remained haunted by the skepticism exemplified by Bayle's critical history, which questioned whether such a thing as historical truth was possible. See J. H. Brumfitt, *Voltaire: Historian* (London: Oxford University Press, 1970).

27 Judith Sklar, "Jean d'Alembert and the Rehabilitation of History," *Journal of the History of Ideas*, 42:4 (1981), pp. 643–64.

28 Georges Canguilhem, "Fontenelle philosophe et historien des sciences," *Etudes d'histoire et de philosophe des sciences* (Paris: Vrin, 1970), p. 55.

29 See d'Alembert's *Encyclopédie* articles "Collège" and "Erudition," and his "Réflexions sur l'histoire," in *Œuvres complètes*, II, pp. 1–10.

30 As permanent secretary of the Académie Française, d'Alembert was responsible for writing the official necrologies of recently deceased *immortels*. These *éloges*, especially those of scientists, have been seen as prototypical scientific history. On d'Alembert as historian of science, see Georges Gusdorf, *De l'histoire des sciences à l'histoire de la pensée* (Paris: Payot, 1966), pp. 47–62.

31 For studies of empowerment in terms of authorial self-production, see Gregory S. Brown, "The Self-Fashionings of Olympe de Gouges, 1784–1789," *Eighteenth-Century Studies*, 34:3 (2001), pp. 383–401; and Geoffrey Turnovsky, "Conceptualising the Literary Market: Diderot and the *Lettre sur le commerce de la librairie*," *SVEC*, 2003:01 (2003), pp. 135–70.

32 This camouflaging is one of the characteristics of ideology, which does not so much hide reality as give it to be seen differently. See Louis Althusser, for whom ideology presents an imaginary representation of real conditions of existence, "Ideology and Ideological State Apparatuses," in *Lenin and Philosophy*, trans. Ben Brewster (New York: Monthly Review Press, 1971).

33 See Michel Guéroult, *Philosophie de l'histoire de la philosophie* (Paris: Aubier, 1979); Alexandre Koyré, *Etudes d'histoire de la pensée philosophique* (Paris: Colin, 1962); Jean Marie Goulemot, *Le Règne de l'histoire: discours historiques*

et révolutions, XVIIe–XVIIIe siècles (Paris: Albin Michel, 1996); Henry Vyverberg, *Historical Pessimism in the French Enlightenment* (Cambridge, MA: Harvard University Press, 1958).
34 Ernst Cassirer, *The Philosophy of the Enlightenment*, trans. Fritz C. A. Koelln and James P. Pettegrove (Princeton: Princeton University Press, 1951), pp. v–vi.
35 Dena Goodman, *The Republic of Letters: A Cultural History of the French Enlightenment* (Ithaca: Cornell University Press, 1994), p. 61.
36 See Lewis P. Hinchman, *Hegel's Critique of the Enlightenment* (Gainesville: University Presses of Florida, 1984).
37 Cassirer, *Philosophy*, p. v.
38 Peter Gay, "The Social History of Ideas: Ernst Cassirer and After," in *The Critical Spirit: Essays in Honor of Herbert Marcuse*, ed. Kurth H. Wolff and Barrington Moore, (Boston, MA: Beacon Press, 1967), pp. 106–20.
39 Robert Darnton, "In Search of the Enlightenment: Recent Attempts to Create a Social History of Ideas," *Journal of Modern History*, 43 (1971), pp. 113–32.
40 Goodman, *Republic of Letters*, p. 63. See her "Difference: An Enlightenment Concept," in *What's Left of Enlightenment? A Postmodern Question*, ed. Keith Michael Baker and Peter Hanns Reil (Stanford: Stanford University Press, 2001), pp. 129–47.
41 See Dominick LaCapra, *Rethinking Intellectual History: Texts, Contexts, Language* (Ithaca: Cornell University Press, 1983).
42 Cassirer, *Philosophy*, p.viii.
43 *Ibid.*, pp.xi–xii.
44 *Ibid.*, p.xi.
45 Cassirer was elected rector of the University of Hamburg in 1929, the first time a Jew had held this position in Germany. In 1932, in his last major speech, which was on the history of modern natural rights, "Vom Wesen und Werden des Naturrechts," he stressed the eighteenth-century notion of inalienable rights, calling for their revival. In 1933, Hitler became Chancellor. In May of that year Cassirer and his family left Germany for Vienna. Coincidentally, it was in the same month that Martin Heidegger, with whom Cassirer had been involved in a series of public debates over the direction of German philosophy, assumed the rectorship of the University of Freiburg.
46 Cassirer, *Philosophy*, p.xi.
47 Johnson Kent Wright, "'A Bright Clear Mirror': Cassirer's *The Philosophy of the Enlightenment*," in *What's Left of Enlightenment? A Postmodern Question*, ed. Keith Michael Baker and Peter Hans Reill (Stanford: Stanford University Press, 2001), p. 96.
48 As Wright notes, this argument is made by the English historian Alfred Cobban, "The Enlightenment and Germany," *Spectator*, 26 (September 1952), pp. 406–7. For another perspective on the 'national' determination of early modern French studies, see Daniel Gordon's discussion of Norbert Elias in *Citizens Without Sovereignty*, ch. 3.

3. THE SUBJECT OF ENLIGHTENMENT: CONSTRUCTING PHILOSOPHERS, WRITING INTELLECTUALS

1 "The progress of human knowledge is a route already laid out, from which it is almost impossible for thought (*l'esprit humain*) to diverge," he writes in the *Encyclopédie* article "Eclectisme," v, p. 283.
2 Condorcet, *Esquisse d'un tableau historique des progrès de l'esprit humain* (Paris: Vrin, 1970), p. 1.
3 On Condorcet's symbolic afterlife, see Jean-Pierre Schandeler, *Les Interprétations de Condorcet: symboles et concepts (1794–1894)*, SVEC, 2000:03 (Oxford: Voltaire Foundation, 2000).
4 On eighteenth-century materialism, see Olivier Bloch, *Le Matérialisme* (Paris: Presses Universitaires de France, 1985); *Etre matérialiste au siècle des Lumières*, ed. Beatrice Fink and Gerhardt Stenger (Paris: Presses Universitaires de France, 1999).
5 "Thinking is feeling" (*Penser, c'est sentir*), writes Helvétius in *De l'esprit* (1758), a claim Destutt de Tracy intensifies, "Thinking ... is always feeling, and it is only feeling" ("Penser ... c'est toujours sentir, et ce n'est rien que sentir"), in *Eléments d'idéologie* (1801) (Paris: Courcier, 1804), p. 25.
6 D'Alembert's debate with Rousseau continues in the *Encyclopédie* article "Genève," to which Rousseau responds in his *Lettre à d'Alembert sur les spectacles*. See Patrick Coleman, *Rousseau's Political Imagination: Rule and Representation in the "Lettre à d'Alembert"* (Geneva: Droz, 1984).
7 This interpretation has been subjected to significant revision. Roger Chartier discusses de Tocqueville's *L'Ancien Régime et la révolution française* in *The Cultural Origins of the French Revolution* (Durham, NC: Duke University Press, 1989), pp. 20–37, 154–62. Alternative views of de Tocqueville's position have been offered by Jürgen Habermas, *The Structural Transformation of the Public Sphere*, trans. Thomas Burger (Cambridge, MA: MIT Press, 1989), and Reinhart Koselleck, *Critique and Crisis* (Cambridge, MA: MIT Press, 1988).
8 "[The great (*les grands*) will begin] to seek out not only the works of writers but the writers themselves." Jean Le Rond d'Alembert, *Essai sur la société des gens de lettres et des grands* (Paris: Belin, 1821), IV, p. 339.
9 See Dena Goodman, *The Republic of Letters: A Cultural History of the French Enlightenment* (Ithaca: Cornell University Press, 1994); Daniel Gordon, *Citizens Without Sovereignty* (Princeton: Princeton University Press, 1994).
10 Other eighteenth-century formulations of sociability are found in François Adrien Pluquet's *De la sociabilité* (1767) and Claude-François-Nicolas Le Maître de Claville's *Traité du vrai mérite* (1736). See Albert O. Hirschman, *The Passions and the Interests: Political Arguments for Capitalism Before Its Triumph* (Princeton: Princeton University Press, 1977).
11 D'Alembert, *Essai*, IV, p. 339.
12 Robert Darnton, *The Literary Underground of the Old Regime* (Cambridge, MA: Harvard University Press, 1982).
13 On the emergence of the writer, see Roger Chartier, *Lectures et lecteurs dans la France d'Ancien Régime* (Paris: Seuil, 1987) and *Culture écrite et société: l'ordre*

des livres, XIVe–XVIIIe siècle (Paris: Albin Michel, 1996); Eric Walter, "Les Auteurs et le champ littéraire," in *Histoire de l'édition française*, ed. Henri-Jean Martin, II: *Le Livre triomphant (1660–1830)* (Paris: Promodis, 1984), pp. 383–409; and Alain Viala, *La Naissance de l'écrivain: sociologie de la littérature à l'âge classique* (Paris: Minuit, 1985).

14 See Erica Harth, *Ideology and Culture in Seventeenth-Century France* (Ithaca: Cornell University Press, 1983), p. 115.

15 From a traditional – and unreconstructed – Marxist perspective, that meaning was designed to reflect and promote the interests of an established, homogeneous class. Louis Althusser offers a more nuanced understanding of ideology, arguing that it provides an imaginary resolution to contradictions that are not reconciled in social reality.

16 See Louis Marin, *Le Récit est un piège* (Paris: Minuit, 1978) and *Le Portrait du roi* (Paris: Minuit, 1981); and Jean-Marie Apostolidès, *Le Roi machine: spectacle et politique au temps de Louis XIV* (Paris: Minuit, 1981).

17 Carolyn Lougee, *Le Paradis des femmes: Women, Salons, and Social Stratification in Seventeenth-Century France* (Princeton: Princeton University Press, 1976), and more recently Joan de Jean, *Tender Geographies: Women and the Origins of the Novel in France* (New York, 1991), have helped revise the regicentric notion of court culture by revealing the structure and workings of other cultural spaces besides that of the court.

18 Pierre Bourdieu, *Distinction: A Social Critique of the Judgment of Taste*, trans. Richard Nice (Cambridge, MA.: Harvard University Press, 1984). On the postrevolutionary development of the intellectual field, see Christophe Charle, *Naissance des "intellectuels," 1880–1900* (Paris: Minuit, 1990). Régis Debray analyzes the transformation of modern French intellectuals in *Teachers, Writers, Celebrities: The Intellectuals of Modern France*, trans. David Macey (London: New Left Books, 1981).

19 Voltaire himself published the article in 1773, and it appeared in an edition of Helvétius's works. See Herbert Dieckmann, *"Le Philosophe": Texts and Interpretation* (St. Louis: n.p., 1948), here p. 9; and Ira O. Wade, *The Clandestine Organization and Diffusion of Philosophic Ideas in France from 1700 to 1750* (Princeton: Princeton University Press, 1938).

20 For a discussion of the ARTFL database and its impact on research on the eighteenth century, see Philip Stewart, "The *Encyclopédie* On-Line," and Fabienne-Sophie Chauderlot, "Encyclopédismes d'hier et d'aujourd'hui: informations ou pensée? Une lecture de l'*Encyclopédie* à la Deleuze," in *Using the "Encyclopédie": Ways of Knowing, Ways of Reading*, ed. Daniel Brewer and Julie Candler Hayes, *SVEC*, 2002:05.

21 Roger Chartier analyzes this shift in "The Man of Letters," in *Enlightenment Portraits*, ed. Michel Vovelle, trans. Lydia Cochrane (Chicago: University of Chicago Press, 1997), pp. 142–89.

22 Quotations from *Le Philosophe* refer to the Dieckmann edition; p. 30.

23 Louis Althusser, *Lenin and Philosophy, and Other Essays*, trans. Ben Brewster (London: Monthy Review Press, 1971), p. 24.

Notes to pages 61–72

24 *Le Philosophe*, pp. 32, 46.
25 See Pierre Naudin, *L'Expérience et le sentiment de la solitude: de l'aube des Lumières à la Révolution* (Paris: Klincksieck, 1995). Juliette Cherbuliez remaps the idea of retreat in *The Place of Exile: Leisure Literature and the Limits of Absolutism* (Lewisburg, PA: Bucknell University Press, 2005).
26 See Norbert Elias, *The Court Society*, trans. Edmund Jephcott (New York: Pantheon, 1983).
27 Goulemot, in Jean Marie Goulemot and Daniel Oster, *Gens de lettres, écrivains et bohèmes: l'imaginaire littéraire, 1630–1900* (Paris: Minerve, 1992), pp. 9, 11. Edward Said extends the idea of the marginalized, alienated writer to include the intellectual whose viewpoint is always 'exilic', as she or he moves away from and against centralizing authority and towards margins; *Representations of the Intellectual* (New York: Pantheon, 1994).
28 In *Lettre sur le commerce de la librairie*, in *Œuvres complètes*, VIII (Paris: Hermann, 1976), pp. 479–567, Diderot maintains that these rights should reside with publishers, which is far preferable to their not being recognized at all. That they could legitimately reside with the writer is not yet arguable.
29 For alternative views of the literary field, see Geoffrey Turnovsky, "Marginal Writers in the 'Literary Market': Defining a New Field of Authorship in Eighteenth-Century France," *Studies in Eighteenth-Century Culture*, 33 (2004), pp. 101–23; and Gregory S. Brown, *Literary Sociability and Literary Property in France, 1775–1793* (Aldershot: Ashgate, 2006). Cf. Elizabeth L. Eisenstein, *Grub Street Abroad: Aspects of the French Cosmopolitan Press from the Age of Louis XIV to the French Revolution* (New York: Clarendon Press, 1992). For a collection of critical responses to Darnton's thesis, see *The Darnton Debate*, ed. Haydn T. Mason (Oxford: Voltaire Foundation, 1998).
30 *Le Philosophe*, pp. 42, 44.
31 *Ibid.*, p. 44.
32 Michael Moriarty, *Taste and Ideology in Seventeenth-Century France* (Cambridge: Cambridge University Press, 1988), p. 52. See Emmanuel Bury, *L'Invention de l'honnête homme, 1580–1750* (Paris: Presses Universitaires de France, 1996).
33 *Le Philosophe*, p. 44.
34 *Ibid.*, p. 60.
35 "I love luxury and even the soft life, / All pleasures, arts of every kind, / Propriety, taste, ornaments: / All decent men have such feelings … / Oh, what a fine time this age of iron!" Although more restrained in his *Défense du Mondain* (1737) and more nuanced in his *Discours en vers sur l'Homme* (1738), Voltaire's epicureanism will remain a constant ideal in his writing.
36 *Le Philosophe*, pp. 91–2.
37 Roland Barthes, "Le Dernier des écrivains heureux," *Essais critiques* (Paris: Seuil, 1964); Jean-Paul Sartre, *Qu'est-ce que la littérature?* (Paris: Gallimard, 1948).
38 Louis Althusser, *For Marx*, trans. Ben Brewster (London: Allen Lane, 1969), p. 234.
39 Denis Diderot, *Le Neveu de Rameau*, in *Œuvres complètes* (Paris: Hermann, 1989), XII, p. 72.

40 Goulemot, in Goulemot and Oster, *Gens de lettres*, p. 8.
41 Lyotard, *Tombeau de l'intellectuel, et autres papiers* (Paris: Galilée, 1984), p. 12.
42 Lyotard explains the historical specificity of this remark and pursues this reflection in his essay, "Discussions, ou: phraser 'après Auschwitz'," in *Les Fins de l'homme* (Paris: Galilée, 1981), pp. 283–308. See also *Le Différand* (Paris: Minuit, 1983).
43 See the special issue of *L'Esprit Créateur* on the subject of the intellectual, including my article, "The French Intellectual, History, and the Reproduction of Culture," 37:2 (1997), pp. 16–33.

4. DESIGNING THE PAST: THINKING HISTORY THROUGH MONTESQUIEU

1 Alain Grosrichard, *La Structure du sérail: la fiction du despotisme asiatique dans l'Occident classique* (Paris: Seuil, 1979).
2 Denis Diderot, *Correspondance*, ed. Georges Roth and Jean Varloot (Paris: Editions de Minuit, 1968), XIV, p. 227.
3 Jean-Jacques Rousseau, *Correspondance complète*, ed. Ralph A. Leigh (Geneva: Institut et Musée Voltaire, 1975), XIII, p. 98.
4 Diderot clings to the belief in the eventually vindicative judgment of posterity, even as he voices counter-arguments through the character Lui in *Le Neveu de Rameau* and debates the issue at length with the sculptor Etienne-Maurice Falconet in *Le Pour et le contre, ou lettres sur la postérité*, *Œuvres complètes*, XIX (Paris: Hermann, 1986).
5 Jean-Claude Bonnet, *Naissance du Panthéon: essai sur le culte des grands hommes* (Paris: Fayard, 1998).
6 See Jean Marie Goulemot and Daniel Oster, *Gens de lettres, écrivains et bohèmes: l'imaginaire littéraire, 1630–1900* (Paris: Minerve, 1992). Cf. Goulemot's *Adieu les philosophes: que reste-t-il des Lumières?* (Paris: Seuil, 2001).
7 For a study of the larger context in which this reconfiguration of Montesquieu occurs, see David Bell, *The Cult of the Nation in France: Inventing Nationalism, 1680–1800* (Cambridge, MA: Harvard University Press, 2001).
8 This tension plays itself out in the divided reception Condorcet's works receive in the nineteenth century. See Jean-Pierre Schandeler, *Les Interprétations de Condorcet: symboles et concepts (1794–1894)*, SVEC, 2000:03.
9 For a schematic view of this reception, see Louis Desgraves, *Répertoire des ouvrages et des articles sur Montesquieu* (Geneva: Droz, 1988). Cf. Corrado Rosso's more analytical *La Réception de Montesquieu, ou, les silences de la harpe éolienne* (Paris: Nizet, 1989); Catherine Larrère, "Montesquieu and the Modern Republic: The Republican Heritage in Nineteenth-Century France," *SVEC*, 2002:09 (2002), pp. 235–49; and Jean Ehrard, "Montesquieu dans les débats politiques français d'aujourd'hui," *SVEC*, 2003:01 (2003), pp. 455–64.
10 *The Eclipse of Reason* (New York: Seabury Press, 1974). For an analysis of this eclipse as it relates to Enlightenment, see Theodor Adorno and Max Horkheimer, *Dialectic of Enlightenment*, trans. John Cumming (New York: Continuum, 1972).

11 In one of the numerous instances of eighteenth-century intellectual self-portraiture, Diderot describes the eclectic as follows: "The eclectic is a philosopher who, trampling prejudice, tradition, ancientness, universal consent, and authority, in short everything that enthralls the horde, dares to think for himself, to return to the clearest general principles, examine and discuss them, to admit nothing that has not been vouchsafed by this experience and reason; and from all the philosophies he has analyzed impartially and without special consideration, he makes his own personal private philosophy," "Eclectisme," *Encyclopédie*, v, p. 270.
12 Benrekassa's own work on Montesquieu represents a challenging attempt to articulate those conditions. See *La Politique et sa mémoire: la politique et l'histoire dans la pensée des Lumières* (Paris: Payot, 1983); *Le Concentrique et l'excentrique: marges des Lumières* (Paris: Payot, 1980), pp. 155–79.
13 Jean Ehrard, in Georges Benrekassa, "Table ronde: Montesquieu et la culture politique d'aujourd'hui," *Dix-Huitième Siècle*, 21 (1989), pp. 179–86.
14 *Œuvres complètes* (Paris: Gallimard, 1951), II, p. 173. For an analysis of Montesquieu and the question of causality that sets him in the frame of Enlightenment philosophy of history, see David Carrithers, "Montesquieu's Philosophy of History," *Journal of the History of Ideas*, 47 (1986), pp. 61–80.
15 Montesquieu, *The Spirit of the Laws*, ed. and trans. Anne M. Cohler, Basia Carolyn Miller, and Harold Samuel Stone (Cambridge: Cambridge University Press, 1989), p. xliii.
16 Possessing a causality, Rome can be explained rationally. Thus the Roman lesson is that "facts are not opaque to reason ... But [Montesquieu's originality] is not to have limited himself to an epistemological reading of the course of events. To him, the logic of history belongs to history itself, and the ultimate *raison d'être* of its movement must be grasped." Simone Goyard-Fabre, *Montesquieu: la nature, les lois, la liberté* (Paris: Presses Universitaires de France, 1993), p. 43.
17 See Louis Marin, *Le Portrait du roi* (Paris, 1981), and Jean-Marie Apostolidès, *Le Roi machine: spectacle et politique au temps de Louis XIV* (Paris: Minuit, 1981).
18 See Simone Goyard-Fabre, *Montesquieu, adversaire de Hobbes* (Paris: Lettres Modernes, 1980).
19 Montesquieu, *The Spirit of the Laws*, 1:2, p. 6.
20 *Ibid.*, 1:1, p. 3.
21 *Ibid.*, 1:3, p. 8.
22 "[Montesquieu] proves that political action is possible, and he defines its conditions." Jean Ehrard, *La Politique de Montesquieu* (Paris: Armand Colin, 1965), p. 9.
23 Bertrand Binoche, "Montesquieu et la crise de la rationalité historique," *Revue Germanique Internationale*, 3 (1995), p. 33.
24 Montesquieu, *The Spirit of the Laws*, 8:2, p. 112.
25 *Ibid.*, 8:5, p. 116.
26 *Ibid.*, 3:10, p. 29.
27 *Ibid.*, 8:10, p. 119.

28 Montesquieu, *Persian Letters*, trans. C. J. Betts (Harmondsworth: Penguin Books, 1973), letter 136, pp. 241–2.
29 *Ibid.*, letter 11, p. 53.
30 Montesquieu, *The Spirit of the Laws*, 8:11, p. 119.
31 *Ibid.*, 11:13, p. 172.
32 This double reading points to what Isaiah Berlin calls an "internal conflict" in Montesquieu's writing, a tension between, on the one hand, an evolutionary, pragmatic development of law, open to meliorative social change, and, on the other, a tradition of codified law, based on general principles of universal, unchanging validity. "Montesquieu," in *Against the Current* (London: The Hogarth Press, 1979), p. 196.
33 See Jean Ehrard and Catherine Volpilhac-Auger, "Théorie des révolutions dans le rapport qu'elles ont avec les divers gouvernements," *Dix-Huitième Siècle*, 21 (1989), pp. 23–46. On the larger eighteenth-century understanding of the sense of the word 'revolution', see Keith Michael Baker, "Revolution," in *The French Revolution and the Creation of Modern Political Culture*, II: *The Political Culture of the French Revolution*, ed. Colin Lucas (New York: Pergamon, 1988), pp. 41–62.
34 Montesquieu, *The Spirit of the Laws*, 5:7, p. 49.
35 See Jean Marie Goulemot, *Discours, histoire et révolution* (Paris: 10/18, 1975), p. 458; and his "Vision du devenir historique et formes de la révolution dans les *Lettres persanes*," *Dix-Huitième Siècle*, 21 (1989), pp. 13–22.
36 Montesquieu, *The Spirit of the Laws*, 11:6, p. 166.
37 Jean Starobinski, *Montesquieu par lui-même* (Paris: Seuil, 1959), p. 74.
38 Henry Vyverberg, *Historical Pessimism in the French Enlightenment* (Cambridge, MA: Harvard University Press, 1958), p. 164.
39 For Georges Benrekassa, this possibility leads to a paradoxical state of affairs in interpreting Montesquieu. "In sacrificing what seems to be the most 'outdated' or 'archaic', we often prevent ourselves from truly understanding what is presented as being the most of the moment (*actuel*)." "Table ronde," p. 183.
40 Nannerl O. Keohane, *Philosophy and the State in France: The Renaissance to the Enlightenment* (Princeton: Princeton University Press, 1980).
41 Montesquieu, *The Spirit of the Laws*, 11:4, p. 155.
42 *Ibid.*
43 *Ibid.*, 11:3, p. 155.
44 *Ibid.*, 19:5, p. 310.
45 "In the long run," writes Kristeva, "only a thorough investigation of our remarkable relationship with both the other and strangeness within ourselves can lead people to give up hunting for the scapegoat outside their group, a search that allows them to withdraw into their own 'sanctum' thus purified." *Nations Without Nationalism*, trans. Leon S. Roudiez (New York: Columbia University Press, 1993), p. 51. For another explicitly textualizing commentary on Montesquieu that addresses the question of nationality and cultural identity and alterity, see Tzvetan Todorov, *On Human Diversity*, trans. Catherine Porter (Cambridge, MA: Harvard University Press, 1993).

46 Ehrard, *La Politique de Montesquieu*, p. 39.
47 Benrekassa, "Table ronde," p. 133.

5. LITERATURE AND THE MAKING OF REVOLUTIONARY HISTORY

1 See Bronisław Baczko, *Comment sortir de la Terreur: Thermidor et la Révolution* (Paris: Gallimard, 1989); and Marc Bouloiseau, *The Jacobin Republic, 1792–94*, trans. Jonathan Mandelbaum (Cambridge: Cambridge University Press, 1983).
2 Baczko, *Comment sortir*, p. 48.
3 Roland Barthes, "Historical Discourse," trans. Peter Wexler, in *Structuralism: A Reader*, ed. Michael Lane (London: Jonathan Cape, 1970), p. 153.
4 John H. Zammito provides an overview of the question in "Are We Being Theoretical Yet? The New Historicism, the New Philosophy of History, and 'Practicing Historians'," *Journal of Modern History*, 65 (1993), pp. 783–814.
5 Dorinda Outram, "'Mere Words': Enlightenment, Revolution, and Damage Control," *Journal of Modern History*, 63 (1991), p. 328.
6 Paul Ricœur, *Histoire et vérité* (Paris: Seuil, 1955), p. 261.
7 I use the term 'political' to refer to "the activity through which individuals and groups in any society articulate, negotiate, implement, and enforce the competing claims they make upon one another and upon the whole. Political culture is, in this sense, the set of discourses or symbolic practices by which these claims are made." Keith Michael Baker, *Inventing the French Revolution: Essays on French Political Culture in the Eighteenth Century* (Cambridge: Cambridge University Press, 1990), p. 5.
8 On this cultural reconfiguration, see Lynn Hunt, *Politics, Culture and Class in the French Revolution* (Berkeley: University of California Press, 1984); Mona Ozouf, *La Fête révolutionnaire, 1789–1799* (Paris: Gallimard, 1976); and Marie-Hélène Huet, *Mourning Glory: The Will of the French Revolution* (Philadelphia: University of Pennsylvania Press, 1997).
9 Jean-Claude Bonnet, *Naissance du Panthéon: essai sur le culte des grands hommes* (Paris: Fayard, 1998).
10 Bronisław Baczko, "Lumières," in vol. "Idées," *Dictionnaire critique de la Révolution française*, ed. François Furet and Mona Ozouf (Paris: Flammarion, 1992), p. 287.
11 Michel de Certeau, "The Historiographical Operation," in *The Writing of History*, trans. Tom Conley (New York: Columbia University Press, 1988), pp. 56–113.
12 Keith Michael Baker, "Enlightenment and Revolution in France: Old Problems, Renewed Approaches," *Journal of Modern History*, 53 (1982), pp. 281–303.
13 Roger Chartier, *The Cultural Origins of the French Revolution*, trans. Lydia G. Cochrane (Durham, NC: Duke University Press, 1991), pp. 4–5.
14 François Furet, *Interpreting the French Revolution*, trans. Elborg Forster (New York: Cambridge University Press, 1978), p. 35.

15 Michel Foucault, "Nietzsche, la généalogie, l'histoire," in *Dits et écrits*, I (Paris: Gallimard, 2001), pp. 1004–24.
16 Chartier, *Cultural Origins*, p. 5.
17 Quoted in James Swenson, *On Jean-Jacques Rousseau Considered as One of the First Authors of the Revolution* (Stanford: Stanford University Press, 2000), p. 10. My discussion of Rousseau's relation to the Revolution owes much to Swenson. Cf. Roger Barny, *Rousseau dans la Révolution: le personnage de Jean-Jacques et les débuts du culte révolutionnaire (1787–1791)* (Oxford: Voltaire Foundation, 1986).
18 See Chartier, *Cultural Origins*, ch. 1.
19 Jean-Jacques Rousseau, *"Letter to D'Alembert" and Writings for the Theater*, ed. and trans. Alan Bloom *et al.*, *The Collected Writings of Rousseau* (Hanover, NH: University Press of New Hampshire, 2004), x, p. 262.
20 Carol Blum, *Rousseau and the Republic of Virtue* (Ithaca: Cornell University Press, 1984).
21 Jean Starobinski analyzes the production of selfhood in *Jean-Jacques Rousseau, Transparency and Obstruction*, trans. Arthur Goldhammer (Chicago: University of Chicago Press, 1988). Paul de Man reveals the figural dimensions and limitations of the self thus constructed in *Allegories of Reading* (New Haven: Yale University Press, 1979); Robert Darnton recounts the experience of an eighteenth-century reader of Rousseau in *The Great Cat Massacre* (New York: Basic Books, 1984).
22 Swenson, *On Jean-Jacques Rousseau*, p. 211.
23 Bernard Manin, "Rousseau," in vol. "Idées," *Dictionnaire critique de la Révolution française*, ed. François Furet and Mona Ozouf (Paris: Flammarion, 1992), p. 478.
24 Maximilien-François Robespierre, *Œuvres complètes*, 10 vols. (Paris: Phénix, 2000), I, pp. 211–12.
25 Maximilien-François Robespierre, *Ecrits*, ed. Claude Mazauric (Paris: Messidor, 1989), p. 320.
26 *Ibid.*, p. 81.
27 In *ibid.*, p. 33.
28 Manin, "Rousseau," p. 459.
29 Robert Darnton, *Mesmerism and the End of the Enlightenment in France* (Cambridge, MA: Harvard University Press, 1968), and *The Business of Enlightenment: A Publishing History of the "Encyclopédie"* (Cambridge, MA: Harvard University Press, 1979). On the role of La Harpe and the Lycée in the institutionalization of knowledge, see Joan DeJean, "Classical Reeducation: Decanonizing the Feminine," in *Displacements: Women, Tradition, Literatures in French*, ed. Joan DeJean and Nancy K. Miller (Baltimore: Johns Hopkins University Press, 1991), pp. 22–7.
30 *Lycée, ou Cours de littérature ancienne et moderne*, 4 vols. (Paris: Verdière, 1818), I, p. 125.
31 Christopher Todd, *Voltaire's Disciple: Jean-François de La Harpe* (London: Modern Humanities Research Association, 1972).

32 Ferdinand Brunetière, *L'Evolution des genres dans l'histoire de la littérature*, 5th edn. (Paris: Hachette, 1910), p. 161.
33 See Jacques Godechot, *The Counter-Revolution: Doctrine and Action, 1789–1804*, trans. Salvator Attanasio (New York: Fertig, 1971).
34 Roland Barthes, "Réflexions sur un manuel," in *L'Enseignement de la littérature*, ed. Serge Doubrovsky and Tzvetan Todorov (Paris: Plon, 1969), pp. 170–7.
35 La Harpe, *Lycée*, IV, p. iv.
36 *Ibid.*, I, p. xix.
37 Louis Althusser, "Idéologie et appareils idéologiques d'Etat," *La Pensée*, 151 (1970), pp. 3–38.
38 Hunt, *Politics, Culture and Class*, p. 24.
39 La Harpe, *Lycée*, IV, p. 168.
40 Quoted in Sylvain Auroux, "Le Sujet de la langue: la conception politique de la langue sous l'Ancien Régime et la Révolution," in *Les Idéologues: sémiotique, théories et politiques linguistiques pendant la Révolution française*, ed. Winfried Busse and Jürgen Trabant (Amsterdam: Benjamins, 1986), p. 265.
41 See Michel de Certeau, Dominique Julia, and Jacques Revel, *Une politique de la langue: la Révolution française et les patois, l'enquête de Grégoire* (Paris: Gallimard, 1975).
42 Quoted in Auroux "Le Sujet de la langue," p. 266.
43 See Sylvain Auroux, *La Sémiotique des encyclopédistes: essai d'épistémologie historique des sciences du langage* (Paris: Payot, 1979); and Daniel Droixhe, *La Linguistique et l'appel de l'histoire (1600–1800): rationalisme et révolutions positivistes* (Geneva: Droz, 1978).
44 La Harpe, *Lycée*, IV, p. 171.
45 François Furet, *Interpreting the French Revolution*, trans. Elborg Forster (Cambridge: Cambridge University Press, 1978), p. 48.
46 Hunt, "Review Essay," *History and Theory*, 20 (1981), p. 317.
47 Claude Lefort, "Interpreting Revolution within the French Revolution," in *Democracy and Political Theory*, trans. David Macey (Minneapolis: University of Minnesota Press, 1988), p. 110.
48 La Harpe, *Lycée*, IV, pp. 182, 194.
49 Ironically, as partisan of their circle, La Harpe himself had defended the philosophes against such attacks. See Jean Balcou, *Fréron contre les philosophes* (Geneva: Droz, 1975).
50 La Harpe, *Lycée*, IV, pp. 323, 396.
51 *Ibid.*, IV, p. 216.
52 Nanette LeCoat, "Philosophy vs. Eloquence: Laharpe and the Literary Debate at the Ecole Normale," *French Review*, 61 (1988), pp. 421–7.
53 See Lucien Jaume, *Le Discours Jacobin et la démocratie* (Paris: Fayard, 1989).

6. INVENTING A LITERARY PAST

1 On the revolutionary reconfiguration of urban life, see Richard A. Etlin, *Symbolic Space: French Enlightenment Architecture and Its Legacy*

(Chicago: University of Chicago Press, 1994), and Priscilla Parkhurst Ferguson, *Paris as Revolution: Writing the Nineteenth-Century City* (Berkeley: University of California Press, 1994).
2 See François Furet, *Revolutionary France, 1770–1880*, trans. Antonia Nevill (Oxford: Blackwell, 1992).
3 Pierre Birnbaum, *The Idea of France*, trans. M. B. DeBevoise (New York: Hill and Wang, 2001), pp. x–xi.
4 François Furet, in François Furet, Jacques Julliard, and Pierre Rosanvallon, *La République du centre: la fin de l'exception française* (Paris: Calmann-Lévy, 1986), p. 18.
5 Hayden White, *The Content of the Form: Narrative Discourse and Historical Representation* (Baltimore: Johns Hopkins University Press, 1987). Christopher Prendergast, *The Order of Mimesis* (Cambridge: Cambridge University Press, 1986), p. 231.
6 R. G. Collingwood, *The Idea of History*, cited in David Lowenthal, *The Past is a Foreign Country* (New York: Cambridge University Press, 1985), p. 187.
7 Ceri Crossley, *French Historians and Romanticism: Thierry, Guizot, the Saint-Simonians, Quinet, Michelet* (New York: Routledge, 1993), p. 1.
8 Heinrich Heine, *De la France* (Paris: Gallimard, 1994), quoted in Birnbaum, *The Idea of France*, p. 133.
9 François Hartog and Jacques Revel, *Les Usages politiques du passé* (Paris: Editions de l'Ecole des Hautes Etudes en Sciences Sociales, 2001), pp. 13–14. See also Jacques Revel, "Le Fardeau de la mémoire," *Correspondances*, 55 (1999), pp. 3–9.
10 See Peter Novick, *That Noble Dream: The "Objectivity Question" and the American Historical Profession* (New York: Cambridge University Press, 1988).
11 Quoted in Hartog and Revel, *Les Usages politiques*, p. 13.
12 Benedict Anderson, *Imagined Communities: Reflections on the Origin and Spread of Nationalism* (London: Verso, 1983). A critical understanding of nationhood and nationalism calls for viewing them not as the natural and positive expression of a popular longing or self-consciousness, but rather as the forgetting, if not the suppression, of their imaginary, constructed status. Ernst Renan sensed this: "The essence of a nation is that all individuals have many things in common, and also that everyone has forgotten many things." "Qu'est-ce qu'une nation?," quoted by Anderson, *Imagined Communities*, p. 6.
13 Eric Hobsbawm and Terence Ranger, eds., *The Invention of Tradition* (New York: Cambridge University Press, 1983).
14 Mona Ozouf, *La Fête révolutionnaire, 1789–1799* (Paris: Gallimard, 1976), and *L'Homme régénéré: essais sur la Révolution française* (Paris: Gallimard, 1989).
15 Marcel Detienne, *Comment être autochtone? Du pur Athénien au Français raciné* (Paris: Seuil, 2003).
16 Quoted in Maurice Gontard, *L'Enseignement secondaire en France de la fin de l'Ancien Régime à la loi Falloux: 1750–1850* (Aix-en-Provence: Edisud, 1984), p. 80.
17 Gontard, *L'Enseignement*, p. 127.

18 Paul Gerbod, *La Condition universitaire en France au XIXe siècle (1842–1880)* (Paris: Presses Universitaires de France, 1965), p. 129.
19 See Roland Mortier, *Le "Tableau littéraire de la France" au XVIIIe siècle* (Brussels: Palais des Académies, 1972).
20 See Luc Fraisse, *Les Fondements de l'histoire littéraire, de Saint-René Taillandier à Lanson* (Paris: Honoré Champion, 2002).
21 For a more extensive discussion of these issues, see David Perkins, *Is Literary History Possible?* (Baltimore: Johns Hopkins University Press, 1992).
22 Eusèbe Salverte, *Tableau littéraire de la France au XVIIIe siècle* (Paris: H. Nicolle, 1809), pp. 1–2.
23 Abel-François Villemain, *Cours de littérature française: tableau de la littérature française au XVIIIe siècle*, 4 vols. (Paris: Didier, 1873), IV, p. 340.
24 *Ibid.*
25 *Ibid.*, I, p. 2.
26 *Ibid.*, I, p. 3.
27 *Ibid.*, III, p. 195.
28 *Ibid.*, IV, p. 315.
29 *Ibid.*, III, p. 195.
30 *Ibid.*, I, p. 3.
31 The *Tableau* ends with praise for Madame de Staël and her critique of Napoleon: "When oppression exists, thinking is protesting" (IV, p. 365).
32 *Ibid.*, IV, pp. 405–6.
33 *Ibid.*, I, p. 391.
34 *Cours*, II, p. 114.
35 *Ibid.*, II, p. 119.
36 *Ibid.*, II, p. 113.
37 *Ibid.*, II, p. 128–9.
38 Charles Baudelaire, "L'Esprit et le style de M. Villemain," in *Œuvres complètes* (Paris: Gallimard, 1976), II, pp. 192–214.
39 For a fine-grained study of the disciplining of literary history during the Third Republic, see Ralph Albanese, *La Fontaine à l'école républicaine: de la critique universitaire aux manuels scolaires (1870–1914)* (Saratoga, CA: Anma Libri, 1992). Jean-Thomas Nordmann provides an overview of nineteenth-century literary criticism in *La Critique littéraire française au XIXe siècle (1800–1914)* (Paris: Livre de Poche, 2001).
40 Nicolas Wagner, "Le XVIIIème siècle de Villemain," *Œuvres et Critiques*, 10:1 (1985), pp. 45–65.
41 See Joseph-Marc Bailbé, *Jules Janin 1804–1874: une sensibilité littéraire et artistique* (Paris: Lettres Modernes, 1974).
42 Charles-Auguste Sainte-Beuve, *Nouveaux lundis*, 13 vols. (Paris: Michel Lévy frères, 1870–9), IX, p. 80.
43 Charles Auguste Sainte-Beuve, *Le Cahier vert*, ed. Raphaël Molho (Paris: Gallimard, 1973), I, p. 159.
44 Charles Auguste Sainte-Beuve, *Portraits littéraires*, ed. Gérald Antoine (Paris: Laffont, 1993), p. 22.

45 Charles Auguste Sainte-Beuve, *Causeries du lundi*, 4th edn., 14 vols. (Paris: Garnier, 1876), II, p. 1.
46 Charles Auguste Sainte-Beuve, *Portraits contemporains*, 3 vols. (Paris: Calmann Lévy, 1876), III, p. 401.
47 Roger Fayolle, *Sainte-Beuve et le XVIIIe siècle, ou comment les révolutions arrivent* (Paris: Armand Colin, 1972).
48 Saint-Beuve, *Causeries*, IV, p. 343
49 *Ibid.*, V, p. 81.
50 *Ibid.*, I, p. 313. The same image appears in 1857, in a passage referring to the *coup d'état* of Louis Napoleon Bonaparte: "All of France was on a raft; after three years of half-measures and misery, it needed to set forth full sail ... The universal acclaim with which France greeted its president in 1852 and crowned him emperor was, among other things, an act that made very good sense" (*Causeries*, XV, p. 315). See Maxime Leroy, *La Politique de Sainte-Beuve* (Paris: Gallimard, 1941).
51 *Causeries*, I, p. 40.
52 *Ibid.*, I, p. 48.
53 *Ibid.*, II, p. 266.
54 Hippolyte Taine, *Les Origines de la France contemporaine* (Paris: Hachette, 1876–85).
55 See Maxine G. Cutler, *Evocations of the Eighteenth Century in French Poetry, 1800–1869* (Geneva: Droz, 1970).
56 Richard Terdiman, *Discourse/Counter-Discourse: The Theory and Practice of Symbolic Resistance in Nineteenth-Century France* (Ithaca: Cornell University Press, 1985).
57 See Julia Kristeva, *Revolution in Poetic Language*, trans. Margaret Waller (New York: Columbia University Press, 1984), and Terry Eagleton, *The Ideology of the Aesthetic* (London: Blackwell, 1990).
58 On sociability, see Didier Masseau, *L'Invention de l'intellectuel dans l'Europe du XVIIIe siècle* (Paris: Presses Universitaires de France, 1994); Dena Goodman, *The Republic of Letters: A Cultural History of the French Enlightenment* (Ithaca: Cornell University Press, 1994); Daniel Gordon, *Citizens Without Sovereignty* (Princeton: Princeton University Press, 1994); Tzvetan Todorov, *On Human Diversity: Nationalism, Racism, and Exoticism in French Thought*, trans. Catherine Porter (Cambridge, MA: Harvard University Press, 1993); Christian Jouhaud, *Les Pouvoirs de la littérature: histoire d'un paradoxe* (Paris: Gallimard, 2000); and Carla Hesse, *The Other Enlightenment: How French Women Became Modern* (Princeton: Princeton University Press, 2001).
59 See Jean Roussel, *Jean-Jacques Rousseau en France après la Révolution, 1795–1830: lectures et légende* (Paris: Armand Colin, 1972).
60 Saint-Beuve, *Causeries*, III, p. 79.
61 Saint-Beuve, *Portraits contemporains*, I, p. 277.
62 Paul de Man shows the complexity of trying to decide even which are the political texts in Rousseau and which the esthetic ones, in *Allegories of Reading* (New Haven: Yale University Press, 1979).

63 Saint-Beuve, *Causeries*, III, p. 78.
64 *Ibid.*, III, p. 79.
65 Charles-Auguste Sainte-Beuve, *Les Grands Ecrivains français* (Paris: Garnier, 1927), p. 172.
66 "Founded on the rupture between a past that is its object, and a present that is the place of its practice, history endlessly finds the present in its object and the past in its practice. Inhabited by the uncanniness that it seeks, history imposes its law upon the faraway places that it conquers when it fosters the illustion that it is bringing them back to life." Michel de Certeau, "Making History," in *The Writing of History*, trans. Tom Conley (New York: Columbia University Press, 1988), p. 36.

7. COMMEMORATING ENLIGHTENMENT: BRINGING OUT THE DEAD, BELATEDLY

1 See Philippe Ariès, *The Hour of Our Death*, trans. Helen Weaver (New York: Vintage Books, 1982), and Michel Vovelle, *La Mort et l'Occident de 1300 à nos jours* (Paris: Gallimard, 1983).
2 Avner Ben-Amos, *Funerals, Politics, and Memory in Modern France, 1789–1996* (New York: Oxford University Press, 2000), p. 146. Cf. Marie-Hélène Huet, *Mourning Glory: The Will of the French Revolution* (Philadelphia: University of Pennsylvania Press, 1997).
3 Juliet Flower MacCannell, *The Regime of the Brother: After the Patriarchy* (New York: Routledge, 1991).
4 Sigmund Freud, *Totem and Taboo*, in *The Standard Edition of the Complete Works of Sigmund Freud*, ed. James Strachey (London: Hogarth Press, 1953–74), XIII, p. 143.
5 Michel de Certeau, *The Mystic Fable*, trans. Michael B. Smith (Chicago: University of Chicago Press, 1992), p. 10 (translation modified).
6 Details of this event are found in Raymond Trousson, *Images de Diderot en France, 1784–1913* (Paris: Champion, 1997).
7 See Eric Walter, "1884: Une consécration ratée: Diderot, Danton et les positivistes," in *Diderot et le XVIIIe siècle en Europe et au Japon*, ed. H. Nakagawa (Nagoya: Centre Kawaï pour la Culture et la Pédagogie, 1988), pp. 187–214.
8 See Jean Marie Goulemot and Eric Walter, "Les Centenaires de Voltaire et de Rousseau," in *Les Lieux de mémoire*, ed. Pierre Nora (Paris: Gallimard, 1984), I, pp. 381–420.
9 Auguste Comte, *Catéchisme positiviste*, ed. P. F. Pecaut (Paris: Garnier, 1909), p. 5.
10 Quoted in Trousson, *Images*, p. 299.
11 As Trousson notes, the 1884 celebration had been "the first important attempt to make the master of the *Encyclopédie* into one of the organizing myths of cultural and political consciousness." *Images*, p. 295.

12 Abbé Antoine Sabatier de Castres, *Les Trois Siècles de littérature française, ou tableau de l'esprit de nos écrivains, depuis François I jusqu'à nos jours*, 5th edn. (La Haye: Gosse junior, 1778), II, pp. 103–10.
13 Eusèbe Salverte, *Eloge philosophique de Denys Diderot* (Paris: Surosne, 1801), p. 85.
14 The first major study in France of Diderot's 'construction' is Jacques Proust, *Lectures de Diderot* (Paris: Armand Colin, 1974), which is amplified more recently by Trousson's *Images de Diderot*.
15 For Diderot's reception in Germany, see Roland Mortier, *Diderot en Allemagne*, rev. edn. (Geneva: Slatkine Reprints, 1986).
16 Michel Foucault, "What Is An Author?," *Partisan Review*, 42 (1975), pp. 603–14.
17 See Arthur Wilson, "The Verdict of Posterity, 1784–1852," in *Essays on Diderot and the Enlightenment in Honor of O. Fellows* (Geneva: Droz, 1974), pp. 400–22.
18 J. Th. de Booy and Alan J. Freer, "*Jacques le fataliste*" *et* "*La Religieuse*" *devant la critique révolutionnaire (1796–1800)* (*Studies on Voltaire and the Eighteenth Century*, 33) (Geneva: Institut et Musée Voltaire, 1965).
19 With the greater possibility for intellectual expression that followed the strict censorship of the Empire, publication of eighteenth-century authors becomes an effective way to oppose the regime during the Restoration. From the pulpit of Saint-Sulpice, bishop Frayssinous declares, "Yes indeed, the ongoing conspiracy against throne and altar is located in this ongoing flow of writings and perverse lampoons that preached revolt ceaselessly and with impiety." Quoted in Trousson, *Images*, p. 113. See Henri Martin, *Histoire de l'édition française*, II–III (Paris: Promodis, 1982–6).
20 In Jules Michelet's *Histoire de la Révolution française* (1847), Danton is characterized as "the true son of Diderot." Quoted in Trousson, *Images*, p. 186.
21 Roland Barthes, "Reflections on a Manual," trans. Sandy Petrey, *Publications of the Modern Language Association of America*, 112:1 (1997), pp. 69–75.
22 Eugen Weber, *Peasants Into Frenchmen: The Modernization of Rural France 1870–1914* (Stanford: Stanford University Press, 1976).
23 Trousson, *Images*, from which the following description of the manual's function is taken (p. 206).
24 Noël La Place, author of *Leçons de littérature*, provides an illuminating example. A defrocked priest, holder of the chair of eloquence in 1810, La Place will become *inspecteur général* of the Université de France in 1831. He defines the aim of *Leçons de littérature* thus: "Each selection in this collection, while offering an exercise in careful reading, memorization, public speaking, analysis, and oratorical development, also provides a lesson in humanity or justice, religion, philosophy, disinterest or the love of the public good, etc. Everything in this collection results from genius, talent, and virtue; everything expresses the most exquisite taste and the purest of morals. Not one thought, not one word goes against the delicacy of decency or the dignity of mores." Quoted in Trousson, *Images*, p. 161. As one might surmise, Diderot was as absent from the 1804 edition of the *Leçons* in 1804 as he would be from the 1862 edition.

25 Quoted in Andreas Huyssens, *Twilight Memories: Marking Time in a Culture of Amnesia* (New York: Routledge, 1995), p. 1.
26 Chateaubriand contrasts the seventeenth century, characterized by "this tender religion ... this harmonious instrument in which the authors of the century of Louis XIV found the tone of their eloquence," with the eighteenth century, represented by "a narrow philosophy that proceeded by dividing things and dividing them again, measuring feelings with a compass, subjecting the soul to calculation, and reducing the universe, including God, to a passing concealment of nothingness. Thus the eighteenth century grows smaller in perspective each day, as the seventeenth grows larger as we become more distant from it." *Le Génie du christianisme* (Paris, Mignaret, 1803), p. 140. See Jean Sareil, "Le Massacre de Voltaire dans les manuels scolaires," *Studies on Voltaire and the Eighteenth Century*, 212 (1982), pp. 83–161.
27 In addition to my "Political Culture and Literary History: La Harpe's *Lycée*," *Modern Language Quarterly*, 58:2 (June 1997), pp. 1–22, see R. Landry, "Le Prisme de La Harpe," *Studies on Voltaire and the Eighteenth Century*, 153 (1976), pp. 1255–85.
28 Antoine Compagnon, *La Troisième République des lettres: de Flaubert à Proust* (Paris: Seuil, 1983).
29 See Lionel Gossman, *Between History and Literature* (Cambridge, MA: Harvard University Press, 1990).
30 Compagnon, *La Troisième République*, p. 134.
31 Quoted in *ibid.*, p. 84.
32 Lanson, *Revue bleue*, September 30, 1905, pp. 422–3, quoted in Compagnon, *La Troisième République*, pp. 110–11.
33 See André Chervel, ed., *L'Enseignement du français à l'école primaire*, I: *1791–1879* (Paris: Institut National de Recherche Pédagogique, 1992).
34 Denis Hollier, "On Literature Considered as a Dead Language," in *The Uses of Literary History*, ed. Marshall Brown (Durham, NC: Duke University Press, 1995), p. 239.
35 See Luc Fraisse, *Les Fondements de l'histoire littéraire, de Saint-René Taillandier à Lanson* (Paris: Champion, 2002).

8. THE VOLTAIRE EFFECT

1 Michel Foucault, "Qu'est-ce qu'un auteur?," *Dits et écrits*, 2 vols. (Paris: Gallimard, 2001), II, pp. 817–49.
2 See Gregory S. Brown, *Literary Sociability and Literary Property in France, 1775–1793: Beaumarchais, the Société des Auteurs Dramatiques and the Comédie Française* (Aldershot: Ashgate, 2006).
3 Robert Darnton, *The Literary Underground of the Old Regime* (Cambridge, MA: Harvard University Press, 1982). Darnton's path-breaking investigation of the 'low' Enlightenment spawned considerable methodological debate and disciplinary reconfiguration. See *The Darnton Debate: Books and Revolution in the Eighteenth Century*, ed. Haydn T. Mason (Oxford: Voltaire Foundation, 1998).

4 Geoffrey Turnovsky plots a middle course between these two views of authorship, suggesting that the literary market of the late eighteenth century should be understood less in an empirical sense as a pre-constituted sphere than as an emerging structural concept and an imaginary space that thus was highly unstable. "The Enlightenment Literary Market: Rousseau, Authorship, and the Book Trade," *Eighteenth-Century Studies*, 36:3 (2003), pp. 387–410.
5 As Roland Barthes puts it, Voltaire was the last of the fortunate writers in France. "Le Dernier des écrivains heureux," *Essais critiques* (Paris: Seuil, 1964), pp. 94–100.
6 Malraux himself had given a major speech some twenty years earlier at the 'pantheonization' of the resistance fighter Jean Moulin. The more recent 'pantheonization' of Alexandre Dumas in 2002 served an equally symbolic function, suggested by the presence of an ethnically 'mixed' figure of Marianne who accompanied the coffin containing Dumas's ashes.
7 Quoted in Catherine Thomas, *Le Mythe du XVIIIe siècle au XIXe siècle, 1830–1860* (Paris: Honoré Champion, 2003), pp. 69–77.
8 Quoted in Stephen Bird, *Reinventing Voltaire: The Politics of Commemoration in Nineteenth-Century France, Studies on Voltaire and the Eighteenth Century*, 2000:09 (Oxford: Voltaire Foundation, 2000), p. 171.
9 <www.adpf.asso.fr/adpf-publi/folio/voltaire/voltaire01.html> (accessed January 15, 2007).
10 See Patricia Mainardi, *Art and Politics in the Second Empire: The Universal Expositions* (New Haven: Yale University Press, 1987).
11 *Les Lieux de mémoire*, ed. Pierre Nora, 7 vols. (Paris: Gallimard, 1984–92). This work itself has become itself a kind of memory site, and its recent translation into English has expanded its impact: *Realms of Memory: Rethinking the French Past*, ed. Lawrence Kritzman, trans. Arthur Goldhammer, 3 vols. (New York: Columbia University Press, 1996–8). Studies of the cult of memory have burgeoned: Annette Becker, *La Guerre et la foi: de la mort à la mémoire* (Paris: Armand Colin, 1994); Robert Gildea, *The Past in French History* (New Haven: Yale University Press, 1994); Pascal Ory, *Une nation pour mémoire: 1889, 1939, 1989, trois jubilés révolutionnaires* (Paris: Presses de la Fondation nationale des sciences politiques, 1992); Daniel J. Sherman, *The Construction of Memory in Interwar France* (Chicago: University of Chicago Press, 1999); and Avner Ben-Amos, *Funerals, Politics, and Memory in Modern France 1789–1996* (New York: Oxford University Press, 2000).
12 François Furet, Jacques Julliard, and Pierre Rosanvallon, *La République du centre: la fin de l'exception française* (Paris: Calmann-Lévy, 1986), p. 18.
13 See for instance Linda Orr, *Headless History: Nineteenth-Century French Historiography of the Revolution* (Ithaca: Cornell University Press, 1990).
14 Cathy Caruth, introduction to "Recapturing the Past," in *Trauma: Explorations in Memory* (Baltimore: Johns Hopkins University Press, 1995), p. 151. See also her *Unclaimed Experience: Trauma, Narrative and History* (Baltimore: Johns Hopkins University Press, 1996).
15 *Scènes et doctrines du nationalisme* (Paris: Plon-Nourrit, 1925), 1, p. 118.

16 Jacques Derrida, in Giovanna Borradori, *Philosophy in a Time of Terror: Dialogues with Jürgen Habermas and Jacques Derrida* (Chicago: University of Chicago Press, 2003), p. 125.

17 See Jean Marie Goulemot, *Adieu les philosophes: que reste-t-il des Lumières?* (Paris: Seuil, 2001).

9. READING AMONG THE RUINS

1 For a stimulating unpacking of this photograph, see Eduardo Cadava, "*Leseblitz*: On the Threshold of Violence," *Assemblages*, 20 (1993), pp. 22–3.

2 For a discussion of the Grand Tour from the British perspective, see Jeremy Black, *The British Abroad: The Grand Tour in the Eighteenth Century* (New York: St. Martin's Press, 1992).

3 Once all the variations of "ruin*" are included ("ruiner," "ruine/s," and "ruiné/e/s"), the semantic grid is much larger – extending to some 950 instances.

4 The epistemological premises of archeology are visible in the collection of plates assembled by Anne-Claude-Philippe, comte de Caylus, in his *Recueil d'antiquités égyptiennes, étrusques, grecques et romaines* (Paris: Desaint et Saillant, 1752–67). The frontispiece of the collection represents the remnants of the past as concealed yet accessible to those who have the techniques – tools and knowledge – to unearth and understand them. The very title of Caylus's collection, "recueil d'antiquités," which is visible on the column in the frontispiece, suggests that archeology, unlike a more disordered antiquarianism, is an acquisitive and proprietary discipline, gathering remnants together in order to register, restore, and resurrect the past. See *Irresistible Decay: Ruins Reclaimed*, ed. Michael Roth (Santa Monica: The Getty Research Institute for the History of Art and the Humanities, 1997). Other influential archeological collections include J. D. Leroy, *Les Ruines des plus beaux monuments de la Grèce* (1758) and the comte de Choiseul-Gouffier, *Voyage pittoresque de la Grèce* (1782).

5 For a wide-ranging and richly documented study of the ruin motif, see Roland Mortier, *La Poétique des ruines* (Geneva: Droz, 1974).

6 *Encyclopédie, ou dictionnaire raisonné des arts, des sciences, et des métiers*, ed. Denis Diderot and Jean Le Rond d'Alembert (Paris, 1751–72), IV, p. 637.

7 Anne-Robert-Jacques Turgot, *Œuvres* (Paris: Guillomin, 1844).

8 "I seemed to hear, in the echo of my footsteps resounding beneath those vast arches, the mighty voices of those who had built them. I was lost, a mere insect, in all this immensity. Yet, even as I saw myself grow small, I felt something, I know not what, that lifted my soul, and I said to myself, sighing: why was I not born a Roman!" Jean-Jacques Rousseau, *Confessions*, trans. Angela Scholar (New York: Oxford University Press, 2000), p. 250.

9 See Dora Wiebenson, *The Picturesque Garden in France* (Princeton: Princeton University Press, 1978), and Diana Ketcham, *Le Désert de Retz: A Late Eighteenth-Century French Folly Garden* (Cambridge, MA: MIT Press, 1994).

10 In similar fashion the rise in interest in the countryside and peasants in mid-eighteenth-century France translates a sense of nostalgic loss, created by

230 Notes to pages 186–200

a period of intense urbanization and the displaced urban sociability it produced. See Amy S. Wyngaard, *From Savage to Citizen: The Invention of the Peasant in the French Enlightenment* (Newark, NJ: University of Delaware Press, 2004). Wyngaard's argument recalls Norbert Elias's analysis of the alienated subjectivity of the displaced rural nobility in the seventeenth century.

11 Victor Hugo, "L'Arc de triomphe," *Les Voix intérieures* (Paris: Gallimard, 1837). In a similar sense, Pierre Puvis de Chavanne writes, "More beautiful than a chef-d'œuvre is its ruin." *La Mémoire des ruines: anthologie des monuments disparus en France*, ed. Claude de Montclos (Paris: Mengès, 1992), p. 8.

12 Denis Diderot, *Diderot on Art*, II: *The Salon of 1767*, ed. and trans. John Goodman (New Haven: Yale University Press, 1995), p. 206.

13 *Ibid.*, II, p. 197.

14 The subjective version of this insight reads as follows, in Diderot's exhortation to artists that they assault his sight and senses: "First touch me, astonish me, tear me to pieces, make me shudder, weep, and tremble, make me angry; then soothe my eyes, if you can." "Notes on Painting," *ibid.*, II, p. 222.

15 Louis-Sébastien Mercier, *L'An 2440* (London [Neuchâtel: Samuel Fauche] 1774), ch. 44, pp. 401–2.

16 In *The Dialectics of Seeing: Walter Benjamin and the Arcades Project* (Cambridge, MA: MIT Press, 1989), Susan Buck-Morss writes: "The ruin ... is the form in which the wish images of the past century appear, as rubble, in the present. But it refers also to the loosened building block (both semantic and material) out of which a new order can be constructed" (p. 212).

17 See Christopher Woodward, *In Ruins* (London: Chatto & Windus, 2001).

18 See Andrew McClellan, *Inventing the Louvre: Art, Politics, and the Origins of the Modern Museum in Eighteenth-Century Paris* (Cambridge: Cambridge University Press, 1994), and Marie-Catherine Sahut and Nicole Garnier, *Le Louvre d'Hubert Robert* (Paris: Editions de la Réunion des Musées Nationaux, 1979).

19 Francis Haskell and Nicholas Penny, *Taste and the Antique: The Lure of Classical Sculpture 1500–1900* (New Haven: Yale University Press, 1981), p. 148.

20 See Brian Lukacher, *Joseph Gandy: An Architectural Visionary in Georgian England* (London: Thames & Hudson, 2006).

21 Didier Maleuvre, *Museum Memories: History, Technology, Art* (Stanford: Stanford University Press, 1999), p. 83.

22 Maleuvre, pp. 87, 85.

23 *Ibid.*, p. 271

24 Constantin François Chasseboeuf, comte de Volney, *Les Ruines ou méditations sur les révolutions des empires* (1791), 10th edn. (Paris: Bossange, 1822), p. 1.

10. EPILOGUE

1 Philippe Ariès, "L'Histoire des mentalités," in *La Nouvelle Histoire*, ed. Jacques Le Goff (Paris: Retz, 1978), p. 411.

2 Jacques Revel, "Histoire et sciences sociales: les paradigmes des *Annales*," *Annales*, 34:6 (1979), pp. 1372–3. Offering another perspective onto this

breakup, François Dosse's study of twentieth-century French historiography suggests that history is "in pieces." *L'Histoire en miettes: des Annales à la 'nouvelle histoire'* (Paris: La Découverte, 1987).

3 Roland Barthes, "The Discourse of History," trans. Peter Wexler, in *Structuralism: A Reader*, ed. Michael Lane (London: Jonathan Cape, 1970), pp. 145–55.

4 Revel, 1372. In *The Order of Things*, Michel Foucault invokes a similar end of man, likening the latter to an image drawn in sand on the beach, which the waves of time will one day wash away.

5 Raymond Aron, *Introduction to the Philosophy of History: An Essay on the Limits of Historical Objectivity*, trans. George J. Irwin (Boston, MA: Beacon Press, 1961).

6 Raymond Aron, *The Opium of the Intellectuals*, trans. Terence Kilmartin (New York: Norton, 1962). See also Tony Judt, *The Burden of Responsibility: Blum, Camus, Aron, and the French Twentieth Century* (Chicago: University of Chicago Press, 1998).

7 Edmund Husserl, "Philosophy and the Crisis of European Humanity," in *The Crisis of European Sciences and Transcendental Philosophy*, trans. David Carr (Evanston: Northwestern University Press, 1970), pp. 269–300.

8 Jacques Derrida, *Rogues: Two Essays on Reason*, trans. Pascale-Anne Brault and Michael Nass (Stanford: Stanford University Press, 2005), p. 127.

9 *Rogues*, p. 158. Derrida characterizes as follows the relation between deconstruction (if such a thing exists, as he puts it), democracy, and crisis: "Deconstruction, if something of the sort exists, would remain above all, in my view, an unconditional rationalism that never renounces – and precisely in the name of the Enlightenment to come, in the space to be opened up of a democracy to come – the possibility of suspending in an argued, deliberated, rational fashion, all conditions, hypotheses, conventions, and presuppositions, and of criticizing unconditionally all conditionalities, including those that still found the critical idea, namely, those of the *krinein*, of the *krisis*, of the binary or dialectical decision or judgment." *Rogues*, p. 142.

10 Richard Terdiman, *Past Present: Modernity and the Memory Crisis* (Ithaca: Cornell University Press, 1993).

11 François Dosse, "La Nouvelle Histoire," in Christian Delacroix, François Dosse, and Patrick Garcia, *Histoire et historiens en France depuis 1945* (Paris: Association pour la Diffusion de la Pensée Française, 2003), p. 112.

12 Jean-François Lyotard, *The Postmodern Explained: Correspondence 1982–1985*, ed. Julian Pefanis and Morgan Thomas (Minneapolis: University of Minnesota Press, 1992), p. 95.

13 Pierre Nora, "The Era of Commemoration," in *Realms of Memory: The Construction of the French Past*, ed. Pierre Nora, trans. Arthur Goldhammer (New York: Columbia University Press, 1998), III, pp. 635–7.

14 Jean-Claude Guillebaud, *La Trahison des Lumières: enquête sur le désarroi contemporain* (Paris: Seuil, 1995), p. 22.

Bibliography of works cited

Adorno, Theodor, and Max Horkheimer. *Dialectic of Enlightenment*, trans. John Cumming. New York: Continuum, 1972.
Albanese, Ralph. *La Fontaine à l'école républicaine: de la critique universitaire aux manuels scolaires (1870–1914)*. Saratoga, CA: Anma Libri, 1992.
Althusser, Louis. *For Marx*, trans. Ben Brewster. London: Allen Lane, 1969.
  "Idéologie et appareils idéologiques d'Etat." *La Pensée*, 151 (1970), pp. 3–38. Eng. trans. "Ideology and Ideological State Apparatuses." In *Lenin and Philosophy*, trans. Ben Brewster. New York: Monthly Review Press, 1971.
  Lenin and Philosophy, and Other Essays, trans. Ben Brewster. London: Monthy Review Press, 1971.
Anderson, Benedict. *Imagined Communities: Reflections on the Origin and Spread of Nationalism*. London: Verso, 1983.
Apostolidès, Jean-Marie. *Le Roi machine: spectacle et politique au temps de Louis XIV*. Paris: Minuit, 1981.
Ariès, Philippe. "L'Histoire des mentalités." In *La Nouvelle Histoire*, ed., Jacques Le Goff *et al.*, pp. 402–23. Paris: Retz, 1978.
  The Hour of Our Death, trans. Helen Weaver. New York: Vintage Books, 1982.
Aron, Raymond. *Introduction to the Philosophy of History: An Essay on the Limits of Historical Objectivity*, trans. George J. Irwin. Boston: Beacon Press, 1961.
  The Opium of the Intellectuals, trans. Terence Kilmartin. New York: Norton, 1962.
Auroux, Sylvain. *La Sémiotique des encyclopédistes: essai d'épistémologie historique des sciences du langage*. Paris: Payot, 1979.
  "Le Sujet de la langue: la conception politique de la langue sous l'Ancien Régime et la Révolution." In *Les Idéologues: sémiotique, théories et politiques linguistiques pendant la Révolution française*, ed. Winfried Busse and Jürgen Trabant, pp. 259–78. Amsterdam: Benjamins, 1986.
Baczko, Bronisław. *Comment sortir de la Terreur: Thermidor et la Révolution*. Paris: Gallimard, 1989.
  "Lumières." In vol. "Idées," *Dictionnaire critique de la Révolution française*, ed. François Furet and Mona Ozouf, pp. 275–91. Paris: Flammarion, 1992.
  Lumières de l'utopie. Paris: Payot, 1978.
Bailbé, Joseph-Marc. *Jules Janin 1804–1874: une sensibilité littéraire et artistique*. Paris: Lettres Modernes, 1974.

Baker, Keith Michael. "Enlightenment and Revolution in France: Old Problems, Renewed Approaches." *Journal of Modern History*, 53 (1981), pp. 281–303.
  Inventing the French Revolution: Essays on French Political Culture in the Eighteenth Century. Cambridge: Cambridge University Press, 1990.
  "Revolution." In *The French Revolution and the Creation of Modern Political Culture*, II: *The Political Culture of the French Revolution*, ed., Colin Lucas. pp. 41–62. New York: Pergamon, 1988.
Balcou, Jean. *Fréron contre les philosophes*. Geneva: Droz, 1975.
Barny, Roger. *Rousseau dans la Révolution: le personnage de Jean-Jacques et les débuts du culte révolutionnaire (1787–1791)*. Oxford: Voltaire Foundation, 1986.
Barrès, Maurice. *Scènes et doctrines du nationalisme*. Paris: Plon-Nourrit, 1925.
Barthes, Roland. "Le Dernier des écrivains heureux." In *Essais critiques*. Paris: Seuil, 1964, pp. 94–100.
  "Historical Discourse," trans. Peter Wexler. In *Structuralism: A Reader*, ed., Michael Lane, pp. 145–55. London: Jonathan Cape, 1970.
  "Réflexions sur un manuel." In *L'Enseignement de la littérature*, ed. Serge Doubrovsky and Tzvetan Todorov, pp. 170–7. Paris: Pion. Eng. trans. "Reflections on a Manual," trans. Sandy Petrey. *Publications of the Modern Language Association of America*, 112:1 (1997), pp. 69–75.
Bates, David. "Cartographic Aberrations: Epistemology and Order in the Encyclopedic Map." In *Using the "Encyclopédie": Ways of Knowing, Ways of Reading*, ed. Daniel Brewer and Julie Candler Hayes. *SVEC*, 2002:05 (2002), pp. 1–20.
  Enlightenment Aberrations: Error and Revolution in France. Ithaca: Cornell University Press, 2002.
Baudelaire, Charles. "L'Esprit et le style de M. Villemain." In *Œuvres completes*, II. Paris: Gallimard, 1976.
Bauman, Zygmunt. *Modernity and the Holocaust*. Ithaca: Cornell University Press, 1989.
Becker, Annette. *La Guerre et la foi: de la mort à la mémoire*. Paris: Armand Colin, 1994.
Bell, David. *The Cult of the Nation in France: Inventing Nationalism, 1680–1800*. Cambridge, MA: Harvard University Press, 2001.
Ben-Amos, Avner. *Funerals, Politics, and Memory in Modern France 1789–1996*. New York: Oxford University Press, 2000.
Benrekassa, Georges. *Le Concentrique et l'excentrique: marges des Lumières*. Paris: Payot, 1980.
  La Politique et sa mémoire: la politique et l'histoire dans la pensée des Lumières. Paris: Payot, 1983.
Benrekassa, Georges. "Table ronde: Montesquieu et la culture politique d'aujourd'hui." *Dix-Huitième Siècle*, 21 (1989), pp. 179–86.
Berlin, Isaiah. *Against the Current*. London: The Hogarth Press, 1979.
Binoche, Bertrand. "Montesquieu et la crise de la rationalité historique." *Revue Germanique Internationale*, 3 (1995), pp. 31–53.
Bird, Stephen. *Reinventing Voltaire: The Politics of Commemoration in Nineteenth-Century France*. *SVEC*, 2000:09. Oxford: Voltaire Foundation, 2000.

Birnbaum, Pierre. *The Idea of France*, trans. M. B. DeBevoise. New York: Hill and Wang, 2001.
Black, Jeremy. *The British Abroad: The Grand Tour in the Eighteenth Century*. New York: St. Martin's Press, 1992.
Bloch, Olivier, ed. *Epistémologie et matérialisme*. Paris: Méridiens Klincksieck, 1986.
    Le Matérialisme. Paris: Presses Universitaires de France, 1985.
Blum, Carol. *Rousseau and the Republic of Virtue*. Ithaca: Cornell University Press, 1984.
Bonnet, Jean-Claude. *Naissance du Panthéon: essai sur le culte des grands hommes*. Paris: Fayard, 1998.
Borradori, Giovanna. *Philosophy in a Time of Terror: Dialogues with Jürgen Habermas and Jacques Derrida*. Chicago: University of Chicago Press, 2003.
Bouloiseau, Marc. *The Jacobin Republic, 1792–94*, trans. Jonathan Mandelbaum. Cambridge: Cambridge University Press, 1983.
Bourdieu, Pierre. *Distinction: A Social Critique of the Judgment of Taste*, trans. Richard Nice. Cambridge, MA.: Harvard University Press, 1984.
Brewer, Daniel. *The Discourse of Enlightenment in Eighteenth-Century France: Diderot and the Art of Philosophizing*. New York: Cambridge University Press, 1993.
    "The French Intellectual, History, and the Reproduction of Culture." *L'Esprit Créateur*, 37:2 (1997), pp. 16–33.
    "Political Culture and Literary History: La Harpe's *Lycée*." *Modern Language Quarterly*, 58:2 (June 1997), pp. 1–22.
Brown, Gregory S. *Literary Sociability and Literary Property in France, 1775–1793: Beaumarchais, the Société des Auteurs Dramatiques and the Comédie Française*. Aldershot: Ashgate, 2006.
    "The Self-Fashionings of Olympe de Gouges, 1784–1789." *Eighteenth-Century Studies*, 34:3 (2001), pp. 383–401.
Brumfitt, J. H. *Voltaire: Historian*. London: Oxford University Press, 1970.
Brunetière, Ferdinand. *L'Evolution des genres dans l'histoire de la littérature*. 5th edn. Paris: Hachette, 1910.
Buck-Morss, Susan. *The Dialectics of Seeing: Walter Benjamin and the Arcades Project*. Cambridge, MA: MIT Press, 1989.
Bury, Emmanuel. *L'Invention de l'honnête homme, 1580–1750*. Paris: Presses Universitaires de France, 1996.
Cadava, Eduardo. "*Leseblitz*: On the Threshold of Violence." *Assemblages*, 20 (1993), pp. 22–23.
Canguilhem, Georges. "Fontenelle philosophe et historien des sciences." *Etudes d'histoire et de philosophe des sciences*. Paris: Vrin, 1970.
Caplan, Jay. *Framed Narratives: Diderot's Genealogy of the Beholder*. Minneapolis: University of Minnesota Press, 1985.
Carrard, Philippe. *Poetics of the New History: French Historical Discourse from Braudel to Chartier*. Baltimore: Johns Hopkins University Press, 1992.
Carrithers, David. "Montesquieu's Philosophy of History." *Journal of the History of Ideas*, 47 (1986), pp. 61–80.

Caruth, Cathy. "Recapturing the Past." In *Trauma: Explorations in Memory*, pp. 151–7. Baltimore: Johns Hopkins University Press, 1995, pp. 151–7.
  Unclaimed Experience: Trauma, Narrative and History. Baltimore: Johns Hopkins University Press, 1996.
Cassirer, Ernst. *The Philosophy of the Enlightenment*, trans. Fritz C. A. Koelln and James P. Pettegrove. Princeton: Princeton University Press, 1951.
Caylus, Anne-Claude-Philippe, comte de. *Recueil d'antiquités égyptiennes, étrusques, grecques et romaines.* Paris: Dessaint et Saillant, 1752–67.
Certeau, Michel de. *The Mystic Fable*, trans. Michael B. Smith. Chicago: University of Chicago Press, 1992.
  The Writing of History, trans. Tom Conley. New York: Columbia University Press, 1988.
Certeau, Michel de, Dominique Julia, and Jacques Revel. *Une politique de la langue: la Révolution française et les patois, l'enquête de Grégoire.* Paris: Gallimard, 1975.
Charle, Christophe. *La Naissance des "intellectuels," 1880–1900.* Paris: Minuit, 1990.
Charles, Mary Louise. *The Growth of Diderot's Fame in France from 1784 to 1875.* Bryn Mawr, 1942.
Chartier, Roger. *The Cultural Origins of the French Revolution*, trans. Lydia G. Cochrane. Durham, NC: Duke University Press, 1991.
  Culture écrite et société: l'ordre des livres, XIVe–XVIIIe siècle. Paris: Albin Michel, 1996.
  "Intellectual History or Sociocultural History: The French Trajectory." In *Modern European Intellectual History*, ed. Dominick LaCapra and Steven L. Kaplan, pp. 13–46. Ithaca: Cornell University Press, 1982.
  Lectures et lecteurs dans la France d'Ancien Régime. Paris: Seuil, 1987.
Chartier, Roger. "The Man of Letters." In *Enlightenment Portraits*, ed. Michel Vovelle, trans. Lydia Cochrane, pp. 142–89. Chicago: University of Chicago Press, 1997.
Chateaubriand, François-René de. *Le Génie du christianisme.* Paris: Mignaret, 1803.
Chauderlot, Fabienne-Sophie. "Encyclopédismes d'hier et d'aujourd'hui: informations ou pensée? Une lecture de l'*Encyclopédie* à la Deleuze." In *Using the "Encyclopédie": Ways of Knowing, Ways of Reading*, ed. Daniel Brewer and Julie Candler Hayes, pp. 37–62. SVEC, 2002:05. Oxford: Voltaire Foundation, 2002.
Cherbuliez, Juliette. *The Place of Exile: Leisure Literature and the Limits of Absolutism.* Lewisburg, PA: Bucknell University Press, 2005.
Chervel, André, ed., *L'Enseignement du français à l'école primaire*, I: *1791–1879*. Paris: Institut National de Recherche Pédagogique, 1992.
Choiseul-Gouffier, Marie-Gabriel-Florent-Auguste, comte de. *Voyage pittoresque de la Grèce.* 3 vols. Paris: Tilliard, 1782–1822.
Cobban, Alfred. "The Enlightenment and Germany." *Spectator*, 26 (September 1952), pp. 406–7.
Coleman, Patrick. *Rousseau's Political Imagination: Rule and Representation in the "Lettre à d'Alembert."* Geneva: Droz, 1984.

Compagnon, Antoine. *La Troisième République des lettres: de Flaubert à Proust*. Paris: Seuil, 1983.
Compte, Auguste. *Catéchisme positiviste*, ed. P. F. Pecaut. Paris: Garnier, 1909.
Condorcet, Jacques-Marie de Caritat de. *Esquisse d'un tableau historique des progrès de l'esprit humain*. Paris: Vrin, 1970.
Crossley, Ceri. *French Historians and Romanticism: Thierry, Guizot, the Saint-Simonians, Quinet, Michelet*. New York: Routledge, 1993.
Cutler, Maxine G. *Evocations of the Eighteenth Century in French Poetry, 1800–1869*. Geneva: Droz, 1970.
d'Alembert, Jean Le Rond. *Essai sur les éléments de philosophie*. In *Œuvres complètes*, 5 vols. (Paris: Belin, 1821), I, pp. 115–348.
 "Réflexions sur l'histoire." In *Œuvres complètes*, 5 vols., Paris: Belin, 1821, II, pp. 1–10.
d'Alembert, Jean Le Rond. *Essai sur la société des gens de lettres et des grands*. In *Œuvres complètes*, 5 vols., Paris: Belin, 1821, IV, pp. 335–72.
 "Sur la destruction des Jésuites en France." In *Œuvres complètes*, 5 vols., Paris: Belin, 1821, II, pp. 11–118.
Darnton, Robert. *The Business of Enlightenment: A Publishing History of the "Encyclopédie."* Cambridge, MA: Harvard University Press, 1979.
 "George Washington's False Teeth." In *La Recherche Dix-Huitiémiste*, ed. Michel Delon and Jochen Schlobach, pp. 149–66. Paris: Honoré Champion, 1998.
 The Great Cat Massacre. New York: Basic Books, 1984.
 Mesmerism and the End of the Enlightenment in France. Cambridge, MA: Harvard University Press, 1968.
 "In Search of the Enlightenment: Recent Attempts to Create a Social History of Ideas." *Journal of Modern History*, 43 (1971), pp. 113–32.
 The Literary Underground of the Old Regime. Cambridge, MA: Harvard University Press, 1982.
de Booy, J. Th., and Alan J. Freer, *"Jacques le fataliste" et "La Religieuse" devant la critique révolutionnaire (1796–1800)*. Geneva: Institute et Musée Voltaire, 1965.
DeJean, Joan. *Ancients Against Moderns: Culture Wars and the Making of a Fin de Siècle*. Chicago: University of Chicago Press, 1997.
 "Classical Reeducation: Decanonizing the Feminine." In *Displacements: Women, Tradition, Literatures in French*, ed. Joan DeJean and Nancy K. Miller, pp. 22–7. Baltimore: Johns Hopkins University Press, 1991.
 Tender Geographies: Women and the Origins of the Novel in France. New York: Columbia University Press, 1991.
de Man, Paul. *Allegories of Reading*. New Haven: Yale University Press, 1979.
De Montclos, Claude, ed. *La Mémoire des ruines: anthologie des monuments disparus en France*. Paris: Mengès, 1992.
Deane, Seamus. *The French Revolution and Enlightenment in English, 1789–1832*. Cambridge, MA: Harvard University Press, 1988.
Debray, Régis. *Aveuglantes lumières: journal en clair-obscur*. Paris: Gallimard, 2006.

Debray, Régis. *Teachers, Writers, Celebrities: The Intellectuals of Modern France*, trans. David Macey, London: New Left Books, 1981.
Delon, Michel, ed. *Dictionnaire européen des Lumières*. Paris: Presses Universitaires de France, 1997.
Denby, David. "Crise des Lumières, crise de la modernité?" *Dix-Huitième Siècle*, 30 (1998), pp. 257–70.
  Sentimental Narrative and the Social Order in France, 1760–1820. New York: Cambridge University Press, 1994.
Derrida, Jacques. *Rogues: Two Essays on Reason*, trans. Pascale-Anne Brault and Michael Nass. Stanford: Stanford University Press, 2005.
Desgraves, Louis. *Répertoire des ouvrages et des articles sur Montesquieu*. Geneva: Droz, 1988.
Destutt de Tracy, Antoine-Louis-Claude. *Eléments d'idéologie*. Paris: Courcier, 1804.
Detienne, Marcel. *Comment être autochtone? Du pur Athénien au Français raciné*. Paris: Editions du Seuil, 2003.
Diderot, Denis. *Correspondance*, ed. Georges Roth and Jean Varloot. Paris: Editions de Minuit, 1968.
  Diderot on Art, ed. and trans. John Goodman. 2 vols. New Haven: Yale University Press, 1995.
  Lettre sur le commerce de la librairie. In *Œuvres complètes*, VIII, pp. 479–567. Paris: Hermann, 1976.
  Le Neveu de Rameau. In *Œuvres complètes*, XII. Paris: Hermann, 1989.
  Pensées sur l'interprétation de la nature. In *Œuvres complètes*, IX. Paris: Hermann, 1981.
  Le Pour et le contre, ou lettres sur la postérité. In *Œuvres complètes*, XIX Paris: Hermann, 1986.
Diderot, Denis, and Jean Le Rond d'Alembert, eds. *Encyclopédie, ou dictionnaire raisonné des sciences, des arts et des métiers*. vols. Paris: Briasson, 1751–65.
Dieckmann, Herbert. *"Le Philosophe": Texts and Interpretation*. St. Louis: n.p., 1948.
Dosse, François. *L'Histoire en miettes: des "Annales" à la "nouvelle histoire."* Paris: La Découverte, 1987. Eng. trans. *New History in France: The Triumph of the "Annales,"* trans. Peter Conroy. Chicago: University of Illinois Press, 1994.
  "La Nouvelle Histoire." In Christian Delacroix, François Dosse, and Patrick Garcia, *Histoire et historiens en France depuis 1945*, pp. 111–27. Paris: Association pour la Diffusion de la Pensée Française, 2003.
Droixhe, Daniel. *La Linguistique et l'appel de l'histoire (1600–1800): rationalisme et révolutions positivistes*. Geneva: Droz, 1978.
Eagleton, Terry. *The Ideology of the Aesthetic*. London: Blackwell, 1990.
Ehrard, Jean. "Montesquieu dans les débats politiques français d'aujourd'hui." *SVEC*, 2003:01 (2003), pp. 455–64.
  La Politique de Montesquieu. Paris: Armand Colin, 1965.
Ehrard, Jean, and Catherine Volpilhac-Auger. "Théorie des révolutions dans le rapport qu'elles ont avec les divers gouvernements." *Dix-Huitième Siècle*, 21 (1989), pp. 23–46.

Eisenstein, Elizabeth L. *Grub Street Abroad: Aspects of the French Cosmopolitan Press from the Age of Louis XIV to the French Revolution*. New York: Clarendon Press, 1992.
Elias, Norbert. *The Court Society*, trans. Edmund Jephcott, New York: Pantheon, 1983.
Etlin, Richard A. *Symbolic Space: French Enlightenment Architecture and Its Legacy*. Chicago: University of Chicago Press, 1994.
Fayolle, Roger. *Sainte-Beuve et le XVIIIe siècle, ou comment les révolutions arrivent*. Paris: Armand Colin, 1972.
Ferguson, Priscilla Parkhurst. *Paris as Revolution: Writing the Nineteenth-Century City*. Berkeley: University of California Press, 1994.
Fink, Beatrice, and Gerhardt Stenger, eds. *Etre matérialiste au siècle des Lumières*. Paris: Presses Universitaires de France, 1999.
Finkielkraut, Alain. *The Undoing of Thought*, trans. Dennis O'Keefe, London: Claridge, 1988.
Fontenelle, Bernard Le Bovier de. *Fontenelle: Entretiens sur la pluralité des mondes*, ed. Robert Shackleton. Oxford: Clarendon Press, 1955.
Foucault, Michel. *The Archaeology of Knowledge*, trans. A. M. Sheridan Smith. New York: Pantheon Books, 1972.
  Discipline and Punish: The Birth of the Prison, trans. Alan Sheridan. New York: Vintage, 1995.
  "Governmentality." In *The Foucault Effect: Studies in Governmentality*, ed. Graham Burchell, Colin Gordon, and Peter Miller, pp. 87–104. Chicago: University of Chicago Press, 1991.
  "Nietzsche, la généalogie, l'histoire." In *Dits et écrits*, I. Paris: Gallimard, 2001, pp. 1004–24. Eng. trans. "Nietzsche, Genealogy, History." In *Language, Counter-Memory, Practice*, ed. Donald F. Bouchard. Ithaca: Cornell University Press, 1977.
  The Order of Things. New York: Vintage Books, 1970.
  "Qu'est-ce qu'un auteur?" In *Dits et écrits*, II, pp. 817–49. Paris: Gallimard, 2001. Eng. trans. "What Is An Author?" *Partisan Review*, 42 (1975), pp. 603–14.
  "Qu'est-ce que les Lumières?" In *Dits et écrits* Paris: Gallimard, 1994, IV, pp. 222–43. Eng. trans. "What is Enlightenment?" trans. Catherine Porter, In *The Foucault Reader*, ed. Paul Rabinow, New York: Pantheon Books, 1984, pp. 32–40.
Fraisse, Luc. *Les Fondements de l'histoire littéraire, de Saint-René Taillandier à Lanson*. Paris: Champion, 2002.
Freud, Sigmund. *Totem and Taboo*. In *The Standard Edition of the Complete Works of Sigmund Freud*, XIII, ed. James Strachey. London: Hogarth Press, 1953–74.
Fumaroli, Marc. *La Querelle des Anciens et des Modernes*. Paris: Gallimard, 2000.
Furet, François. *Le Passé d'une illusion: essai sur l'idée communiste au XXe siècle*. Paris: Robert Laffont, 1995.
Furet, François, *Penser la Révolution française*. Paris: Gallimard, 1978. Eng. trans. *Interpreting the French Revolution*, trans. Elborg Forster. Cambridge: Cambridge University Press, 1981.

Revolutionary France, 1770–1880, trans. Antonia Nevill. Oxford: Blackwell, 1992.
Furet, François, Jacques Julliard, and Pierre Rosanvallon. *La République du centre: la fin de l'exception française*. Paris: Calmann-Lévy, 1986.
Gay, Peter. "The Social History of Ideas: Ernst Cassirer and After." In *The Critical Spirit: Essays in Honor of Herbert Marcuse*, ed. Kurth H. Wolff and Barrington Moore, pp. 106–20. Boston: Beacon Press, 1967.
Gerbod, Paul. *La Condition universitaire en France au XIXe siècle (1842–1880)*. Paris: Presses Universitaires de France, 1965.
Gildea, Robert. *The Past in French History*. New Haven: Yale University Press, 1994.
Godechot, Jacques. *The Counter-Revolution: Doctrine and Action, 1789–1804*, trans. Salvator Attanasio. New York: Fertig, 1971.
Gontard, Maurice. *L'Enseignement secondaire en France de la fin de l'Ancien Régime à la loi Falloux: 1750–1850*. Aix-en-Provence: Edisud, 1984.
Goodman, Dena. "Difference: An Enlightenment Concept." In *What's Left of Enlightenment? A Postmodern Question*, ed. Keith Michael Baker and Peter Hanns Reil, pp. 129–47. Stanford: Stanford University Press, 2001.
  The Republic of Letters: A Cultural History of the French Enlightenment. Ithaca: Cornell University Press, 1994.
Gordon, Daniel. *Citizens Without Sovereignty*. Princeton: Princeton University Press, 1994.
  ed. *Postmodernism and the Enlightenment*. New York: Routledge, 2001.
Gossman, Lionel. *Between History and Literature*. Cambridge, MA: Harvard University Press, 1990.
Goulemot, Jean Marie. *Adieu les philosophes: que reste-t-il des Lumières?* Paris: Seuil, 2001.
  "Vision du devenir historique et formes de la révolution dans les *Lettres persanes*." *Dix-Huitième Siècle*, 21 (1989), pp. 13–22.
  Discours, histoire et revolution. Paris: 10/18, 1975.
  "Literary Practices: Publicizing the Private." In *A History of Private Life*, III: *Passions of the Renaissance*, ed. Roger Chartier, trans. Arthur Goldhammer, pp. 363–95. Cambridge, MA: Harvard University Press, 1989.
  Le Règne de l'histoire: discours historiques et révolutions, XVIIe–XVIIIe siècles. Paris: Albin Michel, 1996.
Goulemot, Jean Marie, and Daniel Oster. *Gens de lettres, écrivains et bohèmes: l'imaginaire littéraire, 1630–1900*. Paris: Minerve, 1992.
Goulemot, Jean Marie, and Eric Walter. "Les Centenaires de Voltaire et de Rousseau." In *Les Lieux de mémoire*, I, ed. Pierre Nora, pp. 381–420. Paris: Gallimard, 1984.
Goyard-Fabre, Simone. *Montesquieu, adversaire de Hobbes*. Paris: Lettres Modernes, 1980.
  Montesquieu: la nature, les lois, la liberté. Paris: Presses Universitaires de France, 1993.
Gray, John. *Enlightenment's Wake: Politics and Culture at the Close of the Modern Age*. New York: Routledge, 1995.

Grosrichard, Alain. *La Structure du sérail: la fiction du despotisme asiatique dans l'Occident classique.* Paris: Seuil, 1979.
Groult, Martine. *D'Alembert et la mécanique de la vérité dans l'"Encyclopédie."* Paris: Honoré Champion, 1999.
Guéroult, Michel. *Philosophie de l'histoire de la philosophie.* Paris: Aubier, 1979.
Guillebaud, Jean-Claude. *La Trahison des Lumières: enquête sur le désarroi contemporain.* Paris: Seuil, 1995.
Gusdorf, Georges. *De l'histoire des sciences à l'histoire de la pensée.* Paris: Payot, 1966.
Habermas, Jürgen. *Autonomy and Solidarity: Interviews,* ed. Peter Dews. London: Verso, 1986.
  The Structural Transformation of the Public Sphere, trans. Thomas Burger. Cambridge, MA: MIT Press, 1989.
Hamilton, Paul. *Historicism.* New York: Routledge, 1996.
Harth, Erica. *Ideology and Culture in Seventeenth-Century France.* Ithaca: Cornell University Press, 1983.
Hartog, François. *Régimes d'historicité: présentisme et expérience du temps.* Paris: Seuil, 2003.
Hartog, François, and Jacques Revel. *Les Usages politiques du passé.* Paris: Editions de l'Ecole des Hautes Etudes en Sciences Sociales, 2001.
Haskell, Francis, and Nicholas Penny. *Taste and the Antique: The Lure of Classical Sculpture 1500–1900.* New Haven: Yale University Press, 1981.
Heine, Heinrich. *De la France.* Paris: Gallimard, 1994.
Heinz, Thoma. *Aufklärung und nachrevolutionäres Bürgertum in Frankreich: zur Aufklärungsrezeption in der französischen Literaturgeschichte des 19. Jahrhunderts (1794–1914).* Heidelberg: Winter, 1976.
Hesse, Carla. *The Other Enlightenment: How French Women Became Modern.* Princeton: Princeton University Press, 2001.
Hinchman, Lewis P. *Hegel's Critique of the Enlightenment.* Gainesville: University Presses of Florida, 1984.
Hirschman, Albert O. *The Passions and the Interests: Political Arguments for Capitalism Before Its Triumph.* Princeton: Princeton University Press, 1977.
Hobsbawm, Eric, and Terence Ranger, eds. *The Invention of Tradition.* New York: Cambridge University Press, 1983.
Hollier, Denis. "On Literature Considered as a Dead Language." In *The Uses of Literary History,* ed. Marshall Brown. Durham, NC: Duke University Press, 1995, pp. 233–41.
Horkheimer, Max. *The Eclipse of Reason.* New York: Seabury Press, 1974.
Huet, Marie-Hélène. *Mourning Glory: The Will of the French Revolution.* Philadelphia: University of Pennsylvania Press, 1997.
Hugo, Victor. *Les Voix intérieures.* Paris: Gallimard, 1983.
Hunt, Lynn. *Politics, Culture and Class in the French Revolution.* Berkeley: University of California Press, 1984.
  "Review Essay, Penser la Révolution française." *History and Theory,* 20:3 (1981), pp. 313–23.

Husserl, Edmund. "Philosophy and the Crisis of European Humanity." In *The Crisis of European Sciences and Transcendental Philosophy*, trans. David Carr, pp. 269–300. Evanston: Northwestern University Press, 1970.
Huyssens, Andreas. *Twilight Memories: Marking Time in a Culture of Amnesia*. New York: Routledge, 1995.
Jacob, Margaret C. *The Cultural Meaning of the Scientific Revolution*. New York: Knopf, 1988.
 Scientific Culture and the Making of the Industrial West. New York: Oxford University Press, 1997.
Jaume, Lucien. *Le Discours jacobin et la démocratie*. Paris: Fayard, 1989.
Jenkins, Keith. *Why History? Ethics and Postmodernity*. New York: Routledge, 1999.
Jouhaud, Christian. *Les Pouvoirs de la littérature: histoire d'un paradoxe*. Paris: Gallimard, 2000.
Judt, Tony. *The Burden of Responsibility: Blum, Camus, Aron, and the French Twentieth Century*. Chicago: University of Chicago Press, 1998.
 Past Imperfect: French Intellectuals, 1944–1956. Berkeley: University of California Press, 1992.
Kant, Immanuel. *Critique of Pure Reason*, trans. Norman Kemp Smith. New York: St. Martin's Press, 1968.
 Kant's Political Writings, ed. Hans Reiss. Cambridge: Cambridge University Press, 1970.
Kaplan, Steven. *Farewell, Revolution: Disputed Legacies, France, 1789–1989*. Ithaca: Cornell University Press, 1995.
 Farewell, Revolution: The Historians' Feud, France, 1789–1989. Ithaca: Cornell University Press, 1995.
Keohane, Nannerl O. *Philosophy and the State in France: The Renaissance to the Enlightenment*. Princeton: Princeton University Press, 1980.
Ketcham, Diana. *Le Désert de Retz: A Late Eighteenth-Century French Folly Garden*. Cambridge, MA: MIT Press, 1994.
Koselleck, Reinhart. *Critique and Crisis*. Cambridge, MA: MIT Press, 1988.
Koyré, Alexandre. *Etudes d'histoire de la pensée philosophique*. Paris: Colin, 1962.
 From the Closed World to the Infinite Universe. Baltimore: Johns Hopkins University Press, 1957.
Kristeva, Julia. *Nations Without Nationalism*, trans. Leon S. Roudiez. New York: Columbia University Press, 1993.
 Revolution in Poetic Language, trans. Margaret Waller. New York: Columbia University Press, 1984.
Kuhn, Thomas S. *The Structure of Scientific Revolutions*. Chicago: University of Chicago Press, 1962.
La Harpe, Jean François de. *Lycée, ou Cours de littérature ancienne et moderne*. 4 vols. Paris: Verdière, 1818.
LaCapra, Dominick. *Rethinking Intellectual History: Texts, Contexts, Language*. Ithaca: Cornell University Press, 1983.
Landry, R. "Le Prisme de La Harpe." *Studies on Voltaire and the Eighteenth Century*, 153 (1976), pp. 1255–85.

Larrère, Catherine. "Montesquieu and the Modern Republic: The Republican Heritage in Nineteenth-Century France." *SVEC*, 2002:09 (2002), pp. 235–49.

Latour, Bruno. *We Have Never Been Modern*, trans. Catherine Porter, New York: Harvester Wheatsheaf, 1993.

Le Goff, Jacques. "Les Mentalités: une histoire ambiguë." In *Faire de l'histoire*, ed. Jacques Le Goff and Pierre Nora, 3 vols., Paris: Gallimard, 1974, III, pp. 76–94.

Le Roy, David. *Les Ruines des plus beaux monuments de la Grèce*. 2nd edn. Paris: H.-L. Guérin et L.-F. Delatour, 1758.

LeCoat, Nanette. "Philosophy vs. Eloquence: Laharpe and the Literary Debate at the Ecole Normale." *French Review*, 61 (1988), pp. 421–7.

Lefort, Claude. "Interpreting Revolution within the French Revolution." In *Democracy and Political Theory*, trans. David Macey, pp. 89–114. Minneapolis: University of Minnesota Press, 1988.

Leroy, Maxime. *La Politique de Sainte-Beuve*. Paris: Gallimard, 1941.

Lilla, Mark. "The Legitimacy of the Liberal Age." In *New French Thought: Political Philosophy*, ed. Mark Lilla, pp. 3–34. Princeton: Princeton University Press, 1994.

Lougee, Carolyn. *Le Paradis des femmes: Women, Salons, and Social Stratification in Seventeenth-Century France*. Princeton: Princeton University Press, 1976.

Lowenthal, David. *The Past is a Foreign Country*. New York: Cambridge University Press, 1985.

Lukacher, Brian. *Joseph Gandy: An Architectural Visionary in Georgian England*. London: Thames and Hudson, 2006.

Lyotard, Jean-François. *Le Différand*. Paris: Minuit, 1983.

"Discussions, ou: phraser 'après Auschwitz'." In *Les Fins de l'homme*, pp. 283–308. Paris: Galilée, 1981.

Political Writings, trans. Bill Readings and Kevin Paul. Minneapolis: University of Minnesota Press, 1993.

The Postmodern Condition, trans. Geoff Bennington and Brian Massumi. Minneapolis: University of Minnesota Press, 1984.

The Postmodern Explained: Correspondence 1982–1985, ed. Julian Pefanis and Morgan Thomas. Minneapolis: University of Minnesota Press, 1992.

Tombeau de l'intellectuel, et autres papiers. Paris: Galilée, 1984.

MacCannell, Juliet Flower. *The Regime of the Brother: After the Patriarchy*. New York: Routledge, 1991.

McClellan, Andrew. *Inventing the Louvre: Art, Politics, and the Origins of the Modern Museum in Eighteenth-Century Paris*. Cambridge: Cambridge University Press, 1994.

McMahon, Darrin M. *Enemies of the Enlightenment: The French Counter-Enlightenment and the Making of Modernity*. New York: Oxford University Press, 2001.

Mainardi, Patricia. *Art and Politics in the Second Empire: The Universal Expositions*. New Haven: Yale University Press, 1987.

Maleuvre, Didier. *Museum Memories: History, Technology, Art*. Stanford: Stanford University Press, 1999.
Mandrou, Robert. "Mentalité." In *Encyclopaedia Universalis*, pp. 436–8. Paris: Encyclopaedia Universalis, 1992–95.
Manin, Bernard. "Rousseau." In vol. "Idées," *Dictionnaire critique de la Révolution française*, ed. François Furet and Mona Ozouf, pp. 457–81. Paris: Flammarion, 1992.
Marin, Louis. *Le Portrait du roi*. Paris: Minuit, 1981.
 Le Récit est un piège. Paris: Minuit, 1978.
Martin, Henri. *Histoire de l' édition française*. 3 vols. Paris: Promodis, 1982–6.
Mason, Haydn T., ed. *The Darnton Debate: Books and Revolution in the Eighteenth Century*. Oxford: Voltaire Foundation, 1998.
Masseau, Didier. *Les Ennemis des philosophes: l'antiphilosophie au temps des Lumières*. Paris: Albin Michel, 2002.
 L'Invention de l'intellectuel dans l'Europe du XVIIIe siècle. Paris: Presses Universitaires de France, 1994.
Mercier, Louis-Sébastien. *L'An 2440*. London [Neuchâtel: Simon Fauche], 1774.
Montclos, Claude de, ed. *La Mémoire des ruines: anthologie des monuments disparus en France*. Paris: Mengès, 1992.
Montesquieu, Charles de Secondat, *Œuvres complètes*. Paris: Gallimard, 1951.
 Persian Letters, trans. C. J. Betts. Harmondsworth: Penguin Books, 1973.
 The Spirit of the Laws, ed. and trans. Anne M. Cohler, Basia Carolyn Miller, and Harold Samuel Stone. Cambridge: Cambridge University Press, 1989.
Moriarty, Michael. *Taste and Ideology in Seventeenth-Century France*. Cambridge: Cambridge University Press, 1988.
Mortier, Roland. *Diderot en Allemagne*. Geneva: Slatkine Reprints, 1986.
 La Poétique des ruines. Geneva: Droz, 1974.
 Le "Tableau littéraire de la France" au XVIIIe siècle. Brussels: Palais des Académies, 1972.
Nancy, Jean-Luc. *The Inoperative Community*, trans. Peter Connor *et al.*, Minneapolis: University of Minnesota Press, 1991.
Naudin, Pierre. *L'Expérience et le sentiment de la solitude: de l'aube des Lumières à la Révolution*. Paris: Klincksieck, 1995.
Nora, Pierre. "The Era of Commemoration." In *Realms of Memory: The Construction of the French Past*, ed. Pierre Nora, trans. Arthur Goldhammer, III, pp. 635–7. New York: Columbia University Press, 1998.
 "Ernest Lavisse: son rôle dans la formation du sentiment national." *Revue Historique*, 228 (1962), pp. 73–106.
 "Lavisse, instituteur national: Le 'Petit Lavisse', évangile de la République." In *Les Lieux de mémoire*, ed. Pierre Nora, I, *La République*, pp. 247–89. Paris: Gallimard, 1984.
 ed. *Les Lieux de mémoire*. 7 vols. Paris: Gallimard, 1984–92.
 ed. *Realms of Memory: Rethinking the French Past*, ed. Lawrence Kritzman, trans. Arthur Goldhammer. 3 vols. New York: Columbia University Press, 1996–8.

Nordmann, Jean-Thomas. *La Critique littéraire française au XIXe siècle (1800–1914)*. Paris: Livre de Poche, 2001.
Novick, Peter. *That Noble Dream: The "Objectivity Question" and the American Historical Profession*. New York: Cambridge University Press, 1988.
Orr, Linda. *Headless History: Nineteenth-Century French Historiography of the Revolution*. Ithaca: Cornell University Press, 1990.
Ory, Pascal. *Une Nation pour mémoire: 1889, 1939, 1989, trois jubilés révolutionnaires*. Paris: Presses de la Fondation nationale des sciences politiques, 1992.
Osler, Margaret J., ed. *Rethinking the Scientific Revolution*. New York: Cambridge University Press, 2000.
Outram, Dorinda. "'Mere Words': Enlightenment, Revolution, and Damage Control." *Journal of Modern History*, 63 (1991), pp. 327–62.
Ozouf, Mona. *La Fête révolutionnaire, 1789–1799*. Paris: Gallimard, 1976.
  L'Homme régénéré: essais sur la Révolution française. Paris: Gallimard, 1989.
Perkins, David. *Is Literary History Possible?* Baltimore: Johns Hopkins University Press, 1992.
Porter, Roy, and Mikulas Teich, eds. *The Enlightenment in National Context*. Cambridge: Cambridge University Press, 1981.
Prendergast, Christopher. *The Order of Mimesis*. Cambridge: Cambridge University Press, 1986.
Proust, Jacques. *Lectures de Diderot*. Paris: Colin, 1974.
Revel, Jacques. "Le Fardeau de la mémoire." *Correspondances*, 55 (1999), pp. 3–9.
  "Histoire et sciences sociales: les paradigmes des *Annales*." *Annales*, 34:6 (1979), pp. 1372–3.
Ricoeur, Paul. *Histoire et vérité*. Paris: Seuil, 1955.
Robespierre, Maximilien-François. *Ecrits*, ed. Claude Mazauric. Paris: Messidor, 1989.
  Œuvres complètes. 10 vols. Paris: Phénix, 2000.
Roger, Jacques. *The Life Sciences in Eighteenth-Century French Thought*, trans. Robert Ellrich. Stanford: Stanford University Press, 1997.
Roger, Philippe. *The American Enemy: A Story of French Anti-Americanism*, trans. Sharon Bowman. Chicago: University of Chicago Press, 2005.
Rosenfeld, Sophia. "Writing the History of Censorship in the Age of Enlightenment." In *Postmodernism and the Enlightenment*, ed. Daniel Gordon, pp. 117–46. New York: Routledge, 2001.
Rosso, Corrado. *La Réception de Montesquieu, ou, les silences de la harpe éolienne*. Paris: Nizet, 1989.
Roth, Michael, ed. *Irresistible Decay: Ruins Reclaimed*. Santa Monica: The Getty Research Institute for the History of Art and the Humanities, 1997.
Rousseau, Jean-Jacques. *Confessions*, trans. Angela Scholar. New York: Oxford University Press, 2000.
Rousseau, Jean-Jacques. *Correspondance*, ed. Georges Roth and Jean Varloot. Paris: Editions de Minuit, 1968.
  "Letter to D'Alembert" and Writings for the Theater, ed. and trans. Alan Bloom et al. In *The Collected Writings of Rousseau*, x. Hanover, NH: University Press of New Hampshire, 2004.

Roussel, Jean. *Jean-Jacques Rousseau en France après la Révolution, 1795–1830: lectures et légende.* Paris: Colin, 1972.
Rousso, Henry. *The Vichy Syndrome: History and Memory in France since 1944*, trans. Arthur Goldhammer. Cambridge, MA: Harvard University Press, 1991.
Sabatier de Castres, Antoine. *Les Trois Siècles de littérature française, ou tableau de l'esprit de nos écrivains, depuis François I jusqu'à nos jours.* 5th edn. La Haye: Gosse junior, 1778.
Sahut, Marie-Catherine, and Nicole Garnier. *Le Louvre d'Hubert Robert.* Paris: Editions de la Réunion des Musées Nationaux, 1979.
Said, Edward. *Representations of the Intellectual.* New York: Pantheon, 1994.
Sainte-Beuve, Charles Auguste. *Le Cahier vert*, ed. Raphaël Molho. Paris: Gallimard, 1973.
  Causeries du lundi. 19 vols. 4th edn. Paris: Garnier, 1876.
  Les Grands écrivains français. Paris: Garnier, 1927.
  Nouveaux lundis. 13 vols. Paris: Michel Lévy frères, 1870–9.
  Portraits contemporaines. 5 vols. Paris: Calmann Lévy, 1876.
  Portraits littéraires, ed. Gérald Antoine. Paris: Laffont, 1993.
Sala-Molins, Louis. *Dark Side of the Light: Slavery and the French Enlightenment*, trans. John Conteh-Morgan. Minneapolis: University of Minnesota Press, 2005.
Salverte, Eusèbe. *Eloge philosophique de Denys Diderot.* Paris: Surosne, 1801.
  Tableau littéraire de la France au XVIIIe siècle. Paris: H. Nicolle, 1809.
Sareil, Jean. "Le Massacre de Voltaire dans les manuels scolaires." *Studies on Voltaire and the Eighteenth Century*, 212 (1982), pp. 83–161.
Sartre, Jean-Paul. *Qu'est-ce que la littérature?* Paris: Gallimard, 1948.
Schandeler, Jean-Pierre. *Les Interprétations de Condorcet: symboles et concepts (1794–1894).* SVEC, 2000:03. Oxford: Voltaire Foundation, 2000.
Schmidt, James. "Inventing the Enlightenment: British Hegelians, Anti-Jacobins, and the Oxford English Dictionary." *Journal of the History of Ideas*, 64:3 (2003), pp. 421–43.
  ed. *What is Enlightenment? Eighteenth-Century Answers and Twentieth-Century Questions.* Berkeley: University of California Press, 1996.
Shapin, Steven. *The Scientific Revolution.* Chicago: University of Chicago Press, 2000.
Sherman, Daniel J. *The Construction of Memory in Interwar France.* Chicago: University of Chicago Press, 1999.
Sklar, Judith. "Jean d'Alembert and the Rehabilitation of History." *Journal of the History of Ideas*, 42:4 (1981), pp. 643–64.
Soboul, Albert. "L'*Encyclopédie* et le mouvement encyclopédique." La Pensée, 39 (1951). Rpt. in Albert Soboul, *Textes choisis de l'Encyclopédie.* Paris: Editions Sociales, 1952.
  The French Revolution, 1787–1799, trans. Alan Forrest and Colin Jones. New York: Vintage, 1974.
Starobinski, Jean. *Jean-Jacques Rousseau: Transparency and Obstruction*, trans. Arthur Goldhammer. Chicago: University of Chicago Press, 1988.
  Montesquieu par lui-même. Paris: Seuil, 1959.

Stewart, Philip, "The *Encyclopédie* On-Line." In *Using the "Encyclopédie": Ways of Knowing, Ways of Reading*, ed. Daniel Brewer and Julie Candler Hayes. *SVEC*, 2002:05. Oxford: Voltaire Foundation, 2002.

Swenson, James. *On Jean-Jacques Rousseau Considered as One of the First Authors of the Revolution*. Stanford: Stanford University Press, 2000.

Taine, Hippolyte. *Les Origines de la France contemporaine*. Paris: Hachette, 1876–94.

Terdiman, Richard. *Discourse/Counter-Discourse: The Theory and Practice of Symbolic Resistance in Nineteenth-Century France*. Ithaca: Cornell University Press, 1985.

 Past Present: Modernity and the Memory Crisis. Ithaca: Cornell University Press, 1993.

Thomas, Catherine. *Le Mythe du XVIIIe siècle au XIXè siècle, 1830–1860*. Paris: Honoré Champion, 2003, pp. 69–77.

Todd, Christopher. *Voltaire's Disciple: Jean-François de La Harpe*. London: Modern Humanities Research Association, 1972.

Todorov, Tzvetan. *On Human Diversity: Nationalism, Racism, and Exoticism in French Thought*, trans. Catherine Porter. Cambridge, MA: Harvard University Press, 1993.

Trousson, Raymond. *Images de Diderot en France, 1784–1913*. Paris: Champion, 1997.

Turgot, Anne-Robert-Jacques. *Œuvres*. Paris: Guillaumin, 1844.

Turnovsky, Geoffrey. "Conceptualising the Literary Market: Diderot and the *Lettre sur le commerce de la librairie*." *SVEC*, 2003:01 (2003), pp. 135–70.

 "The Enlightenment Literary Market: Rousseau, Authorship, and the Book Trade." *Eighteenth-Century Studies*, 36:3 (2003), pp. 387–410.

 "Marginal Writers in the 'Literary Market': Defining a New Field of Authorship in Eighteenth-Century France." *Studies in Eighteenth-Century Culture*, 33 (2004), pp. 101–23.

Van Damme, Stéphane. *Descartes: essai d'histoire culturelle d'une grandeur philosophique*. Paris: Presses de Sciences Po, 2002.

Viala, Alain. *La Naissance de l'écrivain: sociologie de la littérature à l'âge classique*. Paris: Minuit, 1985.

Villemain, Abel-François. *Cours de littérature française: tableau de la littérature française au XVIIIe siècle*. 4 vols. Paris: Didier, 1873.

Volney, Constantin François de Chasseboeuf, comte de. *Les Ruines ou méditations sur les révolutions des empires*. 10th edn. Paris: Bossange, 1822.

Vovelle, Michel. *La Mort et l'Occident de 1300 à nos jours*. Paris: Gallimard, 1983.

 ed. *Enlightenment Portraits*, trans. Lydia Cochrane. Chicago: University of Chicago Press, 1997.

Vyverberg, Henry. *Historical Pessimism in the French Enlightenment*. Cambridge, MA: Harvard University Press, 1958.

Wade, Ira O. *The Clandestine Organization and Diffusion of Philosophic Ideas in France from 1700 to 1750*. Princeton: Princeton University Press, 1938.

Wagner, Nicolas. "Le XVIIIème siècle de Villemain." *Œuvres et Critiques*, 10:1 (1985), pp. 45–65.

Walter, Eric. "1884: Une consécration ratée: Diderot, Danton et les positivistes." In *Diderot et le XVIIIe siècle en Europe et au Japon*, ed. H. Nakagawa, pp. 187–214. Nagoya: Centre Kawaï pour la Culture et la Pédagogie, 1988.
"Les Auteurs et le champ littéraire." In *Histoire de l'édition française*, ed. Henri-Jean Martin, II: *Le Livre triomphant (1660–1830)*, pp. 383–409. Paris: Promodis, 1984.
Weber, Eugen. *Peasants Into Frenchmen: The Modernization of Rural France 1870–1914*. Stanford: Stanford University Press, 1976.
White, Hayden. *The Content of the Form: Narrative Discourse and Historical Representation*. Baltimore: Johns Hopkins University Press, 1987.
Wiebenson, Dora. *The Picturesque Garden in France*. Princeton: Princeton University Press, 1978.
Wilson, Arthur. "The Verdict of Posterity, 1784–1852." In John Pappas, ed., *Essays on Diderot and the Enlightenment in Honor of O. Fellows*, pp. 400–22. Geneva: Droz, 1974.
Woodward, Christopher. *In Ruins*. London: Chatto & Windus, 2001.
Wright, Johnson Kent. "'A Bright Clear Mirror': Cassirer's *The Philosophy of the Enlightenment.*" In *What's Left of Enlightenment? A Postmodern Question*, ed. Keith Michael Baker and Peter Hanns Reil, pp. 70–101. Stanford: Stanford University Press, 2001.
Wyngaard, Amy S. *From Savage to Citizen: The Invention of the Peasant in the French Enlightenment*. Newark, NJ: University of Delaware Press, 2004.
Zammito, John H. "Are We Being Theoretical Yet? The New Historicism, the New Philosophy of History, and 'Practicing Historians.'" *Journal of Modern History*, 65 (1993), pp. 783–814.

Index

Abbey Ste. Geneviève, 167
Académie Française, 26, 55—60, 211; production of dictionaries by, 57, 115; Villemain's position in, 135. SEE ALSO *Dictionnaire de l'Académie Française*
Adorno, Theodor, 17, 34, 201
advent narratives, 4—5, 16, 38, 50
Alice et Valcour (Sade), 69
Althusser, Louis, 82; on bourgeois ideology of universality, 70; on ideology, 113, 211, 214; on words as instruments of knowledge, 60
American Revolution, 14
L'An 2440 (Mercier), 69, 187—8, 189
anachronism in historical understanding, 28
Ancien Régime, 102
Anderson, Benedict, 125, 177, 222
Annales d'histoire économique et politique journal, 6, 200, 204
L'Année littéraire (ed. Fréron), 16
"An Answer to the Question: 'What is Enlightenment'" (Kant), 19—22
"Les Antiquités de Rome" (Bellay), 186
anti-Semitism, 74, 178
Apollo Belvedere statue, 191—2
archeology, 182—3, 229
Ariès, Philippe, 199
Aron, Raymond, 201
L'Art du XVIIIe siècle (Goncourt and Goncourt), 143
Assézat, Jules, 157
Aukflärung, 13
auteur, 57
authors, 55, 57; agency of, 162—3, 228; economic aspects of, 64, 163, 215; Foucault's views of, 126, 153, 162; of history, SEE historical narrative during the Enlightenment; outsider roles of, 62, 63, 215. SEE ALSO constructing the philosophe; Voltaire
autobiography, 26

Baczko, Bronisław, 97—9, 103, 121
Baker, Keith, 11, 104
Balzac, Honoré de, 141, 154
Barante, Prosper de, 130
Barrès, Maurice, 177
Barruel, Augustin, 111—12, 154
Barthes, Roland, 7; on death of historical narrative, 75—8; on 'linguistic turn' of understanding, 99—100; on literature as a pedagogical object, 155; on tautology of literature, 112; on Voltaire, 69
Bastille Day, 123
Baudelaire, Charles, 135—6, 154
Bauman, Zygmunt, 17
Bayle, Pierre, 3, 37
Beaumarchais, Pierre de, 167
Bellay, Joachim du, 186
Ben-Amos, Avner, 148
Benjamin, Walter, 203
Benrekassa, Georges, 83, 84, 95, 217, 218
Berry, Charles Ferdinand, duc de, 128
"La Bibliothèque des histoires" series (ed. Nora), 6
bicentennial of the French Revolution, 10—12, 174
Bird's-eye View of the Bank of England, A (Gandy), 192
Blanc, Louis, 154
Bloch, Marc, 6
Boileau, Nicolas, 159—60
Bossuet, Jacques-Bénigne, 132, 159—60, 173; criticism by Voltaire of, 165; eulogies by, 77; sacred histories of, 85—6; Sainte-Beuve's portrayal of, 139
Boucher, François, 143
Bougainville, Louis-Antoine de, 62
Bourdieu, Pierre, 57—8
Brucker, Johann Jakob, 82, 83
Brunetière, Ferdinand: literary history by, 130, 159; views on La Harpe of, 111, 157
Büchner, Ludwig, 151—2

Index

Buffon, Georges-Louis Leclerc de: *Histoire naturelle* of, 24, 42; La Harpe's view of, 118; philosophy of history of, 42; Villemain's portrayal of, 133
Burke, Edmund, 101

Cabanis, Georges, 115
Les Cacouacs (Palissot), 16
Candide (Voltaire), 39, 49, 68
Canguilhem, Georges, 37
Cartesianism: philosophical idealism of, 50–2; systematic doubt of, 36–8. SEE ALSO Descartes, René
Caruth, Cathy, 176–7
Casanova, Giovanni Giacomo, 166
Cassirer, Ernst, 4, 43–8; critiques of, 44–6; intellectual climate of, 44, 46–7, 212; linkage of present and past traditions of, 43–4, 46; neo-Kantian view of the Enlightenment of, 44; on portrait of mind, 43; three-part narrative structure of, 44
Castres, Antoine Sabatier de, 152
Catéchisme positiviste (Comte), 151
Catholic Church: Enlightenment's response to, 132; La Harpe's defense of, 113; legal separation of church and state, 173; response to Napoleon's educational reforms by, 128–9, 134; response to Voltaire by, 168–71, 172; Voltaire's view of sacred history, 168. SEE ALSO religion
Causeries du lundi column (Sainte-Beuve), 137, 140, 142
Caylus, Anne-Claude-Philippe, 229
Certeau, Michel de: on the historiographical operation, 104; on intellectual history, 7–8; on link between past and present of historiography, 225; on writing about the dead, 149
Challes, Robert, 189
Chartier, Roger: on the limits of new history, 7; on the link between Enlightenment and Revolution, 105; on traditional teleological narrative, 11–12, 104
Chateaubriand, François-René de: on French heritage of ruins, 195; membership in Sainte-Beuve's literary pantheon of, 139; Restoration-era views of, 154; on seventeenth-century Christianity, 227; tour of Rome by, 188
Chénier, André-Marie de, 139
Clérisseau, Charles-Louis, 189
Code de la nature (Morelly), 68, 153
Colbert, Jean-Baptiste, 165
Comédie Française, 164
commemorative activities, 148–9, 161, 225;

bicentennial of the Revolution, 10–12, 174; centennial celebrations of Voltaire and Rousseau, 169, 174; centennial of the Revolution, 151, 174; Certeau on writing about the dead, 149; Diderot's belated posterity, 150–2; eulogies for Enlightenment figures, 77, 75–8, 79–80; legitimizing purpose of, 151; linking of the present with the past of, 149–51; Nora's *Lieux de mémoire* project, 174–7, 204–5; nostalgia in, 205; positivist views of republican sponsors of, 151–2; production of knowledge through, 176; recalling the Revolution in, 10–12, 103, 126, 151, 174; Voltaire's iconic afterlife, 162, 166–71, 173–4
Commune, 123, 174
Compagnon, Antoine, 158, 159
Comte, Auguste, 151, 157
Condillac, Etienne Bonnot de, 82; La Harpe's critique of, 117, 118; narrative of modern knowledge of, 25; on origins of the Enlightenment, 49; response to Montesquieu of, 81; sensationalism of, 3, 34, 51
Condorcet, Marie-Jean Caritat de, 50, 151; narrative of inevitable progress by, 42, 49–50; narrative of modern knowledge of, 25–7; nineteenth-century reception of, 216; publishing of Voltaire by, 167; *Vie de Voltaire*, 168
Les Confessions (Rousseau), 4, 107, 108; imagined readers of, 68; personal style of, 63; on ruins, 184, 229
Confessions d'un enfant du siècle (Musset), 170
Considérations sur les causes de la grandeur des Romans et de leur décadence (Montesquieu), 84–5, 91, 201
Considérations sur les mœurs (Duclos), 24
Constant, Benjamin, 82, 130
constructing the philosophe, 54–72; d'Alembert's *homme de lettres*, 41–8, 52–4, 213; Diderot's Moi and Lui, 71–2, 152, 216; Diderot's views of the eclectic, 77, 82, 217; Dieckmann's historical context of, 67; Dumarsais's views on, 58–61; early definitions and portrayals of, 58–60; economic aspects of, 64, 66; the *honnête homme*, 65–7; imagined freedom from history of, 68; modern role of the public intellectual, 72–4, 78; new social behavior of, 56–7, 61–4; new ways of knowing of, 60–3; production through official institutions of, 55–60, 64; self-representation of, 63; utopian imaginings of, 67–72

constructing the ruin, 179–99; archeological excavations of Herculaneum, 182–3, 229; Désert de Retz folly house, 185; Diderot on, 186–7, 230; *Encyclopédie* on meaning and value of, 182–4, 229; Holland House Library image, 179–82; imaginary ruins, 185–8, 229; Maleuvre on the historicity of museums, 194–5; as part of narrative of progress, 184; portrayal through travel writing, 195–9; Robert's imagery of, 188–95; Romantic versions of, 195; as storehouse of knowledge for the future, 183, 187–8, 189, 230; temporal matrix offered by, 179; the trope of the monument, 183; Volney's *Les Ruines*, 195–9
contestatory discourses of the Enlightenment, SEE resistance to the Enlightenment
contextually determined views of the Enlightenment, 51, 100; Cassirer's Germany of the 1930s, 44, 46–7, 212; gender contexts, 45; historicity of Montesquieu's writing, 93–6; links between present and past, SEE temporal perspectives of Enlightenment historiography; political contexts of revolutionary change, 30; politicized discourse of literary history, 112–18, 130, 131–3, 140, 155, 158, 219, 226; role of situated knowledge in, 15–16, 41–3, 48, 211; Sainte-Beuve's biographical method of literary criticism, 137–9; Sainte-Beuve's prism of political upheaval, 139, 140; social creation of the *homme de lettres*, 41–8, 52–3, 162–3, 213; strategies of reading history, 79, 83; temporal contexts, SEE temporal perspectives of Enlightenment historiography
Contrat social (Rousseau), 105–6
Contre Sainte-Beuve (Proust), 137
Corneille, Pierre, 62, 164, 173
cosmopolitanism, 59
Cours de littérature française (Villemain), 127, 135
Cousin, Victor, 127–8, 129
creation of modern French identity, 6, 123; commemoration of the dead in, 148–9, 161, 172–3, 225; commemoration of the Revolution in, 10–12, 103, 126, 151, 174; education in, 128–9, 132, 136, 155–7, 160, 172–3, 226, 227; emergence of republicanism in, 10, 123–5, 172–3; Enlightenment principles of, 123–5; evolutionary narrative of, 124–7; genealogy of national thought in, 127; historians in,

126–7; imagined communities of nations in, 125, 172–3, 222; linkage of past with present in, 149–51, 166–71; literature and literary history in, SEE literature and literary history; Louis XIV's creation of the state, 131; memory projects in, 123, 124–7, 139, 156, 174–7, 197; national citizenship, 126, 136; political use of the Enlightenment in, 112–18, 130, 131–3, 140, 155, 158, 168–71, 219, 226; positivism of, 151–2; Sainte-Beuve's journalistic criticism, 136–46; Voltaire's iconic afterlife in, 162, 166–71
crisis of French historiography, 6–12, 201; *Annales*'s new economic focus, 6; Barthes's narratological analysis, 7; Certeau's historical objects, 7–8; debates about the Revolution, 10–12; Foucault's genealogical history, 9–10; Furet's political semiotics, 11; *mentalité*, 6–7, 148; new history, 6–7; post-Enlightenment era, SEE post-Enlightenment thought; praxis of history, 8–10; traditional practices, 6, 8–9
Critique of Pure Reason (Kant), 20–1
critique: Descartes's view of critical reflection, 36–8; Foucault's cautions of perspective, 22; Kant's views of reason, 20–1, 24
Critiques (Kant), 44
cultural history, SEE sociocultural history
cultural production in the Enlightenment: development of the intellectual field in, 57–8; emergence of literature in, 57; paradigm of sociability in, 16, 56–7, 61, 142–4, 143–4; production of dictionaries in, 57; role of official institutions in, 55–60, 64. SEE ALSO constructing the philosophe
cultural studies, 100
culture wars, 27
Curie, Marie, 165

d'Alembert, Jean Le Rond, 3, 4, 25; Académie Française participation of, 26, 211; on geometrical paradigms of knowledge, 35–6, 39; on historical narrative, 35–40; the *homme de lettres*, 41–8, 52–4, 213; impact of Descartes on, 36–8, 211; as intellectual historian, 39–48; La Harpe's critique of, 117, 118; on the nature of change, 32–3; portrait of mind of, 24–7, 42, 43, 52; on revolutionary change, 29; on situated knowledge, 41–3; as sociocultural historian, 40–8; structured representations of knowledge of, 33–5, 39. SEE ALSO *Encyclopédie*
Danton, Georges-Jacques, 150

Index

Darnton, Robert, 45, 55, 64, 163, 227
de Gaulle, Charles, 178
De l'esprit (Helvétius), 34
De l'esprit des lois (Montesquieu), 24
De l'homme (Helvétius), 34
De l'interprétation de la nature (Diderot), 153
death, SEE commemorative activities
Debray, Régis, 12
The Decline and Fall of the Roman Empire (Gibbon), 184
Défense du christianisme (Frayssinous), 129
Défense du Mondain (Voltaire), 215
Denby, David, 12
Derrida, Jacques, 202, 231
Descartes, René, 4; critical response to idealism of, 50–2; described as revolutionary, 30; impact on d'Alembert, 30, 36–8, 211; methodical doubt of, 36–8; narrative of modern knowledge of, 25
Deschamps, Dom Léger-Marie, 68
Désert de Retz folly house, 185
Destutt de Tracy, Antoine, 51, 82
determinism, 10, 11
Detienne, Marcel, 126
Dialectic of Enlightenment (Adorno and Horkheimer), 17, 201
Dictionnaire de l'Académie Française, 49, 58–60, 115
Dictionnaire de Trévoux, 59
Dictionnaire historique et critique (Voltaire), 3
Dictionnaire philosophique (Voltaire), 164, 168, 178
Diderot, Denis, 3, 4, 25; art criticism of, 4; belated posterity of, 152–5, 157–8, 226; commemorative activities for, 150–2, 225; Comte's praise of, 151; as critic, 134; on eclecticism, 77, 82, 217; on esthetic role of salon culture, 146, 153, 186–7; failed election to Académie Française of, 26; on geometry, 31; imagined dialogue with Catherine of Russia of, 68; La Harpe's critique of, 111, 118, 157; Lui character of, 71–2, 152, 216; materialism of, 60, 134, 154; Moi character of, 71–2, 152; narrative of inevitable progress of, 49, 213; narrative of modern knowledge of, 25; on the nature of change, 30–3; nineteenth-century critics of, 152; on parameters of scientific knowledge, 30–3, 210; portrayal of convent life by, 73; portrayal of Montesquieu by, 75–8, 82; portrayal of the philosophe by, 58, 71–2; on posterity, 95, 216; on preserving knowledge for the future, 183; publishing history of, 153, 157; revolutionary associations of, 154; on ruins, 186–7, 230; Sainte-Beuve's portrayal of, 145–6, 153, 154, 157; on self-construction for the future, 78–82; on sensationalism, 51; utopian experiments of, 69; Villemain's portrayal of, 134–5; on writing and publishing, 215
disciplinary blind spots, 45
Discours de la méthode (Descartes), 25, 37
Discours en vers sur l'Homme (Voltaire), 215
"Discours préliminaire" to the *Encyclopédie* (d'Alembert), 25–6, 30, 36–8
Discours sur l'histoire universelle (Bossuet), 85–6
Discours sur l'inégalité (Rousseau), 106
Discours sur les sciences et les arts (Rousseau), 24
"The Discourse of History" (Barthes), 75
Le Dix-Huitième Siècle (Houssaye), 143
Dosse, François, 204
Dreyfus Affair, 74
Du Pont de Nemours, Pierre-Samuel, 118
Duclos, Charles-Pinot, 24
Dumarsais, César Chesneau, 58–61, 64–6
Dumas, Alexandre, 228
Dupanloup, Mgr., bishop of Orléans, 172
Durkheim, Emile, 82

"Eclectisme" (Diderot), 58, 76–8, 82–4
"Economie politique" (Rousseau), 106
"Encyclopédie" (Diderot), 25; on the goal of the encyclopedic text, 32; on parameters of scientific knowledge, 210; on preserving knowledge for the future, 183
economics of the philosopher: market for writing and publishing, 64, 163, 215; usefulness of the philosophe, 66
écrivain, 57. SEE ALSO authors
educational reforms: creation of modern French identity, 128–9, 132, 136, 155–7, 172–3, 226, 227; Ferry's work of the 1880s, 136, 160, 173; Lanson's separation of history from literature, 158–60, 161, 173; Napoleonic reforms, 128–9, 134; teaching of history, 173; teaching of literature, 155–7, 159–60, 173; teaching of philosophy, 129
Eglise Sainte-Geneviève, 102
Ehrard, Jean, 83, 95
Emile (Rousseau), 101
Encyclopédie (ed. Diderot and d'Alembert), 24, 72, 153; censorship fears of editors of, 68; critical responses to, 16; "Discours préliminaire" of, 25–6, 30, 36–8; electronic text version of, 58; fascination with ruins of, 182–4, 229; goal of, 32; "Herculanum" essay (de Jaucourt), 182–3; La Harpe's critique of, 111, 117;

new subject positions in, 78; permission for publication of, 26; portrayal of the philosophe in, 58–61; portrayals of Montesquieu in, 76–8, 79–80, 81; as storehouse of knowledge for the future, 183; the trope of the monument in, 183; use of term "revolution" in, 30
English Revolution, 14, 30
Enlightenment, significance of term, 1–2, 13
The Enlightenment: An Interpretation (Gay), 4
epistemological change, 30–3
epistemological knowledge, SEE knowledge
epistolary novels, 26, 89–90, 107
Ermenonville gardens, 185
l'esprit, SEE portraits of mind
"Esprit de la Révolution" (La Harpe), 113–14
L'Esprit des lois (Montesquieu), 84–9; *Encyclopédie*'s references to, 79–80, 81; historical narrative writing of, 38; on the power of the monarch, 188; Villemain's critique of, 133–5
Esquisse d'un tableau historique des progrès de l'esprit (Condorcet), 25–7, 49–50
Essai sur l'origine des connaissances humaines (Condillac), 25, 34, 49
Essai sur la société des gens de lettres et des grands (d'Alembert), 41–8, 52–4, 213
Essai sur les éléments de philosophie (d'Alembert), 24–41; on historical narrative, 35–40; impact of Cartesianism on, 36–8, 211; intellectual history of, 39–48; portrait of mind in, 24–7, 42, 43, 52; on revolutionary change, 29–33; as socio-cultural history, 40–8; *tableau* format of, 33–5, 39
Essai sur les mœurs (Voltaire), 42–3
Essais (Montaigne), 93
Et in Arcadia ego (Poussin), 181
eulogies, 77, 79–80, 75–8
The European Mind, 1680–1715 (Hazard), 4

Fabre, Victorin, 131
Faguet, Emile, 157
Fanaticism in Revolutionary Language (La Harpe), 113
Febvre, Lucien, 6
La Femme au XVIIIe siècle (Goncourt and Goncourt), 143
Fénelon, François, 173
Ferney estate of Voltaire, 166
Ferry, Jules, 136, 160, 173
fiction, SEE literature and literary history
field theory of Bourdieu, 57–8
Finkeilkraut, Alain, 12
Flaubert, Gustave, 168, 170

Fontenelle, Bernard de, 50; on Cartesian historical method, 37; on Cartesian reason, 211; La Harpe's portrayal of, 118; on origins of the Enlightenment, 49
Foucault, Michel, 2; on authorship, 126, 153, 162; on the end of man, 231; on genealogical history, 9–10, 104; on historical praxis, 8–10; on perspective in criticism, 22; on structured representations of knowledge, 34; on traditional teleological narrative, 8–9, 104
Fragonard, Jean Honoré, 143, 188
Franco-Prussian War, 151, 174
Frankenstein (Shelley), 198
Frayssinous, Denis-Luc, 128, 226
French identity, SEE creation of modern French identity
French Revolution, 14, 97–9; association with the Enlightenment of, 29, 102–3, 105, 140–2, 154, 168, 210; bicentennial celebration of, 10–12, 174; centennial celebrations of, 151, 174; Chartier's causal reversal of, 11–12; citizenship, 122; conservative histories of, 111–12; contemporary readings of, 171–2, 176–7; Furet's political semiotics of, 11, 117; impact on nineteenth-century literary histories of, 112–18, 130, 131–3, 140, 155, 158, 219, 226; influence of Rousseau on, 105–10; the Jacobin Terror, 97–9, 109, 111, 117, 170; La Harpe's study of, 109–21, 122; Marxist interpretations of, 10, 11, 104; murder of Condorcet during, 49–50; official commemorations of, 10–12, 103, 126, 151, 174; pantheonization of heroes of, 102–3, 154, 167, 168; political re-theorizing of revolutionaries, 104; reconfigurations of time in, 101–2, 122; Thermidor and its challenges, 97–9, 117, 142, 170; transformation of language by, 11, 113–18, 197
Fréron, Elie-Catherine, 16
Freud, Sigmund, 148, 176
Furet, François: political semiotics of, 11, 117; on the politics of memory, 123, 167; on traditional teleological narrative, 104
Furetière, Antoine, 57, 59

Galerie des portraits du XVIIIe siècle (Houssaye), 143
Gandy, Joseph M., 192
Gautherin, Jean, 150
Gay, Peter, 4, 44–6
gender contexts of history, 45
genealogical narrative, 9–10, 104, 105

Le Génie du christianisme (Chateaubriand), 154, 195, 227
"Gens de lettres" (Voltaire), 24, 58
"Great French Writers" series (pub. Hachette), 173
gens de lettres, SEE constructing the philosophe; *homme de lettres*
geometrical paradigms of knowledge, 31, 35–6
Géricault, Jean-Louis, 141
German historiography, 44
Geruzez, Eugène-Nicolas, 157, 173
Gibbon, Edward, 166, 184
Ginguené, Pierre-Louis, 105
Girardin, marquis de, 185
Goethe, Johan Wolfgang von, 153
Goncourt, Edmond and Jules de, 143, 171
Goodman, Dena, 43, 45
Goulemot, Jean Marie, 12, 63, 178
Graffigny, Françoise de, 187
Gray, John, 208
Grégoire, *Abbé* Henri, 115
Grotius, Hugh, 85–6
Guerre aux démolisseurs (Hugo), 186
Guillebaud, Jean-Claude, 205
Guizot, François, 124, 127, 129, 143

Habermas, Jürgen, 17
Hall, Stuart, 157
Hartog, François, 2, 203–5
Hazard, Paul, 4
Hegel, Georg, 43, 46
Heidegger, Martin, 212
Heine, Heinrich, 125
Helvétius, Claude-Adrien: La Harpe's critique of, 111; response to Montesquieu by, 81; sensationalism of, 34, 51
"La Henriade" (Voltaire), 164
Herculaneum, 182–3
Histoire d'un voyage faict en la Terre de Brésil (Léry), 62
Histoire de France (Lavisse), 6
Histoire de France contemporaine (Lavisse), 6
Histoire de la littérature anglaise (Taine), 138
Histoire de la littérature française (Lanson), 158
"Histoire moderne d'Angleterre" (Jaucourt), 30
Histoire naturelle (Buffon), 24, 42
Historia critica philosophiae (Brucker), 82, 83
historical narrative during the Enlightenment: creation of the *homme de lettres*, 41–8, 52–3, 162–3, 213; critical reflection, doubt, and skepticism in, 24, 36–8, 86–90, 211; d'Alembert's intellectual history, 35–40, 39–48; Diderot on the nature of change, 30–3; Diderot's self-constructing linkage of past with future, 78–82; eulogies, 75–8, 79–80; exploration of causality in, 84–90; the ideal collectivity of humanity in, 21–2; impact of politicized language on, 113–18; interest in peasant life in, 229; *l'esprit général* of, 94–5, 218; meaning and value of ruins in, 182–4, 185–8, 229; memoirs and letters, 38; Montesquieu's impact on, SEE Montesquieu, Charles-Louis Secondat de; narrative of inevitable progress, 42–3, 49–52, 184, 199; narrative of modern knowledge, SEE knowledge; rationality of history in, 86–90, 217; responses to Bossuet in, 85–6; responses to Hobbes in, 85–6; on retrospective history, 40; role of factuality in, 87; shift away from idealism in, 50–2, 59; on transformative change, 88–92, 218; use of narrative style in, 92; Voltaire's historical method, 37, 155–7; writings on Rome in, 84–6, 91, 217. SEE ALSO historiography of the Enlightenment
historical praxis, 8–10
historiographical operation, 104
historiography of the Enlightenment, 12–15, 24–48; advent narratives, 4–5, 16, 38, 50; Anglo-American versions, 13–15, 208; commemorations of the dead, SEE commemorative activities; contextually determined narratives, SEE contextually determined views of the Enlightenment; disciplinary debates on, 99–101; identity narratives, SEE creation of modern French identity; La Harpe's rejection of the philosophes, SEE La Harpe, Jean-François de; literary criticism in, SEE literature and literary history; in new history narratives, SEE new history; political nature of, SEE politicized nature of historical discourse; in the post-Enlightenment age, 199–205; readings of Montesquieu in, 81–4, 93–6, 217, 218; resistance to the Enlightenment in, SEE resistance to the Enlightenment; role of the French Revolution in, SEE French Revolution; role of memory in, SEE memory; sacred history, 37, 85–6, 168; teleological narrative, 8–9, 104; temporal nature of, SEE temporal perspectives of Enlightenment historiography; written during the Enlightenment, SEE historical narrative during the Enlightenment. SEE ALSO sociocultural history
Hobbes, Thomas, 86
Hobsbawm, Eric, 126
Holbach, Paul-Henri d', 33, 81
Holland House Library, 179–82

Hollier, Denis, 160
Holocaust readings on rationality of evil, 17
homme de lettres, 41–8; autonomy and agency of, 54, 162–3; social context of, 52–4, 213. SEE ALSO constructing the philosophe
L'Homme machine (La Mettrie), 24, 25, 60
honnête homme, 65–7
Horkheimer, Max, 17, 34, 82, 201
Houdon, Jean-Antoine, 166
Houssaye, Arsène, 143
Hugo, Victor, 169, 186, 195
human rights discourse, 73–84
Hume, David, 151
Hunt, Lynn, 114, 117
Husserl, Edmund, 201–2, 231

idealism, SEE Cartesianism
identity, SEE creation of modern French identity
ideology, 211
Imaginary View of the Grand Gallery of the Louvre in Ruins (Robert), 189–92
imagined communities, 125, 222
L'Ingénu (Voltaire), 39
Institut de France, 129–31
intellectual history, 4–5; Certeau's historical objects, 7–8; contemporary readings of the French Revolution, 171–2; critiques of Cassirer's idealized version, 44–6; disciplinary blind spot of, 45; origins in d'Alembert's work of, 39–48; textual mediation of knowledge, 43.
  SEE ALSO knowledge
intellectuals, SEE constructing the philosophe
interpretations of the Enlightenment, SEE contextually determined views of the Enlightenment AND temporal perspectives of Enlightenment historiography

'J'accuse' (Zola), 74, 178
Jacques le fataliste (Diderot), 153
Janin, Jules-Gabriel, 130, 137
Jaucourt, Louis de: definition of "revolution" of, 30; "Herculanum" essay of, 182–3; on the philosophe, 58; sensationalism of, 34; on sociability, 54
Jay, Antoine, 131
Jenkins, Keith, 18
Jesuit dictionary, 59
Joan of Arc, 174
Journal de Trévoux, 16
Journal des débats, 137
journalistic criticism, 136–46
Julie, ou la nouvelle Héloïse (Rousseau), 106–7
Juliette (Sade), 34

Kant, Immanuel, 5; on collective identity of humanity, 21–2; on criticism and reason, 20–1, 24, 43, 51; description of the Enlightenment by, 19–22; on public and private spheres of reason, 20–1; utopian experiments of, 68
knowledge, 25–6, 33–5, 60–3; autonomy of, 54; Cartesian idealism, 50–2; d'Alembert's portrait of mind, 24–7, 42, 43, 52; Diderot on scientific knowledge, 30–3, 210; *Encyclopédie*'s goal of revolutionized knowledge, 32; epistemological ways of knowing, 3–4, 30–3; geometrical paradigms of, 31, 35–6; materialism, 51, 59; sensationalism, 3, 51, 59, 117; situated knowledge, 41–3, 48, 211; structured *tableaux* of d'Alembert, 33–5, 39; textual mediation of, 43
Kraft und Stoff (Büchner), 151–2
Kristeva, Julia, 82, 95, 218
Kritik, 20–1
Kuhn, Thomas, 25

La Bruyère, Jean de, 139
La Fontaine, Jean de, 139, 159–60
La Harpe, Jean-François de, 16, 109–21, 122; association with the Lycée of, 110–11, 113; critique of Diderot by, 118, 157; critiques of the philosophes by, 117–19, 132, 133, 221; defense of the Catholic Church by, 113; efforts to move beyond the Revolution of, 111–14; impact of Voltaire's esthetic positions on, 112–13, 157; impact on literary historians of, 130, 138; on importance of esthetic judgment, 112–13; on political and historical nature of literature, 112–18, 132, 219; on the power of words, language, and eloquence, 113–14, 115–18, 119–21; on the role of divine causality, 118, 119–20
La Ligue de la Patrie française, 177
La Mettrie, Julien Offroy, 24, 25, 60
La Rochefoucauld, François de, 65–7, 139
Lafayette, Marie-Madeleine de, 61
Lamartine, Alphonse de, 195
Lamennais, Hugues-Félicité Robert de, 154
Lancret, Nicolas, 143, 171
Lanson, Gustave, 130, 157, 158–60, 161, 173
Latour, Bruno, 26, 209
Lavisse, Ernest, 6
Le Goff, Jacques, 6
Le Père de famille (Diderot), 153
Lefort, Claude, 116, 117
Lemercier, Népomucène, 138
Léry, Jean de, 62
"Lettres" (Voltaire), 58

Les Lieux de mémoire project (ed. Nora), 174–7, 228, 229
letter-writing, 38
Lettre à d'Alembert (Rousseau), 107
Lettre sur la liberté de la presse (Diderot), 215
Lettre sur les aveugles (Diderot), 25, 153
Lettre sur les sourds et muets (Diderot), 25, 153
Lettres d'une Péruvienne (Graffigny), 69
Lettres persanes (Montesquieu), 63, 68, 89–90, 201
Lettres philosophiques (Voltaire), 164
Leviathan (Hobbes), 85–6
Lévy-Bruhl, Lucien, 6
Lilla, Mark, 14
linguistic projections of meaning, 13, 115–18; role of eloquence in language, 119–21; semiotic politics, 117; transformations of language by the Revolution, 11, 113–18, 197
literacy, 57
literature and literary history, 51, 57, 127; anti-philosophy of the nineteenth century, 170–1; Barthes on tautology of, 112; exteriority of the ideological in, 146–7; Ferry's educational reforms of, 160; Hollier's post-literacy age, 160; Institut de France's *tableau* competitions, 129–31; La Harpe's critique of Enlightenment writers, 117–19, 132, 133, 221; La Harpe's emphasis on eloquence, 119–21; La Harpe's portrayal of the French Revolution, 109–21; Lanson's separation of literature from history, 158, 161; as pedagogical object, 155–7; politicized role of, 112–18, 130, 131–3, 140, 155, 158, 219, 226; the power of words, 115–18; Proust's esthetic modernism, 137; Rousseau's impact on the Revolution, 105–10; Sainte-Beuve's journalistic criticism, 136–46, 170; self-reflectivity in epistolary novels, 107; travel writing, 62, 187, 195–9; use of Enlightenment past to reconstruct the present, 129–31; utopian literature, 62; Villemain's reformist portrayal of the Enlightenment, 127–36, 132–6, 135–6; Villemain's *Tableau*, 129
Littré, Emile, 157
Locke, John, 37, 51
Louis XIV, king of France, 57; absolute power of, 95; court culture of, 61, 165; Enlightenment response to, 132; Mercier's imaginary encounter with, 187; pacification goals of, 53; role in creation of French identity of, 131, 132
Louis XV, king of France, 164, 167, 178

Louis XVIII, king of France, 128
Louis-Napoléon, emperor of France, 139, 173, 224
Louis-Philippe, king of France, 139, 141, 157
Louvre museum: Apollo Belvedere statue, 191–2; Enlightenment era reorganization of, 192–5; *Imaginary View of the Grand Gallery of the Louvre in Ruins* (Robert), 189–92
Lowenthal, David, 28
Lycée, ou Cours de littérature ancienne et moderne (La Harpe), 111–14, 157; "Esprit de la Révolution" appendix, 113–14. SEE ALSO La Harpe, Jean-François de
Lycée, 110–11, 113
Lyotard, Jean-François: on broken promise of progress, 204; on Enlightenment as modern narrative, 18; on intellectuals, 72

MacCannell, Juliet, 148
Madame Bovary (Flaubert), 168
Maistre, Joseph de, 111–12, 133
Maleuvre, Didier, 194–5
Mallet du Pan, Jacques, 111
Malraux, André, 167, 228
Manin, Bernard, 107
"Marie Antoinette" (Sainte-Beuve), 139
"The Marseillaise," 123
Marxist views: of the Enlightenment, 10, 55, 214; of human agency, 11; of the Revolution, 104
materialism, 51; of Diderot, 60, 134, 154; shift from idealism to, 51
Méditations métaphysiques (Descartes), 25
Mémoires d'outre-tombe (Chateaubriand), 195
memoirs, 26, 38
memory: crisis of, in new history, 203–5; disruption by French Revolution of, 197; in nineteenth-century literary history, 156; Nora's *Lieux de mémoire* project, 174–7, 204–5; in production of cultural identity, 123, 124–7; Sainte-Beuve's project of, 139
mentalité, 6–7, 148
La Mentalité primitive (Lévy-Bruhl), 6
Les Misérables (Hugo), 169
Mercier, J. S., 115
Mercier, Louis-Sébastien: on "demi-littérateurs," 64; imaginary time travel of, 69, 187–8, 189
Méré, Antoine Gombaud, 65–7
Michelet, Jules, 103, 124, 146, 154
Micromégas (Voltaire), 39
modern French identity, SEE creation of modern French identity
Modernity and the Holocaust (Bauman), 17

modernity narratives, 4–5, 16, 18; Jenkins on failed experiment of, 18; Kant on collective identity in, 21–2; Latour's claim against, 26, 209; seventeenth-century struggles over, 26
Molière, 139, 174
Le Mondain (Voltaire), 66
Montaigne, Michel Eyquem de, 93, 139
Montesquieu, Charles-Louis Secondat de, 24, 118; contemporary readings of, 81–4, 93–6, 217, 218; critique of the absolutist monarchy by, 94, 201; discursive style of, 92; eclecticism of, 82; *Encyclopédie* references to, 79–80, 81; Enlightenment readings of, 78–82; eulogies for, 75–8, 79–80; exploration of causality by, 84–90, 217; historical narrative writing of, 38; historicization of, 79–80; on "*l'esprit général*," 94–5, 218; membership in Sainte-Beuve's literary pantheon of, 139; on moderation of the aristocracy, 75; on the rationality of history, 86–90, 217; on rationality of socio-political culture, 3; response to Bossuet of, 85–6; response to Hobbes of, 85–6; response to skepticism and factuality of, 87–8; on revolution and transformative change, 30, 88–92, 218; on Rome, 84–6, 91, 217; travel writing of, 63, 187; utopian experiments of, 68; Villemain's portrayal of, 133–5; on withstanding time, 91
Monville, François Racine de, 185
Morelly, 68, 153
Moriarty, Michael, 66
Mornet, Daniel, 106
Moulin, Jean, 228
Musset, Alfred de, 170

Nancy, Jean-Luc, 28
Napoleon: art plundering of, 192; educational reforms of, 128–9, 134; political use of the Enlightenment by, 131; on Rousseau, 109
narratives about the Enlightenment, SEE historical narrative during the Enlightenment; historiography of the Enlightenment
national narratives, 12, 207
Natoire, Charles-Joseph, 189
Le Neveu de Rameau (Diderot), 71–2, 152, 153, 216
new history, 6–7; Barthes's narratological analysis, 7; Certeau's historical objects, 7–8; cultural memory crisis in, 203–5; Foucault's genealogical history, 9–10, 104; Furet's political semiotics, 11; Revolution debates in, 10–12; role of *mentalité* in, 6–7, 148

Nietzsche, Friedrich, 164
"Nietzsche, Genealogy, History" (Foucault), 8–10
nineteenth-century France, SEE creation of modern French identity
Nisard, Désiré, 130, 138, 157
Nodier, Charles, 146
Nora, Pierre, 6, 174–7, 204–5, 228
La Nouvelle Héloïse (Rousseau), 4, 68, 106–7
La Nouvelle Histoire (Le Goff), 6, 200
novels, 26

"On the Principles of Political Morality that Must Guide the Convention" (Robespierre), 109
oppositional discourses of the Enlightenment, SEE resistance to the Enlightenment
origins of the Enlightenment, SEE advent narratives

painting of the Enlightenment, 143, 188–91
Palissot, Charles, 16
Panini, Giovanni Paolo, 188, 189
Panthéon, 103, 167, 168, 228
paradigm shift, 25
Pascal, Blaise, 93, 139
Pastoret, Marquise de, 103
"Patrie" (Furetière), 59
patronage system, 64
Pensées (Pascal), 93
Pensées philosophiques (Diderot), 153
Pensées sur l'interprétation de la nature (Diderot), 30–3, 183, 210
Penser la Révolution (Furet), 11
"*le petit Lavisse*" (Lavisse), 6
Phenomenology (Hegel), 44
"Le Philosophe" (Dumarsais), 58–61, 64–6, 71–2; affirmation of rationalism in, 60; Dieckmann's historical reading of, 67; utopian and universalist ideals of, 67–71. SEE ALSO constructing the philosophe
philosophers, SEE constructing the philosophe
"Philosophie de l'histoire" (Voltaire), 42–3
"Philosophique" (Jaucourt), 58
philosophy of history, 42
The Philosophy of the Enlightenment (Cassirer), 4, 43–8
Piranesi, Giovanni Battista, 188, 189
Pius VI, Pope, 192
"Plan de deux discours sur l'histoire universelle" (Turgot), 184
"Plan d'un ouvrage sur la géographie politique" (Turgot), 184
plays, 26

Index

political theory, 14; Furet's political semiotics, 11; impact of Montesquieu on, SEE Montesquieu, Charles-Louis Secondat de
politicized nature of historical discourse, 101, 131–3, 219; in creation of modern French identity, 112–18, 130, 131–3, 140, 155, 158, 168–71, 219, 226; language and semiotics in, 113–18; re-theorizing work of French revolutionaries, 104
Politique tirée de l'Ecriture Sainte (Bossuet), 85–6
Pompadour, Madame de (Antoinette Poisson), 164
Pompeii, 182–3, 188
Portraits intimes du XVIIIe siècle (Goncourt and Goncourt), 143
portraits of mind: Cassirer's restatement of d'Alembert, 43; critical activity, 24; d'Alembert's *l'esprit*, 24–7, 42, 52; new forms of subjectivity, 26. SEE ALSO knowledge
positivism, 151–2
post-Enlightenment thought, 199–205; Ariès's religion of progress, 199; Aron's critique of historical reality, 201; Benjamin's suspicion of linear historicity, 203; crisis of cultural memory, 203–5; Husserl's warning about scientific reason, 201–2, 231; impact of structuralism on, 200–1. SEE ALSO crisis of French historiography
The Postmodern Condition (Lyotard), 18
postmodernist critiques of Enlightenment, 16–18, 18–23, 208; Foucault's cautions on perspective of, 22; Jenkins's view of modernity as failed experiment, 18
Poussin, Nicolas, 181
power, 54
praxis/practice of history, 8–10
Prendergast, Christopher, 124
press, 136–46
La Princesse de Clèves (Lafayette), 61
production of French national identity, SEE creation of modern French identity
Project for the American and French Research on the Treasury of the French Language (ARTFL), 58
Project for the Disposition of the Grand Galerie of the Louvre (Robert), 192–5
Project for Universal Peace (Kant), 68
Proust, Jacques, 226
Proust, Marcel, 137
public intellectuals, 72–4, 78. SEE ALSO constructing the philosophe
publishing industry, 64

pyrrhonisme, 37, 87–8
"Le Pyrrhonisme de l'histoire" (Voltaire), 37, 211

Quesnay, François, 118
Qu'est-ce que la littérature? (Sartre), 69
Quinet, Edgar, 124

Racine, Jean, 62, 159–60, 164
The Raft of the Medusa (Géricault), 141
Rameau, Jean-Philippe, 30
reading: as allegory for the temporal matrix of Enlightenment ruins, 179; contextualization of, 79; of history, contemporary, 83
Realms of Memory (ed. Nora), 174–7, 204–5, 228
reason: Kant's definitions of, 20–1; public and private spheres of, 20–1. SEE ALSO knowledge
reception history, 83
Recueil d'antiquités égyptiennes, étrusques, grecques et romaines (Caylus), 229
Reflections on the Revolution in France (Burke), 101–2
"Réflexions sur l'histoire" (d'Alembert), 40
Réfutation d'Helvétius (Diderot), 51
"régimes d'historicité," 4
La Religieuse (Diderot), 73
Le Rêve de d'Alembert (Diderot), 32–3, 60
Règles pour la direction de l'esprit (Descartes), 37
religion: Enlightenment campaigns against, 73; La Harpe's defense of, 113; La Harpe's view of divine causality, 118, 119–20; replacement by sociability of, 61; sacred paradigms for history, 37, 85–6, 168. SEE ALSO Catholic Church
Remarques pour servir de supplément à l'Essai sur les mœurs (Voltaire), 88
Renaissance history, 136
republicanism, 123–5. SEE ALSO creation of modern French identity
resistance to the Enlightenment, 26; contemporary resistance to the philosophes, 16–18; in identity creation, SEE creation of modern French identity in La Harpe's critiques of the philosophes, 117–19, 132, 133, 221; in post-Enlightenment thought, 199–205; in postmodernist critiques of the Enlightenment, 16–18, 18–23, 208
retreat, 61–2
Revel, Jacques, 200
Rêveries d'un promeneur solitaire (Rousseau), 4, 63, 107

revolutionary change, 29–33; geometrical definition of, 30; scientific revolution, 30–3; as term representing momentous change, 29
revolutions, SEE American Revolution; French Revolution
Revue historique, 125
Richelet, Pierre, 57
Richelieu, Cardinal, 55
Ricœur, Paul, 101
Rivarol, Antoine, 154
Robert, Hubert, 186–7, 188–95; *Imaginary View of the Grand Gallery of the Louvre in Ruins,* 189–92; *Project for the Disposition of the Grand Galerie of the Louvre,* 192–5
Robespierre, Maximilien-François, 170; attempt to justify the Terror, 109; fall and execution of, 97, 142; on Rousseau, 108–10
Roederer, Pierre-Louis, 109
Roland, Jean-Marie, 110
Roman history, 84–6, 91
Romantic historiography, 124, 125, 195.
SEE ALSO creation of modern French identity
Rosenfeld, Sophia, 14
Rousseau, Jean-Jacques, 4, 24, 82; burial at Ermenonville of, 185; centennial celebrations of, 169; on "civilized" theatre, 107; commemorative activities for, 151, 169; exploration of experience by, 4; imagined readers of, 68; influence on the Revolution of, 105–10, 108–10; interest in ruins of, 184, 229; La Harpe's critique of, 111, 118; membership in Sainte-Beuve's literary pantheon of, 139; on Montesquieu's death and funeral, 76; moral works of, 106–7; Mornet's reading of, 106; Napoléon's view of, 109; nineteenth-century rehabilitation of, 127, 133, 144–5; political texts of, 106; Revolutionary pantheonization of, 102–3, 168; Robespierre's view on, 108–10; on the role of the writer, 52; Sainte-Beuve's portrayal of, 144–5, 224; self-representation of, 63, 107, 108; Villemain's portrayal of, 133
"Rousseau juge de Jean-Jacques" (Rousseau), 108
Les Ruines (Volney), 184, 195–9
ruins, SEE constructing the ruin
The Ruins of Palmyra (Wood), 198

sacred history, 37, 85–6, 168
Sade, Donatien de, 34, 69
Said, Edward, 215
Sainte-Beuve, Charles-Augustin, 127, 136–46; biographical method of, 137–9; *Causeries du lundi* column, 137; freedom from the political of, 137–9, 140, 142–3; impact on literary history of, 130; literary pantheon of, 139–40; political contexts of, 139, 140; portrayal of Balzac by, 141; portrayal of Diderot by, 145–6, 153, 154, 157; portrayal of Rousseau by, 144–5, 224; portrayal of Voltaire by, 170; Proust's critique of, 137; on statue of Diderot, 150; valorization of salon sociability of, 142–3; view of the Enlightenment of, 140–2
Saint-Evremond, Charles de, 65–7
salon culture, 56–7, 62; Diderot in, 146, 153, 186–7; resuscitation by the Goncourts of, 171; Sainte-Beuve's view of, 142–3
Salons (Diderot), 153, 186–7
Salverte, Eusèbe, 130, 153
Sartre, Jean-Paul, 69, 178
scientific knowledge, 30–3, 210
Scudéry, Madame Madeleine de, 62
Second Empire, 139, 141, 157, 173, 224
Second Republic, 139, 141
Secondat, Charles de, SEE Montesquieu, Charles-Louis Secondat de
Senancour, Etienne de, 195
sensationalism, 3, 51, 59, 117
seventeenth-century France: cultural production during, 55–60; literacy during, 57; moralism and *honnêteté* in, 65–7; retreat tradition of, 61–2; salon culture during, 62; struggles over modernity during, 26
Sévigné, Marie de, 159–60
Shelley, Mary, 198
Le Siècle de Louis XIV (Voltaire), 24
situated knowledge, 15–16, 41–3, 48, 211
Soane, John, 192
Soboul, Albert, 11
"Sociabilité" (Jaucourt), 54
sociability, 16, 56–7, 61, 142–3, 143–4.
SEE ALSO salon culture
La Société féodale (Bloch), 6
Société positiviste, 150, 151
sociocultural history, 5; in Cassirer's *The Philosophy of the Enlightenment,* 43–8; cultural studies, 100; of Enlightenment resistance, 16–18; gender contexts in, 45; ideological analysis of, 55, 214; paradigm of sociability in, 16, 56–7, 61, 142–3, 143–4; readings of the French Revolution in, 171–2, 197; of the republic of letters, 53; role of cultural memory in, 123, 124–7, 139, 156, 174–7; role of literature in, 51; role of situated knowledge in, 41–3, 48; as written by d'Alembert, 40–8.
SEE ALSO contextually determined views of the Enlightenment

Soufflot, Jacques, 102, 167
speeches, eulogies, 75–8, 79–80; political oratory of the Revolution, 132
"The Spirit and Style of M. Villemain" (Baudelaire), 135–6
Staël, Anne-Louis Germaine de, 130, 133
Starobinski, Jean, 91–2, 93
Stendhal, 154
structuralism, 7
structures of knowledge: geometrical paradigms of knowledge, 31, 35–6; *tableaux* of d'Alembert, 33–5, 39. SEE ALSO knowledge
Supplément au voyage de Bougainville (Diderot), 69, 153
"Sur la destruction des Jésuites" (d'Alembert), 40
Swenson, James, 107
Système de la nature (Holbach), 33

Tableau de la littérature du XVIIIe siècle (Villemain), 129, 135–6; moral chronology of, 133; preface on political use of the Enlightenment of, 131; writers included in, 133–5
Tableau de Paris (Mercier), 64
Tableau historique des progrès de l'esprit (Condorcet), 42
Tableau historique et critique de la poésie française et du théâtre français au XVIe siècle (Sainte-Beuve), 136
"Tableau philosophique des progrès successifs de l'esprit humain" (Turgot), 49
tableaux of d'Alembert, 33–5, 39
Taine, Hippolyte, 138, 142
teleological narrative, 8–9, 104
Temple of Modern Philosophy, 185
temporal perspectives of Enlightenment historiography: advent narratives, 4–5, 16, 38, 50; belatedness of Diderot, 152–5; Cartesian sense of becoming, 37; creation of collective memories, 123, 124–7, 139, 156; d'Alembert's views on, 35–40; future anterior view, 2, 205; linkage between present and past, 42–3, 43–4, 46, 55, 78–151, 149–51; revolutionary reconfigurations of time, 101–2, 122, 197; role of the present in, 5; ruins as storehouses of knowledge for the future, 179, 183, 187–8, 189, 230
Terdiman, Richard, 143, 203
"La Terre et les morts" (Barrès), 177
Thermidor's challenges and significance, 97–9, 117, 142, 170
Thierry, Augustin, 124
Third Republic, 6, 157, 169, 224; commemorative practices of, 103, 151, 174–8; identity production by, SEE creation of modern French identity; legitimizing role of commemorative events in, 151; political cultivation of memory by, 174–7
"To the Memory of Jean-Jacques Rousseau" (Robespierre), 108–10
Tocqueville, Alexis de, 53, 84, 108
Todorov, Tzvetan, 82
Tourneux, Maurice, 157
Traité de dynamique (d'Alembert), 34
Traité des sensations (Condillac), 34
Traité sur la tolérance (Voltaire), 164
travel writing, 62, 187, 195–9
tribunals of reason, 20–1
Les Trois Siècles de littérature française, 152
Turgot, Anne-Robert Jacques, 49, 118, 184
200th anniversary of the French Revolution, 10–12, 174

ultras, 128–9, 134
Universal Exhibition of 1878, 174
Université impériale, 128–9, 132
utopian literature, 62, 67–72; imagined communities, 125, 222; in Mercier's imaginary time travel, 69, 187–8, 189; in Volney's portrayal of the Levant, 197

Valéry, Paul, 178
Versailles's imaginary ruins, 187–8
Vie de Voltaire (Condorcet), 168
Villemain, Abel-François, 127–36, 157; Baudelaire's critique of, 135–6; critiques of skepticism by, 133; impact on literary history of, 130; institutional context of, 128–6, 135–6; as Minister of Education, 135–6; as Minister of Public Instruction, 129; moral chronology of, 133; opposition to the church of, 135; on political use of the Enlightenment, 131–3; reformist discourse of the Enlightenment of, 132–5, 135–6; valorizing of eloquence by, 135; writers considered by, 133–5
Vinet, Alexandre, 157
Volney, Constantin François Chasseboeuf de, 184, 195–9
Voltaire, 4, 24, 163–6; Barthes's characterization of, 69; burial sites of, 167; campaign against religious intolerance by, 73, 164; centennial celebration of, 169, 174; commemorative activities for, 151, 169, 173–4; correspondence of, 166; on creature comforts, 66, 215; critical responses to, 16; critique of sacred history of, 37, 168;

on Dumarsais's "Le Philosophe," 214; *Ecrasez l'infâme* slogan of, 164; iconic afterlife of, 162, 166–71; imagined dialogue with Frederick of Prussia of, 68; impact on La Harpe of, 112–13; inclusion in educational curricula of, 173; La Harpe's critique of, 118; as model for the modern intellectual, 178; narrative of inevitable progress of, 49; on new critical activity, 24; nineteenth-century literary histories of, 170–1; on the philosophe, 58; portrayal of the *canaille*, 64; publication and dissemination of works of, 166–7, 172; publication of Dumarsais's "Philosophe" by, 58–61; response to Montesquieu by, 81; revolutionary pantheonization of, 102–3, 167, 168; Sainte-Beuve's portrayal of, 139, 170; tales of "*l'esprit philosophique*" by, 39; utopian experiments of, 68; view of history of, 3, 37, 42–3, 88, 211; Villemain's portrayal of, 133
Voyage autour du monde (Bougainville), 62
Voyage en Syrie et en Egypte (Volney), 195
Les Vrais principes de l'Eglise gallicane (Frayssinous), 129
Vyverberg, Henry, 92

Watteau, Jean-Antoine, 143, 171
Weber, Eugen, 156
White, Hayden, 124
Why History? (Jenkins), 18
Wood, Robert, 198
Wright, Johnson, 47
writers, SEE authors

Zola, Emile, 74, 178